Monsters

A BEDFORD SPOTLIGHT READER

Monsters

A BEDFORD SPOTLIGHT READER

Andrew J. Hoffman
San Diego Mesa College

Bedford/St. Martin's

A Macmillan Education Imprint

Boston • New York

For Bedford/St. Martin's

Vice President, Editorial, Macmillan Higher Education Humanities: Edwin Hill
Editorial Director, English and Music: Karen S. Henry
Publisher for Composition, Business and Technical Writing, and Developmental Writing: Leasa Burton
Executive Editor: John E. Sullivan III
Developmental Editor: Leah Rang
Publishing Services Manager: Andrea Cava
Production Supervisor: Lisa McDowell
Marketing Manager: Joy Fisher Williams
Project Management: Books By Design, Inc.
Director of Rights and Permissions: Hilary Newman
Senior Art Director: Anna Palchik
Text Design: Castle Design; Janis Owens, Books By Design, Inc.
Cover Design: John Callahan
Cover Art: © ArtMarie/Getty Images
Composition: Achorn International, Inc.
Printing and Binding: LSC Communications

Manufactured in the United States of America.

0   9
f

For information, write: Bedford/St. Martin's, 75 Arlington Street, Boston, MA 02116   (617-399-4000)

ISBN 978-1-4576-9030-3

Acknowledgments

The Bedford Spotlight Reader Series is a line of single-theme readers, each featuring Bedford's trademark care and quality. The readers in the series collect thoughtfully chosen readings sufficient for an entire writing course—about thirty selections—to allow instructors to provide carefully developed, high-quality instruction at an affordable price. Bedford Spotlight Readers are designed to help students make inquiries from multiple perspectives, opening up topics such as borders, monsters, happiness, money, food, sustainability, and gender to critical analysis. An editorial board of more than a dozen compositionists whose programs focus on specific themes have assisted in the development of the series.

Spotlight Readers offer plenty of material for a composition course while keeping the price low. Each volume in the series includes multiple perspectives on the topic and its effects on individuals and society. Chapters are built around central questions such as "What Is the Attraction of Monsters?" and "What Rituals Shape Our Gender?" and so offer numerous entry points for inquiry and discussion. High-interest readings, chosen for their suitability in the classroom, represent a mix of genres, disciplines, and accessible and challenging selections to allow instructors to tailor their approach to each classroom. Each chapter thus brings to light related—even surprising—questions and ideas.

A rich editorial apparatus provides a sound pedagogical foundation. A general introduction, chapter introductions, and headnotes supply context. Following each selection, writing prompts provide avenues of inquiry tuned to different levels of engagement, from reading comprehension ("Understanding the Text"), to critical analysis ("Reflection and Response"), to the kind of integrative analysis appropriate to the research paper ("Making Connections"). A Web site for the series offers support for teaching, with sample syllabi, additional assignments, Web links, and more: **macmillanhighered.com/spotlight**.

Preface for Instructors

Monsters seem to be everywhere, and it's easy to see why: they're fun. Young and old pile into movie theaters to watch the latest releases from Hollywood featuring both the scary and the attractive—carnivorous zombies, love-struck vampires, bloodthirsty werewolves, even methodical serial killers. Some of the best-selling books of recent years have been those that feature monsters and murderers. Television series now use monsters not as enemies to be combated, but as protagonists saving humans from even worse evils. Pop culture analysis has become a serious focus in many college classrooms. In this setting, such monsters can be seen as manifestations of our cultural fears and desires and so can provide excellent material for deep critical analysis. In the very being of these monsters lies a sense of what we do not comprehend and yet should be familiar with: the Other, who may be another embodiment of ourselves. Could that love-struck vampire represent a longing for eternity—perhaps a love that lasts literally forever? Does that werewolf connect to primordial fears of the forest and our own animalistic past? Zombies might indeed be all around us each and every day in the form of struggles and crises that never seem to end. We fight them off valiantly for fear of succumbing to them. And Dr. Frankenstein's monster might be a repository for fears that science is running too far ahead of human ethics. Monsters, therefore, tie in with many of the concerns, anxieties, and desires that our students bring to class daily. By providing students with an analytical framework, this text helps channel that energy into productive activity, conversation, and writing.

The notion of monsters has deep roots in human history, going back as far as writing records the human imagination. Through time and across cultures, the shapes and types of monsters have varied, but monsters have always existed. In *The Epic of Gilgamesh*, which dates to 2700 BCE, the character of Enkidu is introduced as a hairy man-beast, a human who has been raised among animals.* His friendship with Gilgamesh elevates him to a more human status. In fact, the animal and the human are often blurred in monsters of the past: the sphinx of ancient Egypt has the head of a man and the body of a lion; the ancient Greek version has a woman's head and wings. The Minotaur and centaur of the ancient

---

*The names and titles of monsters have been standardized and formatted for clarity. [Editor's note]

Greeks also combine human and animal features. More recently, Mary Shelley's *Frankenstein*, first published in 1818 with a creature that sprang from Shelley's imagination, continues to be popular today because we have so many of the same anxieties about science and "playing God" with nature as people in the early nineteenth century did. Aliens from outer space arrived in H. G. Wells's novel *The War of the Worlds* (1897), and we've never let go of aliens since then, whether they're monsters intent on conquering us or intelligent beings sent to save us from ourselves. The study of these more recent monsters is no less valuable than investigations into monsters with longer histories. Indeed, studying a wide range of imaginary monsters that embody our fears and desires might help us cope with the existence of real monsters, such as the German dictator Adolf Hitler and the serial killers John Wayne Gacy, Ted Bundy, and Jeffrey Dahmer—all ordinary-seeming people who performed extraordinarily evil deeds. Could the monster inside them also be inside us, in one guise or another?

The idea of using monsters as the theme for this reader came easily for two main reasons: First, monsters are universal. They appear throughout recorded human history in all parts of the globe. The topic of monsters enables students to explore something they are already familiar with but in all likelihood have never studied in a classroom before, and as a result students may realize there's much they never knew about monsters—and about the possibilities for academic inquiry. Second, teaching monsters provides an opportunity to introduce students to interdisciplinary learning. *Monsters* features viewpoints based in art, literature, science, history, philosophy, sociology, psychology, religion, and even criminal justice. There's something for everyone when it comes to monsters.

Monsters offers instructors important advantages in creating and teaching a course. The textbook provides flexibility in designing a syllabus. Instructors can focus on assigning just a few readings in each chapter or explore one chapter in depth while skipping another. The types of sources are varied: some primary texts, some pop culture texts, and some scholarly works, which introduce first-year composition students to the nature of academic discourse. The sources span genres as well, including excerpts from monographs, poems, journal articles, magazine articles, biographies, bestiaries, and even an astrology book. To encourage critical inquiry, each reading has three levels of questions: the first set of questions focuses on reading comprehension, to help students understand the selection's core concepts; the second set calls for students to analyze important issues in the reading; the third set requires students to make connections between the reading and another work—either another selection in the textbook or a work outside the textbook, leading the student to do research. The last two sets of questions can be used as prompts for compositions requiring argumentation and/or research. In addition, *Monsters* allows instructors to take a variety of approaches in the classroom. There are opportunities to discuss personal experiences, literature, film, pop culture, history, science, and more, making *Monsters* a resource that is adaptable to instructors' individual approaches in the classroom.

Ultimately, whether students decide to focus on scientific research surrounding monsters or respond to an instructor's creative writing prompt, studying monsters will raise their awareness of the variety of human experiences and human comprehension and encourage them to ask these fundamental questions: If the monster is the Other—the thing outside ourselves—when we look at it more closely, can we see ourselves within it? And do we like what we see?

Acknowledgments

I would like to acknowledge the many people who made the writing of *Monsters* possible. I wish to first thank Amy Shefferd, sales representative for Bedford/St. Martin's, and Lauren Arrant, humanities specialist. For years, Amy and Lauren have shown up at my office at San Diego Mesa College and pushed me to write for Bedford/St. Martin's, and I can only hope that I have repaid their trust. The editors at Bedford/St. Martin's have been outstanding, including Edwin Hill, Vice President, Editorial, Macmillan Higher Education Humanities; Leasa Burton, Publisher for Composition, Business and Technical Writing, and Developmental Writing; and John Sullivan, Executive Editor, who offered me this wonderful opportunity. Without their leadership and guidance, this book would never have been published. I am grateful for the help of Andrea Cava and Nancy Benjamin, who guided the book through production; Barbara Jatkola for her careful copyediting; John Callahan for the cover design; and Barbara Hernandez and Connie Gardner for obtaining permissions. An enormous thank-you goes to Leah Rang, my developmental editor *extraordinaire*, who went over my work with a fine-tooth comb, corrected my errors, tightened my use of language, and generally made *Monsters* a far better textbook than it would have been without her.

As the poet John Donne wrote, "No man is an island," and he could have added "textbook writers least of all." We depend on the advice and counsel of our colleagues throughout the writing process, and I want to thank those who reviewed this book: John Edgar Browning, Georgia Institute of Technology; James Doan, Nova Southeastern University; Lynée Gaillet, Georgia State University; Michelle Hardy, Prince George's Community College; Christine Howell, Metropolitan Community College; Samantha Looker, University of Wisconsin Oshkosh; and Richard Newman, Nassau Community College. I also wish to thank Devin Milner, librarian at San Diego Mesa College, as well as Anna Kalina and Michael Boyd, librarians at the San Diego Central Library. A library is a valuable resource, and librarians are even more valuable. Thank you.

Last, I would like to thank my wife, Cathy Hoffman. I am fortunate to be married to the best teacher I've ever known. Cathy teaches at San Diego State University in the Department of Rhetoric and Writing Studies, and with nearly thirty years of classroom experience, she has a keen eye for what will work with students and what will not. She was the first reviewer of nearly every word I wrote and steered me clear of many bad decisions. She has been my biggest critic and biggest supporter throughout this process. Without her, *Monsters* could not have been written.

Andrew J. Hoffman

Get the Most Out of Your Course with *Monsters*

B edford/St. Martin's offers resources and format choices that help you and your students get even more out of your book and course. To learn more about or to order any of the following products, contact your Bedford/St. Martin's sales representative, e-mail sales support (**sales_support@bfwpub.com**), or visit the Web site at **macmillanhighered.com/spotlight/catalog**.

Select Value Packages

Add value to your text by packaging one of the following resources with *Monsters*. To learn more about package options for any of the following products, contact your Bedford/St. Martin's sales representative or visit **macmillanhighered.com/spotlight**.

Writer's Help 2.0 is a powerful online writing resource that helps students find answers whether they are searching for writing advice on their own or as part of an assignment.

- **Smart search**
  Built on research with more than 1,600 student writers, the smart search in *Writer's Help* provides reliable results even when students use novice terms, such as *flow* and *unstuck*.

- **Trusted content from our best-selling handbooks**
  Choose *Writer's Help 2.0 for Hacker Handbooks* or *Writer's Help 2.0 for Lunsford Handbooks* and ensure that students have clear advice and examples for all of their writing questions.

- **Adaptive exercises that engage students**
  Writer's Help includes LearningCurve, game-like online quizzing that adapts to what students already know and helps them focus on what they need to learn.

Student access is packaged with *Monsters* at a significant discount. Contact your sales representative to order a package ISBN for *Writer's Help 2.0 for Hacker Handbooks* or *Writer's Help 2.0 for Lunsford Handbooks* to ensure your students have easy access to online writing support. Students who rent a book or buy a used book can purchase access to *Writer's Help 2.0* at **macmillanhighered.com/writershelp2**.

Instructors may request free access by registering as an instructor at **macmillanhighered.com/writershelp2**. For technical support, visit **macmillanhighered.com/getsupport**.

LaunchPad Solo for Readers and Writers allows students to work on whatever they need help with the most. At home or in class, students learn at their own pace, with instruction tailored to each student's unique needs. *LaunchPad Solo for Readers and Writers* features:

- **Pre-built units that support a learning arc**
  Each easy-to-assign unit is comprised of a pre-test check, multimedia instruction and assessment, and a post-test that assesses what students have learned about critical reading, the writing process, using sources, grammar, style, mechanics, and help for multilingual writers.

- **A video introduction to many topics**
  Introductions offer an overview of the unit's topic, and many include a brief, accessible video to illustrate the concepts at hand.

- **Adaptive quizzing for targeted learning**
  Most units include LearningCurve, game-like adaptive quizzing that focuses on the areas in which each student needs the most help.

- **The ability to monitor student progress**
  Use our Gradebook to see which students are on track and which need additional help with specific topics.

LaunchPad Solo for Readers and Writers can be **packaged at a significant discount**. Contact your local Bedford/St. Martin's sales representative for a package ISBN to ensure that your students can take full advantage. Visit **macmillanhighered.com/catalog/readwrite** for more information.

Critical Reading and Writing: A Bedford Spotlight Rhetoric, **by Jeff Ousborne**, is a brief supplement that provides coverage of critical reading, thinking, writing, and research. It is designed to work with any of the books in the Bedford Spotlight Reader Series. *Critical Reading and Writing: A Bedford Spotlight Rhetoric* (a $10 value!) can be packaged for **free** with your book. Contact your sales representative for a package ISBN.

Portfolio Keeping, **Third Edition, by Nedra Reynolds and Elizabeth Davis,** provides all the information students need to use the portfolio method successfully in a writing course. *Portfolio Teaching*, a companion guide for instructors, provides the practical information instructors and writing program administrators need to use the portfolio method successfully in a writing course. To order *Portfolio Keeping* packaged with this text, contact your sales representative for a package ISBN.

Make Learning Fun with *Re:Writing 3*
bedfordstmartins.com/rewriting

Bedford's free and open online resource includes videos and interactive elements to engage students in new ways of writing. You'll find tutorials about using common digital writing tools; an interactive peer review game, Extreme Paragraph Makeover; and more. Visit **bedfordstmartins.com/rewriting**.

Instructor Resources
macmillanhighered.com/spotlight

You have a lot to do in your course. Bedford/St. Martin's wants to make it easy for you to find the support you need — and to get it quickly.

Additional resources for *Monsters* can be downloaded from the Bedford/St. Martin's online catalog at the URL above. In addition to suggestions for books or media to pair with reading selections, the instructor resources feature sample syllabi.

Teaching Central offers the entire list of Bedford/St. Martin's print and online professional resources in one place. You'll find landmark reference works, sourcebooks on pedagogical issues, award-winning collections, and practical advice for the classroom — all free for instructors. Visit **macmillanhighered.com/teachingcentral**.

Bedford *Bits* collects creative ideas for teaching a range of composition topics in a frequently updated blog. A community of teachers — leading scholars, authors, and editors, such as Andrea Lunsford, Elizabeth Losh, Jack Solomon, and Elizabeth Wardle — discuss assignments, activities, revision, research, grammar and style, multimodal composition, technology, peer review, and much more. Take, use, adapt, and pass the ideas around. Then come back to the site to comment or share your own suggestions. Visit **bedfordbits.com**.

Contents

Introduction for Students   1

Chapter 1   Why Do We Create Monsters?   13

One of the most popular horror writers of our time examines the attraction of horror: why do we want to be scared? King argues that we need a release for the negative, uncivilized emotions that swim around in the basement of our psyche like alligators looking for fresh meat.

On the basis of a challenge, a young woman created a story that has thrilled and horrified people for two centuries. In this excerpt, Victor Frankenstein wakes up to find, to his horror, that his efforts to control the laws of nature have been successful: out of dead matter, he has reanimated life—and created a monster.

A professional writer of biographical and literary histories tells the story of the summer of 1816, when the famous poets Lord Byron and Percy Bysshe Shelley; Shelley's young lover, Mary Godwin; and Byron's doctor, John Polidori, challenged themselves to write horror stories, leading to two of the most enduring monsters in literature: Dr. Frankenstein's creature and the vampire.

A popular filmmaker joins with a writer of vampire novels to describe why the myths of vampires are so prevalent across time and culture: because vampires, for good or bad, connect us to the idea of eternity.

Contents by Discipline

Literature and Writing

Philosophy and Religion

Sciences

Social Sciences

Contents by Theme

Introduction for Students

In Maurice Sendak's *Where the Wild Things Are*, young Max, wearing a wolf costume, is sent to bed without any supper. Angry and still rebellious, he sails off to the land where the wild things are, where they "roared their terrible roars, gnashed their terrible teeth, rolled their terrible eyes and showed their terrible claws." How many young children have delighted in Sendak's words and images, wanting to be like Max, leading a wild rumpus filled with monstrous creatures? For young children, Max's journey echoes many childhood desires — to break free of dependence on parents, to dance and howl at the moon, to send monsters to bed without any supper.

Our childhood experiences with monsters might also go in a different direction, far less benign than in Sendak's tale. Some monsters may come from our own imaginations: the creature in the dark corner of the closet, the monster lurking under the bed, the beast outside the window whispering our name. The irrationality of the experience is unimportant in the mind of the child: what's real is the fear. A parent telling the child the monster is gone clearly misses the point, for the monster will come back as soon as Mom or Dad leaves.

Some of the monsters that stalk our imaginations we inherited from writers of the past — even the far past. In the nineteenth century, Mary Shelley dreamed of a monster and gave us the creature from *Frankenstein*, and Bram Stoker brought together centuries of vampire mythology in the character Count Dracula. Ancient cultures in Egypt, Greece, and Rome left us with Medusa and the Minotaur, centaurs and sphinxes, Sirens and a vast array of other mythological creatures. Explorers of new worlds expected to find strange and marvelous monsters, and their imaginations rose to the occasion, interpreting foreign creatures as mythical beasts and conceiving fantastical figures as a way to explain the unknown. And the modern world is still creating monsters — Godzilla and space aliens, zombies and the chupacabra — which fill some sort of need we have to be terrorized and amused.

Monsters are creatures not only *from* but also *of* their times. While today's teachers and parents might have grown up on Sendak's tale, today's college students may associate monsters with creatures on the Yu-Gi-Oh! or Pokémon cards they played with as children. An older generation may have experienced monsters most powerfully in black-and-white films featuring Lon Chaney or Bela Lugosi. Instead of the creepy and frightening vampires of the past, today's young audience may think of the model-quality good looks of Robert Pattinson playing Edward Cullen in the Twilight movies. Yesterday's villain is today's hero, and recognizing such shifts can enrich critical inquiry into the representations of monsters, opening up questions about good and evil, and about monsters' roles in a cultural moment.

Recognizing the evolution from villain to hero is not to say today's monsters are without teeth. There are plenty of evil vampires, rapacious werewolves, creepy zombies, and other creatures to keep us checking under the bed and behind the door even in the twenty-first century. The need to express our fears, to make sense of a world that so often seems in chaos and confusion, has hardly disappeared. Into this need steps the monster as an embodiment of all that is unmanageable around us. We might call this repository of our fears the Other, and no matter what monstrous shape the Other assumes, it is not going away any more than the fear is going away. This is an era in which genetically modified foods evoke the specter of Dr. Frankenstein working to give life to his creature; when the relentless buzz of everyday life threatens to turn us into zombies; when flesh-eating bacteria, Ebola, and AIDS — resisting the best efforts of modern medicine — duplicate the destruction of a vampire or werewolf; and when horrific crimes evoke images and memories of the most terrible monsters of all, human beings. Monsters are arguably as much a part of our collective consciousness as ever.

Why Should I Study Monsters?

You may be tempted to dismiss the study of monsters in the college classroom if you approach monsters solely as a frivolous pop culture fad or the product of ignorant superstition. But monsters have long lived in the minds of humans, going back to the dawn of recorded civilization, and anything that is such an integral part of human culture deserves study. There must be, after all, a reason that monsters have appeared across cultures and times. Stories of werewolves, for instance, can be traced to ancient Greece; stories of vampire-like creatures have been around for thousands of years all around the world. Over the past century, new monsters, such as Godzilla and space aliens (both friendly and hostile), have been created to give expression to newfound fears and anxieties. The fact that monsters vary in many aspects but also have many qualities in common should only enhance our curiosity about the subject.

Monsters are not merely entertainment. The study of monsters is the study of what it means to be human in a world that provides much to fear and avoid. Since time immemorial, people have had to deal with fear: fear of the wild, fear of the unknown, even fear of each other. Monsters may be a repository for much that is negative in the human experience. In this way, monsters provide us with the opportunity to connect to important issues of society, psychology, science, medicine, art, and religion. Indeed, much of the research about monsters is published in the scholarly journals of those fields. There are also a growing number of peer-reviewed scholarly journals that focus on monsters exclusively, such as the *Journal of Dracula Studies*, *Golem: Journal of Religion and Monsters*, *Monsters and the Monstrous*, and the *Irish Journal of Gothic and Horror Studies*, to name a few. In addition, there are many scholarly books written about monsters, as well as more general audience–oriented books, blogs, and magazines. It's rather hard to escape the reach of monsters!

Many times in composition courses, the instructor will teach several themes in a term, often from a textbook that contains many different topics to choose from. Other times, there may be no theme at all, as the instructor wants the students to come up with their own writing topics. So why focus on a single theme? First and foremost, having a single theme allows you to explore the topic in much greater detail than if you worked on multiple themes. There is a sustained involvement in the topic — in this case,

Max and the Wild Things from Maurice Sendak's classic children's book *Where the Wild Things Are* (1963).
Photofest

monsters. Rather than picking up only a superficial impression of the theme — which is often quite complex — you can acquire a deeper, more substantial understanding of the topic. When you do that, you are able to write more serious, sophisticated papers, which can be more informative and interesting for any reader. Such assignments allow you to practice and hone your critical reading, thinking, and writing skills. You might ask, then, "Why monsters? Why not something else?" Good question.

Monsters are relevant figures in society, history, and culture. They appear in virtually every culture and time in the world. The particular details of monsters may be different — how they were created, what they look like, what they do — but there are always monsters. This fact alone makes the topic important and worthy of investigation. The psychology behind the creation of monsters and monster myths is important as well. What do the monsters tell us about ourselves? When we examine monsters, we're really examining human nature and experience.

Monsters are a diverse, multicultural phenomenon. Throughout many times and places, monsters have made their appearance. From the sphinxes and Sirens of the classical Western world, to the giant roc of the Middle Eastern tales of Sinbad the Sailor, to the stories of mermaids and mermen that have appeared all around the world, monsters have an extensive global history. They can be as interesting in their diversity as the cultures that spawn them. Even the same type of monster might take on different characteristics to reflect different times. The history of vampire myths alone shows an evolution, as vampires have progressed from lurid cannibals arising from the grave to feed on humans to glamorous heroes who save people.

Monsters are extremely personal. Even though every culture has its own variations of monsters, each individual has his or her unique relationship to them. This may often be connected to early childhood experiences, perhaps through comic books, television shows, movies, or Halloween costumes — even the antics of an older brother or sister who took a certain sadistic delight in donning a werewolf mask and leaping out of the closet. Some monsters may be deeply personal and unique — an unnamed, unshaped Thing that haunts the darkness. Others may be so popular as to spawn their own fan clubs. One monster may be particularly loathsome or frightening to one person, but it may hardly strike a chord in another. As an adult, you might have put aside the fear of monsters long ago — at least of the jumping-out-of-the-closet kind — only to discover new monsters that might go unnamed though not unfelt.

The study of monsters is an interdisciplinary pursuit. An entire cottage industry has been created around the study of monsters. Indeed, the advent of the discipline of monster studies — and the associated scholarly publications in which research on monsters is published — no doubt spring from the recognition that monsters are complex and important phenomena. After all, if monsters are reflections of us — and humans are notoriously complex already — then the monsters we create and fill with meaning are complex, too. What we fear, what we avoid, what we don't know how to assimilate in our lives — all these can give rise to monsters. Monsters are discussed in many different areas of study — from art, literature, and history to psychology and science. This interdisciplinary approach to studying monsters may help you see possibilities for further study in your own field. For instance, an art history major could explore the representations of monsters in classical paintings and sculpture, or a psychology major might examine the emotional human dynamic reflected in certain monsters. A science student might examine how and why certain physical or biological phenomena could lead people to think they have witnessed the actions of a monster. You may not wish to pursue further study of monsters after your composition course is over, but you will have gained some valuable insight into and experience with processes of inquiry, research, and critical thinking that will be useful in any course of study.

The in-depth study of monsters will give you discourse knowledge. All intellectual endeavors involve participation in an ongoing conversation called a *discourse*. This is not the same type of conversation you might have with a roommate or a group of friends. It is the type of conversation that takes place among many people over many years using various methods of expression, including books, essays, articles, speeches, and more. All college students are expected to develop the skills to absorb, assimilate, and synthesize information gathered from many different sources within a variety of discourses and to find their own voice within them. This is a basic pattern in the production of knowledge. This book offers a range of interrelated readings focusing on the discourse about monsters. Learning how to evaluate and analyze that discourse and how to shape your own voice and perspective within it is an important part of your college education.

How Is This Book Organized?

Monsters is organized as a progression of topics, starting with the creation of monster myths; moving on to an examination of the different aspects of monsters, including their form, their history, and their attraction; and concluding with the human monsters that prey on us in real life. The chapters feature primary texts (the stories that first gave us some popular monsters), general-interest articles from books and magazines, and scholarly research from peer-reviewed journals. The variety in types of sources offers different levels of analysis from various perspectives. The selections represent a span of nearly three thousand years — from a passage from Homer's *The Odyssey* to more contemporary discussions of vampires in Hollywood blockbusters like the Twilight movies — which makes the text relevant, easy to use, informative, and fun.

Chapter 1: Why Do We Create Monsters?

Monsters are not self-made, but are instead human creations, developed at specific times in specific places. This chapter introduces you to the origins of monsters: why we create them and what that says about us and our cultural moment. For instance, Mary Shelley created her monster in the midst of exciting and disturbing scientific experimentation in order to highlight the potential dangers of scientific knowledge and of "playing God." Though of a different era, Godzilla also represents the dangers of modern science: the monster arose from the radioactive ashes of post–World War II Japan to embody the devastation, both physical and psychological, experienced by that nation as a result of two atomic blasts. Other monsters have been resurrected and reinvented today — such as vampires, werewolves, zombies, and even lesser-known creatures like the chupacabra — to provide a catharsis or to give form to a shared, lived experience. Learning about the creation of monsters may lead you to ask further questions — for instance, why certain monsters, such as the vampire or the creature in *Frankenstein*, have had such strong staying power in our imaginations, while others, such as the Chimera and centaur, no longer resonate today.

Chapter 2: Is the Monster Animal or Human?

Some monsters seem to be perversions of the animal kingdom, such as the Cerberus, sphinx, and giant roc. Others seem to be perversions of human beings, such as vampires and zombies. Then there are monsters that blend the two, such as werewolves and mermaids. This chapter explores how monsters connect to what it means to be human and to what we expect from the natural world. Early people lived much closer to nature than we do today, and their monsters reflect that connection, as they combine human and animal forms. Some of the oldest stories recorded feature animal-human combinations, such as the wild man Enkidu in *The Epic of Gilgamesh* or the mermaids and mermen in tales that predate the classical era of the Greeks and Romans. The classical age gave us the Minotaur and centaur, among others. Modern cultures continue to invent new animal-human combinations, such as the "things" in H. G. Wells's novel *The Island of Dr. Moreau* and the part-human, part-insect creature in *The Fly*. Exploring these combinations, and the very fact that they exist, can tell us a lot about how we think about nature and our place in it.

Chapter 3: How Do Monsters Reflect Their Times?

To explore a monster is to explore the time and place that created it. If the monster can embody our fears, it can tell us what those fears are — whether it is fear of the unknown, fear of the different, or fear of the confusing. For much of human history, much of the world was unknown. When Alexander the Great fought his way into India, bands of Vikings sailed in Scandinavian waters, or European explorers ventured into the New World, they encountered many things they had never seen before. They described unusual animals they saw as monstrous, and labeled people who didn't fit their mold as half-human demons or even witches. Their accounts may seem like tall tales to us today, but their monster stories tell us about the times in which they lived. Monsters in many ways represent their times, and that includes our monsters today, as evidenced by our fascination with vampires, werewolves, and zombies.

Chapter 4: What Is the Attraction of Monsters?

In spite of the danger inherent in monsters, they have an allure, too. We know we should keep away, but we cannot. What is the appeal of monsters such as vampires and mermaids? In particular, how is sexuality mixed in with monsters, and how does that reflect our own sexual desires, fears, and anxieties? Some monsters have a strong erotic appeal combined with their danger. The vampire is an example, and it's no accident that movies and television series in recent years have used handsome leading actors such as Brad Pitt, Robert Pattinson, Alexander Skarsgård, and Ian Somerhalder to play the role of vampires. Women, too, can be dangerous monsters, such as the Sirens who lured Odysseus with their song. Analyzing what attracts us to these dangerous figures can reveal our own values and desires.

Chapter 5: Is the Monster within Us?

Sometimes *we* are the monsters. How can we account for the actions of human monsters such as serial killers, murderous autocrats, cannibals, and others who do things that go far beyond the realm of what is typically termed "human"? This is when we find the Other — that unknown, fearsome presence — in ourselves. No longer can the monster be seen as a perverse product of nature, or even a result of science gone terribly wrong. The monster is in us, and there's something about that awareness that is likely to be more disturbing than any thoughts we might have about werewolves or zombies.

What Do We Mean by Critical Reading, Thinking, and Writing?

You have already attained a strong level of competence in the ability to read, or you wouldn't be taking this course. However, you can develop and hone your skills further. At the college level, when instructors talk about reading, they're actually talking about a much more proactive approach to reading than what you might do casually on your own. The term frequently used is *critical reading*. The word "critical" does not simply mean "fault-finding" as it often does in everyday conversation. A better sense of the word is that we are questioning what we read. Critical reading is not only about comprehension — that's just a first step. Many times texts have some vocabulary words you don't know. *Monsters* includes definitions of some unusual, difficult, or technical terms, but if you encounter others that you don't know, look them up in a dictionary. Similarly, you may find allusions to works, writers, characters, cultures, or monsters that you have never heard of before. Do some research on your own so that you are able to understand more fully what the author is trying to communicate. Most texts will reveal more if you give them a second or third reading as well. Only then will you be truly ready to ask questions.

One of the features of this textbook is that there are three sets of questions with each selection. The first group is labeled "Understanding the Text." You may use these questions to make sure you understand the selection and can recognize the key ideas in it. Your instructor may have additional reading comprehension questions as well.

When you read a text critically, you will be asking questions of the text as well as responding to it. Depending on the text itself, you may question its form and the author's use of language. Why is the text written the way it is and not in other ways? Why did the author choose a particular word and not another? You also might ask questions about the attitude present in the text: Is the author biased in favor of or against an issue? Is the author neutral? How is that position revealed? Whenever you have a question or make a particular observation, record your comments in the margins of your textbook, on note cards, on paper, or in a computer file. Your composition instructor may have additional ideas on how to read critically, but a common theme is that a critical reader is an *active* reader. Do not see yourself as a passive consumer of the text; instead, get actively involved in what you're reading — exploring, pushing, and questioning as you go.

Critical thinking is a term that is frequently used in college classrooms. When you read critically, you're thinking critically about a particular text and using reading strategies such as annotation to help you work with the text. But critical thinking can involve much more. When you think critically, you may ask questions that involve your own reactions to the text. Or you may extend your inquiry further and ask questions of the text and its relationship to other selections you've read in this book. Even more, you may respond to the text by doing research beyond this book and then asking additional questions. For example, after reading one of the selections here, you might ask a question such as "What does this reading reveal about our cultural attitudes toward this type of monster?" or "How does the author's argument about the significance of this monster compare to the origin story of the monster from a classical text or a Hollywood movie interpretation of it?" Then you might log on to your campus library's Web site to research other discussions of the monster or other representations of it in order to answer your questions and support your own ideas about the topic.

This is why, along with the "Understanding the Text" questions, there are two sets of writing questions that may be used as prompts for writing assignments. The questions labeled "Reflection and Response" focus on the issues present in the text. They require critical reading skills and analytical thinking. The "Making Connections" questions require not only critical reading and analytical thinking but also that you engage multiple texts. Sometimes the other texts are from this book or refer to films you may have seen, but other times the questions require you to do library research. Your instructor may assign only one type of question or both types, depending on his or her preference. However, even if the questions are not assigned, reading them can provide useful ways for you to approach and think through the selection.

Writing in college is different from writing that you may do elsewhere. When you write in college, you're creating what can be called *academic writing*. Academic writing is an opportunity to engage with an idea, develop an argument, examine an idea from all sides, present a new approach that will change a reader's perspective, fit into a conversation, and fully learn and understand the material and its context. Whether expository or persuasive, academic writing is typically more formal in tone and style than other writing, addresses serious topics, and is usually less personal. You are expected to really engage with and develop your ideas and the ideas of others. That doesn't necessarily mean that your opinions won't be present in your writing, but you will be required to support your ideas with evidence. In terms of types of support, instructors vary in how much importance or value they place on personal experience: some may encourage you to bring your own life experiences into a composition; others may require that you use only the text and library research. Generally, though, academic writing demands a high level of competence in the use of language. Grammar errors, misspellings, and awkward sentences negatively affect the quality of your compositions. All instructors have certain expectations about the structure of each composition and its development. The particulars will vary from instructor to instructor, but in many cases academic writing is marked by the use of logic and reason and by ideas presented in a clear and orderly fashion.

All of the questions following each reading ask you to write academically — to use a tone and style that follows the conventions of academic discourse, to use logic and reason to present and support your arguments, and to really engage with texts and your own ideas to offer an interesting or unique perspective on a topic. Some questions may be answered in a few short sentences, but other questions will require longer compositions that could even be adapted into multimedia presentations with visuals, film clips, and more. Reading through the questions provided after each reading might even inspire you to ask and answer your own questions about the selections and monsters in general.

My ultimate goal is that you enjoy your experience with this book as you explore the worlds of vampires, zombies, werewolves, mermaids, centaurs, and many others. Learning to write compositions can sometimes seem to be an arduous task, and often in college students read texts they are not engaged with at all. With *Monsters* as your guide, I hope neither of these occurs, and I hope you find that the subject of monsters can be fun and educational at the same time. Happy studies!

Andrew J. Hoffman
San Diego Mesa College

P.S. Don't be afraid to use a night-light.

1 Why Do We Create Monsters?

With our current culture's emphasis on reason and science, the notion of a monster seems quaint, possibly romantic — harking back to a time when people believed more readily in fantastic phenomena. Yet the allure of monsters today is still strong. Whether it is the vampire, the zombie, the werewolf, Frankenstein's creature, or some other being of a mystical but threatening character, the twenty-first century does not seem to lack for monsters. Perhaps, as many psychologists, historians, social critics, and others have suggested, we need monsters to symbolize our fears. If so, we need to investigate how monsters encapsulate those fears and what those fears suggest about us and the values of our time. Vampires are as popular today as ever, yet the vampire stories told by Stephenie Meyer are a far cry from the one written by Bram Stoker in the nineteenth century. The zombie enjoys wide popularity these days, but its close cousin, the mummy, no longer resonates within the popular imagination. Why is the brain-eating zombie an appropriate monster for today's fears while a suffocating mummy is not?

Monsters reflect the anxieties of the cultures that create them. In analyzing these monsters, we can learn something about the people of those periods. Stephen King, perhaps the most famous and prolific horror writer today, explains the attraction we have to being frightened. We cannot always be calm and rational because inside all of us is the inner madman or madwoman who needs to be let out once in a while to race about and howl at the moon. Mary Shelley anticipated the great upheavals that science and industry would bring to the nineteenth century. She tells the story of Dr. Victor Frankenstein, who builds a monster from the various parts of dead people. Reanimated by the power of electricity, the creature's awakening horrifies even its own creator. As Shelley would later explain, her creative inspiration came not out of a void, but out of chaos: the chaos of her time. Susan Tyler Hitchcock describes the political, social, scientific, personal, and even environmental anxieties of the particular time in which Shelley wrote *Frankenstein*. A pair of contemporary filmmakers, Guillermo del Toro and Chuck Hogan, examine the enduring popularity of the vampire myth, which goes back to ancient times and is arguably as strong in modern imaginations as ever. They point out that the vampire connects us to the concept of eternity. Chuck Klosterman examines the zombie phenomenon and argues that the zombie is a suitable metaphor for the obstacles we must conquer just to get through our daily lives. Mike Davis takes a look at the chupacabra, a monster whose popularity among the Latino community draws attention to the difficulties they face, and showcases the humor that community uses at times to defuse them. Peter H. Brothers examines the influences behind the making of the movie *Godzilla* in post–World War II Japan. Director Ishirô Honda created a monster that seemed to encapsulate the fears of a nation that experienced the trauma of atomic warfare and the humiliation of defeat. The monster, with its destructive potential, serves as a symbol of science — and human ambition — run amok. Examining threats at a national level, Stephen T. Asma argues that events such as the terrorist attacks of September 11 and the Great Recession drive our need for monsters. The promise is that if we can control the monster, we can control our lives.

The monster is a response to the world around us, and since the world never stops bringing crises, threats, and uncertainties, our need for monsters doesn't end either. Sometimes we modify a long-standing monster such as the vampire to fit the psychological needs of our times; other times we construct a new monster, as Mary Shelley did in the nineteenth century or the Latino community has done today. Whatever the case, these monsters are sure to both frighten and, ironically, reassure us that there may after all be a good reason for our fears.

Why We Crave Horror Movies

Stephen King

Stephen King is one of the most popular and prolific horror writers of our time. His works include *Carrie* (1974), *The Shining* (1977), *The Dead Zone* (1979), and *Misery* (1987), all of which have been made into popular movies. A native of Maine, King began writing for his college newspaper at the University of Maine. Later, he wrote short stories for men's magazines and received his first big break when he published *Carrie* in 1974. The following essay, which initially appeared in *Playboy* magazine in January 1981, is an excerpt from King's book *Danse Macabre* (1981). King argues that the horror movie performs a helpful task, taking on feelings, urges, and impulses that don't fit neatly into the rational, reasonable, and sane parts of our lives. Indeed, King proposes that the horror movie gives "psychic relief" because in most parts of our lives, "simplicity, irrationality and even outright madness" are so rarely allowed. As such, the horror film functions like a pressure-release valve for the inner monster we must typically repress.

I think that we're all mentally ill; those of us outside the asylums only hide it a little better—and maybe not all that much better, after all. We've all known people who talk to themselves, people who sometimes squinch their faces into horrible grimaces when they believe no one is watching, people who have some hysterical fear—of snakes, the dark, the tight place, the long drop . . . and, of course, those final worms and grubs that are waiting so patiently underground.

When we pay our four or five bucks and seat ourselves at tenth-row center in a theater showing a horror movie, we are daring the nightmare.

Why? Some of the reasons are simple and obvious. To show that we can, that we are not afraid, that we can ride this roller coaster. Which is not to say that a really good horror movie may not surprise a scream out of us at some point, the way we may scream when the roller coaster twists through a complete 360 or plows through a lake at the bottom of the drop. And horror movies, like roller coasters, have always been the special province of the young; by the time one turns 40 or 50, one's appetite for double twists or 360-degree loops may be considerably depleted.

We also go to re-establish our feelings of essential normality; the horror movie is innately conservative, even reactionary. Freda Jackson as the horrible melting woman in *Die, Monster, Die!* confirms for us that no matter how far we may be removed from the beauty of a Robert Redford or a Diana Ross, we are still light-years from true ugliness.

And we go to have fun.   5

Ah, but this is where the ground starts to slope away, isn't it? Because this is a very peculiar sort of fun, indeed. The fun comes from seeing others menaced—sometimes killed. One critic has suggested that if pro football has become the voyeur's version of combat, then the horror film has become the modern version of the public lynching.

It is true that the mythic "fairy-tale" horror film intends to take away the shades of gray. . . . It urges us to put away our more civilized and adult penchant for analysis and to become children again, seeing things in pure blacks and whites. It may be that horror movies provide psychic relief on this level because this invitation to lapse into simplicity, irrationality and even outright madness is extended so rarely. We are told we may allow our emotions a free rein . . . or no rein at all.

If we are all insane, then sanity becomes a matter of degree. If your insanity leads you to carve up women like Jack the Ripper or the Cleveland Torso Murderer, we clap you away in the funny farm (but neither of those two amateur-night surgeons was ever caught, heh-heh-heh); if, on the other hand, your insanity leads you only to talk to yourself when you're under stress or to pick your nose on your morning bus, then you are left alone to go about your business . . . though it is doubtful that you will ever be invited to the best parties.

The potential lyncher is in almost all of us (excluding saints, past and present; but then, most saints have been crazy in their own ways), and every now and then, he has to be let loose to scream and roll around in the grass. Our emotions and our fears form their own body, and we recognize that it demands its own exercise to maintain proper muscle tone. Certain of these emotional muscles are accepted—even exalted—in civilized society; they are, of course, the emotions that tend to maintain the status quo of civilization itself. Love, friendship, loyalty, kindness—these are all the emotions that we applaud, emotions that have been immortalized in the couplets of Hallmark cards and in the verses (I don't dare call it poetry) of Leonard Nimoy.°

When we exhibit these emotions, society showers us with positive rein-   10
forcement; we learn this even before we get out of diapers. When, as children, we hug our rotten little puke of a sister and give her a kiss, all the aunts and uncles smile and twit and cry, "Isn't he the sweetest little thing?" Such coveted treats as chocolate-covered graham crackers often follow. But if we deliberately slam the rotten little puke of a sister's fingers in the door,

Leonard Nimoy (1931–2015): American actor best known for playing Spock in the original *Star Trek* television series. He later turned to poetry, music, and other artistic pursuits.

sanctions follow—angry remonstrance from parents, aunts and uncles; instead of a chocolate-covered graham cracker, a spanking.

But anticivilization emotions don't go away, and they demand periodic exercise. We have such "sick" jokes as, "What's the difference between a truckload of bowling balls and a truckload of dead babies?" (You can't unload a truckload of bowling balls with a pitchfork . . . a joke, by the way, that I heard originally from a ten-year-old.) Such a joke may surprise a laugh or a grin out of us even as we recoil, a possibility that confirms the thesis: If we share a brotherhood of man, then we also share an insanity of man. None of which is intended as a defense of either the sick joke or insanity but merely as an explanation of why the best horror films, like the best fairy tales, manage to be reactionary, anarchistic, and revolutionary all at the same time.

> "The mythic horror movie . . . deliberately appeals to all that is worst in us."

The mythic horror movie, like the sick joke, has a dirty job to do. It deliberately appeals to all that is worst in us. It is morbidity unchained, our most base instincts let free, our nastiest fantasies realized . . . and it all happens, fittingly enough, in the dark. For those reasons, good liberals often shy away from horror films. For myself, I like to see the most aggressive of them—*Dawn of the Dead*, for instance—as lifting a trap door in the civilized forebrain and throwing a basket of raw meat to the hungry alligators swimming around in that subterranean river beneath.

Why bother? Because it keeps them from getting out, man. It keeps them down there and me up here. It was Lennon and McCartney who said that all you need is love, and I would agree with that.

As long as you keep the gators fed.

Understanding the Text

1. King states that when we see a horror film, we are "daring the nightmare" (par. 2). What does he mean by that?

2. King uses the metaphor of "emotional muscles" that need exercise (par. 9). Some of these emotions are seen as positive in that they maintain civilization. What are some of the emotions that don't maintain the social status quo, and why do they still need to be exercised?

3. King relies heavily on metaphors and allusions to create a humorous tone while making his argument. What is the advantage of approaching the topic of horror in this way?

Reflection and Response

4. Consider your own experience with horror films. Are you a fan of horror or not? If so, what about horror attracts you, and if not, what repels you? Now consider your response in light of King's statement "We also go [to horror films] to re-establish our feelings of essential normality" (par. 4). Does your response to horror connect to your feelings of normality? If so, how?

5. King argues that we have some emotions that are affirming of civilization and its norms and others that are not — or, "anticivilization emotions," as he terms them (par. 11). Identify and analyze how these negative emotions are "exercised" (to use King's metaphor) in your own life experiences beyond watching horror films.

Making Connections

6. Compare King's essay with Chuck Klosterman's "My Zombie, Myself: Why Modern Life Feels Rather Undead" (p. 40). How does Klosterman differ from King in his analysis of the need for horror in people's lives? In what ways are the two in agreement? Explain your responses using specific textual support from both essays.

7. King reports that one critic said, "The horror film has become the modern version of the public lynching" (par. 6). King continues the metaphor when he claims, "The potential lyncher is in almost all of us" (par. 9). Do some research on the history of lynching in the United States. After your research, argue whether the comparison between public lynching and horror films is either fair and accurate or overdone and exaggerated. Defend your response.

From Frankenstein: The Modern Prometheus

Mary Shelley

Mary Wollstonecraft Godwin was born in 1797 to celebrated radical thinkers William Godwin and Mary Wollstonecraft, the pioneering feminist writer, who died just days after Mary was born. Godwin recognized his daughter's intellect and gave her a rich education, raising her to follow his liberal political ideals and become a writer. However, he withdrew his support when sixteen-year-old Mary became attached to the twenty-one-year-old poet Percy Bysshe Shelley, who was already famous and married to another woman. In 1816, Mary traveled with Shelley to Geneva, where she answered a writing challenge with one of the most enduring works and characters of Western literature. Mary's creation, *Frankenstein*, was first published in 1818 and has lived on in the popular imagination ever since. In this passage, after almost two years of hard work in his laboratory, Victor Frankenstein beholds his own creation, only to react with horror at what he has done.

It was on a dreary night of November that I beheld the accomplishment of my toils. With an anxiety that almost amounted to agony, I collected the instruments of life around me, that I might infuse a spark of being into the lifeless thing that lay at my feet. It was already one in the morning; the rain pattered dismally against the panes, and my candle was nearly burnt out, when, by the glimmer of the half-extinguished light, I saw the dull yellow eye of the creature open; it breathed hard, and a convulsive motion agitated its limbs.

How can I describe my emotions at this catastrophe, or how delineate the wretch whom with such infinite pains and care I had endeavored to form? His limbs were in proportion, and I had selected his features as beautiful. Beautiful! Great God! His yellow skin scarcely covered the work of muscles and arteries beneath; his hair was of a lustrous black, and flowing; his teeth of a pearly whiteness; but these luxuriances only formed a more horrid contrast with his watery eyes, that seemed almost of the same color as the dun-white sockets in which they were set, his shriveled complexion and straight black lips.

The different accidents of life are not so changeable as the feelings of human nature. I had worked hard for nearly two years, for the sole purpose of infusing life into an inanimate body. For this I had deprived myself of rest and health. I had desired it with an ardor that far exceeded moderation; but now that I had finished, the beauty of the dream vanished, and breathless horror and disgust filled my heart. Unable to endure the aspect of the being I had created, I rushed out of the room and continued a long time traversing my bed-chamber, unable to compose my mind to sleep. At length lassitude succeeded to the tumult I had before endured, and I threw myself on the bed in my clothes, endeavoring to seek a few moments of forgetfulness. But it was in vain; I slept, indeed, but I was disturbed by the wildest dreams. I thought I saw Elizabeth, in the bloom of health, walking in the streets of Ingolstadt.° Delighted and surprised, I embraced her, but as I imprinted the first kiss on her lips, they became livid with the hue of death; her features appeared to change, and I thought that I held the corpse of my dead mother in my arms; a shroud enveloped her form, and I saw the grave-worms crawling in the folds of the flannel. I started from my sleep with horror; a cold dew covered my forehead, my teeth chattered, and every limb became convulsed; when, by the dim and yellow light of the moon, as it forced its way through the window shutters, I beheld the wretch—the miserable monster whom I had created. He held up the curtain of the bed; and his eyes, if eyes they

> "By the dim and yellow light of the moon, as it forced its way through the window shutters, I beheld the wretch — the miserable monster whom I had created."

may be called, were fixed on me. His jaws opened, and he muttered some inarticulate sounds, while a grin wrinkled his cheeks. He might have spoken, but I did not hear; one hand was stretched out, seemingly to detain me, but I escaped and rushed downstairs. I took refuge in the courtyard belonging to the house which I inhabited, where I remained during the rest of the night, walking up and down in the greatest agitation, listening attentively, catching and fearing each sound as if it were to announce the approach of the demoniacal corpse to which I had so miserably given life.

Oh! No mortal could support the horror of that countenance. A mummy again endued with animation could not be so hideous as that wretch. I had gazed on him while unfinished; he was ugly then, but when those muscles and joints were rendered capable of motion, it became a thing such as even Dante could not have conceived.

Ingolstadt: a city in Germany along the River Danube.

Understanding the Text

1. Immediately after he animates the creature, Frankenstein calls the act a "catastrophe" (par. 2). Why? Examine the details of Frankenstein's description of the creature to support your answer.

2. Frankenstein awakens from a bad dream only to confront the reality of his creation. What effect does Shelley create by juxtaposing the dream with the curious monster's invasion of Frankenstein's bedchamber?

3. Why does Frankenstein call his own creation a "demoniacal corpse" (par. 3)? If his creation is a demon, what does that say about Frankenstein as a creator?

Reflection and Response

4. Analyze Frankenstein's immediate repulsion toward his creation. What is the basis of his repulsion? Note that Frankenstein claims he had "selected [the creature's] features as beautiful" (par. 2). What is the relationship between beauty and horror? Cite specific passages from the text to support your position.

5. Frankenstein's nightmare begins with a healthy Elizabeth (his love interest), who then turns into the corpse of his dead mother in his arms. How does this dream sequence relate to Frankenstein's actions in giving life to the creature?

6. How does the creature act? Does the lack of aggression surprise you, given the typical popular culture depictions of Frankenstein's monster? Describe the action in this passage from the point of view of the monster.

Making Connections

7. In his essay "Monsters and the Moral Imagination" (p. 61), Stephen T. Asma argues that there are cultural uses for monsters — that they somehow reflect the anxieties of their time. Investigate the culture and time in which Mary Shelley was writing (1816) and argue how time and place came to influence the story of Frankenstein.

8. Compare the passage of the creature's awakening with film depictions of the same. Some choices include the classic movie *Frankenstein* (1931), an updated version of *Frankenstein* (1994), and an even more recent take on the story, *I, Frankenstein* (2014). What differences do you see from the original story by Shelley, and what is the significance of those differences?

Conception

Susan Tyler Hitchcock

Susan Tyler Hitchcock is a book editor for the National Geographic Society and has written more than thirteen books. In this excerpt from *Frankenstein: A Cultural History* (2007), Hitchcock describes two of the leading literary figures of their day — Lord Byron and Percy Bysshe Shelley — and the challenge they took part in during the summer of 1816. The two men — accompanied by Byron's physician, John Polidori; Shelley's young lover, Mary Wollstonecraft Godwin, and their newborn son; and Mary's stepsister Claire Clairmont — had settled in Geneva that summer. The weather was unusually cold and rainy, probably the result of a volcanic eruption in far-off Indonesia. But the time, place, climate, and personal relationships of the companions made possible the creation of not one but two famous monster stories, neither by the famous poets: *Frankenstein* by Mary Godwin (later Mary Shelley) and *The Vampyre* by John Polidori.

> Archetypes make their way into the conscious part of the mind seemingly from the outside and of their own accord. They are autonomous, sometimes forcing themselves in overpoweringly. They have a numinous quality; that is, they have an aura of divinity which is mysterious or terrifying. They are from the unknown.
>
> — WILSON M. HUDSON, *Folklorist*

> It would have been naive to think it was possible to have prevented this.
>
> — IAN WILMUT, *Embryologist Responsible for Dolly, the Cloned Sheep*

The weather was strange all summer long in 1816. Twice in April the year before, Indonesia's Mount Tamboro had erupted—the largest volcanic eruption in history—spewing masses of dust into the atmosphere, which lingered and dimmed the sun's rays throughout the northern latitudes. Temperatures stayed at record lows. In New England killing frosts occurred all summer. In Europe crops—deprived of light and bogged down with too much rain—did not ripen. Grain prices doubled. In India food shortages triggered a famine, which very likely led to the cholera epidemic that spread west during the next two decades, infecting thousands in Europe and North America. Fierce storms of hail, thunder, and lightning swept through many regions. It was a dreary season indeed.

"An almost perpetual rain confines us principally to the house," wrote eighteen-year-old Mary Godwin to her half sister Fanny. "The thunder storms that visit us are grander and more terrific than I have ever seen before." She wrote from a house on the eastern bank of Lake Geneva, into which she had just moved with three fellow travelers: Percy Bysshe Shelley, her twenty-three-year-old lover; Claire Clairmont, her stepsister, also eighteen; and little William, the infant son born to her and Shelley in January. Nearly five months old, the baby—"Willmouse," as they called him—would have been smiling and reaching out to grasp a finger offered to him. One calm evening when they had first arrived, just the three of them—father, mother, child—had gone out on the lake in a little skiff at twilight. They skimmed noiselessly across the lake's glassy surface, watching the sun sink behind the dark frown of the Jura Mountains. Since then, though, storms had moved in. They did at least provide entertainment. "We watch them as they approach," Mary wrote Fanny,

observing the lightning play among the clouds in various parts of the heavens. . . . One night we enjoyed *a finer storm than I had ever before beheld. The lake was lit up—the pines on Jura made visible, and all the scene illuminated for an instant, when a pitchy blackness succeeded, and the thunder came in frightful bursts over our heads amid the darkness.*

Beyond the weather there was an excitement simply in being in Geneva, the intellectual birthplace of the French and American Revolutions. Mary described in her letter to Fanny the obelisk just outside the city, built in honor of Jean-Jacques Rousseau, once banished from his city but now recognized as an intellectual hero. Rousseau had declared that the imperfections and suffering in human life arose not from nature but from society. Human beings had only to free themselves from social oppression and prejudice in order to regain their native joy and liberty. A shared commitment to that idea had bonded her mother and father in an all-too-brief partnership; had drawn the young poet Percy Bysshe Shelley to her father, William Godwin, the radical philosopher he most revered; and had flamed the passion between herself and Shelley from the moment they met.

That first meeting had taken place in 1814, when she was sixteen and he was twenty-one. Now, two years later, they were making a household together. She could find pleasure simply in that: In those two years they had been such wanderers. First this odd threesome, she and Shelley and Claire, had sneaked out of London on a dark night in July 1814 and trekked through France and Germany on barely any money. Three months later they returned to London and found themselves roundly shunned. Shelley was, after all, married to another and father to a child. That No-

Mary Wollstonecraft Godwin Shelley, author
of *Frankenstein*, circa 1840.
© G. L. Archive/Alamy

vember, Harriet Shelley had given birth to a second child. Now, in the
summer of 1816, the legal Mrs. Shelley was raising Ianthe and Charles—
a girl aged three, a boy eighteen months—on her own. Shelley rational-
ized his behavior with a philosophy of free love. "Love," he would write,
"differs from gold and clay:/That to divide is not to take away." His passions—Mary, liberty, poetry, atheism—meant more to him than his responsibility for an estranged and earthly family.

Life with Mary, however, soon developed its own earthly obligations. 5
She had become pregnant during the 1814 escapade and stayed wretch-
edly sick through it all. In those times, and especially in Mary's own experience, birth and death mingled inextricably. Her own mother, Mary
Wollstonecraft, had never risen from bed after giving birth to her. An
infection developed, the fever never ceased, and Wollstonecraft died ten
days after childbirth. Fear certainly exacerbated young Mary Godwin's
condition. On February 22, 1815, a daughter was born prematurely, "unexpectedly alive, but still not expected to live," as Shelley wrote in a

journal. One week later parents, baby, and Claire moved from one end of London to the other, from Pimlico to Hans Place. "A bustle of moving," Mary wrote in her journal on March 2. Four days later she wrote: "find my baby dead——. . . a miserable day." She managed to write a letter to a friend: "It was perfectly well when I went to bed—I awoke in the night to give it suck[. I]t appeared to be *sleeping* so quietly that I would not awake it—it was dead then but we did not find *that* out till morning—from its appearance it evedently [*sic*] died of convulsions." The child was never given a name.

Meanwhile Harriet Shelley pleaded for help for her two children from the fathers of both her husband and his runaway lover. Timothy Shelley, a baronet of ample means, felt fury over family shame more than anything else and clamped down viciously on his son's access to any inheritance. William Godwin, now remarried, no longer enjoyed popularity as a radical author. He and his wife barely made ends meet by running a bookshop and publishing books for children. They shared the baronet's parental outrage, however, and Godwin turned Shelley's kidnapping, as he termed it, of his daughter and stepdaughter into an opportunity for a gentlemanly sort of blackmail. By the summer of 1816, to meet the demands of Harriet Shelley and William Godwin, not to mention his own household obligations, Percy Bysshe Shelley was negotiating with moneylenders and solicitors for post-obit bonds—loans against his future estate.

Mary, Percy, and Claire moved restlessly, often hiding from creditors, Shelley all the while corresponding frantically with William Godwin about money. On January 25, 1816, though, at the end of a letter full of logistics concerning loans and payments, Shelley wrote: "Mrs. Godwin will probably be glad to hear that Mary has safely recovered from a very favorable confinement, & that her child is well." Mary Godwin and Percy Bysshe Shelley, unmarried, welcomed a son into the world. In a decision rife with contradictions, they named him William, after her father.

As if that weren't enough, now, in the cold and rainy summer of 1816, there was a new secret to keep from the Godwins.

Claire Clairmont—Mary's stepsister, the daughter of the second Mrs. Godwin—had been the one who selected Geneva as the destination of their upstart band. She was chasing after the outlandish yet irresistibly popular poet George Gordon, Lord Byron. Some speculate that early on Claire, as well as Mary, had had her eyes on Percy Bysshe Shelley. But by 1816 she was feeling like the odd woman out and, presented with the opportunity to meet the notoriously libertine Byron, Claire Clairmont had plotted—and pounced. Exploiting a tenuous personal connection, she approached Lord Byron. "An utter stranger takes the liberty of addressing you," her first letter to him began. It grew more presumptuous with every paragraph: "It may seem a strange assertion, but it is not the less true that I place my happiness in your hands." Rebuffed, Claire wrote again, explaining that she had drafted a play and sought Byron's advice on her composition. "You think it impertinent that I intrude on you," she wrote. "Remember that I have confided to you the most important secrets. I have withheld nothing." Slyly she implied submission even before he pursued her.

Claire was an annoying distraction during a troubled period of Byron's life. He had married Annabella Milbanke in January 1815, but the marriage swiftly self-destructed, despite the birth of a daughter, Ada. The new wife and mother could not ignore Byron's fascination with his half sister, Augusta, and she had heard rumors of his sexual relations with men. She hired a doctor to investigate his mental condition. Byron was diagnosed sane. If he wasn't insane, he was immoral and dangerous, Annabella reasoned, and presented him with separation papers. Evidences of his incest and sodomy were whispered, even published, throughout Britain. "He is completely lost in the opinion of the world," wrote one London socialite. Byron decided to leave England. He would travel to Switzerland, birthplace of the Enlightenment, tolerant of iconoclasts like Rousseau — and himself.

So when Claire's letters began appearing, Byron was not in a particularly amorous mood. Sometime in late April, though, Claire's plot achieved consummation. As Byron wrote a friend some months later, "A man is a man, and if a girl of eighteen comes prancing to you at all hours there is but one way." It was a heartless fling, Byron said later: "I never loved nor pretended to love her." He probably thought he would shake her loose once he departed from England, but Claire Clairmont did not let go. Learning where Byron was going, she persuaded her friends to head for Geneva, too.

Diodati Escapades

According to Byron's physician and traveling companion, John William Polidori, the Shelley party first encountered Lord Byron on May 27, 1816. "Getting out [of a boat]," wrote Polidori in his diary, "L.B. met M. Wollstonecraft Godwin, her sister, and Percy Shelley." Byron's fame made the younger poet somewhat diffident, yet Byron hosted Shelley for dinner that very night. Polidori described him as "bashful, shy, consumptive, twenty-six: separated from his wife; keeps the two daughters of Godwin, who practise his theories; one L.B's." He got Shelley's age wrong by two years but immediately grasped the dynamics between Claire and Byron.

The scene was set for the momentous summer of 1816. Byron rented the Villa Diodati, an elegant estate house above Lake Geneva. John Milton himself, the author of *Paradise Lost*, had stayed in the house in 1638, while visiting the uncle of his dear friend Charles Diodati. Byron must have enjoyed communing with such an eminent forebear. Shelley, Mary, and Claire rented a humbler house down the hill, closer to the lake's edge, and visited Villa Diodati often. One wonders whether Mary ever brought her baby with her into that environment, electric with testosterone and nerves. She hired a Swiss nursemaid, but she still must have felt torn between her duties as a mother and her fascination with her poet friends. Sometimes fierce lightning storms broke open the skies above Villa Diodati. Together with the storms, sharp wit and intellectual sparring may have kept her at the villa longer than she planned.

They spoke of literature, debating the virtues of the writers of the time. Robert Southey, then Britain's poet laureate, had published *Thalaba the Destroyer* and *The Curse of Kehama*, passionate epics set in mysterious Eastern realms and peopled by unknown deities. Shelley so respected these poems that he used them as models, but Byron mocked them for their pageantry and melodrama. William Wordsworth presented an entirely different aesthetic, finding poetry in the language of the common folk—shepherds, idiots, children. Samuel Taylor Coleridge's poems evoked powers unseen and unnamed. Meanwhile Walter Scott, already revered for poems that sang of his native Scotland, was suspected of being the author of *Waverley*. What a shock if it were true—that a popular poet would descend to write a novel, a new and not altogether respected literary form.

No poet of any renown would write a novel; no elevated person would 15 stoop to read one. Yet in the wee hours of the night, their tongues unleashed by sherry or other elixirs, those present at the Villa Diodati might admit a fascination with an occasional Gothic romance, Mrs. Radcliffe's *Mysteries of Udolpho* or Matthew Gregory Lewis's *The Monk*, perhaps. Set in a dimly imagined past, these popular books of the time pitted established strictures against native human desire, raising the very questions that radical philosophers had been asking about convention and society. Ghosts and spirits haunted the churchyards, vaults, and abbeys; gore, horror, lust, and crime oozed onto the printed page. There was something in the human imagination that made such stories irresistibly fascinating.

- - -

John Polidori, Lord Byron's physician and author
of *The Vampyre*, circa 1820.
Hulton Archive/Getty Images

Electrifying Science

Poetry was much on the minds of those gathered at the Villa Diodati,
but science charged the conversation as well. Polidori, after all, had been
trained in medicine, and Shelley had intended to become a doctor when
he entered Oxford in 1810. A friend described his college quarters as
cluttered with chemistry flasks and retorts.° Early-nineteenth-century
advances in science opened up realms of thought as fantastic as any
coming from the imagination of a poet. In fact, to some, philosophy,
poetry, and science converged to promise revolutionary changes in human knowledge and worldview.

Erasmus Darwin, for example, grandfather to Charles, had proffered
an early theory of evolution. "Organic life beneath the shoreless

---

retorts: a vessel, commonly a glass bulb with a long neck bent downward, used for
distilling or decomposing substances by heat.

waves / Was born and nurs'd in ocean's pearly caves," he wrote in his epic poem *The Temple of Nature; or, the Origin of Society*, published in 1803. As Darwin described it, life forms "new powers acquire, and larger limbs assume / Whence countless groups of vegetation spring, / And breathing realms of fin, and feet, and wing." Notions of evolving life forms led logically back to questions about the origin of life itself. Joseph Priestley, discoverer of oxygen, used mold on vegetables to demonstrate the spontaneous generation of life. Darwin saw similar things going on in aging wheat-flour slurry: "In paste composed of flour and water, which has been suffered to become acescent [to sour], the animalcules called eels, vibrio anguillula, are seen in great abundance." The eggs of such creatures could not possibly "float in the atmosphere, and pass through the sealed glass phial," Darwin reasoned, so they must come into being "by a spontaneous vital process." Evolution and spontaneous generation may be concepts difficult to accept, Darwin granted, but "all new discoveries, as of the magnetic needle, and coated electric jar, and Galvanic pile" seemed just as incredible.

Once Benjamin Franklin and others had managed to harness naturally occurring electricity, experimenters went to work on devices to collect, control, and generate electrical power. The galvanic pile, as Darwin called it—precursor of the electric battery—was named for the Italian scientist Luigi Galvani, whose famous experiments of the 1790s tested the effect of electrical current on the bodies of animals. When a charged metal rod caused disembodied frog leg muscles to move, Galvani glimpsed that electricity motivated living nerve and muscle. His work advanced understanding of what was called "animal electricity," soon renamed "galvanism." By 1802 the *Journal of Natural Philosophy* announced that "the production of the galvanic fluid, or electricity, by the direct or independent energy of life in animals, can no longer be doubted." Galvani's nephew, Luigi Aldini, toured Europe during the first years of the nineteenth century, demonstrating how electrical charges could move not only the legs of frogs but also the eyes and tongues of severed ox heads as well.

In a famous presentation to the president of the Royal College of Surgeons, Aldini demonstrated galvanism with the body of a recently executed murderer. Aldini connected wires from a massive battery of copper and zinc to the corpse's head and anus. As an eyewitness described it:

On the first application of the process to the face, the jaw of the deceased criminal began to quiver, the adjoining muscles were horribly contorted, and one eye was actually opened. In the subsequent part of the process, the right hand was raised and clenched, and the legs and thighs were set in motion. It appeared to the uninformed part of the by-standers as if the wretched man was on the eve of being restored to life.

London newspapers reported the phenomenon, and Aldini mounted 20 shows for the public. Even the Prince Regent attended one. It did not seem farfetched to consider this newly entrapped natural force, electricity, the quintessential force of life. "Galvanism had given token of such things," Mary Godwin wrote as she later recalled how discussions at Villa Diodati of these scientific marvels had filled her with ideas. "Perhaps the component parts of a creature might be manufactured, brought together, and endued [*sic*] with vital warmth."

The Challenge

Poetry and science, Gothic horror and reanimation—those topics tingled in the Geneva air that summer of 1816. Somebody pulled out a collection of tales of the supernatural, *Phantasmagoriana*, which became one evening's entertainment. The book had been translated from German into French in 1812 and subtitled *Recueil d'histoires d'apparitions, de spectres, revenans, fantomes, &c. traduit de l'allemande, par un amateur*—"a collection of stories about apparitions, specters, dreams, phantoms, etc., translated from the German by an amateur." The book must have enjoyed popularity at the time, be-

> "Poetry and science, Gothic horror and reanimation — those topics tingled in the Geneva air that summer of 1816."

cause an English edition came into print in 1813, with the simple title *Tales of the Dead*. The group at Villa Diodati read the stories to one another from the French edition.

"There was the History of the Inconstant Lover," Mary later recalled—its French title "La Morte Fiancée"—which told of an Italian courtier in love with a woman whose identical twin had died mysteriously the year before. "There was the tale of the sinful founder of his race," as she called "Les Portraits de Famille," in which ancient portraits hanging on cold stone walls assumed supernatural powers. "I have not seen these stories since then," she wrote in 1831, "but their incidents are as fresh in my mind as if I had read them yesterday."

After listening to a few of these tales, chilling yet clumsily written, Byron challenged his companions. Any one of them could do better. "'We will each write a ghost story,' said Lord Byron; and his proposition was acceded to," Mary Shelley recounted in 1831. "There were four of us," she begins, although there were five. The one she left out was Claire

Clairmont—maybe Claire was not present, or she simply chose not to write, or maybe Mary was deliberately ignoring her stepsister. Byron only started a story, "a fragment of which he printed at the end of his poem of Mazeppa," Mary reported—a two-thousand-word passage that introduces two Englishmen in a Greek landscape: Augustus Darvell, celebrated, mysterious, and haunted by "some peculiar circumstances in his private history"; and the story's narrator, younger, ingenuous, and mesmerized by Darvell. "This is the end of my journey," Darvell whispers. He has led his young friend into an old Muslim cemetery, full of fallen turban-topped tombstones. He hands him a ring engraved with Arabic characters, with strict instructions to fling it into Eleusinian springs after he dies. A stork alights on a nearby tombstone, a snake writhing in her beak. As she flies away, Darvell breathes his last. The narrator buries him in an ancient grave. "Between astonishment and grief, I was tearless," he says—and at that, Byron abandoned the story.

Percy Shelley appears not to have composed even a fragment in response to the challenge. His wife's explanation, written after his death, was that storytelling was just not his style. Spirits did seem to haunt him—in 1813 he had fled a Welsh cottage, convinced that a ghost had fired a gun at him—but grotesques were not the stuff of his poetry in 1816. Shelley, she wrote, was "more apt to embody ideas and sentiments in the radiance of brilliant imagery, and in the music of the most melodious verse that adorns our language, than to invent the machinery of a story." Ironically, therefore, Byron and Shelley—the two poets destined for the highest echelons of English Romantic literature—fizzled out in response to the ghost-story challenge, but their two companions wrote pieces that would evolve into the two greatest horror stories of modern times.

John Polidori was inspired to write two works, both published three 25 years later. One was a short novel, *Ernestus Berchtold*, little known by anyone but professors of English today. The other, he freely admitted, began with Byron's unfinished story. "A noble author having determined to descend from his lofty range, gave up a few hours to a tale of terror, and wrote the fragment published at the end of Mazeppa," Polidori explained. "Upon this foundation I built the Vampyre," as he titled his story. "In the course of three mornings, I produced that tale."

Like Byron's fragment, Polidori's *Vampyre* tells the tale of two Englishmen—Aubrey, a young gentleman, orphaned and innocent, and Lord Strongmore, a shadowy nobleman "more remarkable for his singularities, than for his rank." Strongmore suggests, much to Aubrey's amazement, that the two tour the Continent together. Repelled by Strongmore's appetite for sex and gambling, Aubrey takes off on his own and falls in love with Ianthe, a Greek country maid, who soon turns up dead, her throat pierced with "marks of teeth having opened the vein of the neck." "A Vampyre! a Vampyre!" the villagers all cry. The assailant turns out to be Lord Strongmore, who next sets his sights on Aubrey's own sister. Aubrey warns his family and mysteriously dies at midnight, leaving others to discover that "Lord Strongmore had disappeared, and Aubrey's sister had glutted the thirst of a VAMPYRE!" The story, borrowed from a poet and written by a man of little talent, would in a few years burst back on the literary scene and then proliferate through the nineteenth century, influencing Bram Stoker as he wrote *Dracula*, the vampire classic, in 1897. Thus on the same night in Geneva in 1816 were born the world's two most famous monsters.

While vampires populated Polidori's imagination, Mary Godwin worried that hers seemed so vacant. "I busied myself *to think of a story,*—a story to rival those which had excited us to this task," she wrote fifteen years later. Conscious exertion seemed to get her nowhere. "I felt that blank incapability of invention which is the greatest misery of authorship, when dull Nothing replies to our anxious invocations. *Have you thought of a story?* I was asked each morning, and each morning I was forced to reply with a mortifying negative." Her mind remained as if a blank slate, and discussions between Byron and Shelley concerning "various philosophical doctrines" including "the nature of the principle of life" made impressions on it. They cited examples; they speculated as to extremes—sometimes the discussion was detailed and technical, sometimes visionary. Details of Aldini's galvanic demonstrations may have mingled with descriptions of gruesome phantasms or translucent° fairies.

With such ideas swirling in her head, Mary Godwin went to bed. "I did not sleep, nor could I be said to think," she recalled. A story presented itself, as she described it, the life force less in her than in the visions appearing to her.

My imagination, unbidden, possessed and guided me, gifting the successive images that arose in my mind with a vividness far beyond the usual bounds of reverie. I saw—with shut eyes, but acute mental vision,—I saw the pale student of unhallowed arts kneeling beside the thing he had put together. I saw the hideous phantasm of a man stretched out, and then, on the working of some powerful engine, show signs of life, and stir with an uneasy, half vital motion.

To enter the original moment of the creation of Frankenstein's monster, strip away all the modern imagery created to portray it. No more white

translucent: clear, transparent.

lab coat, no more electrical coils and transformers, not even a dank stone tower. The author herself gives us very little: a "pale student," "kneeling" on the floor; beside him, "the thing he had put together"—a "hideous phantasm," "some powerful engine" whose force only made him "stir."

Granted, these few words are themselves just garments wrapped by 30 the author around wordless moments of inspiration. It is as if she, one with her character, had gazed for the first time upon "the horrid thing" standing at the bedside, staring at her with its "yellow, watery, but speculative eyes"—for, at the moment that she glimpsed this kernel of her story, she opened her own eyes "with terror," seeking the comfort of the outside world.

The idea so possessed my mind, that a thrill of fear ran through me, and I wished to exchange the ghastly image of my fancy for the realities around. I see them still; the very room, the dark parquet, *the closed shutters, with the moonlight struggling through, and the sense I had that the glassy lake and white high Alps were beyond. I could not so easily get rid of my hideous phantom; still it haunted me. I must try to think of something else. I recurred to my ghost story,—my tiresome unlucky ghost story! O! if I could only contrive one which would frighten my reader as I myself had been frightened that night!*

Soon the two thoughts merged into one: her waking dream *was* her ghost story. "On the morrow I announced that I had *thought of a story*," Mary later recalled. "I began that day with the words, *It was on a dreary night of November*, making only a transcript of the grim terrors of my waking dream."

Mary Godwin Shelley's account of the genesis of her novel, written for its 1831 edition, may contain a few fabrications, a few exaggerations, a few skewed memories. But it is still the most reliable rendition we have of how the story of Frankenstein began, and therefore a good starting point.

Understanding the Text

1. This article begins with two quotations. What is the significance of the quotations to the text and to each other?
2. How is the relationship between Percy Bysshe Shelley and Mary Godwin complicated by issues on both sides?
3. Identify some of the details of Lord Byron's history as detailed in this passage. In what ways did he come to embody the Romantic hero?

Reflection and Response

4. Hitchcock writes, "No poet of any renown would write a novel; no elevated person would stoop to read one" (par. 15). In what ways are certain styles or genres of art connected with class consciousness? What specific styles or genres of art today are affected by awareness of social class, and how is such art restricted or liberated by that?

5. Hitchcock takes some time to document the lives and celebrity of Lord Byron and Percy Bysshe Shelley. In particular, both Byron and Shelley were notorious for their lifestyles, rejecting social conventions and morality, living only for their art. To what extent does the lack of social conventions allow and inspire artists to be more creative? Consider this question in light of the fact that in the challenge, Shelley and Byron were not successful, and Mary Godwin and John Polidori were.

Making Connections

6. Mary Godwin Shelley later wrote about how difficult it was *"to think of a story"* (par. 27). Instead, the idea of *Frankenstein* came to her in a dream. What kinds of connections are there between dreaming and the creative imagination? Reread the excerpt from Shelley's *Frankenstein* that describes the creation of the monster (p. 20) and argue whether the scene has dreamlike qualities or not.

7. Hitchcock cites the work of Luigi Galvani, who sent electric charges through the bodies of dead frogs to watch their muscles move. How did scientific experiments and advances shape the environment in which Mary Godwin Shelley created the story *Frankenstein*? How do current developments, such as the creation of genetically modified organisms or other advances in medical technology, create the conditions in which scientists or doctors act like God? Are developments in medical technology as threatening today as they were in Shelley's time? Why or why not?

Why Vampires Never Die

Guillermo del Toro and Chuck Hogan

Why are vampires as popular now as ever? The stories of vampires — found in different languages, cultures, and times dating back to prehistory — have a strength and power that suggests not only an archetypal origin connected to cannibalism but also a contemporary need. According to Guillermo del Toro and Chuck Hogan in this *New York Times* column, the essential qualities of the modern vampire — combining lust and death — still speak to deep desires and fears. Fascination with the vampire is driven by the desire to move beyond the mortal to the immortal and, in a way, regain the sense of wonder that the modern world often removes. Del Toro is a writer and director of films such as *Pan's Labyrinth* (2006) and the Hellboy series. Hogan is the author of such novels as *Prince of Thieves* (2004) and *Devils in Exile* (2010). Together, del Toro and Hogan wrote the Strain vampire trilogy, which has been adapted into an FX television series.

Tonight, you or someone you love will likely be visited by a vampire— on cable television or the big screen, or in the bookstore. Our own novel describes a modern-day epidemic that spreads across New York City.

It all started nearly 200 years ago. It was the "Year without a Summer" of 1816, when ash from volcanic eruptions lowered temperatures around the globe, giving rise to widespread famine. A few friends gathered at the Villa Diodati on Lake Geneva and decided to engage in a small competition to see who could come up with the most terrifying tale—and the two great monsters of the modern age were born.

One was created by Mary Godwin, soon to become Mary Shelley, whose Dr. Frankenstein gave life to a desolate creature. The other monster was less created than fused. John William Polidori stitched together folklore, personal resentment, and erotic anxieties into *The Vampyre*, a story that is the basis for vampires as they are understood today.

With *The Vampyre*, Polidori gave birth to the two main branches of vampiric fiction: the vampire as romantic hero, and the vampire as undead monster. This ambivalence may reflect Polidori's own, as it is widely accepted that Lord Ruthven, the titular creature, was based upon Lord Byron—literary superstar of the era and another resident of the lakeside villa that fateful summer. Polidori tended to Byron day and night, both as his doctor and most devoted groupie. But Polidori resented him as well: Byron was dashing and brilliant, while the poor doctor had a rather drab talent and unremarkable physique.

But this was just a new twist to a very old idea. The myth, established 5
well before the invention of the word "vampire," seems to cross every
culture, language and era. The Indian Baital, the Ch'ing Shih in China,
and the Romanian Strigoi are but a few of its names. The creature seems
to be as old as Babylonia and Sumer. Or even older.

The vampire may originate from a repressed memory we had as pri-
mates. Perhaps at some point we were—out of necessity—cannibalistic.
As soon as we became sedentary, agricultural tribes with social boundaries, one seminal° myth might have featured our ancestors as primitive
beasts who slept in the cold loam of the earth and fed off the salty blood
of the living.

Monsters, like angels, are invoked by our individual and collective
needs. Today, much as during that gloomy summer in 1816, we feel the
need to seek their cold embrace.

Herein lies an important clue: in contrast to timeless creatures like the
dragon, the vampire does not seek to obliterate us, but instead offers a
peculiar brand of blood alchemy.° For as his contagion bestows its nocturnal gift, the vampire transforms our vile, mortal selves into the gold
of eternal youth, and instills in us something that every social construct
seeks to quash: primal lust. If youth is desire married with unending possibility, then vampire lust creates within us a delicious void, one we long
to fulfill.

In other words, whereas other monsters emphasize what is mortal in
us, the vampire emphasizes the eternal in us. Through the panacea° of its
blood it turns the lead of our toxic flesh into golden matter.

In a society that moves as fast as ours, where every week a new "block- 10
buster" must be enthroned at the box office, or where idols are fabricated
by consensus every new television season, the promise of something everlasting, something truly eternal, holds a special allure. As a seductive
figure, the vampire is as flexible and polyvalent° as ever. Witness its slow
mutation from the pansexual, decadent Anne Rice creatures to the current permutations—promising anything from chaste eternal love to wild
nocturnal escapades—and there you will find the true essence of immortality: adaptability.

Vampires find their niche and mutate at an accelerated rate now—in
the past one would see, for decades, the same variety of fiend, repeated in
multiple storylines. Now, vampires simultaneously occur in all forms

seminal: creative, original; containing the seeds of later development.
alchemy: the process of transforming something ordinary into something special.
panacea: a cure-all; a remedy for all illnesses or difficulties.
polyvalent: having multiple powers of attraction.

and tap into our every need: soap opera storylines, sexual liberation, noir detective fiction, etc. The myth seems to be twittering promiscuously to serve all avenues of life, from cereal boxes to romantic fiction. The fast pace of technology accelerates its viral dispersion in our culture.

But if Polidori remains the roots in the genealogy of our creature, the most widely known vampire was birthed by Bram Stoker in 1897.

Part of the reason for the great success of his *Dracula* is generally acknowledged to be its appearance at a time of great technological revolution. The narrative is full of new gadgets (telegraphs, typing machines), various forms of communication (diaries, ship logs), and cutting-edge science (blood transfusions)—a mash-up of ancient myth in conflict with the world of the present.

Today as well, we stand at the rich uncertain dawn of a new level of scientific innovation. The wireless technology we carry in our pockets today was the stuff of the science fiction in our youth. Our technological arrogance mirrors more and more the Wellsian° dystopia of dissatisfaction, while allowing us to feel safe and connected at all times. We can call, see or hear almost anything and anyone no matter where we are. For most people then, the only remote place remains within. "Know thyself" we do not.

"Despite our obsessive harnessing of information, we are still ultimately vulnerable to our fates and our nightmares."

Despite our obsessive harnessing of information, we are still ultimately 15 vulnerable to our fates and our nightmares. We enthrone the deadly virus in the very same way that *Dracula* allowed the British public to believe in monsters: through science. Science becomes the modern man's superstition. It allows him to experience fear and awe again, and to believe in the things he cannot see.

And through awe, we once again regain spiritual humility. The current vampire pandemic serves to remind us that we have no true jurisdiction over our bodies, our climate or our very souls. Monsters will always provide the possibility of mystery in our mundane "reality show" lives, hinting at a larger spiritual world; for if there are demons in our midst, there surely must be angels lurking nearby as well. In the vampire we find Eros and Thanatos fused together in archetypal embrace, spiraling through the ages, undying.

Forever.

Wellsian: H. G. Wells (1866–1946): British writer best known for his science fiction.

Understanding the Text

1. What are the two main branches of vampire lore that John Polidori fused in his story *The Vampyre*? How does this relate to what the authors call his "ambivalence" about Lord Byron (par. 4)?

2. How do vampires relate to practices of cannibalism? If cannibalism is far in our past, why do vampires still have such popularity today?

3. According to the authors, "As a seductive figure, the vampire is as flexible and polyvalent as ever" (par. 10). What do they mean by that? Explain, citing specific examples.

Reflection and Response

4. The authors state that Bram Stoker's *Dracula* welded together the old vampire mythology with the technological revolutions going on in Stoker's time. What about today's technological advances can be looked at as modern instances of the "new gadgets" (par. 13) of Stoker's time, and how do they influence more current renditions of the vampire myth?

5. The authors argue that "we are still ultimately vulnerable to our fates and our nightmares" (par. 15). Has science and technology taken away our sense of "fear and awe"? If so, how does the vampire myth help return that to us? If not, has science become "the modern man's superstition" (par. 15), as argued by the authors? Use examples to develop your response.

Making Connections

6. The authors state that the vampire combines lust and death. Read the selection from Bram Stoker's *Dracula* (p. 196) and use specific details to argue how that passage combines both of these elements. How do our current cultural attitudes toward lust and death influence more recent vampire stories?

7. Using a current vampire myth, such as the Twilight series by Stephenie Meyer, the Anne Rice books, or even Guillermo del Toro and Chuck Hogan's Strain trilogy, show how it helps us, as the authors say, "regain spiritual humility" (par. 16). Consider also the assumption in the same statement that spiritual humility has been lost and that we now believe we have "true jurisdiction over our bodies." Is this belief a result of our advances in medicine or technology? How does the vampire myth you have chosen serve to help us regain that humility? Support your argument with specific examples.

8. Research the human history of cannibalism and the history of vampires in older cultures and myths. (The authors have named several that will give you a good starting point.) Analyze how the practice of cannibalism, whether from the prehistoric past or more recent times, relates to the stories of vampires.

9. Research past medical practices, such as the widespread use of leeches, and argue how vampires can be seen as connected with disease.

My Zombie, Myself: Why Modern Life Feels Rather Undead

Chuck Klosterman

The zombie is a relatively recent monster: a creation that is not alive, is not particularly intelligent, and simply seeks to eat the brains of humans. In the process, it can reproduce itself. In this article that originally appeared in the *New York Times*, Chuck Klosterman argues that the zombie is a metaphor for our modern, task-filled world, in which the problems we face seem to multiply faster than we can solve them. Thus, zombies neatly encapsulate our fears and anxieties about modern life. Klosterman is a popular writer of nonfiction, including *Sex, Drugs, and Cocoa Puffs* (2003) and *I Wear the Black Hat* (2013). He has also written two novels, *Downtown Owl* (2008) and *The Visible Man* (2011).

Zombies are a value stock. They are wordless and oozing and brain dead, but they're an ever-expanding market with no glass ceiling. Zombies are a target-rich environment, literally and figuratively. The more you fill them with bullets, the more interesting they become. Roughly 5.3 million people watched the first episode of *The Walking Dead* on AMC, a stunning 83 percent more than the 2.9 million who watched the Season 4 premiere of *Mad Men*. This means there are at least 2.4 million cable-ready Americans who might prefer watching Christina Hendricks if she were an animated corpse.

Statistically and aesthetically that dissonance° seems perverse. But it probably shouldn't. Mainstream interest in zombies has steadily risen over the past 40 years. Zombies are a commodity that has advanced slowly and without major evolution, much like the staggering creatures George Romero popularized in the 1968 film *Night of the Living Dead*. What makes that measured amplification curious is the inherent limitations of the zombie itself: You can't add much depth to a creature who can't talk, doesn't think and whose only motive is the consumption of flesh. You can't humanize a zombie, unless you make it less zombie-esque. There are slow zombies, and there are fast zombies—that's pretty much the spectrum of zombie diversity. It's not that zombies are changing to fit the world's condition; it's that the condition of the world seems more like a zombie offensive. Something about zombies is becoming more intriguing to us. And I think I know what that something is.

dissonance: inconsistency between the beliefs one holds and one's actions.

KLOSTERMAN My Zombie, Myself **41**

Zombies are just so easy to kill.

When we think critically about monsters, we tend to classify them as personifications of what we fear. Frankenstein's monster illustrated our trepidation about untethered science; Godzilla was spawned from the fear of the atomic age; werewolves feed into an instinctual panic over predation and man's detachment from nature. Vampires and zombies share an imbedded anxiety about disease. It's easy to project a symbolic relationship between vampirism and AIDS (or vampirism and the loss of purity). From a creative standpoint these fear projections are narrative linchpins; they turn creatures into ideas, and that's the point.

But what if the audience infers an entirely different metaphor? 5

What if contemporary people are less interested in seeing depictions of their unconscious fears and more attracted to allegories of how their day-to-day existence feels? That would explain why so many people watched the first episode of *The Walking Dead*: They knew they would be able to relate to it.

A lot of modern life is exactly like slaughtering zombies.

If there's one thing we all understand about zombie killing, it's that the act is uncomplicated: you blast

> "The principal downside to any zombie attack is that the zombies will never stop coming; the principal downside to life is that you will never be finished with whatever it is you do."

one in the brain from point-blank range (preferably with a shotgun). That's Step 1. Step 2 is doing the same thing to the next zombie that takes its place. Step 3 is identical to Step 2, and Step 4 isn't any different from Step 3. Repeat this process until (a) you perish, or (b) you run out of zombies. That's really the only viable strategy.

Every zombie war is a war of attrition. It's always a numbers game. And it's more repetitive than complex. In other words, zombie killing is philosophically similar to reading and deleting 400 work e-mails on a Monday morning or filling out paperwork that only generates more paperwork, or following Twitter gossip out of obligation, or performing tedious tasks in which the only true risk is being consumed by avalanche. The principal downside to any zombie attack is that the zombies will never stop coming; the principal downside to life is that you will never be finished with whatever it is you do.

The Internet reminds us of this every day. 10

Here's a passage from a youngish writer named Alice Gregory, taken from a recent essay on Gary Shteyngart's dystopic novel *Super Sad True Love Story* in the literary journal *n+1*: "It's hard not to think 'death drive' every time I go on the Internet," she writes. "Opening Safari is an

Andrew Lincoln as Rick Grimes in the zombie television series *The Walking Dead*.
© AMC/Photofest

actively destructive decision. I am asking that consciousness be taken away from me."

Ms. Gregory's self-directed fear is thematically similar to how the zombie brain is described by Max Brooks, author of the fictional oral history *World War Z* and its accompanying self-help manual, *The Zombie Survival Guide*: "Imagine a computer programmed to execute one function. This function cannot be paused, modified or erased. No new data can be stored. No new commands can be installed. This computer will perform that one function, over and over, until its power source eventually shuts down."

This is our collective fear projection: that we will be consumed. Zombies are like the Internet and the media and every conversation we don't want to have. All of it comes at us endlessly (and thoughtlessly), and—if we surrender—we will be overtaken and absorbed. Yet this war is manageable, if not necessarily winnable. As long as we keep deleting whatever's directly in front of us, we survive. We live to eliminate the zombies of tomorrow. We are able to remain human, at least for the time being. Our enemy is relentless and colossal, but also uncreative and stupid.

Battling zombies is like battling anything . . . or everything.

Because of the Twilight series it's easy to manufacture an argument in   15
which zombies are merely replacing vampires as the monster of the moment, a designation that is supposed to matter for metaphorical, non-
monstrous reasons. But that kind of thinking is deceptive. The recent
five-year spike in vampire interest is only about the multiplatform success of Twilight, a brand that isn't about vampirism anyway. It's mostly
about nostalgia for teenage chastity, the attractiveness of its film cast and
the fact that contemporary fiction consumers tend to prefer long serial-
ized novels that can be read rapidly. But this has still created a domino
effect. The 2008 Swedish vampire film *Let the Right One In* was fantastic,
but it probably wouldn't have been remade in the United States if Twilight
had never existed. *The Gates* was an overt attempt by ABC to tap into the
housebound, preteen Twilight audience; HBO's *True Blood* is a camp reaction to Robert Pattinson's flat earnestness.

The difference with zombies, of course, is that it's possible to like a
specific vampire temporarily, which isn't really an option with the undead. Characters like Mr. Pattison's Edward Cullen in Twilight and Anne
Rice's Lestat de Lioncourt, and even boring old Count Dracula can be
multidimensional and erotic; it's possible to learn why they are and who
they once were. Vampire love can be singular. Zombie love, however, is
always communal. If you dig zombies, you dig the entire zombie concept. It's never personal. You're interested in what zombies signify, you
like the way they move, and you understand what's required to stop them.
And this is a reassuring attraction, because those aspects don't really shift.
They've become shared archetypal knowledge.

A few days before Halloween I was in upstate New York with three
other people, and we somehow ended up at the Barn of Terror, outside a
town called Lake Katrine. Entering the barn was mildly disturbing, although probably not as scary as going into an actual abandoned barn that
didn't charge $20 and doesn't own its own domain name. Regardless, the
best part was when we exited the terror barn and were promptly herded
onto a school bus, which took us to a cornfield about a quarter of a mile
away. The field was filled with amateur actors, some playing military per-
sonnel and others that they called the infected. We were told to run
through the moonlit corn maze if we wanted to live; as we ran, armed
soldiers yelled contradictory instructions while hissing zombies emerged
from the corny darkness. It was designed to be fun, and it was. But just
before we immersed ourselves in the corn, one of my companions sardoni-
cally critiqued the reality of our predicament.

"I know this is supposed to be scary," he said. "But I'm pretty confident about my ability to deal with a zombie apocalypse. I feel strangely
informed about what to do in this kind of scenario."

I could not disagree. At this point who isn't? We all know how this goes: If you awake from a coma, and you don't immediately see a member of the hospital staff, assume a zombie takeover has transpired during your incapacitation. Don't travel at night and keep your drapes closed. Don't let zombies spit on you. If you knock a zombie down, direct a second bullet into its brain stem. But above all, do not assume that the war is over, because it never is. The zombies you kill today will merely be replaced by the zombies of tomorrow. But you can do this, my friend. It's disenchanting, but it's not difficult. Keep your finger on the trigger. Continue the termination. Don't stop believing. Don't stop deleting. Return your voice mails and nod your agreements. This is the zombies' world, and we just live in it. But we can live better.

Understanding the Text

1. What are the inherent limitations of zombies, according to Klosterman? In what way do those limitations make zombies different from other monsters, such as vampires?

2. Klosterman writes, "When we think critically about monsters, we tend to classify them as personifications of what we fear" (par. 4). What are those fears, and how does Klosterman connect them to specific monsters?

3. Klosterman quotes Alice Gregory as stating, "Opening Safari is an actively destructive decision. I am asking that consciousness be taken away from me" (par. 11). What is Safari, and what does she mean by this?

Reflection and Response

4. Analyze the difference between the zombie as a monster and the vampire. What different fears do they represent, and how are those fears to be combated? What does the presence of the zombie in popular imagination say about people's anxieties about modern life?

5. One metaphor that Klosterman uses is the computer, and in particular the Internet. Examine how zombies can be seen as a metaphor for the Internet. Based on your experience with the Internet, do you think this is an apt metaphor? Explain, using specific types of Web sites or other Internet functions to illustrate and support your answer.

6. Klosterman poses a key question in paragraph 6: "What if contemporary people are less interested in seeing depictions of their unconscious fears and more attracted to allegories of how their day-to-day existence feels?" If we are attracted to the zombie as an allegory for a boring daily existence filled with repetitive, seemingly meaningless tasks, do these tasks prove more persistent and resilient than zombies? After all, Klosterman argues, "zombies are just so easy to kill" (par. 3), but real-life tasks often are not. Give examples from everyday life to support your position.

Making Connections

7. Read Matt Kaplan's "Cursed by a Bite" (p. 164). Pay particular attention to Kaplan's argument about the origin of the myth of zombies. How does the argument that zombies may have existed on plantations in the Caribbean connect to contemporary society? Cite both Klosterman's and Kaplan's articles in your response.

8. Klosterman references several movie and television versions of the zombie myth: *Night of the Living Dead* (1968), *World War Z* (2013), and *The Walking Dead* (AMC). View at least one of these and argue whether his metaphor of zombies as incarnations of our daily challenges (e.g., "reading and deleting 400 work e-mails," par. 9) seems correct or not. Develop your response with specific examples from both Klosterman's essay and the movie or television version of the zombie myth you viewed.

Monsters and Messiahs

Mike Davis

The chupacabra (translated from the Spanish as "goatsucker") is a monster that combines elements of the dog, coyote, bat, rat, and possibly even alien. While no chupacabra has ever been found, its legend has gained popularity. Initially said to have appeared in Puerto Rico, the chupacabra has migrated to northern Mexico, the American Southwest, and even into the city of Los Angeles. In this article that appeared in the literary magazine *Grand Street*, Mike Davis examines the notion of what is real versus what is imaginary as a conflict between civilization and the wild, and he explores how the Latino population finds in the chupacabra a symbol of fear, then deflects that fear with humor. Davis is a professor of creative writing at the University of California, Riverside. His distinguished nonfiction often focuses on urban politics.

The wild is predator. It is the unexpected and the unpredictable. It is also dream. The Tongva of [what is now] Los Angeles, like other first peoples, made no ontological° distinction between everyday animals and those that appeared only in dreams or at the end of vision quests. Their bestiary,° for example, encompassed the *nunas-i-s*, dreaded creatures who survived from the time of the Ancestors, like the monster scorpion living in a cave at the eponymous Rancho El Escorpion in the west San Fernando Valley. There were also different species of were-animals—were-cougars, were-bears, were–sea lions, and so on—in whom masqueraded the spirits of the most powerful shamans. And, most astonishing perhaps, there was the great inland whale that lived in Big Bear Lake (in Tongvan, "the lake that cries"), high in the San Bernardino Mountains.

The cougar on the cover of the *Los Angeles Times*, of course, is not necessarily less imaginary than a giant scorpion or a mountain whale. Our bestiaries, deprived of the Tongva's continuous, intimate, and deep knowledge of their fauna, are animal cartoons based on random encounters and behavioralist clichés. Too often we equate wildness with urban disorder, and wild animals end up as the symbolic equivalents of street criminals. Or, conversely, they acquire all the psychopathic connotations of sentimentalized pets and surrogate people. The Otherness of wild ani-

---

ontological: relating to or based on being or existence.
bestiary: a collection or description of real or imagined beasts.

mals is the gestalt° that we constantly refashion in the image of our own urban misunderstanding and alienation. Where nature is most opaquely unknowable, as it is in the "character" of animals, we intensely crave the anthropomorphic comfort of definition and category. Bestiaries, by definition, are hierarchies of allegorical fauna (including familiar species in their double role as social symbols) crowned by monsters. And monsters, which embody fears in sensual forms, are sometimes messiahs of consolation.

If Los Angeles's bad dreams in recent years have conjured monsters, like man-eating cougars, out of the city's own wild periphery, they have also laid out a welcome mat for monstrous tourists. In early July of 1996, for example, the famous goat-sucking vampire from Puerto Rico, *el chupacabra*, took up residence in the Latino barrio of Pacoima, in the northwest San Fernando Valley. A hybrid fad, midway between the hula hoop and the Devil in Salem, mass culture and mass hysteria, the chupacabra was simultaneously an avatar° of poor people's deepest fears and an exuberant, tongue-in-cheek emblem of Latino cultural populism. I am not sure that the notoriously ill-tempered creature, with its bottomless appetite for *cabra*, *gallina*, and *pato*° (not to mention the odd Doberman pinscher or two), would enjoy being called a messiah, but it certainly has been a lightning rod for immigrant anxiety. In a vast, strange city—sometimes more desolate than a desert and more dangerous than a jungle—the chupacabra has brought the reassurance of a familiar monstrosity.

Like Southern California's parched coyotes of the early 1990s, the chupacabras were brought out of the hills and into the city by drought. Both in Puerto Rico, where the goatsucker first appeared in the town of Canóvanas, twenty miles east of San Juan, in December 1994, and in northern Mexico, where scores of incidents were reported throughout 1996, there is good reason to credit local claims of a dramatic increase in mysterious attacks on livestock and pets. Puerto Rico is recovering from two years of drought and massive hurricane damage, while northern Mexico, together with the American Southwest, has been suffering through the driest period since the dust-bowl era of the 1930s. In both cases, as Puerto Rican veterinarians and Mexican agricultural officials have demonstrated in detailed investigations, there has been an unusual, drought-related hike in the number and ferocity of wild-dog and coyote attacks. (In

---

gestalt: a structure or configuration derived from examining the properties of the parts so as to indicate the whole.
avatar: an incarnation in human form; an embodiment or personification of an idea, attitude, or view of life.
cabra, *gallina*, **and** *pato*: goat, hen, and duck.

An illustration of *el chupacabra.*
Courtesy of David Pirkle

Sinaloa, [Mexico,] a zoological task force blamed pollution rather than drought: "There's no goatsucker, but pollution is now so bad that it's driving ordinary animals mad, giving them the behavioral trappings of crazed alien creatures.")

From the beginning, how- 5 ever, folk culture was suspicious of "expert" explanations—"Who, after all, has ever seen a dog kill a goat like that?"—and preferred the agency of monsters and vampires. Indeed, the chupacabra may be an echo of the mythic bestiary of the Tainos, Puerto Rico's extinct aboriginal culture. At any event, its image underwent a fascinating evolution as sightings passed from the oral grapevine into the Spanish-speaking tabloid press, then into prime-time tabloid television, before a final apotheosis as an episode of *The X-Files.* Thus the original witness at Canóvanas described an apparition "just like the Devil . . . four or five feet tall with red eyes and a hideous forked tongue." A month later, the chupacabra grew a horn, which a mechanic, attacked by the creature just before Christmas 1995, amended to long, spiked hair or fur. Its body was portrayed as a hideous combination of a rat and kangaroo. After the chupacabra's immigration to Mexico in early 1996, however, its image was remodeled yet again, as the bug-eyed rat face and punk-rocker hairstyle were replaced by bat wings and a space alien's head. In Puerto Rico, there had been intense speculation that the chupacabra was a mascot or pet left behind by extraterrestrial visitors; now, according to Mexican UFO experts, there was proof that the chupacabra was E.T. himself.

The Mexican left, on the other hand, declared that the chupacabra was actually Carlos Salinas de Gortari, the runaway ex-president, who "had sucked the blood of his country," and T-shirts with Salinas's visage, bald and big-eared, on the body of a chupacabra soon became a popular rage. So did El Chupacabra, a masked wrestler and social activist, who began to appear regularly at some of the nearly one thousand anti-government protests held in turbulent Mexico City during 1996. Elsewhere in Mexico, the beloved devil-rat-alien, Latino if not literally *raza,*°

raza: race.

was supplanting Mickey Mouse and the Power Rangers as a popular icon: bars offered *chupacervezas*, food stands sold *chupatacos*, and mariachis sang *chupacarridos*. The delirious embrace of *chupacabrismo* by Mexico was, first and above all, a celebration of the national sense of humor. Despite all the setbacks and infamies of the Salinas era, Mexico still owned its laughter. Yet, as in Puerto Rico and Florida (where a chupacabra panic broke out in the Sweetwater district of Miami in March 1996), there was also genuine terror. Scientists, government ministers, and even President Zedillo [of Mexico] went on television to calm hysteria, while local investigators gathered irrefutable evidence of feral dog and coyote attacks on farm corrals.

In Los Angeles, the chupacabra craze was something of an antidote to the monomania of the Simpson trial. While O.J. was saturating English-language television in late spring and summer of 1996, the Spanish-language media, dominated by the huge Televisa chain, was covering chupacabra sightings in Sinaloa and Baja California, and debating whether the terror would strike in Southern California. In early July, two rabbits and a goat were found dead in a Pacoima barnyard. (Pacoima may possess some kind of occult locational significance since the Virgin Mary was widely believed to have appeared in nearby Lopez Canyon in 1990.) Although no one actually saw the chupacabra, there were telltale puncture wounds on the animals' necks and their bodies were totally drained of blood. Some people locked themselves in their houses and refused to send their children to school. Others had trouble sleeping and were afraid to take the trash out at night. The majority, however, simply chuckled: Los Angeles had recently acquired a first-rate *futbol* team; now it also had a genuine chupacabra to prove its Latin-Americanness. Meanwhile, in the chaparral-covered hills above Pacoima, a pair of well-fed coyotes were howling their own delight.

> "The delirious embrace of *chupacabrismo* by Mexico was, first and above all, a celebration of the national sense of humor."

Understanding the Text

1. Davis begins by discussing ancient bestiaries — collections of real or mythical animals. Consider this statement: "Our bestiaries, deprived of the Tongva's continuous, intimate and deep knowledge of their fauna, are animal cartoons based on random encounters and behavioralist clichés" (par. 2). What is his point about the bestiaries of native peoples and how they differ from modern concepts of animals?
2. What is the origin of the chupacabra?

3. Davis calls the Spanish-language media coverage of chupacabra attacks "an antidote to the monomania" of the English-language coverage of the O. J. Simpson trial (par. 7). What point is he making here?

Reflection and Response

4. Analyze the role that the chupacabra plays in Latino culture, as described by Davis. How does it create both fear and humor? What do you think Mexicans' simultaneous embrace of both the fear and the humor reveals about Latinos' attitudes and values? Can you think of other examples of a culture identifying with a negative figure or event and the reasons for that cultural embrace?

5. Why does Davis use the word "messiah" in discussing the chupacabra (pars. 2 and 3)? In what ways might the creature be considered a savior, and what might this image of the chupacabra reveal about Latinos' attitudes and values? Can you think of other examples of a culture identifying with a negative figure or event and the reasons for that cultural embrace?

6. An undercurrent in the article is a conflict of both class and culture. For the well-educated and scientifically minded, the chupacabra is a myth, perhaps arising from the effects of feral dogs or coyotes suffering from the drought. For the poor and uneducated, the chupacabra is a symbol of their suffering and alienation. Examine how Davis compares the two lines of thinking. Does he pick a side? Defend your answer.

Making Connections

7. Compare Davis's article on the chupacabra with Kenneth H. Simonsen's "The Monstrous and the Bestial: Animals in Greek Myths" (p. 89). What similarities do you find between the contemporary story of the chupacabra and the mythical creatures of ancient Greece? What role do such creatures play not only in the imagination but also in the culture of a people?

8. Research more recent articles on the chupacabra — articles about people claiming to have captured a chupacabra, only to find out the animal is actually a raccoon, dog, or coyote. Why do stories of the chupacabra persist, despite no concrete evidence of the animal's existence? Does the chupacabra meet a specific cultural need? Explain your answer.

Japan's Nuclear Nightmare: How the Bomb Became a Beast Called Godzilla

Peter H. Brothers

One of the most popular monster films of all time is *Godzilla* (1954), made in Japan less than a decade after atomic bombs devastated the cities of Hiroshima and Nagasaki. Still reeling from the trauma of atomic annihilation and the subsequent effects of radioactive poisoning, a team of Japanese filmmakers created a monster that embodied the fears and anxieties in Japan resulting from nuclear warfare. Originally conceived as a response to other film beasts, especially *King Kong* (1933), Godzilla in many ways surpassed them: the reptilian monster (and the film) stands as an enduring symbol of what happens when people tamper with science in such a way that the consequences extend beyond the imagination. Peter H. Brothers is an actor, director, lecturer, and author of several books, including *Mushroom Clouds and Mushroom Men: The Fantastic Cinema of Ishiro Honda* (2009), *Devil Bat Diary: The Journal of Johnny Layton* (2011), and *Terror in Tinseltown: The Sequel to "Devil Bat Diary"* (2012). This article was first published in 2011 in *Cineaste*, a magazine that covers the art and politics of film.

In 1954, while barely recovering from a devastating defeat in the Second World War and a humiliating seven-year-long American occupation, the Japanese were once again reminded of their unwilling participation in the Atomic Age, which began with the bombings of Hiroshima and Nagasaki. In March of that year a Japanese tuna trawler named *The Lucky Dragon No. 5* returned to port after finding itself covered in radioactive ash following the detonation of the first underwater nuclear explosion from the American "Operation Crossroads" atomic-bomb tests, which brought home to the Japanese the recurring and haunting images of the death, destruction, and demoralization befalling them at the end of WWII. It also gave Toho Studios producer Tomoyuki Tanaka a way to save face, following an aborted coproduction film project with Indonesia, by initiating a Japanese production unprecedented in that nation's history.

Inspired by the success of *The Beast from 20,000 Fathoms* (1953) and influenced by *King Kong* (1933), the film that resulted is singularly Japanese. *Godzilla* (*Gojira*) is a film less about a giant dinosaur running amuck and more about the psychological recovery of a people trying to rebuild their cities, their culture, and their lives threatened by radioactive fall-out. Just as those individuals who were once a part of America's "Greatest Generation" are rapidly fading from the scene, so too are those Japanese for whom the possibility of a nuclear catastrophe was never far away. Caught—if not in the cross hairs then decidedly in the line of fire—between two feuding superpowers, Japan's island nation had every reason to believe that their time could come again in dealing with the terrifying consequences of the Atomic (soon Nuclear) Age.

Tanaka saw a way to make a monster movie and cash in on a current craze while special-effects master Eiji Tsuburaya saw it as an opportunity to make his personal tribute to *King Kong*, the film that had motivated him to go into effects work in the first place. But for forty-year-old journeyman director Ishirô Honda, who was handed the assignment after the original director Senkichi Taniguchi turned it down, he resolved to use the monster as a metaphor for the growing fears of a nation living in the shadow of doomsday. As Honda said years later, "I wanted to make radiation visible." As a result, the Bomb became the Beast.

Honda knew firsthand the horrors of war. With over seven years of duty as an infantryman in China behind him, he had not only experienced combat but while on leave had also witnessed some of the fire raids on Japanese cities. After the surrender he spent six months as a POW, and after being repatriated he walked through the rubble of what was once the city of Hiroshima. As a result of these events, this film (and it is every inch his film) is a somber testimony of those experiences, continually reinforcing the feeling that nothing can be settled by armed conflicts and that potential destruction still looms over a Japanese populace helpless to prevent it.

In later years Honda stated that a direct reference to the real-life *Lucky* 5 *Dragon* incident was intentionally avoided so as to not make an obvious connection and thereby upset and dismay the moviegoing public. He wanted to make a film that was entertaining yet not preachy, to dramatize and not traumatize. Yet this intention is difficult to accept in light of the film's opening scene:

Japanese sailors are relaxing in the hot summer sun when suddenly a bright flash of light appears that justifiably gets their attention. While getting a closer look they are blinded for their efforts, and those staggering to get away are awash in atomic fire, which will melt the flesh off their bones as the radio operator sends a fervent, final, and futile message before he dies.

The bright light the sailors saw was a representation of a phenomenon known to the survivors of Hiroshima and Nagasaki as the *"pikadon"* or "flash-boom" caused by the explosion of the atomic bombs, and the sinking of the ship calls to mind the destruction of the Japanese Merchant Marine by U.S. submarines during the war. The fact that we witness the death of the radio operator is not a coincidence, for it was Aikichi Kuboyama—the real-life radio operator of *The Lucky Dragon*—who died of radiation poisoning from that fatal encounter just one month before the film was released. If that weren't enough, the life raft visible on the ship's railing in the film reads *Eiko-Maru No. 5.* A more direct parallel is difficult to imagine.

Godzilla is in fact a virtual re-creation of the Japanese military and civilian experience during the final months of WWII, even to Godzilla itself, as Honda insisted that the monster's roar sound like an air-raid siren while its footsteps should sound like exploding bombs. Numerous other WWII analogies in *Godzilla* (the WWII events are in bold and the movie scenes are italicized) can be cited.

On the night of March 9, 1945, American B-29s laid down tons of incendiaries on the city of Tokyo, destroying 250,000 homes, burning out ten square miles of the city, leaving one million homeless and 100,000 dead.

The "sea of fire" engulfing Tokyo during Godzilla's rampage.   10

The Japanese Home Defense mobilizes to fight the invasion of the Japanese mainland from the sea in what was known to the Americans as "Operation Olympic."

The Japanese Home Defense gets ready to repel Godzilla's second attack, which is an invasion from the sea.

In the last months of the war the Japanese military is overwhelmed by superior enemy technology and sheer weight of numbers.

The Japanese military is helpless in their attempts to stop Godzilla.

Japan will face America alone, Germany and Italy having already   15
surrendered.

Japan faces Godzilla alone with no other country giving or offering aid.

Radio bulletins warn of impending evening American air raids as searchlights are employed and sirens alert residents to seek shelter.

Reports come over the radio notifying the citizens of Tokyo that the monster is approaching, as searchlights slice through the sky and sirens wail.

The Kamikaze (Divine Wind) unit flyers wore *hachimaki* headbands, usually anointed with religious symbols and inspirational words, in a desperate last-ditch attempt to defeat the Allied powers.

Ogata and Serizawa prepare to fight Godzilla with an unconventional   20
weapon (the "Oxygen Destroyer") as they don their headbands.

Japanese cities are reduced to rubble by means of conventional bombings, fire raids, and the atomic bombings.

After Godzilla's final assault on Tokyo, the camera pans over a devastated landscape of broken buildings and burning rubble.

Hospitals in Japan are overflowing with victims, known as the "gembakusha," of the two atomic-bomb attacks.

After Godzilla's second attack Japanese hospitals are filled with patients suffering from terrible radiation burns.

Ironically, when the film was released in America two years later (as 25 *Godzilla; King of the Monsters!), Boston Traveler* critic Alta Maloney stated of the hospital scenes: "They look suspiciously like actual films taken after the dropping of the atom bombs in Japan. They are uncomfortable views." This backhanded compliment is typical of the condescending attitude most Western critics had towards Japanese cinema at large, yet Honda's "uncomfortable views" were not pilfered from American-occupation footage but were solely the work of Honda and his chief cameraman Masao Tamai.

As it happens, these scenes are far less shocking and graphic than the real thing and the reason for this was simple. Honda was a man of extreme good taste and decency and did not want to disturb or horrify his audience; it was for this same reason that the scars on the scientist Serizawa's face were toned down considerably in the film from their original conception seen in production photos. Honda wanted his public to concentrate on the suffering within the individuals and not be sickened or distracted by their physical deformities.

Godzilla is a film that deserves to be taken seriously, but to accept what the movie is saying on its own terms one must understand its subtle anti-American tone and dissertation of destruction, which has been difficult for American critics to acknowledge, for to do so is to admit the guilt belonging solely to the society that had dropped the bombs in the first place (in America the Bomb is viewed as a necessary evil; in Japan the Bomb is evil, period).

To view this film objectively is to come face to face with the burden of responsibility for having laid waste to entire Japanese cities with fire and radiation. While it has been argued that there never would have been a Hiroshima had there never been a Pearl Harbor, what is also true is that without Hiroshima there would never have been a *Godzilla*. The relevancy of Honda's intention, however, has now faded with time. With the end of the Cold War, and the beginning of Strategic Arms Limitation Talks and test-ban treaties, and with some (but not all) of the nations of the world slowly dismantling their nuclear arsenals, the Black Shadow of Death that was the original conception of *Godzilla* has become merely camp to some and corny to others. What they fail to see is the deeper meaning of the film, but because of the efforts of those involved with its creation, *Godzilla* remains a superbly-crafted and engaging motion picture with more conviction, drama, and mood than any other so-called

A movie poster for the 1956 American adaptation of *Godzilla*, starring Raymond Burr.

"monster movie" before or since. *King Kong* may be considered the greater film, but *Godzilla* is better.

While technically brilliant from an effects standpoint, *Kong* is a stylized melodrama suffering from dated dialog, stagy machismo overtones, and graphically-shocking images, whereas *Godzilla* is a subdued and contemporary film dealing with an issue that is pertinent and real, one that hangs over our heads today as did the mushroom clouds over Japan in 1945. *Kong* is pure fantasy told in storybook style meant to entertain, *Godzilla* is a window to an alternate reality meant to enlighten. *Kong* is a film about a giant gorilla, *Godzilla* is a film about men. There is a difference.

Godzilla is also a far more emotionally powerful viewing experience. 30 In *King Kong*, as the giant ape shakes screaming sailors off a tree trunk into a deep chasm, we witness their deaths from a distance, thus maintaining an objective viewpoint and are not particularly appalled or saddened. Japanese commuters in *Godzilla* are killed riding on their train into Tokyo and Honda pulls his camera in close on the reactions of female onlookers, and as a result we are much more involved, intimately experiencing their shock and horror. *Kong* is an exaggeration of an ape representing the summation of the fears and frustrations of a time long since passed, the Great Depression of the early 1930s, whereas *Godzilla* is a metaphor of man's tampering with science, as relevant a message today as it was over fifty years ago.

> "*[King] Kong* is a film about a giant gorilla, *Godzilla* is a film about men. There is a difference."

• • •

In America the film was altered substantially (to tone down, intentionally or not, the Atomic Bomb connection), incorporating new scenes with the American actor Raymond Burr so as to make the film more acceptable for Western viewers (the distributor, Embassy Pictures, felt there was no way Americans would attend an all-Japanese production just fifteen years after Pearl Harbor). Even then director/editor Terry Morse handled the film with extraordinary care, retaining the spirit, if not the letter, of the original (happily all of Ifukube's brilliant score was retained, which was not always the case, as his films were usually mutilated for their American release).

The differences between the two versions is worthy of an article in itself, but essentially the original ninety-eight-minute version was cut to only eighty minutes (which included the insertion of twenty minutes of

Americanized footage). Lost on the cutting-room floor were scenes focusing on the "love triangle" relationship between Emiko (engaged to Serizawa) and her lover Ogata, and the tension they feel in having to inform Serizawa of their relationship, as well as the adoption of the Odo Island native boy Shinkichi by Dr. Yamane after the boy's parents have been killed by Godzilla.

Also eliminated were important dialog scenes, which were substituted with new scenes of Burr—posing as newspaper reporter Steve Martin— interacting with characters not in Honda's film informing him of what is happening; in some instances Burr simply narrates over the source material. Burr also has "conversations" with the actors in Honda's film, thanks to intercutting between close-ups of the new and original footage, with Burr often seen chatting with extras with their backs to the camera clothed in wardrobes similar to the original actors!

The biggest alteration involves the distillation of the atomic bomb connection, such as the deletion of a scene where train commuters complain about Nagasaki and once again having to seek refuge in bomb shelters, as well as Yamane's crucial soliloquy at the end of the film in which he warns the audience of the dangers of atomic experimentation. Also deleted was an argument between Ogata and Yamane where the younger man mentions the "atomic cloud that still haunts us Japanese." The American "A-Bomb" becomes the Russian "H-Bomb" and the word "radiation"—used consistently in Honda's film—is never heard in the new footage, with the scars the survivors are experiencing now referred to as "strange burns" (for those interested in comparing the two versions, they are available on the *Gojira/Godzilla* DVD "Collector's Edition" from Classic Media).

Sadly, the film's desperately serious message was disavowed by critics 35 both in Japan and in America, largely because they considered *Godzilla* as a monster movie not worthy of serious consideration, whereas many able to see beneath the surface discovered the film's moral. Strangely, the fact that *Godzilla* was a great commercial success may have worked against it, spawning as it has over two dozen sequels of inferior quality that have tended to cheapen the original film's intent by simply attempting to cash in on a major merchandising enterprise.

For his part, Honda felt most moviegoers missed the point by getting caught up in the visuals, often musing that the kids would eventually get it once they reached adulthood. He was right, yet Honda wanted it both ways: by not making a direct statement and discreetly avoiding the real issue, he nevertheless made a picture so stunning that it succeeds as entertainment, thereby distracting many viewers from its moral compass. Whether or not he ultimately succeeded depends on the interpretation gleaned by the individual viewer; some understand the "hidden" meaning while others are simply captivated by the intriguing story, or just enjoy watching the fantasy elements. In his later years, Honda acknowledged his naive hope that the film would persuade the nations of the world to cease and desist their nuclear development. He did live long enough to see the end of the Cold War, nuclear tests, and the beginning of nuclear disarmament treaties, but his hope for a world without nuclear energy never came to pass.

• • •

There are a number of reasons to appreciate *Godzilla's* role in film history, one of which was its enormous impact on the Japanese film industry. *Godzilla* was not only the first Japanese film to be made under a security lid and the first to be storyboarded, it was also the studio's most expensive and daring production up to that time. More important still is that before *Godzilla* all movies produced in Japan were indigenous products: domestic stories made only for their domestic audiences and where stories involving monsters were not to be taken seriously as authentic living creatures. The resultant production that premiered on November 3, 1954, was not only the first film in the longest running movie series originating from a single studio and the birth of a still-popular genre, but has also become the greatest international success in the history of Japanese filmmaking. It remains to this day the most famous Japanese film ever made.

It was also a gamble without precedent as no such film had ever been made in Japan before and there was no guarantee that Tsuburaya could pull off the heretofore untried special effects; nor was there any way of knowing how Japanese audiences would react to a thinly-disguised version of the horrific events that befell them during the war.

As it happened, *Godzilla* drew in nearly ten million Japanese viewers who were now able to deal with images that were indelibly integrated into their national psyche. Indeed the cathartic effect° the film apparently had was quite possibly the main reason for *Godzilla's* success; the horrific sufferings of the past could be addressed and soothed by the most horrific fiction of the present.

The film was a supreme collaborative effort created by individuals 40
whose lives were forever changed by the specter of the mushroom cloud, many of whom were either directly involved or profoundly affected by

cathartic effect: the release of strong emotions, such as pity or fear, especially through an interaction with art.

the traumatic events of those times, including special-effects photographer Sadamasa Arikawa, who told a crowd at a screening of the film in 2003 that "*Godzilla* was very much a picture of its time." Just as the explosions over Hiroshima and Nagasaki were watershed moments in the archives of the twentieth century, representing an initial gaze into a frightening new world of terror, *Godzilla* will forever remain a portal to a past many Americans would prefer to forget and that the Japanese can never forget. It is now recognized as not only the cinema's first antinuclear film but also the finest re-creation of the mood and desperation of a civilian population devastated by the worst weapon ever used.

Moreover it stands as the greatest achievement of a team that would collaborate on many more fantasy films, including the producer who needed a last-minute replacement for an aborted coproduction, a special-effects maverick and an iconoclastic musician, and, ultimately, a sensitive and thoughtful director named Ishirô Honda, who made more films seen by more people around the world than any other Japanese filmmaker.

The terrible irony in all of this is that if *Godzilla* is indeed the representation of the dangers of man's tampering with atomic and nuclear power, it has more recently surfaced in such places as Three Mile Island, Chernobyl, and now in Fukushima, where at the time of this writing a possible nuclear-reactor meltdown threatens consequences beyond even the imagination of the men who brought such a terrible fiction to life (a recent e-mail sent by one of the workers at the plant desperately trying to avert catastrophe reads like dialog from *Godzilla*: "If we're in hell now, all we can do is to crawl up towards heaven. Who could stand this reality?").

Regarded by many today as merely "pop culture," at its time the movie *Godzilla* was a warning about a newly-christened crisis, one which has yet to be fully appreciated, and a legacy which should never be forgotten.

Understanding the Text

1. What is important about the movie's opening scene with the Japanese sailors? How does it create a context for the film?

2. *Brothers* details a number of parallels between the events at the end of World War II and scenes in the movie. What connections is he pointing out between the real events and the film?

3. Why did Ishirô Honda deliberately make the physical injuries and scarring to victims "far less shocking and graphic than the real thing" (par. 26)? What is the ultimate effect?

4. What are the principal differences between the original Japanese version of *Godzilla* and the first remake for American audiences, starring Raymond Burr? What were the reasons for those differences?

Reflection and Response

5. Brothers asserts that *Godzilla* is more about people than a monster. In what ways is this true? How does Godzilla the monster function as a representation of the very real fear of atomic destruction as well as the trauma of humiliating defeat in war?

6. Why has *Godzilla* had such staying power in people's imaginations? Consider that there are more than two dozen feature-length remakes or sequels to the film, not to mention two separate American television series and a large number of video games that feature Godzilla.

Making Connections

7. Brothers states that "*Godzilla* is a metaphor of man's tampering with science, as relevant a message today as it was over fifty years ago" (par. 30). Compare and contrast *Godzilla* and Mary Shelley's *Frankenstein* (p. 20), another story that springs from anxieties about meddling with science. What similarities are there in the creatures from *Frankenstein* and *Godzilla*, and how does the fact that Honda's Godzilla is a distinctly nonhuman monster create differences between it and Shelley's invention?

8. View the original Japanese version of *Godzilla* and compare it with a later version, either the one with Raymond Burr, presented as *Godzilla, King of the Monsters!* (1956), or a more contemporary version, such as *Godzilla* (1998) or *Godzilla* (2014). How do they differ, and what is the significance of the differences? Support your response with details from both films.

9. *Godzilla* was partially inspired by *King Kong* (1933). View the original *King Kong* and research the background of that film and its era. Then compare and contrast *Godzilla* and *King Kong*. How was *King Kong* an expression of the fears and anxieties of its time, and how were those fears different from the ones expressed in *Godzilla*? What in society has changed over time that makes *King Kong* less popular than *Godzilla* today?

Monsters and the Moral Imagination

Stephen T. Asma

In this article, Stephen T. Asma, a professor of philosophy at Columbia College Chicago, argues that monsters have a purpose — not merely to express our fears but also to test our sense of morality. While the likelihood of a real-life zombie attack seems negligible, other crises and traumas can and do occur. In fact, in our post-9/11 world, monsters have seen a sort of resurgence. Perhaps, as Asma argues, we create monsters as a reaction to the fears we experience and our inability to control the world around us. This article first appeared in the *Chronicle of Higher Education* in October 2009.

Monsters are on the rise. People can't seem to get enough of vampires lately, and zombies have a new lease on life. This year and next we have the release of the usual horror films like *Saw VI* and *Halloween II*; the campy mayhem of *Zombieland*; more-pensive forays like *9* (produced by Tim Burton and Timur Bekmambetov), *The Wolfman*, and *The Twilight Saga: New Moon*; and, more playfully, *Where the Wild Things Are* (a Dave Eggers rewrite of the Maurice Sendak classic).

The reasons for this increased monster culture are hard to pin down. Maybe it's social anxiety in the post-9/11 decade, or the conflict in Iraq—some think there's an uptick in such fare during wartime. Perhaps it's the economic downturn. The monster proliferation can be explained, in part, by exploring the meaning of monsters. Popular culture is re-enchanted with meaningful monsters, and even the eggheads are stroking their chins—last month saw the seventh global conference on Monsters and the Monstrous at the University of Oxford.

The uses of monsters vary widely. In our liberal culture, we dramatize the rage of the monstrous creature and Frankenstein's is a good example—then scold ourselves and our "intolerant society" for alienating the outcast in the first place. The liberal lesson of monsters is one of tolerance: We must overcome our innate scapegoating, our xenophobic° tendencies. Of course, this is by no means the only interpretation of monster stories. The medieval mind saw giants and mythical creatures as God's punishments for the sin of pride. For the Greeks and Romans, monsters were prodigies—warnings of impending calamity.

---

xenophobic: relating to the fear of outsiders or foreigners.

After Freud, monster stories were considered cathartic journeys into our unconscious[;] everybody contains a Mr. Hyde, and these stories give us a chance to "walk on the wild side." But in the denouement° of most stories, the monster is killed and the psyche restored to civilized order. We can have our fun with the "torture porn" of Leatherface and Freddy Krueger or the erotic vampires, but this "vacation" to where the wild things are ultimately helps us return to our lives of quiet repression.

Any careful reading of Bram Stoker's *Dracula*, for example, will reveal not only a highly sexualized description of blood drinking, but an erotic characterization of the count himself. Even John Polidori's original 1819 vampire tale *The Vampyre* describes the monster as a sexually attractive force. According to the critic Christopher Craft, [the] Gothic monster tales *Frankenstein*, *The Strange Case of Dr. Jekyll and Mr. Hyde*, *Dracula*, [and] Anne Rice's *Vampire Chronicles* rehearse a similar story structure. "Each of these texts first invites or admits a monster, then entertains and is entertained by monstrosity for some extended duration, until in its closing pages it expels or repudiates the monster and all the disruption that he/she/it brings," he writes.

● ● ●

A crucial but often-ignored aspect of monsterology is the role those beasties play in our moral imaginations. Recent experimental moral psychology has given us useful tools for looking at the way people actually do their moral thinking. Brain imaging, together with hypothetical ethical dilemmas about runaway trolley cars, can teach us a lot about our real value systems and actions. But another way to get at this subterranean territory is by looking at our imaginative lives.

Monsters can stand as symbols of human vulnerability and crisis, and as such they play imaginative foils for thinking about our own responses to menace. Part of our fascination with serial-killer monsters is that we (and our loved ones) are potentially vulnerable to sadistic violence — never mind that statistical probability renders such an attack almost laughable. Irrational fears are decidedly unfunny. We are vulnerable to both the inner and the outer forces. Monster stories and films only draw us in when we identify with the persons who are being chased, and we tacitly ask ourselves: Would I board up the windows to keep the zombies out or seek the open water? Would I go down to the basement after I hear

---

denouement: the ending of a story; the climax and resolution, when everything is explained and made clear.

the thump, and if so, would I bring the butcher knife or the fireplace poker? What will I do when I am vulnerable?

The comedy writer Max Brooks understands that dimension of monster stories very well. In books like *The Zombie Survival Guide* and *World War Z*, Brooks gives us painstaking, haunting, and hilarious advice about how best to meet our undead foes. For its April Fools' edition, the otherwise serious journal *Archaeology* interviewed Brooks, asking him (tongue firmly in cheek): "Does the archaeological record hold any zombie-related lessons for us today? What can our ancestors teach us about meeting and, ultimately, defeating the undead menace?" Brooks replied: "The greatest lesson our ancestors have to teach us is to remain both vigilant and unafraid. We must endeavor to emulate the ancient Romans; calm, efficient, treating zombies as just one more item on a rather mundane checklist. Panic is the undead's greatest ally, doing far more damage, in some cases, than the creatures themselves. The goal is to be prepared, not scared, to use our heads, and cut off theirs."

Brooks is unparalleled in parodying a well-worn monster tradition, but he wouldn't be so funny if we weren't already using monster stories to imagine strategies for facing enemies. The monster is a virtual sparring partner for our imagination. How will I avoid, assuage, or defeat my enemy? Will I have grace under pressure? Will I help others who are injured? Or will I be that guy who selfishly goes it alone and usually meets an especially painful demise?

In a significant sense, monsters are a part of our attempt to envision 10 the good life or at least the secure life. Our ethical convictions do not spring fully grown from our heads but must be developed in the context of real and imagined challenges. In order to discover our values, we have to face trials and tribulation, and monsters help us imaginatively rehearse. Imagining how we will face an unstoppable, powerful, and inhuman threat is an illuminating exercise in hypothetical reasoning and hypothetical feeling.

You can't know for sure how you will face a headless zombie, an alien face-hugger, an approaching sea monster, or a chainsaw-wielding psycho. Fortunately, you're unlikely to be put to the test. But you might face similarly terrifying trials. You might be assaulted, be put on the front lines of some war, or be robbed, raped, or otherwise harassed and assailed. We may be lucky enough to have had no real acquaintance with such horrors, but we have all nonetheless played them out in our mind's eye. And though we can't know for sure how we'll face an enemy soldier or a rapist, it doesn't stop us from imaginatively formulating responses. We use the imagination in order to establish our own agency in chaotic and uncontrollable situations.

People frequently underestimate the role of art and imagery in their own moral convictions. Through art (e.g., Shelley's *Frankenstein*, Hitchcock's *Psycho*, King's and Kubrick's *The Shining*), artists convey moral visions. Audiences can reflect on them, reject or embrace them, take inspiration from them, and otherwise be enriched beyond the entertainment aspect. Good monster stories can transmit moral truths to us by showing us examples of dignity and depravity without preaching or proselytizing.

But imagining monsters is not just the stuff of fiction. Picture yourself in the following scenario. On the evening of August 7, 1994, Bruce Shapiro entered a coffee bar in New Haven, Conn. Shapiro and his friends had entered the cafe and were relaxing at a table near the front door. Approximately 15 other people were scattered around the bar, enjoying the evening. One of Shapiro's friends went up to the bar to get drinks. "Suddenly there was chaos," Shapiro explained in the *Nation* the next year, "as if a mortar shell had landed." He looked up to see a flash of metal and people leaping away from a thin, bearded man with a ponytail. Chairs and tables were knocked over, and Shapiro protected one of his friends by pulling her to the ground.

> "Good monster stories can transmit moral truths to us by showing us examples of dignity and depravity without preaching or proselytizing."

In a matter of minutes, the thin man, Daniel Silva, had managed to stab and seriously injure seven people in the coffee shop. Using a six-inch hunting knife, Silva jumped around the room and attacked with lightning speed. Two of Shapiro's friends were stabbed. After helping some others, Shapiro finally escaped the cafe. "I had gone no more than a few steps," he recalled, "when I felt a hard punch in my back followed instantly by the unforgettable sensation of skin and muscle tissue parting. Silva had stabbed me about six inches above my waist, just beneath my rib cage."

Shapiro fell to the pavement and cried out, "Why are you doing this?" Standing over him, Silva plunged the knife into Shapiro's chest, beneath his left shoulder. "You killed my mother" was the incoherent response that Silva offered his victim. Silva then pulled the knife out of Shapiro and rode off on a bicycle. He was soon apprehended and jailed.

Was Silva a monster? Not exactly. He was a mentally ill man who snapped and seemed to think that his mother had been wronged and felt some obscure need to avenge her. (She was, in fact, in a nearby hospital at the time, being treated for diabetes.) But from the perspective of raw experience, this horrifying event shares many qualities with the imagined monster attack. Shapiro and his unfortunate company were suddenly presented with a deadly, irrational, powerful force that sent them reeling for mere survival. And yet the victims demonstrated an impressive ability to reach out and help each other. While the victims were leaping away from Silva's angry knife blade, I suspect that he was for them, practically speaking, a true monster. I would never presume to correct them on that account. In such circumstances, many of us are sympathetic to the use of the monster epithet.

One of the fascinating aspects of Shapiro's experience is how people responded to his story after the fact. I have been suggesting that monster stones are encapsulations of the human feeling of vulnerability — the monster stories offer us the "disease" of vulnerability and its possible "cures" (in the form of heroes and coping strategies). Few monster stories remain indefinitely in the "threat phase." When fear is at a fever pitch, they always move on to the hero phase. Hercules slays the Hydra, George slays the dragon, medicine slays the alien virus, the stake and crucifix slay the vampire. Life and art mutually seek to conquer vulnerability. "Being a victim is a hard idea to accept," Shapiro explained, "even while lying in a hospital bed with tubes in veins, chest, penis, and abdomen. The spirit rebels against the idea of oneself as fundamentally powerless."

This natural rebellion may have prompted the most repeated question facing Shapiro when he got out of the hospital. When people learned of Daniel Silva's attack on seven victims, they asked, "Why didn't anyone try to stop him?" Shapiro always tried to explain how fast and confusing the attack was, but people failed to accept this. Shapiro, who was offended by the question, says, "The question carries not empathy but an implicit burden of blame; it really asks 'Why didn't you stop him?' It is asked because no one likes to imagine oneself a victim." We like to see ourselves as victors against every threat, but of course that's not reality.

* * *

Believers in human progress, from the Enlightenment to the present, think that monsters are disappearing. Rationality will pour its light into the dark corners and reveal the monsters to be merely chimeric. A familiar upshot of the liberal interpretation of monsters is to suggest that when we properly embrace difference, the monsters will vanish. According to this view, the monster concept is no longer useful in the modern world. If it hangs on, it does so like an appendix — useful once but hazardous now.

I disagree. The monster concept is still extremely useful, and it's a 20 permanent player in the moral imagination because human vulnerability is permanent. The monster is a beneficial foe, helping us to virtually represent the obstacles that real life will surely send our way. As long as there are real enemies in the world, there will be useful dramatic versions of them in our heads.

In 2006, four armed men in Kandahar, Afghanistan, broke into the home of an Afghan headmaster and teacher named Malim Abdul Habib. The four men held Habib as they gathered his wife and children together, forcing them to watch as they stabbed Habib eight times and then decapitated him. Habib was the headmaster at Shaikh Mathi Baba high school, where he educated girls along with boys. The Taliban militants of the region, who are suspected in the beheading, see the education of girls as a violation of Islam (a view that is obviously not shared by the vast majority of Muslims). My point is simply this: If you can gather a man's family together at gunpoint and force them to watch as you cut off his head, then you are a monster. You don't just seem like one; you are one.

A relativist might counter by pointing out that American soldiers at Abu Ghraib tortured some innocent people, too. That, I agree, is true and astoundingly shameful, but it doesn't prove there are no real monsters. It only widens the category and recognizes monsters on both sides of an issue. Two sides calling each other monsters doesn't prove that monsters don't exist. In the case of the American torturer at Abu Ghraib and the Taliban beheader in Afghanistan, both epithets sound entirely accurate.

My own view is that the concept of monster cannot be erased from our language and thinking. It cannot be replaced by other more polite terms and concepts, because it still refers to something that has no satisfactory semantic° substitute or refinement. The term's imprecision, within parameters, is part of its usefulness. Terms like "monster" and "evil" have a lot of metaphysical residue on them, left over from the Western traditions. But even if we neuter the term from obscure theological questions about Cain, or metaphysical questions about demons, the language still successfully expresses a radical frustration over the inhumanity of some enemy. The meaning of "monster" is found in its context, in its use.

So this Halloween season, let us, by all means, enjoy our fright fest, but let's not forget to take monsters seriously, too. I'll be checking under my bed, as usual. But remember, things don't strike fear in our hearts unless our hearts are already seriously committed to something (e.g., life, limb, children, ideologies, whatever). Ironically then, inhuman threats are great reminders of our own humanity. And for that we can all thank our zombies.

---

semantic: relating to the study of meanings.

Understanding the Text

1. What are the different interpretations of monster stories that Asma cites, including those of the ancient Greeks and Romans, the medieval era, and Sigmund Freud?

2. Asma connects monsters with the "moral imagination." What does he mean by this term? Cite specific examples from the article.

3. What is the point Asma makes with the story of Bruce Shapiro? How does that connect to the idea of monsters? How does it relate to Shapiro's statement that "no one likes to imagine oneself a victim" (par. 18)?

Reflection and Response

4. Asma speaks of learning from scientific "brain imaging" about people presented with "hypothetical ethical dilemmas" (par. 6). Do you find him convincing when he goes from real-life situations to situations regarding monsters? Why or why not?

5. According to Asma, "The monster concept is still extremely useful, and it's a permanent player in the moral imagination because human vulnerability is permanent" (par. 20). Apply this statement to a monster of your choice and argue how that particular monster concept can be useful.

Making Connections

6. Is Asma's thesis in "Monsters and the Moral Imagination" compatible with other explanations of monsters in this book? Consider, for example, the explanations given by Guillermo del Toro and Chuck Hogan for the popularity of vampires (p. 36), Chuck Klosterman's discussion about zombies (p. 40), or Skye Alexander's discussion of mermaids (p. 232). Do these ideas dovetail with Asma's, or do they contradict his assertions?

7. Asma makes the connection between imaginary monsters and serial killers or other real-life monsters. Investigate the impact of serial killers in Chapter 5 of this book or in other sources. Do real-life monsters have the same impact on the moral imagination as fictional creatures, or are there substantial differences? Defend your answer.

© ArtMarie/Getty Images

Is the Monster Animal or Human?

The composite creature—built from different parts of animals or humans — seems particularly marked as monstrous, standing as a gross violation of nature. It challenges our understanding of how certain things belong together and other things do not. Yet the composite monster has taken firm hold in the human imagination. Indeed, the ancient world created many composites. Some of these combinations are solely distortions of the animal kingdom, such as the fifty-headed dog Cerberus or the Chimera, a creature commonly depicted with the head of a lion, the head of a goat, and the head of a snake. Others, such as the Minotaur or sphinx, horrifically combine animal and human characteristics. The composite monster calls into question the very nature of its being, for its strangeness pushes the boundaries of what we can accept in nature and ourselves.

Such monsters attract as much curiosity as horror, and the stories of their origins may contain the keys to their nature. Introducing imaginary monsters to the reader, Jorge Luis Borges, the famous writer of magical realism, tells stories about the centaur, Minotaur, sphinx, and the Sirens. He examines their origins and their special place within the myths of the cultures that created them. Another tale, attributed to the Greek historian Apollodorus, recounts how Minos wanted to be king of Crete, but he paid a steep price when he backed out of a deal he made with the god Poseidon to get his kingdom: after coupling with a sacred bull, Minos's wife gave birth to the half-man, half-bull Minotaur. The Roman poet Ovid tells the tale of some very poorly behaved wedding guests: the half-man, half-horse centaurs. Inflamed with wine and lust, the centaurs try to make off with the women at the banquet. A deadly pitched battle ensues, in which most of the centaurs are killed. Commenting on the importance of composite creatures in Greek myths, Kenneth H. Simonsen explores two categories of imaginary creatures — those that are merely bestial and others that are truly monstrous. The distinctions we make reveal what we see as positive or negative attributes in animals and people. Bruce F. Kawin looks at more recent portrayals of animal-human combinations: H. G. Wells's novel *The Island of Dr. Moreau* and the films *Island of Lost Souls*, *The Fly* (two different versions), and *Creature from the Black Lagoon*. Konstantinos, a practicing occultist, turns our attention to werewolves, presenting a different spin on the myth of when werewolves make their appearance. Finally, Elizabeth A. Lawrence, a cultural anthropologist, examines different variations of the werewolf myth to interpret the long and sometimes contentious relationship wolves and humans have had and to ask why we might find ourselves taking on their characteristics.

Exploring the nature of such unnatural creatures offers opportunities for investigation into how people feel about nature, as well as their relationship to it. Human attitudes toward creatures found in nature — horses, wolves, lions, bulls, fish, and others — are reflected in the composite monsters of our imaginations. These monsters may alternately express qualities we admire or find abhorrent. The very notion of violating the boundaries of nature invokes a terror of its own: all sense of order is tested, and chaos — the loss of civilization — may be the result.

The Origins of Half-Human, Half-Animal Creatures

Jorge Luis Borges

The following excerpts from Jose Luis Borges's *Book of Imaginary Beings* (originally published in 1957) examine the origins of monstrous combinations of human and animal. The monsters are terrifying because of their perversion of what nature has kept separate: the human combined with a horse, bull, bird, fish, or lion. Borges was an Argentine writer whose works helped create the genre known as *magical realism* — a rendering of day-to-day life imbued with magical events. Among his many works are *Ficciones* (1944), *El Aleph and Other Stories* (1949), and *Labyrinths* (1962).

A child is taken for the first time to the zoo. The child may grow up to be you or me, or, conversely, we may once have been that child but have forgotten. At the zoo, that terrible "zoological garden," the child sees living animals he has never seen before—jaguars, vultures, buffalo, and, strangest of all, giraffes. He sees for the first time the confused variety of the animal kingdom, and the spectacle, far from alarming or frightening him, delights him. It delights him so much, in fact, that a trip to the zoo becomes part of the "fun" of childhood, or what passes for fun. How is one to explain this common and yet mysterious occurrence?

We can, of course, deny it. We can tell ourselves that children brusquely led into that garden become, twenty years down the line, neurotic, and the truth is, there's not a child who has not discovered the zoo and not an adult who is not, when carefully examined, discovered to be neurotic. Or we may assert that the child is, by definition, a discoverer, and that discovering the camel is no more remarkable than discovering mirrors, or water, or stairs. We may assert that the child trusts his parents, those who take him into that place filled with animals. Besides, the stuffed tiger on his bed and the tiger in the encyclopedia have prepared him to look without fear upon the tiger of flesh and blood. Plato (should he join in this discussion) would tell us that the child has already seen the tiger, in the world of archetypes, and that now, seeing it, he but *recognizes* it. Schopenhauer (still more startlingly) would say that the child looks without fear on tigers because he knows that he is the tigers and the tigers are he, or, more precisely, that tigers and he are of one essence—Will.

Let us move now from the zoo of reality to the zoo of mythology, that zoological garden whose fauna is comprised not of lions but of sphinxes and gryphons and centaurs. The population of this second zoo should by all rights exceed that of the first, since a monster is nothing but a combination of elements taken from real creatures, and the combinatory possibilities border on the infinite. In the centaur, horse and man are mingled; in the Minotaur, bull and man (Dante imagined it with the face of a human and the body of a bull). Following this lead, it seems to us, any number of monsters, combinations of fish, bird, and reptile, might be produced—the only limit being our own ennui° or revulsion. That, however, never happens; the monsters that we make would be stillborn, thank God. In the last pages of *The Temptation of St. Anthony*, Flaubert brought together all sorts of medieval and classical monsters, and even (his commentators tell us) attempted to invent some of his own; the total is not great, and those creatures that exert power over mankind's imagination are really very few. Readers browsing through our own anthology will see that the zoology attributable to dreams is in fact considerably more modest than that attributable to God.

> "A monster is nothing but a combination of elements taken from real creatures, and the combinatory possibilities border on the infinite."

We do not know what the dragon *means*, just as we do not know the meaning of the universe, but there is something in the image of the dragon that is congenial to man's imagination, and thus the dragon arises in many latitudes and ages. It is, one might say, a *necessary* monster, not some ephemeral° and casual creature like the Chimera or the catoblepas.

We would add that we have no illusions that this book, perhaps the first of its kind, contains within its covers every fantastic animal. We have pored through the classics and through Oriental literature, but we are perfectly aware that the subject we have undertaken is infinite.

The Centaur

The centaur is the most harmonious creature in fantastic zoology. In the *Metamorphoses*, Ovid calls it "biform," but it is easy enough to overlook its heterogeneous nature and to think that in the Platonic world of essences there is an archetype of the Centaur just as there is of the Horse or of Man. The discovery of that archetype took many centuries; primitive and archaic monuments portray a nude man to which a horse's rump

---

ennui: a feeling of boredom or dissatisfaction.
ephemeral: very short-lived.

can only uncomfortably be fitted. On the western facade of the Temple of Zeus on Olympia, the centaurs have equine limbs; at the place from which the animal's neck should emerge, there emerges the torso of a man.

Ixion, the king of Thessaly, was said to have engendered the race of centaurs upon a cloud to whom Zeus gave the shape of Hera; another legend has it that they are the children of Apollo. (It has been said that the word "centaur" derives from "gandharva"; in Vedic° mythology, the Gandharva are minor deities who rule over the horses of the sun.) Since the Greeks of Homer's time did not ride horses, it is conjectured that the first nomad they saw seemed to them to be one with his steed, and it is also alleged that the Indians of the New World saw Pizarro's and Hernán Cortés's soldiers as centaurs. William H. Prescott's *History of the Conquest of Peru* gives the following account of that first meeting:

It might have gone hard with the Spaniards, hotly pressed by their resolute enemy so superior in numbers, but for a ludicrous accident reported by the historians as happening to one of the cavaliers. This was a fall from his horse, which so astonished the barbarians, who were not prepared for this division of what seemed one and the same being into two, that, filled with consternation, they fell back, and left a way open for the Christians to regain their vessels!

But unlike the Indians of the New World, the Greeks did know the horse. It seems more likely that the centaur was a deliberately drawn image, not some ignorant confusion.

The most popular of the fables in which the centaurs figure is that of their battle with the Lapiths, who had invited them to a wedding feast. The guests were unused to wine; in the midst of the celebration, a drunken and lustfully inflamed centaur, Eurytus, seized the bride and, overturning tables, set in motion the famous Centauromachia that Phidias or one of his followers sculpted on the Parthenon, Ovid sang in the twelfth book of the *Metamorphoses*, and Rubens took for inspiration. The centaurs, defeated by the Lapiths, had to flee to Thessaly. In another battle, Hercules's arrows extinguished the entire race.

Anger and rustic barbarism are symbolized in the centaur, though Achilles and Aesculapius were tutored by Chiron, "the most gentlemanly" of the centaurs (*Iliad*, Book XI), who instructed his charges in the arts of music, hunting, warfare, and even medicine and surgery. Chiron figures memorably in the twelfth canto of Dante's *Inferno*, which is gen-

10

Vedic: relating to sacred Hindu writings, especially the Rig Veda, Sama Veda, Atharva Veda, and Yajur Veda.

erally called the "centaur canto." See, in this regard, the fine observations made by Momigliano, in his 1945 edition.

Pliny says that he saw a Hippocentaur, preserved in honey, which was sent to the emperor from Egypt.

In his *Dinner of the Seven Wise Men*, Plutarch tells the humorous story of one of the youths who tended the flocks of Periander, despot of Corinth. It seems the herdsman brought the ruler the foal, wrapped in a leather bag, that a certain mare had given birth to just that morning; the newborn's face, neck, and arms were human, while the rest of its body was that of a horse. It cried like a baby, and everyone thought this a terrifying omen. The wise Thales looked at it, however, laughed, and told Periander that he should either not employ such young men as keepers of his horses or provide wives for them.

In the fifth book of his poem *De Rerum Natura*, Lucretius declares the centaur an impossible creature:

Centaurs never existed, nor at any time can there be creatures of double nature and twofold body combined together of incompatible limbs, such that the powers of the two halves can be fairly balanced. Here is a proof that will convince the dullest wit.

Firstly, the horse is at the best of his vigour when three years have passed round; not so the boy by any means, for even at this time he will often in sleep seek his mother's milky breast. Afterwards, when the strong powers of the horse are failing in old age and his body faints as life recedes, then is the time of the flower of boyhood, when youth is beginning and is clothing the cheeks with soft down.

The Minotaur

The idea of a house built expressly so that people will become lost in it may be stranger than the idea of a man with the head of a bull, and yet the two ideas may reinforce one another. Indeed, the image of the Labyrinth and the image of the Minotaur seem to "go together": it is fitting that at the center of a monstrous house there should live a monstrous inhabitant.

The Minotaur, half man, half bull, was born out of the lovemaking of 15 Pasiphae, the queen of Crete, with a white bull sent by Poseidon from the sea. Daedalus, the artificer who built the device that allowed such a passion to be consummated, also built the Labyrinth destined to house, and hide, the monstrous offspring. The Minotaur ate human flesh; to satisfy its hunger, the king of Crete required that Athens render Crete a yearly tribute of seven youths and seven maidens. Theseus resolved to save his kingdom from that terrible taxation, and volunteered to go. Ariadne, the daughter of the king, gave the young man a spool of thread so that he would not become lost in the mazy corridors of the Labyrinth; the hero killed the Minotaur and followed the thread out of the maze.

Ovid, in an attempt at a witty turn of phrase, speaks of the "man half bull and the bull half man"; Dante, who was familiar with the words of the ancients but not with their coins and monuments, pictured the Minotaur with the head of a man and the body of a bull (*Inferno*, XII, 1–30).

The worship of the bull and the double-headed axe (whose name was *labrys*, and so might well have evolved into "labyrinth") was characteristic of pre-Hellenic religions, which held sacred festivals in their honor, known as Tauromachias. To judge from murals, human figures with the heads of bulls figured in Cretan demonology. The Greek fable of the Minotaur is probably a late and somewhat uncouth version of very ancient myths—the shadow of other, still more horrific, dreams.

Sirens

Through the centuries, the Sirens' shape has changed. The first historian of these creatures, the rhapsodist of *The Odyssey* (Book XII), does not describe them; Ovid tells us they are birds with golden plumage and the face of a virgin. For Apollonius of Rhodes, the top half of their body is a woman's and the bottom, a seabird's; for Tirso de Molina (and for heraldry), they are half fish, half woman. Nor is their nature any less disputed: Lemprière's dictionary says that they are nymphs, while Quicherat's says they are monsters and Grimal's, demons. They inhabit one of the Western Isles, near the island of Circe, but the body of one Siren, Parthenope, was found in the Campagna. She gave her name to the famous city that we now know as Naples; the geographer Strabo saw her tomb and witnessed the gymnastic games that are periodically held in her memory.

The Odyssey says that the Sirens' singing would lure sailors to shipwreck and death by drowning, and that in order to hear the Sirens' song and yet not perish, Ulysses commanded his rowers to stop their ears with beeswax and tie him to the mast. The Sirens tempted the warrior with the knowledge of all things on earth:

> Sea rovers here take joy
>   Voyaging onward,
> As from our song of Troy
> Greybeard and rower-boy
>   Goeth more learned.

All feats on that great field
   In the long warfare,
Dark days the bright gods willed,
   Wounds you bore there,

Argos' old soldiery
   On Troy beach teeming,
Charmed out of time we see.
No life on earth can be
   Hid from our dreaming.

A legend contained in the *Library* of the mythologer Apollodorus tells 20 that Orpheus, in the Argonaut's ship, sang sweeter than the Sirens, and that upon hearing him, the Sirens threw themselves into the sea where they were transformed into rocks, for they were fated to die whenever a man did not fall under their spell. (The sphinx also threw itself from a mountaintop when its riddle was guessed.)

Sometime in the sixth century, a Siren was captured in the north of Wales and baptized, and even listed as a saint in certain ancient calendars, under the name Murgen. Another came through a break in a dike in 1403, and lived in Haarlem until her death. No one could understand her, but she taught people to spin and she worshipped the cross, as though instinctively. A sixteenth-century chronicler reasoned that she was not a fish, for she knew how to spin, nor yet was she a woman, for she could live in water.

The English language makes a distinction between the classical Siren and that creature with a fish's tail that is called a mermaid. It was no doubt an analogy with the Tritons, deities in the court of Poseidon, that influenced the shape of these latter creatures.

In the tenth book of the *Republic*, eight Sirens preside over the revolution of the eight concentric spheres of the heavens.

"Siren: an imaginary marine animal," we read in one particularly uncouth dictionary.

The Sphinx

The sphinx found on Egyptian monuments (called "Androsphinx" by 25 Herodotus, to distinguish it from the Greek creature) is a recumbent lion with the head of a man; it is believed to represent the authority of the pharaoh, and it guarded the tombs and temples of that land. Other sphinxes, on the avenues of Karnak, have the head of a lamb, the animal sacred to Amon. Bearded and crowned sphinxes are found on monuments in Assyria, and it is a common image on Persian jewelry. Pliny includes sphinxes in his catalog of Ethiopian animals, but the only description he offers is that it has "brown hair and two mammae on the breast."

The Greek sphinx has the head and breasts of a woman, the wings of a bird, and the body and legs of a lion. Others give it the body of a dog and the tail of a serpent. Legend recounts that it devastated the countryside of Thebes by demanding that travelers on the roads solve riddles that it put to them (it had a human voice); it devoured those who could not answer. This was the famous question it put to Oedipus, son of Jocasta: "What has four feet, two feet, or three feet, and the more feet it has, the weaker it is?"[1]

Oedipus answered that it was man, who crawls on four legs as a child, walks upon two legs as a man, and leans upon a stick in old age. The sphinx, its riddle solved, leapt to its death from a mountaintop.

In 1849 Thomas De Quincey suggested a second interpretation, which might complement the traditional one. The answer to the riddle, according to De Quincey, is less man in general than Oedipus himself, a helpless orphan in his morning, alone in the fullness of his manhood, and leaning upon Antigone in his blind and hopeless old age.

---

[1]This is apparently the oldest version of the riddle. The years have added the metaphor of the life of man as a single day, so that we now know the following version of it: "What animal walks on four legs in the morning, two legs at midday, and three in the evening?"

Understanding the Text

1. Why does Borges say that the child is a "discoverer" (par. 2)? What are the different types of discovery he cites?

2. What does Borges mean when he calls the dragon a *"necessary"* monster, as opposed to the Chimera or catoblepas (par. 4)?

3. What are the different relationships that humans have had with horses in history? How does that seem to have worked its way into the creation of the centaur?

4. The inventor Daedalus figures in both the conception of the Minotaur and the creation of the Labyrinth. In what ways does he serve as a contrast to Theseus, the hero in the Minotaur myth?

Reflection and Response

5. In his Introduction, Borges writes, "The zoology attributable to dreams is in fact considerably more modest than that attributable to God" (par. 3). Do you agree or disagree with this statement? Give examples from both the world of mythology and the world of nature to support your argument.

6. Note that there are both positive and negative portrayals of the centaur in mythology. Why do you think these contradictory attitudes exist?

Making Connections

7. Borges says that the Sirens tempted Ulysses (Odysseus) "with the knowledge of all things on earth" (par. 19). Compare that with the temptation of Adam and Eve to eat from the Tree of Knowledge in the Garden of Eden, as described in the Bible (Genesis 3:1–24). What does this temptation say about human nature — and about the creation of monsters? Find other examples of this sort of temptation.

8. Borges quotes Lucretius's argument for why the centaur could never have existed. How does his logic differ from contemporary arguments about why different species such as human and horse could never create offspring?

9. Research other combinations of species that appear in mythology, such as the Chimera, griffin, or catoblepas, or misshapen animals, such as the Cerberus or Hydra. Argue whether such monsters have the same impact on the human imagination as ones that combine human and animal qualities, using evidence from your research to support your answer.

The Birth of the Minotaur

Apollodorus

In a story of pride and arrogance brought down, Minos prays to the god Poseidon that a bull be brought forth from the sea, so that he could be seen to have the favor of the gods. In return, Minos promises to sacrifice the bull to Poseidon. Poseidon provides the bull, but when Minos reneges on his part of the deal, the god has his revenge. He causes Minos's wife, Pasiphae, to fall in love with the bull, mate with it, and produce a horrific child: the half-man, half-bull Minotaur. The story is recorded in the *Library*, a three-book collection of ancient myths and legends traditionally attributed to the Greek historian Apollodorus. That authorship has been discounted, however, as Apollodorus lived four centuries before the *Library* was written.

Asterius° dying childless, Minos wished to reign over Crete, but his claim was opposed. So he alleged that he had received the kingdom from the gods, and in proof of it he said that whatever he prayed for would be done. And in sacrificing to Poseidon he prayed that a bull might appear from the depths, promising to sacrifice it when it appeared. Poseidon did send him up a fine bull, and Minos obtained the kingdom, but he sent the bull to the herds and sacrificed another. [Being the first to obtain the dominion of the sea, he extended his rule over almost all the islands.]

> "Poseidon made the animal savage, and contrived that Pasiphae should conceive a passion for it."

But angry at him for not sacrificing the bull, Poseidon made the animal savage, and contrived that Pasiphae should conceive a passion for it. In her love for the bull she found an accomplice in Daedalus, an architect, who had been banished from Athens for murder. He constructed a wooden cow on wheels, took it, hollowed it out in the inside, sewed it up in the hide of a cow which he had skinned, and set it in the meadow in which the bull used to graze. Then he introduced Pasiphae into it; and the bull came and coupled with it, as if it were a real cow. And she gave birth to Asterius, who was called the Minotaur. He had the face of a bull, but the rest of him was human; and Minos, in compliance with certain oracles, shut him up and guarded him in the

---

Asterius: prince of the Cretans and stepfather to Minos.

The Minotaur depicted on an ancient Greek eye-cup, with an inscription that reads, "The boy is beautiful."
© Heritage Partnership Ltd./Alamy

Labyrinth. Now the Labyrinth which Daedalus constructed was a chamber "that with its tangled windings perplexed the outward way." The story of the Minotaur, and Androgeus, and Phaedra, and Ariadne, I will tell hereafter in my account of Theseus.

Understanding the Text

1. Why does Minos make the deal with Poseidon?
2. While the text is not specific, infer why Minos does not fulfill his end of the bargain.
3. What is the role of Daedalus in this story?

Reflection and Response

4. In your opinion, why does Poseidon choose the form of revenge that he does? What specifically about the revenge would be satisfying to the god?
5. How is this story a tale of overreaching ambition? What other tales of greed or hubris do you know of that make the same point?

Making Connections

6. Compare this tale with the description of the Minotaur provided by Jorge
    Luis Borges (p. 72). How do the two accounts of the Minotaur differ? What
    is significant about the differences?

7. In Borges's account, he mentions that worship of a bull and a double-
    headed ax, called a labrys, was characteristic of pre-Hellenic religions
    (meaning those before the time of the ancient Greeks). Research the his-
    tory of the labrys as a symbol of female power. How does the tale of the
    Minotaur attributed to Apollodorus bring together ancient ideas about
    the bull and the labrys? Considering Apollodorus's account, do you think
    the labrys is an appropriate symbol of female power or not? Support your
    answer.

The Battle of the Lapiths and Centaurs

Ovid

The legendary Greek hero Nestor tells Achilles the story of a wedding banquet gone terribly wrong. Invited to the wedding of Pirithous and Hippodamia are the centaurs — half-man, half-horse creatures. When the centaurs get drunk, they attempt to abduct the women at the banquet. A pitched battle ensues, in which many humans and centaurs are killed. The story is told by Ovid in Book 12 of *Metamorphoses*, one of the most important works of mythology. Along with Virgil and Horace, Ovid is considered one of the most important writers of the Roman era. [Editor's note: line numbers follow the Raeburn translation.]

"Piríthoüs, son of Ixíon and king of the Lapiths,   210
had married Hippodamía. He invited the cloud-born centaurs
to join the banquet at tables arranged in a leafy glen.
The chieftains of Thessaly came; I, Nestor, also attended.
The palace was filled with the festive hubbub of thronging guests.
Now hark to the wedding-hymn! Torches and rising smoke in the
          great hall!   215
Enter the bride, escorted by matrons and younger women,
and looking a picture. We all declared how blessed Piríthoüs
was in his beautiful wife. But our praise's effect as a lucky
omen was almost undone, when the wildest of all the wild centaurs,
Eúrytus, drunk already, was further inflamed by the sight   220
of the bride, and the power of wine reinforced by desire took over.
Tables were upside down in a flash, the feast was reduced
to a shambles, as Eúrytus seized Piríthoüs' newly-wed bride
by the hair and forced her away, while each of the other centaurs
grabbed any woman he fancied or found. The chaos resembled   225
a captured city, and women were screaming all over the palace.
We quickly rose from our couches. 'Eúrytus!' shouted Théseus,
taking the lead, 'you must be crazy! How dare you provoke
Piríthoüs while *I* live and foolishly injure us both?'
The centaur said nothing—he couldn't defend his outrageous
          behavior   230
by words—but used his unruly fists to punch the prince
on the jaw and to pummel his chest. On a table nearby there
          chanced
to be lying an antique wine-bowl, richly embossed with figures   235
in high relief. The bowl was huge, but Theseus was huger;

he lifted it up and hurled it directly in Eúrytus' face.
As globules of blood and fragments of brain poured out of the
wound,
the centaur, vomiting wine from his mouth, fell backwards and
drummed
with his heels on the sodden sand. His brothers, enraged by the
carnage,

240

"Eúrytus, drunk already, was further inflamed by the sight of the bride, and the power of wine reinforced by desire took over."

vied with each other in shouting as
one, 'To arms, to arms!'
Inspired by the wine with courage,
they started the battle by sending
their goblets flying, then breakable jars
and round-lipped vessels,
objects intended for feasts, now used
for war and for slaughter.

"Amycus, son of Ophíon, was first among the rampaging   245
centaurs to raid the inner rooms of the palace and plunder
an iron stand which supported a cluster of burning candles.
He lifted the whole thing high, like a priest at a sacrifice straining
to raise the axe which will cleave the neck of a pure white bull,
then dashed it down on the forehead of Céladon, one of the
Lapiths.   250
This fractured his skull and mangled his face past all recognition.
His eyes burst out of their sockets, the bones of his cheeks were
shattered,
the nose smashed inwards and jammed beneath the roof of his
mouth.
But another Lapith called Pélates wrenched the leg from a
maplewood
table and used it to hammer Amycus down to the ground,   255
with his chin forced into his chest. As the centaur sputtered his
teeth out
mingled with gore, a second blow dispatched him to Hades.
"Next to the fore came Grýneus, who'd stood there, grimly
inspecting
the smoking altar and said, 'Why don't we make use of this?'
With a frightening glare in his eyes, he lifted the hefty structure, 260
fires and all, and hurled it into a group of the Lapiths.
Two were crushed by the mountainous weight, Bróteas and Oríos
(Orios' mother was Mýcale, said to have often succeeded
in drawing down the horns of the moon with her incantations).
'You won't get away with this, if I can get hold of a weapon!' 265

Exádius said, and then caught sight of some antlers nailed
to a tall pine tree as a votive offering. There was his weapon!
Armed with the horns of a stag, Exadius aimed for the centaur's
eyeballs and gouged them out. One eye stuck fast on the antlers,
and one rolled down on to Gryneus' beard, blood-coated, and clung
    there.   270

                          • • •

"How about Caeneus? He killed five centaurs: Antímachus,
    Stýphelus,
Élymus, Bromus and lastly Pyrácmus, who fought with an axe.   460
(I can't remember their wounds, but only their names and the
    number.)
Then Látreus, a centaur of massive physique, rushed forward to face
    him,
armed with the spoils of Halésus, a Macedonian he'd slaughtered.
In age he was past his youth and his temples were flecked with gray,
but his strength was still a young man's. His helmet, shield and
    exotic   465
pike attracted all eyes as he proudly turned to each army,
brandished his weapons and pranced around in a well-traced circle,
flinging a torrent of insolent taunts in the empty air:
'Caenis,° you bitch! Must I tolerate *you*? You will always be female   470
and Caenis to *me*. Perhaps you forget your original sex.
Do you ever recall what you did to deserve your reward? Do you
    think
of the price which you paid to achieve this specious masculine body?
Look at the girl you were born and the shame that she suffered.
    Then go,
return to your distaff and basket of wool. Go back to your spinning,   475
and leave the fighting to *men*!' As Latreus was galloping past him,
shouting these insults, Caeneus let fly with his spear, which made a
    great
gash in the mocker's side where man and horse are united.
Maddened by pain, the centaur cast at the hero's uncovered
head with his pike. The weapon rebounded like hail off a rooftop   480
or pebbles dropped on a drum. Then Latreus attacked at close
    quarters

Caenis: the female form of Caeneus. Caeneus was originally born as a woman and was
raped by Neptune, who then fulfilled her request to be transformed into a man so he
could never be raped again.

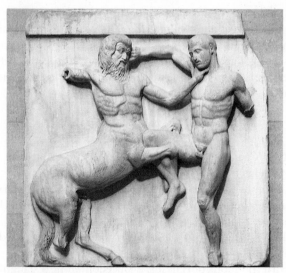

A marble tablet with a sculpture relief from the Parthenon in Athens, depicting the battle between the Lapiths and centaurs.

© World History Archive/Alamy

and struggled to bury his sword in the young man's side, but the side
was too hard; there was no way in. 'You won't escape me,' he
    shouted.
'You'll die on the edge of my sword, since the point's been blunted!'
    So turning   485
his weapon sideways, he reached to slash him around his thighs,
but the blow produced no more than a thud—the flesh might well
    have been
marble. The metal was broken to splinters on striking such tough
    skin.
Caeneus was tired of exposing his still unwounded limbs
to the stupefied centaur. 'Come on!' he said to him, 'now let's see   490
how your body responds to *my* steel'; and he plunged his death-
    dealing sword
right up to the hilt in his enemy's trunk and compounded the
    damage
by turning and twisting the sunken blade right into his vitals.
On came the centaurs, shouting and yelling, rushing in frenzy,
everyone hurling or thrusting their weapons against one foe.   495
Those weapons were blunted and fell to the ground, while Caeneus
    remained

unscathed by all of their blows; not a drop of his blood had been
    spilt.
   "This turn of events left the centaurs dumbfounded. 'Shameful,
    disgraceful!'
Mónychus cried. 'Our whole tribe worsted by one man, hardly
a man at that! No, *he* is a man and we are behaving   500
as feebly as women. What use is this massive girth of our bodies?
What of our double strength? Has nature combined in ourselves
the courage and force of the world's two mightiest creatures for
    nothing?
Our mother a goddess? I don't believe it. Our father cannot
have been Ixion, a mortal with pride enough to aspire   505
to sleep with Juno on high, when *we* are defeated by someone
whose sex is in doubt! Let us roll the boulders, the trees, whole
    mountains
on top of this upstart. Let's hurl the forests and crush the life
from his living body. His throat will be choked by the bulk of it all,
and the weight will prove good as a wound.' So saying, he seized   510
a trunk knocked down, as it chanced, by the south wind's fury, and
    threw it
against his unwoundable foe. The rest did the same; in a short while
Othrys° was stripped of its trees and Pelion° empty of shade.
Crushed beneath that enormous layer, the hero sweltered
under the weight of the trees, and heaved with his sturdy shoulders   515
to raise the pile, but after the load grew greater and greater
over his head and he couldn't breathe through his mouth any longer,
consciousness left him. But then he recovered and vainly attempted
to roll the trees off his body and lift himself up to obtain
some air. For a while he succeeded in moving the surface, as if   520
Mount Ida, which look! we can see over there, was disturbed by an
    earthquake.
No one is certain what happened next. Some said that his body
was thrust right down by the mass of the trees to the shadows of
    Hades.
Mopsus the seer said no. He'd noticed a rust-winged bird
emerging out of the pile and soaring into the air.   525
I also sighted the bird that day for the first and the last time.
Mopsus watched it gently circling the camp and he heard it

Othrys: a mountain in Greece that in Greek mythology was the home of the Titans,
who were later overthrown by Zeus.
Pelion: a mountain in Greece that in Greek mythology was the home of the centaurs.

loudly clapping its wings. As he thoughtfully followed it round
with his eyes, he exclaimed, 'All hail! Hail Caeneus, pride of the
  Lapiths,   530
once unique among men, and now sole bird of your kind.'
The prophet said it and we believed it. Grief made our anger
all the more bitter. That one man's life should be crushed by so many!
To vent our sorrow, we turned on the centaurs and didn't cease
  fighting
till most had been killed and the rest were in rout or were rescued by
  night."   535

Understanding the Text

1. How do Theseus and the other Greeks respond to the centaurs' disruption
   of the wedding banquet?

2. What makes Caeneus a unique person? What is behind the special rage
   that the centaurs feel toward him? How do they eventually kill him?

Reflection and Response

3. How does the behavior of the centaurs at the wedding reflect both human
   and animal behaviors? Explain.

4. The fight escalates quickly into a battle to the death. It is human action —
   Theseus kills Eurytus with a wine bowl — that turns the disruption into a
   mortal fight. As Ovid writes, "Objects intended for feasts [were] now used
   for war and slaughter" (l. 244). What does this quick turn of events say
   about the combination (or overlap) of human and animal traits?

5. Ovid seems to revel in his descriptions of gory wounds as he details the
   events of the battle. What advantage in storytelling does this give Ovid?
   Use specific examples from the poem to support your position.

Making Connections

6. While the story is told by Nestor, a Greek, and features Greek characters, it
   is recorded by Ovid, a Roman author. Research the story of the rape of the
   Sabine women, an event that allegedly occurred several hundred years
   before Ovid, in which Roman men, lacking wives, kidnapped Sabine
   women to take as their own. You might also analyze visual depictions of
   this event by looking at the famous sculpture by Giambologna or paintings
   by Pietro da Cortona, Jacques-Louis David, and Pablo Picasso. Compare
   the behavior of the Romans in that event with the behavior of the centaurs
   in this selection. What does this comparison suggest about monsters?

7. Research the history of the character Caeneus. Can Caeneus be regarded
   as a type of monster? Why or why not? Note the spelling change to
   "Caenis" in line 470. In your research, consider issues of sexual violation and
   how they are handled in mythology. What does this say about male and
   female sexuality as viewed in those times — and in our own?

The Monstrous and the Bestial: Animals in Greek Myths

Kenneth H. Simonsen

The relationship between humans and animals in mythology is complex — sometimes positive and sometimes negative. Humans' negative attitudes toward animals typically arise when animals behave in monstrous ways. Sometimes they exhibit aggressive behavior beyond the norm; other times they are abnormally formed freaks of nature, comprising different animal parts or even animal and human parts. In other words, some of these animals are truly monstrous, while others are merely bestial. Kenneth H. Simonsen was a professor of philosophy at the College of Lake County. This article originally appeared in 1986 in *Between the Species*, a peer-reviewed journal for the study of philosophy and animals published by California Polytechnic State University at San Luis Obispo.

In the myths, the ancient Greeks were at times rather positive toward animals. The Olympian gods were often represented as wild animals, usually symbolizing some divine attribute. Zeus was associated with the eagle, a reference to his dominance as sky god and, perhaps, also to his epithet as "Far Seeing." Ares' fierceness was symbolized by the wild boar, Aphrodite's lecherousness by the dove or sparrow (Morford and Lenardon, p. 69). Oddly, Athena's wisdom was symbolized by the owl, a bird not known for its brightness. The Olympians could also acquire animal associations by their roles as cult figures. Artemis was associated with bears because of the Brauron cult in central Attica, in which little girls involved in the festival were dressed up as bears (Kirk, p. 233). Apollo Lyceius has been interpreted as a wolf god, and Dionysis Bromius, as depicted in *The Bacchai*, appears as a roaring bull (Kirk, p. 130).

But, as in the case of the three evangelists and their symbolic animals,° it may be rash to draw any hard conclusions from these Hellenic eagles, owls, or bears. The association of god and beast may be more a matter of literary convention than anything else. Or, in the case of Apollo Delphinios, the connection may be etymological, an attempt to explain the origin of names. Or, the epithet may be ambiguous, e.g., Apollo Lyceius may refer to "wolf" or "light" or to Lycia, one of the prophetic

---

three evangelists and their symbolic animals: a reference to the writers of the first three Gospels in the New Testament—Matthew, Mark, and Luke. Their symbolic animals are the winged-man (or angel), the winged-lion, and the winged-ox, respectively.

god's supposed places of origin (Burkert, p. 21). In any event, there is enough ambiguity here to impede any firm conclusions.

A stronger case can be made for the presence in Greek myths of what may be called "friendly animals," animals who befriend, instruct, protect, or somehow aid humans. Foremost among these animals is a creature who is actually half animal and half human but deserves to be mentioned in this context. Cheiron the centaur was renowned as a teacher, "the greatest educator of his day," who instructed Jason and Aesclepius (Kirk, p. 208). The winged horse Pegasus, although born from the blood of Medusa, was a great aid to Bellerophon in his exploits. Hesiod tells us that Pegasus was even favored by the gods; he was brought to Olympus, where he carries the thunder and lightning of Zeus (Hesiod, p. 140). Ario, a horse born from the union of Poseidon and Demeter, who had coupled in the form of horses, rescued King Adrastus from Thebes (Kirk, p. 225). Even non-mythical animals are presented at times with sympathy. When Odysseus returns to Ithaca in disguise after an absence of twenty years, one of the few creatures who recognizes him is his faithful dog:

But when he knew he heard Odysseus' voice nearby, he did his best to wag his tail, nose down, with flattened ears, having no strength to move nearer his master. And the man looked away, wiping a salt tear from his cheek. (Homer, p. 320)

This touching scene, a parallel in reverse of the famous stele° of the dog lamenting his dead master, shows a profound sympathy between human and beast. Clearly, there are instances in Greek myth when animals are viewed with compassion, respect, and, at times, companionable friendship.

But there seem to be many more instances in the myths when animals 5 are not depicted in such favorable light. Rather than clever horses or trustworthy dogs, one is more likely to encounter fierce and savage beasts, often in monstrous and grotesque form. It is to that disparaging, often terrible, portrayal of animal life that we must turn. In very broad terms, one can distinguish various kinds of mythic animals. Some are monstrous abnormalities and freaks of nature; others are more ordinary but possess great strength and/or size. Some are part human and part animal; others are wholly animal. And some are cruel and vicious, while others are merely lustful and uncontrollable. Taken all together, they form an unsavory collection. They represent everything that is terrifying and hateful

stele: a stone pillar or slab, usually with a carved inscription or design, serving as a monument.

in the animal kingdom, everything that should be feared and avoided by humans.

Hesiod presents a powerful picture of these bizarre, mythical animals, monstrous in the sense of being hideous or grotesque. The terrible aspect of these monsters is that they are abnormal; they deviate from what is normal or natural. Echidna, a progenitor° of many of these monsters, is herself half nymph and half snake. She mates, somehow, with the "law-less and violent" Typhoeus, who possesses one hundred "inhuman" snake-like heads, from which issue the sounds of bulls, lions, and dogs, as well as whistles, hisses, and speech comprehensible to the gods (Hesiod, p. 141). One offspring of this union is the vicious, fifty-headed dog, Cerberus; another is the Hydra, a many-headed serpent who, in turn, gives birth to Chimera, a monster with a lion head, a goat head, and a snake head. Echidna also gives birth to the dog Orthus, with whom she mates in typ-ical animalistic fashion to produce the sphinx and the Nemean lion (Hesiod, p. 142). Echidna's relative Thaumas (the word "uncle" seems in-appropriate) sires the harpies "of the lovely hair," says Hesiod, while Ovid quaintly refers to them as "girl-faced vultures" (Ovid, p. 187). But it is not necessary to mention all the monstrous animals in Hesiod's menagerie; the bizarre contrast with the wise Cheiron or the faithful dog of Odys-seus is apparent.

There are other animal monstrosities in Greek myth, but only two more will be added to this ghastly catalog. They are important not only as enduring images in art or speech but also because, like Orthus and Cerberus, they are domesticated rather than purely wild animals. The most famous of the two is the Minotaur, half man and half bull, whose image readily comes to mind from Picasso's drawings. The Minotaur, born of the unnatural union of Pasiphae and the Cretan bull, is cruel enough to be included in Hesiod's collection, particularly since he regu-larly feasts on Athenian youths (Ovid, p. 220). The other monster, whose name has become a literary catchword, is so bizarre that she has evaded any Picasso: poor Scylla, driven mad by Circe's witchcraft. Upon entering a pool enchanted by Circe, a belt of vicious snarling dogs sprouted around her belly:

> And there she sat, half naked girl,
>   half monster,
> With mad dogs barking round her
>   lower regions. (Ovid, p. 385)

---

progenitor: someone or something who is first; an ancestor.

This is a strange catalog, found in Hesiod and other writers of antiquity, of monstrous animals. If we are not adequately repelled by the gruesome description of these monsters, Hesiod instructs us on how to respond by his use of adjectives. These monsters are "furious," "cruel," "inhuman," "unmanageable," "lawless," "violent," "voracious," "terrible," and "savage." Insofar as Hesiod has any effect on our unthinking subconscious attitudes toward animals, it is a most negative one. These animal monsters are vicious and unrestrainably violent. They are repellent and terrifying. We would be doing all of creation a favor, if we could rid the earth of them. And this is in fact what heroes like Heracles actually do.

> "It is conceivable that what is terrible or repelling about these creatures is not their animal traits but, rather, their abnormalities."

But is the image of animals drawn from this horrendous catalog really a picture of animals as we know them? Or are they merely literary creations that no one takes seriously? After all, some of Hesiod's monsters are humanoid. The three-headed Geryon, the one-eyed cyclopes, and the one hundred–armed, fifty-headed brothers Cottus, Briareus, and Gyes are also abnormal monsters. Of course, some of Hesiod's humanoid monsters aren't as savage and cruel as his animals. The one hundred–armed brothers are clever enough to form an alliance with Zeus, and the cyclopes are craftsmen, gifted enough to produce the thunderbolt for Zeus. Echidna and her offspring apparently lack such human attributes. Furthermore, Hesiod lumps together both domesticated and wild animals. Perhaps fear, terror, or repulsion is appropriate for snakes, vultures, and lions, but such responses seem peculiar when applied to the dog, the goat, and the bull. Evidently, the loyal dog of Odysseus can also appear in myth as the fifty-headed (or three-headed, if you will) Cerberus.

There is a possible explanation for the peculiarities found in Hesiod's 10 catalog of monstrous animals. It is conceivable that what is terrible or repelling about these creatures is not their animal traits but, rather, their abnormalities. They are repugnant because they are unnatural monstrosities, not because they are more or less animals. This at least is the view of H. J. Rose, who would prefer to believe that the Greek imagination could never generate such unclassical images. He regards these monsters as the product of a non-Greek mind. The origins of Echidna, Cerberus, Chimera, and the sphinx are to be found in Assyria, or India, or in the Levant. Hesiod's "hideous brood," Rose claims, is alien to the Greek mind because his brood is filled with abnormal and unnatural creatures:

It is not surprising, considering how little the Greeks like monstrosities, that these products of an imagination not their own are represented as living in the lower world. (Rose, p. 31)

In reply to Rose, it should be pointed out that even though the Greeks may not have created these pre-Olympian animal monstrosities, they nonetheless retained them in their myths. They evidently served a purpose in the myths, and, perhaps, in the Greek psyche. As such, they influenced, consciously and subconsciously, subsequent generations of readers of the myths.

But if one is really to answer Rose fully, one must abstract the monstrous element from the image of animals in myth. If it is only abnormality or unnaturalness that causes a negative response, then non-monstrous animals should appear in myth as benign and friendly, like Pegasus, or they should at least be ordinary or neutral. If, on the other hand, non-monstrous animals still are depicted as savage and vicious, then there may be grounds for concluding that it is not just abnormality but also "beastliness" that is disparaged. Thus, it is necessary to turn to those animals who are not hideous, grotesque, abnormal, or unnatural. These animals may be inhuman, brutish, cruel, stupid, or violent, but they are not monstrous. Rather, they are merely bestial.

Greek myths do contain a number of animals who are bestial rather than monstrous. They often differ from ordinary animals in that they are larger or much stronger, but usually this powerfulness is invested in them by the gods, whose will they serve. These bestial animals lack the cosmic power of Typhoeus, but they don't lack the vicious, lawless, violent nature. The Calydonian boar described by Ovid does not seem grotesquely unnatural as wild boars go. Although inspired by divine power from Diana, he is not a hideous, abnormal monster. But he is vicious:

> But blood and fire wheeled in his great eyes;
> His neck was iron; his bristles rose like spears . . . and streams
>   of lightning
> Poured from his wide lips, and when he smiled or sighed
> All vines and grasses burnt beneath his breath. (Ovid, p. 224)

The "she-dragon" killed by Apollo the Far Shooter in the *Hymn to Apollo* may very well have been a monstrous dragon, but the reference to her "rapidly thrusting" coils and the use of the name "Pytho," now applied to the python, suggest that this creature may have been a gigantic, bloodthirsty snake (Athanassakis, p. 27). Ovid is less ambiguous in his depiction of "Mars' serpent," a "sea blue snake" who emerges from his cave to destroy Cadmus' men. Ovid's serpent is distinctly python-like; he kills by crushing the Phoenicians with his tail, i.e., by constriction. Others die, however, by his forked tongue, rather than by biting, and some even are killed by his bad breath (Ovid, p. 86). Ovid's description of this snake is gory and monstrous, but the snake itself, however terrifying, does not seem to be an unnatural monstrosity. His only abnormality is his fire-flashing eyes, but this fire generating power Ovid also attributes to boars and bulls (see above and below) and may very well be symbolic of the beasts' power and savageness. Or it may be a symbol of the divine power infused in the beasts by the gods. The bulls encountered by Jason have a similar fire-snorting capacity. In his quest for the golden fleece, Jason must harness these ferocious bulls for King Aeetes:

> Look! Now bronze-footed bulls charged the field,
> Whose steel ringed nostrils poured forth a blast of fire;
> Grass withered at their feet. (Ovid, p. 91)

The various bestial animals encountered by Heracles in his twelve 15 labors should be added to this catalog. The boar of Erymanthus, the Cretan bull, and the human flesh–eating horses of Diomedes are, presumably, fierce and dangerous. If they were not, they would not be a challenge to Heracles' valor and might. But they are not monsters. Yet, they appear in the same context as Hesiod's monstrosities, viz., the Hydra, the Nemean lion, and Cerberus (Rose, pp. 211–5). Clearly, both monstrous and bestial animals in the legend of Heracles' labors share vicious and savage behaviors.

This catalog of monstrous and bestial creatures should be indicative of the role played by animals in many Greek myths. Such creatures are often forbidding, threatening, savage, cruel, and violent. The presence of friendly or even neutral animals in myth, a minor strain, cannot offset the powerful impression made by these ferocious beasts. They are part of our artistic and literary heritage, in which they re-appear, transformed into Grendel or St. George's dragon. (Of course, the Greek myths are not the only source of our traditional disparagement of animals. Snakes are not beloved in the Biblical tradition, either, where they are divested of their positive, Greek association with rebirth and regeneration.)

Animals, when they are not presented as savage and cruel in Greek myth, often appear as merely sub-human; they are, not surprisingly, merely "animalistic" or "brutish." This characteristic is found in the many transformations described in myth, e.g., Odysseus' men transformed into pigs by Circe. The violence is missing here, but the poet provides a vivid picture of a groveling, swinish existence (Homer, p. 172). It gives concreteness to J. S. Mill's remark that it is better to be Socrates dissatisfied than a pig satisfied. In Ovid's many transformations, this same theme of trading a civilized, human life for a brutish, bestial one is repeated ad nauseam. Poor Acteon, seeing Diana naked by accident, is transformed into a stag and killed by his own hounds. Symbolically, he loses his most human attribute, the power of articulate speech, and is unable to call off his hounds (Ovid, p. 91). Calisto, who had the misfortune of kindling the lust of Zeus, is transformed into a bear:

> Her gift of speech was ripped away and from her throat
> Came guttural noises horrible to hear;
> Though her emotions were of a human kind,
> She was a bear . . . (Ovid, p. 70)

Cadmus is transformed into a snake in the midst of speech, as his tongue splits and his words become hisses (Ovid, p. 128). And Lycaon is reduced to a "terror which words cannot utter." Symbolic of his own tyranny, he is transformed into a savage and inhuman wolf, "his foaming lips and jaws quick with thoughts of blood" (Ovid, p. 37).

Even the gods can transform themselves into beasts, usually as a matter of convenience. In the *Hymn to Dionysus*, the effeminate god of wine cannot intimidate the pirates by his gentle appearance, so he transforms himself into a terrible roaring lion (Athanassakis, p. 53). Most often, the gods become beasts in order to satisfy their lusts and, when necessary, commit the violence of rape. Zeus assumes the shape of a dove, a swan, and a bull for these purposes. Demeter becomes a mare to escape the attentions of Poseidon, but is foiled when the earthshaker in turn transforms himself into a lusty stallion. So, even the anthropomorphic gods, with all their human traits, take on animal form in order to engage in bestial behaviors.

In these transformations, a basic pattern emerges. A rational, civilized 20 life is exchanged for an animalistic, sub-human life. The human or the god still retains human consciousness, but his/her behavior becomes bestial. Symbolically, the humans are deprived of articulate speech, human society, and the amenities of civilization. Not being gods, they illustrate Aristotle's famous comment that a man without a city state is either a beast or a god.

There is one species of mythical beast which clearly embodies this rigid distinction between the human and the bestial, viz., the centaurs. Centaurs share with Pan and the satyrs a mixed nature, in which the animal parts symbolize baser or "animalistic" passions. But unlike the satyrs, who are driven by perpetual lust, the centaurs seem to be of a higher sort, since they are capable of a superficial degree of civilization. The wise Cheiron, in particular, is supremely civilized; he is the "paradigm of Culture" (Kirk, p. 85). But Cheiron is, evidently, exceptional. Only he remains aloof when the rowdy centaurs, drunken and violent, break up the marriage of the Lapith princess, Hippodamia. Civilized restraint in centaurs is very fragile; it quickly disintegrates when they are exposed to wine, allowing their beastly, uncontrollable natures to emerge. Plato, in discussing the conflict of reason and desire in the human psyche, uses the example of the charioteer and his horses. But he could have readily used centaurs as examples, who are human in their civilized, albeit rare restraint, but animal in their lack of it. Kirk has this distinction in mind when, following Lévi-Strauss, he sees the centaurs as symbolic of the conflict between nature and culture (Kirk, p. 85). Cheiron, the humanized centaur, is civilized and restrained. The other centaurs, wild and uncontrollable, are brutish and bestial; as Kirk says, they act like "animals" or "beasts" (Kirk, p. 208).

This second, pervasive image of animals is a familiar common-place in the philosophies of Plato and Aristotle, but it has strong roots in myth, as well. It is this Hellenic, rather than the Hebraic, tradition which has associated being human with reason and restraint and "beastliness" with passion, violence, lack of control, and brutishness. It is not surprising that the humanistic Greeks, who saw their gods anthropomorphically, would see the non-human, living creatures as inferior and brutish. Although St. Thomas would never have done such a thing, he could have easily cited a number of Greek myths, instead of Aristotle, to illustrate his belief that animals are lower on the chain of being and, therefore, unworthy of respect.

After distinguishing between animals who are monstrous or bestial and between those who are primarily violent or lustful, we have arrived at two conclusions. First, animals are more commonly portrayed in Greek myth as savage and violent than as friendly and peaceful. Second, animals are generally, but not always, depicted as lawless, undisciplined, and uncontrollable, thus serving as a symbol for unrestrained, human passions. Of course, many humans and gods in the myths fit this description as well, but at least they are capable of civilization. Animals, being part of nature, are not. It is these two disparaging views that have contributed to our traditional, negative attitude toward the animal kingdom.

Works Cited

Athanassakis, A., editor, *The Homeric Hymns* (Baltimore: Johns Hopkins University Press, 1976).

Burkert, Walter, *Homo Necans* (Berkeley: University of California Press, 1972).

Hesiod, *Theogony* (Lattimore translation) (Ann Arbor: University of Michigan Press, 1977).

Homer, *The Odyssey* (Fitzgerald translation) (New York: Doubleday, 1963).

Kirk, G. S., *The Greek Myths* (Baltimore: Penguin, 1974).

Morford, Mark P. O., and Lenardon, Robert J., *Classical Mythology* (New York: Longman, 1971).

Rose, H. J., *A Handbook of Greek Mythology* (London: Dutton, 1960).

Understanding the Text

1. What are some examples of how the Greeks viewed animals positively, according to Simonsen? What is a common factor in all these examples?

2. Many monsters are said to have been mothered by Echidna, a half-nymph, half-snake creature. How are these monsters seen negatively?

3. What is the distinction that Simonsen makes between "monstrous" and "bestial"? Why is this distinction important?

Reflection and Response

4. Focus on Simonsen's argument that the centaurs have a mixed nature. How is their nature different from that of the satyrs, creatures that combine human and horse features (according to the ancient Greeks) or human and goat features (according to the Romans)? How do mixed creatures function to show approval or disapproval of certain kinds of human behavior? Compare them with mixed creatures that do not incorporate human parts. How are creatures that possess a human element different from those that do not? What is symbolically important about that distinction?

5. Analyze the importance of how — and why — speech separates humans from animals. Give specific examples from Simonsen's essay to support your position.

6. Simonsen argues that animals serve as "a symbol for unrestrained, human passions" (par. 23). Do you agree? Defend your answer.

Making Connections

7. How does contemporary culture portray animals differently than the ancient Greeks? Are there current examples that reflect Odysseus's loyal dog? Are there examples of animal depictions that border on the monstrous? What does that say about our own time's attitude toward the monstrous and bestial?

8. The stories of the ancient Greeks differ from those in the Bible, which come from the Hebraic tradition. Nevertheless, there are some similarities. For example, Echidna has characteristics of a nymph (woman) and a snake, which is reminiscent of the story of Eve and the serpent in the Garden of Eden. Simonsen remarks how such stories may reappear in other times and places, such as in the character of Grendel in *Beowulf* (p. 151) or in Saint George's dragon. Choose one myth and research how it has been modified or told differently across time and cultures — including contemporary tellings of the myth.

Composite Monsters: *Island of Lost Souls* and *The Fly*

Bruce F. Kawin

The horror film genre has many types of monsters, but one of the most interesting is the composite monsters who are part-animal, part-human. In his book *Horror and the Horror Film*, Bruce F. Kawin, a professor of English and film studies at the University of Colorado, looks to horror movies to explore our relationships with monsters. In this excerpt, he examines how in the fictional world of films, animal and human can be combined in horrible ways that nature never allows, giving us an opportunity to ask questions about ourselves and our potential to be monstrous as well as human.

One of the early uses of "monster" in English refers to an imaginary creature made up of the parts of two or more animals, one of which might be human. It can also refer to a malformed fetus, usually born dead and resembling several animals, or a mix between human and animal. Ancient mythology includes such composite creatures as the sphinx and the centaur. Film gives us the *Creature from the Black Lagoon* (Jack Arnold, 1954, US), where the Gill Man, whose species has survived since the Devonian Age,° has the characteristics of a man and a fish, and *The Fly* (Kurt Neumann, 1958, US), where a man has the head and arm of a fly, and a fly has the head and arm of a man—or the remake of *The Fly* (David Cronenberg, 1986, Canada/US), where the man and the fly are completely integrated on a molecular level. These creatures raise the question of the definition of man, the species, which stands—as it is said in *The Creature Walks Among Us* (John Sherwood, 1956, US)—"between the jungle and the stars." The horror of the monster, the challenge to human nature and the threat of a new category of life are found together in the dangerous mix.

It is part of the horror film's job to tell us about our nature. The genre is charged with the investigation of all forms of life, from the natural to the unnatural, with a special interest in human nature, which it continually defines and redefines in relation to other kinds and ways of being.

Devonian Age: a geologic period dating from 416 million years ago; part of the Paleozoic Era, it is also known as the Age of Fishes.

The Gill Man (Ben Chapman) holds Kay Lawrence (Julie Adams) in *The Creature from the Black Lagoon* (1954).

© Universal International Pictures/Photofest

It proposes a fable of who we are, often showing the image of our condition and our potential in a monster or in those who oppose it.

A composite creature, a combination of animal forms, the fruit of anything from mythology or surgery to genetic anomaly, disturbs our sense of the orderly classification of species—of the way things ought to be, much as the Frankenstein Monster displays life and death at once. These monsters are not human, yet they are not entirely some other animal. One of their most human characteristics is that they may find people sexually attractive. The Creature from the Black Lagoon (played by Ricou Browning in the water and Ben Chapman on land) is practically a romantic, so intensely does he concentrate on the only woman in each of the three films. When he carries the unconscious Kay (Julia Adams) into his grotto in *Black Lagoon*, it is expected, iconic (p. 100). Yet we do not consider them a human couple but see them as "the monster and the girl," as the phrase went. With his gills and dormant lungs, with his webs and claw-like fingers, with his arms and legs and fins, the Creature is a fork in the road between marine and land life: the point at which his species stopped evolving millions of years ago.

Composites can be especially dangerous, for they may have the intelligence of humans or something like it. Cronenberg's man-fly has all of his former intelligence along with an insect-like selfishness that perverts it. The Creature from the Black Lagoon has cunning and the ability to plan; he is almost a human opponent.

Island of Lost Souls (Erle C. Kenton, 1932, US) has creatures that describe themselves as "Not men, not beasts" but "things." The film was loosely based on H. G. Wells's novel *The Island of Dr. Moreau*—"loosely" because it added women to the story and changed the ending—but Wells had much the same monsters, and he had "the Law" and "the House of Pain." Dr Moreau (Charles Laughton), a mad scientist who respects no moral or physical boundaries, takes animals into his laboratory, the House of Pain, and, after somehow altering their germ plasm, vivisects them. Sometimes (in the novel, often) he grafts several animals together—parts of a dog and a bear, for instance—and works on the results, cutting the animals into human form. It is horrible, and so are the screams. His assistant is a disgraced, drunken doctor, Montgomery (Arthur Hohl), who had probably been doing abortions, another forbidden operation, back in civilization. The humanoid beasts, the only inhabitants of the island aside from those in Moreau's compound, have a village where they recite to each other the Law that Moreau has conditioned into them: "not to run on all fours," for example. ("What is the Law?" Moreau ritually demands, cracking his whip. "Not to spill blood," says the leader, the Sayer of the Law [Bela Lugosi], "that is the Law. Are we not men?" "Are we not men?" the monsters chant in unison.) The Law keeps the monsters in line, and so does the ritual reminder, "His is the House of Pain."

Moreau has only two problems: the "stubborn beast flesh" keeps growing back—making it necessary to take the monsters back to the House of Pain—and he has a nosy, shipwrecked observer, Edward Parker (Richard Arlen). Before being abandoned on Moreau's island, Edward had telegrammed his fiancée, Ruth (Leila Hyams), when to expect him at the port where they were planning to marry. She and a local captain (Donahue, played by Paul Hurst) go to Moreau's island. In the meantime Moreau has decided to experiment with Edward, to see whether his prized creation, Lota, the Panther Woman (Kathleen Burke), who looks entirely human, will be attracted to a human male. She is. As mentioned before, neither she nor Ruth is in the novel. The movie has made sex, particularly the prospect of sex between species, an important element of the confrontation between human and monster. Explaining his experiments to Edward, Moreau asks, under creepy lighting, "Do you know what it means to feel like God?" This desire seems to be what was most feared about mad scientists and doctors in the 1930s and 40s, though they were still playing God much later, as in *The Human Centipede (First Sequence)* (Tom Six, 2009, Netherlands), where a mad scientist cuts and stitches three people into a composite organism.

When Ruth and Donahue arrive, one of the monsters, the violent Ouran (Hans Steinke), is attracted to her. After a scene in which Ruth gets partly undressed for bed, Ouran pries away the bars on her bedroom window and comes through the opening as Ruth screams (this example of the bedroom-window scene is clearly about sex). Later, on Moreau's orders, Ouran strangles Donahue. Then Ouran tells the Sayer of the Law, "Law no more"—because Moreau told him to spill blood.

> "Not men, not beasts. Part men, part beast — Things!"

The beast-men confront Moreau at his house, where he asks whether they have forgotten the House of Pain. The Sayer of the Law says, "You made us in the House of Pain. You made us things! Not men, not beasts. Part men, part beast—Things!"—and the monsters advance on the camera in one chilling shot after another. The monsters pursue Moreau into the House of Pain and cut him to pieces. Edward, Ruth and Montgomery escape, and Lota, the film's ritual sacrifice, is killed protecting them from Ouran. Fire consumes all of Moreau's work (the work of a mad scientist doesn't last). The final shot fades out on Edward and Ruth, as Montgomery rows their boat away from the fiery island. Now, having passed through the horror phase of their relationship, which in this case has forced them to deal with the nature of life, and to undergo trials and perils proving themselves right for each other, they can marry.

Moreau is a mad scientist, and this could be called a mad-scientist picture, but its primary horror is centered in the monsters, composite "things" that clearly manifest, in their own terms, the threat that Moreau represents to the spontaneous course of evolution and to biology itself.

Understanding the Text

1. According to Kawin, what is the danger of the composite creature? Why does it pose such a threat?

2. What is the key difference between the 1958 version of *The Fly* and the 1986 version? Why is that difference important?

3. Why does Kawin refer to the Creature from the Black Lagoon (or the Gill Man) as "practically a romantic" (par. 3)?

4. Dr. Moreau, the mad scientist in *Island of Lost Souls*, says, "Do you know what it means to feel like God?" (par. 6). In what ways is Moreau like God? In what ways is he not?

Reflection and Response

5. Consider your own experience with monsters in films. Do you find humanoid horror monsters more frightening than animalistic ones? Why or why not? Why might filmmakers focus on half-human creatures instead of completely monstrous ones?

6. Note that H. G. Wells's novel *The Island of Dr. Moreau* (the original source for *Island of Lost Souls*) has no women, but women were added in the movie. Kawin calls sex "an important element of the confrontation between human and monster" (par. 6). Why do you think women were added in the film? What role does sex play in movies about composite monsters?

7. In *Island of Lost Souls*, Dr. Moreau's creations are trained in the Law, intended to make the creatures more human. However, the transformation of the creatures is never complete: "the 'stubborn beast flesh' keeps growing back" (par. 6). As a result, the creatures must continually undergo painful surgeries to retain the shapes Moreau wants them to have. How does this reflect a battle between nature and nurture? How is the inability to control the return of the natural flesh a sign of human limitations?

Making Connections

8. How do the composite monsters of movies differ from the composite monsters of the classical (and preclassical) era, such as the Minotaur, centaurs, sphinxes, and mermaids? You may wish to investigate other movies that feature composite monsters beyond the ones listed in Kawin's article, including another movie version of H. G. Wells's novel, *The Island of Dr. Moreau* (1996), starring Marlon Brando.

9. Compare Kawin's article with Jeffrey Jerome Cohen's "Fear of the Monster Is Really a Kind of Desire" (p. 190). How does Cohen's thesis connect with Kawin's statement that "the prospect of sex between species [is] an important element of the confrontation between human and monster" (par. 6)? Explain your answer, drawing on additional selections from this book or other sources if necessary.

Birthright

Konstantinos

For many people, Christmas is filled with positive feelings — happy memories, traditions, carols, family. However, long ago in some parts of Europe, people believed that a child born on Christmas (or sometimes Christmas Eve) was destined to be a werewolf. Konstantinos, a self-described neo-pagan and practicing occultist, tells the story of a child born on Christmas Eve who seems to be able to live a normal life except for one day each year, when things go horribly wrong. This excerpt is from Konstantinos's book *Werewolves: The Occult Truth* (2010).

Werewolf lore can give a whole new meaning to being born to . . . well, to do whatever amazing thing you do. Unlike being a blistering guitar player or natural comedian, though, imagine being born to transform into a wolf. Not what the typical child would hope for, right? On the topic of children's hopes, werewolves are uncannily associated with the ultimate holiday for children.

Being born on Christmas was considered a bad sign in seemingly isolated parts of Europe. It's not difficult to imagine why people from the Middle Ages might have had mixed feelings about the holiday. Christmas is a few days after the longest night of the year, and obviously a cold night at that. Wolves would have been extra hungry and on the hunt for food during these cold nights, and remote villagers would have felt trapped indoors during the majority of this approximate time of year. Hungry, howling wolves, combined with bitter winds outside, would take their toll on the sanity of those who had a fair share of superstition to begin with. A common Scandinavian belief, for instance, was that on this night werewolves would gather and steal liquor from villagers, and then engage in drunken revelry . . . now there's a type of werewolf most people can relate to!

The association between lycanthropy° and Christmas also manifested in the idea that any child born on this mysterious holiday was destined to become a werewolf. The exact day of the holiday that counts in effecting this curse, Christmas Eve or Christmas Day, varies by culture. Despite the startling idea that roughly one in 365 people would have been werewolves if the belief were true, the idea did flourish. Guy Endore picked up on this interesting bit of folklore and used it in his novel *The*

---

lycanthropy: the belief that one has become a wolf; the possibility of developing wolf-like characteristics by magic or witchcraft.

Werewolf of Paris. The most well-known folktale involving this belief, however, comes from the village of Sant'Angelo dei Lombardi, which is east of Naples in Italy.

It's unclear what year this legend was supposed to have occurred, but it likely began circulating in the sixteenth or seventeenth century. As Christmas Eve approached (it was the eve, not the twenty-fifth, that applied in this tale), the village watched with suspicion and fear as a young couple prepared for the birth of their child. Apparently, everyone in Sant'Angelo knew what it would mean if the little one arrived on Christmas Eve. He would be doomed to a life of hideous transformations, and they would be doomed to defending themselves against such a beast.

Sure enough, the little boy arrived on the very night everyone feared. 5 Despite their fears, the villagers couldn't bring themselves to punish the little one or his parents. In time it seemed as if their good will toward the family was rewarded. The child was sweet and pleasant, and played nicely with the other children.

Most days and nights, that is. For each Christmas Eve, the little one would turn into a little wolf. And not a cuddly cub, either. He would snap at anyone who came near, including his parents.

> "For each Christmas Eve, the little one would turn into a little wolf."

While he was young and relatively weak, the lycanthrope was easy to contain as each Christmas Eve came around. Every year found him a little bigger and stronger in wolf form, however, and it became increasingly difficult to restrain him when the inevitable change came. The villagers eventually had to change tactics and began locking themselves and their animals in each Christmas, allowing the growing werewolf to venture off into the wilderness. He would return every Christmas morning in human form, fall asleep, and basically awaken as if he were any other child.

While growing up, the boy knew he was actually a werewolf, but also saw that the villagers accepted him. The acceptance ran deep, too, for when he reached his twenties, he was allowed to marry a local girl he had grown up with. They were happy together, and of course had to make special preparations for their first and every Christmas together. Rather than worrying about where to hide the presents, the couple worked out a system where she would lock herself in before his change, and wouldn't open the door until he knocked on the door with three distinct knocks. This simple code would mean he was human again, and ready for her to let him in. After each transformation, she would let him in and wash off the leaves and probably worse material from his gruesome night adventures.

After a few years, the couple's arrangement seemed foolproof, which, of course, meant the wife was destined to become a little too comfortable with the routine. She eventually made a mistake that cost her. No witnesses were there that night when she either didn't lock the door or opened it at a time when she just assumed hubby must have changed back into human form. When they found the naked man walking around, still covered in the night's gore, the villagers knew his wife hadn't washed and cared for him as she had on other Christmas mornings. Taking him home, the villagers found the horribly mangled remains of his wife.

Surprisingly, the folktale doesn't end with the villagers punishing the werewolf. Instead his own guilt did him in, and the man soon after committed suicide.

Merry Christmas.

Understanding the Text

1. What reasons does Konstantinos give for why people might naturally be more fearful around Christmas?

2. Konstantinos states that one Scandinavian belief was that werewolves would gather and steal liquor and get drunk. How does such a belief reinforce or contradict other depictions of werewolves?

3. In the legend about the young man who turns into a werewolf each Christmas Eve, why is he allowed to marry?

Reflection and Response

4. Analyze the relationship between the Christian holiday of Christmas and werewolves. What about this connection seems to make sense and what does not?

5. Note that in the folktale about the young man who becomes a werewolf, he kills himself out of guilt. Given that the story takes place within the belief system of Christians (who would be celebrating Christmas), how is the suicide of the werewolf a more appropriate conclusion than being killed by the villagers? How does the story reinforce traditional Christian teachings about good and evil?

Making Connections

6. In many ways, Christianized Europeans held on to vestiges of their pre-Christian (or pagan) past. Research ways in which the werewolf might be a holdover from that era, a repository of fears and superstitions that Christianity did not completely erase.

7. Compare Konstantinos's telling of the origin of werewolves with Matt Kaplan's version in "Cursed by a Bite" (p. 164). In what ways are the two compatible and in what ways are they not? How do the authors' different points of view (Konstantinos is an occultist; Kaplan is a science journalist) affect their conclusions? Cite quotations from their texts as evidence.

Werewolves in Psyche and Cinema: Man-Beast Transformation and Paradox

Elizabeth A. Lawrence

In this article originally published in the *Journal of American Culture*, former veterinarian and cultural anthropologist Elizabeth A. Lawrence analyzes the relationship between werewolves and humans throughout history and film. The werewolf has existed in the human imagination for thousands of years, with at least one recorded story of human transformation occurring as early as around 2700 BCE, in *The Epic of Gilgamesh*. It combines the animal and the human in a different way than do creatures such as the centaur and Minotaur: the human loses his or her humanity in a complete transformation, albeit only briefly. Perhaps in our past — even longer ago than recorded history — wolves were seen more as friendly competition in the hunt for food than as predators to be feared. As people grew more civilized and began to cultivate crops and animals for food, wolves became their enemies.

The phenomenon of human beings undergoing transformations into other species has been a prevalent notion since the dawn of consciousness. It occurs readily when boundaries between humans and animals are perceived as indistinct or when the presence of those boundaries is being tested or established. Such changes may be voluntary — brought about in an effort to obtain certain desirable characteristics possessed by an animal — or they may be involuntary — inflicted wantonly by an outside force upon an innocent person or intentionally upon a guilty individual as a punishment. Over the course of history, this so-called "shape-changing" has involved many animals, with the wolf being one of the most frequent and persistent. From the Anglo-Saxon *wer*, meaning man and *wulf* meaning wolf comes the term werewolf, defined as a man temporarily or permanently transformed into a wolf (Spence 426). Lycanthropy is the magical ability to assume the form and characteristics of a wolf, and is also used to denote a mental disorder in which a person believes himself to be a wolf.

Our contemporary technological world is imbued with positivism that leaves little room for human-animal forms like werewolves to prowl the night. For industrialized society, belief in the actuality of werewolves has all but vanished; yet the creatures still exist in the human psyche, lying in wait to disturb our dreams. They remain "alive and well in the twentieth century," according to recent psychiatric case studies (Keck 113; Kulick 134). They survive in popular culture through fantasy fiction, Gothic horror novels, tabloids, and even in a 1978 song about werewolves in London. No single classic gave rise to the werewolf image in the way that Mary Shelley's work established Frankenstein and Bram Stoker's novel created Dracula. Rather the contemporary human-wolf has been inspired largely by cinematic representations. The werewolf is the subject of films which have recurred quite regularly over the last six decades and in which the idea of becoming a werewolf is a real possibility, depicted with creativity and enthusiasm, encoding many symbolic meanings.

The 1994 Hollywood hit, *Wolf,* described as "the thinking man's werewolf movie" (Janusonis D5), stars Jack Nicholson, whose "normal feral intensity and lupine features" including "demonically" arched eyebrows are said to fit him for the role ("Wolf" 13; James 13). He plays Will Randall, book editor of a New York publishing house who, when the story begins, is a polite, intelligent individual described as the "last civilized man." He is known as "a good man," but as someone remarks, "the worst things happen to the best people." His character changes after being bitten by a wolf while traveling in the wilds of Vermont. Not only does this event occur during a full moon, but also on the very night the moon was closer to the earth than it had been in 100 years. The first sign that anything unusual had happened to him is the reaction of extreme fear that he inspires in a horse. Later, birds fly in panic out of the trees when he approaches. Soon, dense hair grows around the bite wound on his hand. Then he develops an extraordinarily keen sense of smell, allowing him to detect the odor of another man on his wife's clothes, betraying her infidelity. He no longer needs glasses, hears conversations through closed doors, and can move each ear separately. Hair grows on his face. He twitches his nose and sniffs the air. His habits change to sleeping by day and being active at night. He makes love to his wife after a long abstinence, first pulling off her bathrobe belt with his teeth. She responds by calling him "You animal!" He feels 20 years younger and suddenly has courage to decide to start his own company. He beats up three thugs who attempt to rob him and leaps over a wall when policemen chase him out of a zoo where he has gone to feed. He gives up his former vegetarian lifestyle and craves meat—the bloodier the better.

Randall's conversion is complete when at the next full moon he jumps out of a window, growls revealing fangs instead of teeth, chases a deer through the woods and brings it down. His face is transformed to that of a wolf as he bites the animal's throat, and consumes its flesh. His face and hands are covered with blood. He develops paws with talons and runs on all fours. His eyes glow green. At one point he urinates to mark his territory, and later manages to urinate on the shoes of a fellow-worker who schemed to get his job. Ultimately, he attacks humans, and after his first experience, spits out the fingers of a child. He kills his wife. His arch-enemy and his lover are turned into werewolves after he bites them.

Randall describes his rejuvenation: "I feel as if the wolf passed some- 5 thing along to me, a scrap of its spirit in my blood." A Hindu expert on animal possession tells him that his wolf spirit is a "gift"; not everyone who is bitten has the talent for such transformation. "There must be something wild within, an analogue of the wolf." Through his lupine identity, Randall can experience "power without guilt and love without doubt." This contemporary depiction of the legend has been called "the male version of the heroines in *Women Who Run with the Wolves*," with Randall's "analogue of the wolf" resembling the "Wild Woman Soul" (James 13). *Wolf* is an allegory depicting the viciousness of modern life as represented in the corporate business world. And, following the werewolf tradition, the film reinforces the concept of social and sexual restraint, with loss of control having disastrous consequences. Because wolves are sexual symbols, it has also been suggested that "wolves infecting other people and turning them into other werewolves could be seen as symbolizing the spread of AIDS" (Weinraub 1, 22).

A more innocent film with some of the same motifs, *Teen Wolf* (1985), stars Michael J. Fox as Scott, a frail but handsome schoolboy who is failing both at basketball and at winning the class beauty for his girlfriend. He is bored with working at his dad's hardware store and is "sick of being average." The first sign of his transformation comes when the sounds from a "silent" dog whistle being blown hurt his ears. His ears soon become pointed, his teeth change to fangs, his face and hands become hairy and his nails grow long. Like other werewolves before him, he howls at the full moon. When he participates in a party kissing game, his partner hits him and emerges from the closet with her dress ripped down the back as though by claws. The boy's changing into a wolf is a genetic trait inherited from his father, who explains that, "being what we are is not all bad. There are some advantages. We have great power, and with power goes responsibility. You can do things other people can't do."

Scott has a problem in that he sometimes turns into a wolf when he does not want it to happen. But at first he uses his new strength to great advantage. He becomes an extremely skillful basketball player, making his team victorious and winning popularity with the cheerleaders. He is able to seduce the glamorous girl who once spurned him. And he is suddenly assertive toward the school principal who formerly intimidated him. The whole town goes "wolf crazy" in its adulation for his new achievements, making him a hero and wearing tee-shirts marked "wolf buddy" in his honor. But ultimately his role as wolf fails to bring happiness. He realizes that he loves the quiet girl who has always been his friend, and asks her to the prom. She will only accept, however, if he goes as Scott, not as the wolf. She says she has missed the real Scott. He decides then to be himself, even though the championship game is coming up and he will be letting the team down. In spite of his friends' pleas and his teammates' chant of "wolf, wolf, wolf," he tells the coach "no wolf. I want to play and be myself." The team wins anyway, and Scott is a hero. The experience of being a wolf gave him residual power to excel by instilling confidence.

A more sinister 1981 film, *An American Werewolf in London*, also involves a teen-age boy, David, who travels to northern England accompanied by his friend Jack. The movie opens with the song, "Blue Moon," but soon becomes more ominous as the pair of hikers tries to take refuge from a stormy night at a pub called "The Slaughtered Lamb"—a portent of events to come. The boys notice a five-pointed star on the wall of the pub, a "pentangle" which is associated with witchcraft. The hostile occupants do not allow the boys to stay, driving them away into the dark with the warning, "beware of the moon, avoid the moors, and stick to the roads." But the moon rises, howls are heard, and before they have traveled far a wolf attacks, killing Jack and rendering David unconscious. He wakes up in the hospital with nail scratches on his chest and a bloody mouth after dreaming of killing and eating a deer. Jack appears as a ghost and tells David that the attack by a werewolf made him a lycanthrope. He will remain in limbo, he says, until the last werewolf is destroyed.

Conforming to the familiar pattern, David makes love to his nurse, who has fallen for him. He is shown urinating. A frightened cat spits at him. On the next full moon, he tears off his clothes, revealing a hairy body; he develops fangs and paws with long nails. He feels invigorated and his body seems very strong. He howls while "Blue Moon" plays, and heads for the zoo, where he climbs into the cage with wolves, who accept him, then jumps out and runs through the park. The next morning, six people are found murdered and mutilated. David considers suicide and wonders whether he needs a silver bullet. After a harrowing chase in which he is pursued like a mad dog through Picadilly Circus, the werewolf is shot and changes back into the boy, David, as soon as he is dead.

The Howling, a 1981 film, also features the full moon, yellow, shining 10 eyes, howling, and the idea that werewolves can be killed only with fire or silver bullets. It begins with comments that humankind has lost something valuable in evolution; man is still part savage and we should not deny the animal in us. The plot involves Marcia, a TV reporter who had been kidnapped by a maniac and rescued and who goes on a country retreat with her husband in order to regain her composure. But instead, she encounters werewolves, among them her abductor and her trusted psychiatrist. A graphic scene that is the delight of film makers shows a human transformation into wolf in minute detail. When the heroine is attacked by a werewolf, she fights back with a hatchet and manages to cut off one of the beast's front paws. Upon returning home, she finds her husband with a bandage covering his missing hand.

Eventually, she is caught by a pack of werewolves, who tell her that they once raised cattle for prey but they now feed on people. They explain, "You can't tame what's meant to be wild. . . . From the day we're born, there is a struggle between what is peaceful and what is violent." Finally, the police surround the pack and shut the wolves into an enclosure that is set on fire. But one werewolf gets away and succeeds in biting Marcia. She cries out, "We have to warn people, we have to make them believe." Her inevitable transformation into a werewolf is televised as proof of the reality of the phenomenon. The most striking symbolic element of this movie is an avowedly evil woman in a restaurant ordering a rare hamburger. The final scene consists of a close-up of a raw, red hamburger on a grill, with a spatula patting the meat causing the blood to drip down into the fire. The meat is turned over for cooking on the other side and again pressed, emitting bloody juice, and is served up rare.

Although the noble character of wolves is occasionally portrayed in the films just described, that aspect receives more emphasis in a fascinating movie entitled *Wolfen*, also dated 1981. The plot stresses the likeness between American Indians and wolves: they evolved together and both are superb hunters that do not overpopulate the earth. Unlike most werewolves, who live in remote surroundings, the ones in this story live in New York City. The reason for this becomes clear when a native elder explains to a white man that the creatures he has seen are not wolves, but "wolfen." "For twenty thousand years—ten times your Christian era—the great hunting nations lived together in balance with nature," he points out. "Then came the slaughter" of wolves as well as Indians and buffalo by the white man. "The smartest went underground into the new wilderness." The great hunters became scavengers of garbage in urban areas. "They might be gods. They can see two looks away and they can hear a cloud pass overhead. In their world there are no lies, and no crime. In their eyes, you are the savage. You got technology but lost your senses." They are "other nations, their world is older, more complete, finished. They kill to survive, to protect their families. Man does less." Because of human arrogance, he warns, there will be "life that will prey on us as we prey upon the earth." He tells the white man "You don't have the eyes of the hunter, you have the eyes of the dead."

Flashback films of wolves being mercilessly gunned down from helicopters drive home the history of human cruelty perpetrated upon the species. Yet the people violently killed by the wolfen are restricted to those who directly threaten their survival, individuals involved in urban renewal projects that destroy the old buildings where the creatures live in order to build luxury condos. The wolfen must protect their hunting ground. Mutilation and cannibalism represent their retribution against the humans who wrong them. Otherwise, they thoughtfully prey only upon victims who will not be missed—the sick, the old, and drug addicts. Abandoned people have become their new sources of meat.

In this film, scenes of shape-shifting take place, like other werewolf transformations, under a full moon. Belief holds that the soul can transfer the body into a different form. The shape-shifter goes to the water's edge, takes off his clothes, and with his hand makes paw prints on the shore. He goes down on all fours and laps water containing the moon's reflection and blows water out of his mouth, illustrating the ancient notion of water as a facilitator of transformation. He dashes about in a frenzy and then runs into the water and howls. His teeth grow huge. The moon turns red.

The 1941 definitive cinematic version, *The Wolf Man*, became the "key 15 generating text for the modern figure of the werewolf" (Douglas 244). Set in Wales, this film contrasts in many ways with the recent *Wolf*, demonstrating the evolution of the werewolf image over the past five decades. The titles indicate the emphasis on the human side of the man-beast in the earlier film, with more focus on the animal in the later. In *The Wolf Man*, Lon Chaney, Jr. plays the doomed hero, Larry Talbot, a huge, hulking figure, who is at home with tools, not philosophy. He has no special "gift" like the editor in *Wolf*, and does not resemble a wolf at all, except in the slang sense of chasing a pretty girl and telling her "What big eyes you have, Grandma!" From the very beginning, the script makes clear that

> Even a man who is pure in heart,
> And says his prayers by night
> May become a wolf when the wolfbane blooms
> And the autumn moon is bright.

Larry's innocence cannot save him from his fate when the pentagram, the sign of the werewolf, appears on his hand as a warning he is the next victim of the creature's bite. A simple man, he is a passive victim who cannot be blamed for the hideous murders he commits as a savage wolf, representing the evil side of man. The gypsy woman chants over Larry's body, "The way you walked was thorny through no fault of your own, but as the rain enters the soil, the river enters the sea, so tears run to a predestined end." Her blessing ensures death will release the werewolf from further suffering.

In the recent Jack Nicholson film, despite bloody killings, there is the message, however ambivalent, that wolves can be wholesome, even noble. A new theme enters the old legend: the werewolf can be good or bad according to the character of the transformed human. In *The Wolf Man*, the "everyday world is benign, well-ordered," and Christian, whereas in the 1994 version [*Wolf*], "everyday life is a wolf pack, with rivals contending for power, sex and dominance" and with definite pagan elements (Rutherford 55).

The werewolves' vulnerability to silver, mentioned in subsequent films, is a prominent theme in *The Wolf Man*, in which a silver cane, rather than a silver bullet, is used to kill the creatures. Other patterns set in 1941 for future films are the influence of the moon, the vividly detailed transformation of man to wolf, terrified dogs that bark furiously in recognition of the human form of the werewolf, a frightened horse that rears and whinnies when such a person appears, and a charm provided by a soothsayer to protect the werewolf, who gives it to his sweetheart to protect her from himself. Eerie scenes in a misty forest, wolfbane flowers that wilt when the werewolf is about to strike, a bite wound that heals overnight and then turns into a pentagram, and gypsies with a werewolf among them who return every autumn are noteworthy elements.

The important contribution of this film is articulation of the tension between the physical aspects of the werewolf as an actual entity and the idea that the phenomenon is a mental illness. For Larry, the pragmatist who understands only what can be touched, his transformation is real. For his father, a brooding theorist, the werewolf is more complex. He explains that the werewolf legend, like all legends, has some truth; it is an "ancient explanation of the dual personality in all of us." For him, lycanthropy is a variety of schizophrenia, expressing "the good and evil in every man's soul. In this case, evil takes the shape of an animal." For some people, he says, "life is simple, black and white, with no shades of gray." For others, good and bad are complex and not so easily distinguished. Although he does not believe in the physical form of the werewolf, he feels that "anything can happen to a man in his own mind." He thinks his son has conjured up an evil thing and wants to help him "get out of this mental quagmire." The doctor who is consulted agrees that "a man lost in the mazes of his mind may imagine he is anything." He argues that lycanthropy is "mind over matter," mental suggestion, a kind of self-hypnotism like the stigmata. Larry, he says, is a sick man with a psychic maladjustment who could be cured if he cooperated. But therapy does not intervene. The savage wolf who, while attacking his next victim, is killed by strokes with the silver-tipped cane, turns into the dead body of Larry.

Tales of human-wolf transformations date to the remote past and oc- 20 cur in many cultures. The earliest known description of such a change is found in the Akkadian *Epic of Gilgamesh*, dating from the early second millennium BC, in which the goddess Ishtar turns a shepherd into a wolf who is then devoured by his own dogs. Ovid's *Metamorphoses* describes Jupiter's punishment of Arcadian king Lycaon for giving him a banquet of human flesh: Instantly Lycaon howled, "his clothes changed into bristling hairs, his arms to legs, and he became a wolf." His "savage nature showed in his rabid jaws, and he now directed against the flocks his innate lust for killing" and his mania for shedding blood. "Though he was a wolf, he retained some traces of his original shape" and "presented the same picture of ferocity" (35). Virgil's *Eighth Eclogue* mentions a werewolf as a magician who voluntarily undergoes transformation through use of herbs.

Although these epics gave brief sketches of the phenomenon, the first substantial literary description of a werewolf that became the progenitor of all later versions is included in a Roman work, *Trimalchio's Banquet*, written by Petronius in the first century AD. The tale is narrated by a former slave, Niceros, who was going to visit his mistress and asked a soldier to accompany him. The two men set out under a full moon and after a time stopped to rest among some tombstones that lined the road. During that sojourn, the soldier began stripping off his clothes, putting them down by the roadside. Then he urinated in a circle around his clothes and suddenly turned into a wolf who began to howl and ran away into the woods. His clothes turned into stone. When Niceros reached his mistress's house, she informed him that a wolf had just been there and had butchered many of her herd. The wolf had escaped, but a slave had managed to stab the animal in the neck with a spear. On returning to his master's house at dawn, Niceros notices that the clothes have been removed from the roadside, leaving a pool of blood in their place. Back at home, he finds the soldier lying in bed with a doctor treating his wounded neck. Niceros realized then that the man was a werewolf—using the Latin word *versipellem*, meaning literally "turn skin" (Otten 231–233; Douglas 39, 41–42).

With this story the major elements that recur in werewolf traditions over the ages, including the Hollywood versions, were established. The transition from man to wolf must take place under the full moon. On a practical level, the moonlight enabled Niceros to see an event that had transpired at night and thus make his story believable to his listeners. But the moon also has deep associations with lycanthropy. Symbolically, the moon is associated with the hunt in almost all cultures. This may relate to the fact that for hunter-gatherers the collection of plant food was a daily chore whereas hunting was a periodic activity that may have been stimulated by the phase of the moon acting as a signal to begin the chase. This sign would be reinforced by the howling of the wolves—the predators that hunters most closely imitated. In prehistoric times the lunar cycle was a recognizable unit of time, a natural clock. In many traditions there is an association between the moon and a female deity concerned with hunting. The classic example of this association is the Graeco-Roman figure of Artemis, or Diana, called "the mistress of animals," who is known for changing a man into a stag when he saw her bathing (Douglas 38–40). The moon, of course, as the archetypal symbol of change, has a logical connection with the profound alteration inherent in the man–to–wild beast transformation.

Petronius' story also established the feature that a person must remove his clothes in order to become a werewolf, discarding the things that make him human before changing into an animal. Also initiated was the tradition that some form of magic is used to bring about the transformation, as in the case of the soldier urinating in a circle around his clothes. The urination theme became part of many versions of the werewolf, and relates to the lupine habit of territory marking. In order for the werewolf to become human again, he must return to the same spot where he left his clothes to retrieve them. The conversion of the clothes into stone would prevent anyone from taking or moving them while the owner was in wolf form. Another important motif that persists to the present day is the sympathetic wound—an injury inflicted on the werewolf that will still appear after he returns to human form. In Petronius' tale, as in others to follow, this wound is proof that the phenomenon of changing into a werewolf actually happened and confirms the shared identity of man and wolf. In cinematic versions of the werewolf, as just described, many of these motifs have been retained and others have been added. Water has been an important element in effecting human-to-wolf transformation, and its power could be imparted by drinking from a wolf's paw print, rolling in the dewy grass, bathing in a fountain or spring, or plunging into and swimming across a body of water. Charms or secret ointments rubbed on the body were also used to cause the transition, and wolf pelts or magic belts or girdles provided by a supernatural being and donned by a human could bring about the change to beast.

In order to understand the werewolf and the emotions it evokes, one must take a close look at the extraordinary history of human relationships with the wolf and the crusade of annihilation. The species was long ago extirpated in the British Isles and Scandinavia and wolf populations were decimated in its former range throughout the world (Lopez 13–14). As one wolf researcher points out, the destruction of that animal represents "the first time in the history of the planet [that] one species made a deliberate organized attempt to exterminate a fellow species." Ingrained hatred of the wolf was brought with the colonists to the New World. The American war against the species was "one of the most successful programs ever carried out by the federal government." The original wolf population in what is now the lower forty-eight states before the arrival of European settlers is estimated to have been two million. "By the 1950s, except for isolated populations of a few hundred wolves in the Upper Midwest, the gray wolf had been exterminated in those areas" (McIntyre 69, 77).

• • •

W. M. S. Russell and Clare Russell, two scholars who would be expected   25 to know better, wrote on the social biology of werewolves in 1978, giving a diatribe against wolves that more properly belongs in the Dark Ages: "To propose conserving [wolves] in the wild" is "analogous to suggesting the conservation of desert locusts or malarial mosquitoes. . . . It can only be explained by something like totemic survivals." Referring to Australian *totemism,*° they present the misleading argument that "so long as totems were valuable food species, the totemic system was ecologically sound." But when it spread to embrace objects of "no actual service to the natives," this was no longer true. "The conservation of a pest species is, therefore, intelligible in totemic terms, though obviously not in terms of rational ecology" (178–179). What an unfortunate discussion to be published during this time of ecological crisis, when modern science has demonstrated the vital role predators, particularly wolves, play in the integrity of the natural environment and even in the health of the entire planet!

The Russells argue against the validity of what they call the "sentimental attitude" to wolves, citing the adverse opinions of stock-tenders who must deal with predators in real life, such as the reindeer-herding Lapps. In that society, the Boy Scout movement was resisted by the

totemism: the belief in the connection between an animal or bird that serves as an emblem of a tribe, clan, or family.

children, who "objected strongly to being called Wolf-cubs" (179). The authors trace the origin of the Boy Scout wolf cubs to Akcla, the wolf in Kipling's *Jungle Book*, and argue that through that figure "generations of urban children have been familiarized with the wolf totem." They assert that this may help to explain the appearance in recent years of movements to conserve wild wolf populations, and even reintroduce them into regions where they have been exterminated, a practice that is deplorable because of wolves' "depredations on livestock" and their being "dangerous carriers of rabies" (178). To advocate a cultural materialist view which excludes psychological and cultural motivations denies the preeminent influence of human symbolic capacities.

Admittedly, the utilitarian concerns associated with the rise of stock-tending have been strong factors in evoking hatred for the wolf. In that regard it is relevant that a human-wolf phenomenon exists among the Navajo, a tribe that is deeply involved with sheep-raising. However, the anthropologist who studied Navajo human-wolves, which are a type of witch, did not find that they have any direct relationship to the killing of sheep, but did note that they may steal sheep, motivated by "the jealousy and envy which accrues to the owner of much jewelry and many sheep" (Morgan 11, 40).

Navajo shape-shifters or human-wolves represent belief in fluidity between the human and animal worlds. Human-wolves possess great speed and the ability to cover a lot of territory without effort and then to disappear, demonstrating their supernatural power. As recently as 1992, a Navajo driving a truck at 75 miles an hour reported that the figure of a man ran alongside him and then veered off, changing into a wolf just before disappearing into the bush (Burbank 1994, 1, 5, 6). A Navajo human-wolf can be distinguished from a real wolf because his tail hangs straight down, in contrast to an actual wolf, who puts his tail out behind him as he runs. The morning after shooting a wolf, a Navajo may follow its tracks for miles, only to discover a man bleeding from a suspicious wound. Or, if a suspected werewolf is shot, the next morning a Navajo miles away may fall from his horse, wounded in exactly the same place where the werewolf had been shot. Human-wolves, also called skin walkers, are believed to climb to the top of a family's hogan° and look through the smoke hole. Occupants see a pair of pointed ears and a wolfish face with glowing eyes. The wolf then drops some powder made from the skin of a dead person, called corpse poison, into the fire below, which

---

hogan: a house constructed of dirt and branches, and then covered with mud or sod, used by the Navajo Indians.

flares and causes the people to breathe the deadly fumes. Or the wolf may sprinkle the poison on the victim's nose or mouth or blow it at him, causing bad luck, illness or death (Burbank 1994, 7, 8; Burbank 1990, 49; Morgan 18).

William Morgan argues that the psychological and cultural meanings of Navajo werewolves lie in the fear of the "ravenous cannibalism" they represent and their association with tribal belief in "night wandering" that allows a person to be in two places at the same time (11). Also prominent is the idea that a human-wolf will dig up and eat bodies or take the jewelry that has been buried with the deceased for use in the afterlife. Navajo have "an excessive fear of the dead," shunning contact with a corpse, for the spirit is still in the physical body and must be avoided. The main defining characteristic of a Navajo witch is "trifling with the dead or the possessions of the dead." While in wolf skin, witches break powerful taboos by engaging in necrophilia, sexual excess, incest, bestiality, and cannibalism. Thus they negate world order and bring chaos, destroying the tenets of social propriety not only by obliterating the demarcation between humans and animals but also by transgressing the boundary between life and death (Morgan 11, 25–26; Burbank 1994, 6; Burbank 1990, 49, 51).

The most vivid archetypes of fearful werewolves, however, are those 30 of the Old World, still remembered with dread by each generation who shudders anew at the retelling of their history. During the fifteenth to seventeenth centuries, when belief in werewolves was most prevalent, countless hundreds of people accused of undergoing transformation to wolves were punished, usually by death, often with confessions obtained through torture. Many were burned alive. Details of these cases were carefully recorded. One of the most notorious was the German, Stubbe Peeter, who, over a twenty-five year period allegedly committed many crimes including rape, incest, murder, eating the raw flesh of people as well as animals, and adultery. He confessed to having made a pact with the devil, who had given him a girdle to transform him into a wolf. Above the instrument of torture used in his 1589 execution in Cologne was hung the likeness of a wolf "to show unto all men the shape wherein he executed those cruelties" (Otten 9, 53, 76).

Another self-confessed werewolf, Jean Grenier, tried in France in 1603, revealed that he had become a werewolf by applying a salve and wearing a wolf skin provided by "The Man of the Forest," an affiliate of the devil. The young lycanthrope admitted he had clawed and bitten several girls and had killed and eaten babies and children. The court, unusual for its time, took into account his mental derangement and low intelligence that made him "incapable of rational thought," and sentenced him to life in a monastery for moral and religious instruction. There a visitor noted that he had nails like claws and ran on all fours, eating rotten meat. He died at age twenty, considered to be "scarcely human" (Otten 9, 51; Lopez 244).

During the height of the werewolf craze, a person who was antisocial or marginal, living apart from others, might be accused of being a werewolf. Anyone who was conceived at the full moon, born feet first or with a caul, had a hairy body, scabbed legs, or lupine features, or whose eyebrows met in the middle might be suspect. Lack of visible fur was not a protection as one accused werewolf found when he told his tormentors his hair was on the inside and they gashed his arms and legs to verify his claim (Summers 160–161). Werewolves never had the long, bushy tails of ordinary wolves, and were distinguished from them by being tailless or having truncated tails. Werewolves might also have smaller heads or appear different in color. Many theories involving disease as the cause of belief in werewolves have been advanced. Foremost among these proposed etiologies is porphyria, a rare blood disorder whose symptoms include excessive hair growth on face, hands, arms, and legs, reddish teeth, and claw-shaped fingernails and toenails, as well as facial scarring and disfigurement from lesions resulting from a toxic reaction to sunlight that might make the sufferer prefer to travel at night ("Porphyrias" 7). Other diseases implicated are rabies and ergot poisoning, which could account for the victims' irrational actions; hypertrichosis giving a bestial appearance; malnutrition stimulating an appetite for flesh; demonic possession; melancholia, autism, schizophrenia, and various psychoses; or the ingestion of pharmacological hallucinogens leading to delusions of lupine identity. Though provocative, probably none of these factors played a substantial role in the werewolf phenomenon.

Far more significant is the cultural context in which fear and implacable hatred of predators became nearly universal at a certain stage of human history. Many indigenous predator species take human-beast form in various areas of the world, such as were-jaguars in South America, were-bears in northern Europe and Asia, were-leopards in Africa, were-tigers in China, and were-foxes in Japan. But the concept of werewolves is by far the most widespread and deeply-entrenched image of violence and aggression, occurring throughout the whole range of the wolf's former habitat: from the northern tundra of Europe and Asia down to the shores of the Mediterranean, east to India and China, and to western North America (Douglas 21).

Thousands of years ago the wolf was celebrated as a protector; thus a spiritual leader who acquired its powers to become a wolf-man was regarded with awe. But as human societies became sedentary and adopted the agricultural way of life, attitudes toward wolves, and hence were-wolves, changed. They became identified with hostile forces, outcasts who lived in the woods and preyed upon humans, and were perceived as dangerous misfits or deviates with savage qualities that made them uncivilized and untamable. Originally, primitive societies had generally viewed the werewolf positively because it represented integration of the cultural and wild elements of humans. "To learn to howl with the wolves" meant "opening oneself up to the essence of nature," a process through which it was possible to achieve self-awareness. To live in a social order, a person must have spent time in the wilderness, for only by going outside the self could one's inner nature be made clear. By the Middle Ages, however, the werewolf had lost its benign ritual meaning and was considered destructive, bloodthirsty, and cunning. In the late Middle Ages, it became associated with the devil. At the end of the fifteenth century, the official Catholic position switched from considering belief in werewolves nonsensical and sinful to full belief in their existence as accomplices of Satan who, according to the 1484 Papal Bull,° must be annihilated. This change was "connected to the holy dictum to believe in witches. Along with cats, werewolves were allegedly the favorite cohorts of witches, and in many werewolf trials of the sixteenth and seventeenth centuries there was no real distinction made between werewolf and witch." The greatest fear in both Catholic and Protestant minds was chaos, which was associated with sensuality and an uncontrollable nature, and that fear was projected upon human-wolves (Zipes 68–69, 71).

> "Preeminently, the werewolf phenomenon articulates humankind's overwhelming penchant for symbolizing with animal images, making sense of life with metaphors from nature."

Preeminently, the werewolf phenomenon articulates humankind's 35 overwhelming penchant for symbolizing with animal images, making sense of life with metaphors from nature. The wolf is an extraordinarily rich vehicle of expression, carrying a complex web of embedded codes, some of which stand in paradoxical relationship to the actual animal but most of which are rooted in emphasis on its predation and meat-eating. The wolf bears projected guilt for the human predatory past and a present replete not only with consumption of animal flesh but with all manner of exploitation of and barbarity toward our own species and others. In Christian symbolism, Jesus is the lamb of God and the Good Shepherd for whom the wolf is enemy. Thus, Satan acquired lupine imagery. Christ

Papal Bull: a letter or announcement by which the pope addresses all Catholics.

warns his followers to "beware of false prophets, who come to you in sheep's clothing, but inwardly are ravenous wolves" (Matthew 7:15). Evil wolves became embedded in literary masterpieces. Chaucer's *Parson's Tale* includes the devil's wolves that strangle the sheep of Jesus Christ. Dante's *Inferno* depicts the wolf as a symbol of greed and fraud, for those who are condemned to hell for the sins of the wolf are seducers, hypocrites, thieves, and liars. Rude eating is described as "wolfing" one's food, and hunger is the "wolf at the door." A "discordant note on the violin is still called a wolf." An aggressive sexual signal is a "wolf whistle," and immoral acts are epitomized by the use of the French idiom "she's seen the wolf" meaning "she's lost her virginity" as well as by calling prostitutes "wolves" because they are viewed as "consuming the souls" of men (Lopez 219, 221, 239). Not only human evil, but even that emanating from nature itself is foisted upon the wolf. Lupus is the word for a dread disease that may eat away the flesh.

The uprooting of graves for devouring corpses gave wolves an association with death and their attraction to body-strewn battlefields linked them to war and desolation. Human savagery is couched in lupine terms. The fifteenth century French nobleman known as Bluebeard, who tortured, killed, and ate hundreds of children and bathed in their blood, was categorized as a werewolf by folklorist Sabine Baring-Gould (181–237), even though no man-beast transformation was reported. A Nazi terrorist organization called "Operation Werewolf" carried out a regime of murders in 1920 and in World War II one of Hitler's headquarters was named Werewolf (Douglas 26; Russell and Russell 165). Robert Eisler, following his imprisonment at Buchenwald and Dachau, argued for an evolutionist derivation of human violence, titling his study of sadism and masochism *Man into Wolf* (1951). American World War II propaganda was interwoven with opposition to Aldo Leopold's wolf preservation program. An advocate of the bounty for wolf killers wrote, "The wolf is the Nazi of the forest. He takes the deer and some small fry. . . . Can Professor Leopold justify their existence because deer meant for human consumption should be fed to the Nazi because we must have that protection for the trees? Can he justify the Jap or Nazi because he eats a rabbit or a grouse which are meant for human food, or the songbird on its nest, which are meant by the Lord for our pleasure?" A poster promoting the sale of US Savings Bonds depicts a snarling wolf, and states "There's one 100-proof way to guard your door against this fellow's visit. There's wolf poison in every US Savings Bond you buy" (Thiel 107–108).

A werewolf, according to one account, had "eyes glaring like marshfires" (Baring-Gould 3). A recent Broadway musical production of *Beauty and the Beast* featured snarling wolves with crimson eyes lit up like burning coals. But where many observers described a hideous red or orange glow in the werewolf's eyes, Aldo Leopold saw in the last wolf he had shot "a fierce green fire dying in her eyes." The experience made him think "like a mountain" with an ecological perspective that changed his role from wolf-killer to wolf-preserver (Flader 1). Since that day in 1944, attitudes about wolves have been gradually shifting to becoming more sympathetic, though with many fluctuations. Now, fifty years later, the principal cellist in a California symphony orchestra quit her job in protest against performing Prokofiev's 1936 work, *Peter and the Wolf.* She urged the public to boycott the performance of the work that teaches children "to hate and fear wolves and to applaud a hunter who kills a wolf" ("Wolf Pact" D1). Presently, wolves are being reintroduced to various regions of the United States where stockmen, hunters, and those who fear the wild can be out-voted. School children may visit wolf education centers and are encouraged to adopt a wolf through donations of money.

But the evil werewolf still prowls. Two 1990 British sex criminals were called the "werewolf rapist" and the "Wolfman." Yet strangely the recent multiple murders and cannibalism of Jeffrey Dahmer which resemble deeds recounted at the old European werewolf trials did not elicit those titles (Douglas 262–263). A currently popular song tells about the "Werewolf of London" with "a Chinese menu in his hand. . . . Going to get himself a big dish of beef chow mein." The lyrics warn "If you hear him howling around your kitchen door/Better not let him in. Little old lady got mutilated late last night. . . . He's the hair-handed gent who ran amuk in Kent. . . . Better stay away from him/He'll rip your lungs out. . . . I saw a werewolf drinking a piña colada at Trader Vic's/His hair was perfect/Werewolves of London draw blood" (Zevon). The human-wolf form continues to represent our species' carnivorous nature and our staggering propensity for violence. Likely, werewolves will continue to be important in the future, representing as they do the paradox of our projection into animals of traits unacceptable in humans and the assignment of human behavior patterns to animals. Both processes are deeply entrenched in human cognition and are becoming more, not less, prevalent in modern times. As the wild domain becomes ever more engulfed by the tame and we are concerned with measuring one against the other, the man-beast figure that combines them both holds renewed fascination. Werewolves embody the conflict between instinctual urges and rational behavior—a source of ongoing controversy regarding the question of establishing valid distinctions between people and animals. The werewolf concept represents the need to deal with animality, wildness, and otherness—

urgent issues in modern life—and bridges the man-beast gulf, challenging the ingrained Cartesian dualism° that divides humankind from animals in Western society. The sense of identification we feel with wolves
horrifies us, but at the same time captivates us as we acquire deeper appreciation for the wild realm and our place within it.

Works Cited

An American Werewolf in London. Polygram Pictures, 1981.

Baring-Gould. Sabine. *The Book of Were-Wolves.* New York: Causeway Books, 1973.

Burbank, James C. *Vanishing Lobo: The Mexican Wolf and the Southwest.* Boulder:
Johnson Books. 1990.

Burbank, James C. "Yenaldloosh: The Shape-Shifter Beliefs of the Navajos." *The
Indian Trader* 25.6 (June 1994): 1, 5–8, 10.

Douglas, Adam. *The Beast Within.* London: Chapmans, 1992.

Eisler, Robert. *Man into Wolf: An Anthropological Interpretation of Sadism, Masochism
and Lycanthropy.* London: Routledge and Keegan Paul, 1951.

Flader, Susan L. *Thinking Like a Mountain.* Lincoln: U of Nebraska P, 1974.

The Howling. Avco Embassy Pictures Corporation, 1981.

James, Caryn. "The Werewolf Within Dances with Abandon." *New York Times*
19 June 1994: 13, 18.

Janusonis, Michael. "A Ponderous Wolf Could Use More Howling." *Providence
Journal-Bulletin* 17 June 1994: D5.

Keck, Paul E., et al. "Lycanthropy: Alive and Well in the Twentieth Century." *Psychological Medicine* 18 (1988): 113–120.

Kulick, Aaron R., Harrison G. Pope, Jr., and Paul E. Keck, Jr. "Lycanthropy and Self-
Identification." *Journal of Nervous and Mental Disease* 178.2 (1990): 134–137.

Lopez, Barry Holstun. *Of Wolves and Men.* New York: Charles Scribner's Sons, 1978.

McIntyre, Rick. *A Society of Wolves: National Parks and the Battle over the Wolf.* Still-
water, MN: Voyageur Press, 1993.

Matthew 7:15.

Morgan, William. "Human Wolves among the Navajo." Yale University Publications in Anthropology no. 11, 1936.

Otten, Charlotte F., ed. *A Lycanthropy Reader: Werewolves in Western Culture.* Syracuse: Syracuse UP, 1986.

Ovid. *Metamorphoses.* New York: Penguin, 1955.

"Porphyrias." *Mayo Clinic Health Letter* 7.10 (1986): 7.

Russell, W. M. S., and Claire Russell. "The Social Biology of Werewolves." *Animals
in Folklore.* Ed. J. R. Porter and W. M. S. Russell. Totowa, NJ: Rowman and Lit-
tlefield, 1978.

Cartesian dualism: the belief that the mind and body are separate, as described by the
French philosopher René Descartes.

Rutherford, Brett. "*Wolf* and Other Wolves—An Appreciation." *Haunts* 28 Summer/Fall 1994: 55–56.

Spence, Lewis. *The Encyclopedia of the Occult.* London: Bracken Books, 1988.

Summers, Montague. *The Werewolf.* New York: E. P. Dutton, 1934.

Teen Wolf. Wolfkill Productions, 1985.

Thiel, Richard P. *The Timber Wolf in Wisconsin: The Death and Life of a Majestic Predator.* Madison: U of Wisconsin P, 1993.

Trotti, Hugh. *Beasts and Battles: Fact in Legend and History?* New York: Rivercross, 1989.

Weinraub, Bernard. "Who's Afraid of the Big Bad Book Editor?" *New York Times* 12 June 1994: Section 2: 1, 22–23.

Wolf. Columbia Pictures, 1994.

"Wolf." *People* 41.24 (27 June 1994): 13.

The Wolf Man. Universal City Studio, 1941.

"Wolf Pact." *USA Today* 6 October 1994: D1.

Wolfen. Orion Pictures, 1981.

Zevon, Warren. "Werewolves of London." *A Quiet Normal Life.* Audiotape. New York: Elektra/Asylum Records, 1986.

Zipes, Jack, ed. *The Trials and Tribulations of Little Red Riding Hood.* New York: Routledge, 1993.

Understanding the Text

1. Lawrence begins her article by recounting the plots from a number of movies from the 1980s and 1990s, including such hits as *Wolf* (1994), with Jack Nicholson; *Teen Wolf* (1985), with Michael J. Fox; and *An American Werewolf in London* (1981). What specific points does she make about the portrayals of werewolves in these movies in terms of how they either reinforce or contradict traditional werewolf mythology?

2. Examine the story told by Petronius about the Roman soldier who turned into a wolf. In what ways does this story encapsulate a number of key elements of werewolf lore?

3. How do the Navajo shape-shifters differ in their actions from European werewolves? What do the shape-shifters represent, especially in respect to those differences?

Reflection and Response

4. Why are accounts of human savagery described in wolf-related terms? Cite specific examples from this selection. Can you think of other wolf-related examples that are not in the text?

5. The werewolf is an embodiment of both the animal and the human simultaneously. In what ways does it serve as a symbol of the conflict between the "instinctual urges and rational behavior" that all humans experience (par. 38)? Be specific in your answer.

6. Much is made of the role the wolf plays as a predator, hunting livestock and game that humans want to reserve for themselves. Lawrence argues that the wolf — and by extension the werewolf — is also connected to disease and human death. What specific evidence does she use to support this claim? Do you find her claim to be convincing? Why or why not?

7. Lawrence recounts a number of cases in which people in Europe were convicted of being werewolves, and she also details the behavior of Navajo shape-shifters. In your opinion, what accounts for the belief in the literal existence of werewolves? Consider that in different times and places, there may be different reasons for this belief.

Making Connections

8. Lawrence suggests that many attitudes toward wolves have changed of late, due to more positive representations in popular culture (the Michael J. Fox movie and the more recent television series *Teen Wolf*; the Wolf rank in the Cub Scouts; Professor Remus Lupin in the Harry Potter series), urbanization, and the conservation movement. Do you agree? Research efforts to reintroduce wolves into the wild and the resistance to those attempts by ranchers and hunters, and argue whether or not wolves still represent a meaningful threat, either physically or psychologically.

9. Research the history of human attitudes toward other predatory animals around the world, such as bears, tigers, and lions. Those animals were (and in some cases still are) a threat to human life, yet the wolf seems particularly vilified — sometimes even as a metaphor (e.g., "wolfing" one's food is rude; the memoir and 2013 movie *The Wolf of Wall Street* are about a criminal; a "wolf whistle" is a degrading whistle directed toward an attractive woman). Why this poor regard for the wolf?

How Do Monsters Reflect Their Times?

Records of monsters date back to the earliest traces of the human experience, when people sparred with nature and the unknown just to stay alive. Monsters have never left our consciousness, although the characteristics of monsters have often changed. Certain monsters seem tied to particular times: the sphinx, for instance, belongs to the classical world, and it seems lost in today's monster landscape. By contrast, aliens from other planets have a prominent role in our imaginations today. Examining monsters and the times from which they come can open pathways of analysis and investigation of specific cultural values, practices, attitudes, and historical events.

Sometimes it's easy to laugh at other people's fear and confusion: we can look at descriptions of various monsters and know they could not possibly exist. However, as Ted Genoways recalls, many Americans were terrified by Orson Welles's radio broadcast *The War of the Worlds* in 1938. For many listeners, already nervous about an approaching war in Europe, an alien invasion from the sky seemed all too believable. Daniel Cohen examines the connection between culture and monsters in his look at centaurs, griffins, and rocs, as well as more exotic creatures such as the Persian *senmurv* and the *garuda* of India. Cohen reveals that earlier humans may have had better reasons for believing these creatures existed than modern observers are willing to admit. David D. Gilmore explores the monsters of the ancient world and how well they fit into the societies of their times. He takes a close look at some that incorporate women's features, including the Harpies, the Furies, and Medusa. In the centuries after the fall of Rome, the fearsome forests of northern Europe brought rise to the creature Grendel, who slaughters those trying to build a new civilization in the epic poem *Beowulf*. Stephen T. Asma details how Alexander the Great wrote to his teacher Aristotle about the creatures he came across during his invasion of India. We know they could not possibly have existed as he describes them, but they were as alien to Alexander as a Martian would be to us. His descriptions tell us much about perception and misperception — both his and our own. Supporting the idea that monsters are derived from logical combinations of the cultures, values, and knowledge of the times, Matt Kaplan uses scientific and historical facts to show how people have been enticed to believe in vampires and zombies. W. Scott Poole shifts the focus to the monsters of the New World. Early explorers and settlers found plenty to be afraid of there, so they created monsters to accommodate their religious beliefs and their experiences of the natural world. For instance, the Puritans, struggling to bring control and order to their surroundings, felt that the devil, in all his disguises, was among them. The Salem witch trials were only one result of this mentality, which found monsters in those who were poor, elderly, or different.

If monsters are truly our own creations, paying attention to them can tell us a lot about ourselves, our past, and our present. Witches, aliens, women with serpent hair — all can be symbols for much more. Rational, scientific analysis can offer explanations for why a certain creature may appear to have the qualities that it does, but the monster remains monstrous. The values of a society and a culture are revealed in what it approves of and in what it rejects.

Here Be Monsters

Ted Genoways

Ted Genoways, former editor of the prestigious *Virginia Quarterly Review*, explores the connections between the monsters of the past and those of the present in an editorial introduction. In the early days of exploration, the unknown regions were thought to be populated with strange and dangerous creatures. To reflect that thinking, maps included the warning "Here Be Monsters." Today, though we've charted the planet, we still find monsters. Sometimes the monster is of our own creation, such as the threat of the nuclear age. Other times the monster is a real enemy, such as Adolf Hitler or Al Qaeda. How we react to the monster, real or imagined, says a lot about who we are. Genoways is the author of *The Chain: Farm, Factory, and the Fate of Our Food* (2014) and is currently editor-at-large for *onEarth*, an online publication of the Natural Resources Defense Council. He received a Guggenheim Fellowship in the Humanities in 2010.

On old nautical maps, cartographers inscribed uncharted regions with the legend "Here Be Monsters." Sometimes they would draw pictures of these fanciful beasts rising from the waters, and occasionally would even show them devouring wayward ships. This fear of the unknown, of that future that lies just past the horizon, has been with us always. To contain and put a face to it, our imagination has conjured everything from leviathans of the deep to beasts part-human and part-animal to a woman with snakes for hair and a gaze that turns men to stone. Imagining what we cannot truly imagine, we brace ourselves for the worst.

In the pages of this magazine in 1939, as the United States teetered on the brink of entering World War II, Eleanor Roosevelt reflected on this very subject. By then, however, we had monsters of a different sort: space aliens. Discussing the public panic that occurred after Orson Welles's famous broadcast of *War of the Worlds*, Roosevelt wrote:

> [T]hese invaders were supernatural beings from another planet who straddled the skyway and dealt in death rays. . . . A sane people, living in an atmosphere of fearlessness, does not suddenly become hysterical at the threat of invasion, even from more credible sources, let alone by the Martians from another planet, but we have allowed ourselves to be fed on propaganda which has created a fear complex.

Even after we defeated the Nazis and the Axis powers, the new technology that ended the war also brought new anxieties.

A monster threatens to devour a ship in *The Arrival of the Englishmen in Virginia* (1588) by Theodor de Bry.

At the dawn of the nuclear age and the space age, we grappled with these fears—similar in many ways to our old ones, but arriving now from more infinite shores. Splitting the atom awoke the public to a universe almost too small for comprehension and aroused the fear that tampering with such elemental forces of nature might stir unknown monsters or, through the horrors of radiation, transform us into monsters ourselves. Likewise, propelling astronauts beyond the reaches of our own atmosphere seemed to heighten the possibility of alien encounters. And whenever we imagined the motives of these alien visitors, we again pictured the worst. They wanted earth women for breeding or men as slaves. Or, worse yet, they just wanted us for food.

. . . George Garrett reflects on his loopy and ill-fated role in writing one 5 of these pictures. (In *Frankenstein Meets the Space Monster* [1965] the aliens aren't just after earth women; they're singling out go-go dancers!) These movies feel like high camp to us today, a kind of kitsch° that seems trapped in time, but what held thousands of viewers at drive-ins across America in thrall? Surely, it didn't feel safe and distant then. It must have

kitsch: something that appeals to popular, lowbrow tastes.

something to do with deep-seated anxieties about the future of our own planet, about our place in an uncompromising universe. Or even new parts of the world we thought we knew. Steve Ryfle, in his essay on *Godzilla*, reveals that the original 1954 Japanese version of the film—before the bad over-dubbing and the cheeseball scenes with Raymond Burr inserted—was an overt commentary on the dangers we pose to ourselves in the nuclear age. The film's central figure, a scientist, has developed a weapon more terrible than the bomb and faces the dilemma of whether or not to use it against the monster awoken from the ocean floor by an atomic test. If we unleash this weapon, won't it only lead to another? Won't every new unknown be more horrific than the last?

> "This fear of the unknown, of that future that lies just past the horizon, has been with us always."

Today we must grapple with the reality of these problems more than ever before. The unknown evil, in this case, will not turn out to be a stuntman in a rubber suit. In this one way, we can all agree: those who mean to do us harm are real and they are among us. Now the President of the United States must decide how to defend us without purveying fear and its conjoined twin, hatred. The evil intentions of Al Qaeda are not in doubt, any more than the evil intended—and carried out—by the Nazis was evident. And yet, it is not a simple matter of out-muscling a weaker foe. As Eleanor Roosevelt concluded:

It is not only physical courage which we need, the kind of physical courage which in the face of danger can at least control the outward evidences of fear. It is moral courage as well, the courage which can make up its mind whether it thinks something is right or wrong, make a material or personal sacrifice if necessary, and take the consequences which may come.

If we do not hew to this standard, if we give in to our fear, we face the real possibility of the permanent loss of liberty.

In the wake of the tragic school massacre in Beslan [in 2004], Russian President Vladimir Putin unveiled sweeping governmental reforms in the name of increased security. Stephen Boykewich, a Fulbright scholar in Moscow, writes . . . about the aftermath and impact. Succumbing to their fear, most Russians have chosen to allow Putin whatever control he desires. When [Secretary of State] Colin Powell expressed concern over these changes and suggested that Putin should instead seek a peaceful resolution with the Chechen separatists, Putin angrily replied, "Why don't you meet Osama Bin Laden, invite him to Brussels or to the White

House and engage in talks, ask him what he wants and give it to him so he leaves you in peace?"

Obviously, this is impossible; nevertheless, we must resolve to find new ways to reach out to the world community, to be seen as a strong and benevolent power again, not simply a lion with a thorn in its foot. If we cannot right ourselves, regain our focus, and steady our nerves, we will be forever jumping at shadows and strong-arming those who we perceive as threats. We will retreat further from our fellow travelers on this lonely planet and everywhere we look, we will see monsters.

Understanding the Text

1. What does Eleanor Roosevelt suggest was the cause of the fears sparked by Orson Welles's *War of the Worlds* broadcast?

2. What does Genoways mean when he says that at the dawn of the nuclear age, our fears were "arriving now from more infinite shores" (par. 4)? Why should this be so if by that time the earth itself was completely charted? What does this suggest about how people's fears had changed?

3. What is the main conflict, according to Steven Ryfle, in the original *Godzilla* movie? How does that reflect the time period in which it was made?

Reflection and Response

4. Genoways lists a variety of monsters of different times, from the monsters that appeared on ancient maps in places that were uncharted, to the space aliens who threatened America prior to World War II, to Godzilla in the postwar world. What are the prominent monsters today, and how do they reflect our current fears and anxieties?

5. When Genoways says that the president of the United States must respond to threats "without purveying fear and its conjoined twin, hatred" (par. 6), what attitude does this reflect toward the real-life monsters that threaten us? Is such an attitude realistic? Support your response with specific examples and reasons.

Making Connections

6. Genoways writes that in the post-9/11 world, our responses toward those who mean us harm will in many ways determine who we are: "If we give in to our fear, we face the real possibility of the permanent loss of liberty" (par. 6). Do some research on legal changes in the United States in regard to freedom, privacy rights, laws pertaining to search and seizure, and other areas. Have we become a nation that sees monsters all around us and so have given up liberty for security? Or have we avoided the trap that Genoways warns us about? Explain your answer.

7. Pick an era in America's past and research the monsters that figured prominently in the culture at that time, whether in literature, film, television, or another medium. Analyze how the culture is reflected in those monsters.

The Birth of Monsters

Daniel Cohen

How do monsters such as centaurs, griffins, and rocs come into the human imagination? Daniel Cohen explores how people encountering strange beasts, or unfamiliar combinations such as a man on horseback, could be confused. He circles the globe to find examples of animal combinations, such as the Persian *senmurv* and the *garuda* of India. Some of these creatures are seen as good, but most are dangerous monsters. Cohen is the author of more than one hundred books, many directed to children, such as *Southern Fried Rat and Other Gruesome Tales* (1989) and *Railway Ghosts and Highway Horrors* (1991). This selection comes from a more serious, adult-oriented book, *A Modern Look at Monsters* (1970).

When Hernán Cortés invaded Mexico he had fifteen cavalry men under his command. This handful of mounted men had an effect far exceeding their limited number. The Aztecs, who had never seen a horse before, much less a man on horseback, were terrified. They thought that man and horse were one.

The Incas of Peru reacted even more violently to Pizarro's horsemen. When one of the riders fell from his horse, the Inca warriors fled in panic, thinking that somehow the monster had broken in two.

William Prescott, who wrote the classic history of the conquest of Latin America, drew the analogy between the first impressions of the Aztecs and Incas upon seeing a man on horseback and the centaur, the half-man, half-horse monster of Greek mythology. Unlike the Indians, the early Europeans knew horses or at least horselike creatures. Early civilizations had used horse-drawn wagons, and somewhat later the horse-drawn war chariot became a standard part of the equipment of armies throughout the Middle East and North Africa. But riding was a comparatively late introduction in the civilized world.

The first riders that civilized peoples of the Middle East saw were probably nomadic tribesmen who swept out of the Eurasian steppe° as robbers and invaders. Riding almost certainly developed on the steppe, and the nomads were traditionally superb horsemen. Even later invaders like the Huns continued to inspire an almost supernatural terror among

steppe: a vast, treeless tract of land in southeastern Europe or Asia.

the peoples of the Roman world. Roman writers mentioned again and again how Hunnish rider and horse seemed to be one. It is not hard to imagine that those civilized city dwellers who faced the first invasion of mounted men reacted exactly the same way that the Aztecs and Incas had: they believed that horse and rider were one. And thus began the legend of the centaur. In Greek mythology centaurs were described as fierce, wild, and tribal—words which could well apply to the nomadic horsemen.

It is comforting to begin a search for the origins of ancient monster legends with this story of the centaur. If only one could speak with such easy assurance about the origins of the other monsters. A search for the beginning of the stories of the griffin (or gryphon), that fearsome half lion, half eagle, is typically tangled. Most of us probably became acquainted with the griffin through *Alice in Wonderland*: "They very soon came upon a Gryphon, lying asleep in the sun. (If you don't know what a Gryphon is, look at the picture.) . . . Alice did not quite like the look of the creature. . . ." As it turned out Lewis Carroll's griffin was a harmless even vapid° creature. This, however, was far from typical of griffins. A medieval bestiary warns men to stay away from the griffin "because it feasts upon them at any opportunity." The warning continues: "It is also extremely fond of eating horses."

Some people have suggested that, despite its frequent mention in literature, the griffin was never seriously believed to be a real animal. The griffin, they say, owes its origin to a heraldic practice called dimidiation. When two noble families were joined in marriage the elements that had dominated the coat of arms of each side were combined into a new design. Thus, the family of the eagle might at some point have married into the family of the lion, and the result was a hybrid, the griffin, which adorned the new coat of arms. The griffin was a common creature of heraldry.

This solution, though theoretical, is attractive but for one small detail—the griffin is far older than the practice of heraldry. One medieval bestiary speaks of the griffin as living mostly in "high mountains or in Hyperborean lands"—that is somewhere to the far north. The Romans had heard rumors of griffins in Central Asia. The depredations of these wild creatures were cited by refugees who came to Rome from the East as one of the major reasons for the mass movement of barbarian peoples which ultimately brought down the Roman Empire. The griffin was also a common element in the art of the nomadic Scythians of the steppe,

5

---

vapid: dull, lacking liveliness.

and it seems likely that they picked it up from peoples to the north and east.

But the griffin was not associated solely with the northland. Pliny wrote of "the Gryphon in the country of the Moors." Pliny, you will recall, did not believe that such a monster existed.

Throughout the Middle Ages, objects reputed to be "griffin's claws" were brought to the markets of Europe. Those that came from the north were usually the tusks of extinct mammoths or the horns of the equally extinct woolly rhinoceros. Those "griffin's claws" from the southern regions were most often the horns of antelopes.

The griffin is not unique in the animal mythology of the world. A 10
variety of fierce mammal-birds play an important role in the legends of many parts of the Middle East and India. The Persian *senmurv* or *sinamru* (perhaps "dog-bird"), while terrible in appearance and power, was thought to be a protector of mankind. The *garuda* of India is also benevolent. This deity is part bird and part man and closely associated with the god Vishnu. In Japan

"The roc, says the story, fed elephants to its young."

there was the troublesome *tengu*, a part-bird, part-man creature. In China the *T'ien Kou* or Heaven Dog was more terrifying than troublesome. It was an omen of evil often associated with comets and other frightening meteorological phenomena.

Are these various Oriental mammal-birds ancestral to the griffin? It is hard to say, for the family tree is not at all clear, but it seems reasonable to suspect that all of these various mythological conceptions developed in response to the same sort of creature in the natural world—the eagle or some other large bird of prey. The eagle might indeed seem fierce as a lion when compared with the other birds. Perhaps thousands of years ago men described the eagle or hawk as a "lionlike bird" or even a "lion bird." What began as a descriptive phrase might have been transformed by the artist into a hybrid which combined features of both eagle and lion. Ultimately the origins of this hybrid would be lost and the griffin, half lion and half eagle, would be enshrined in medieval bestiaries as a real animal that lived in a distant land. This myth would be reinforced by the occasional appearance of griffin's claws on the market. In addition there were doubtless tales told by travelers who said they had actually seen the monster firsthand, or had at least talked to people who had seen it firsthand.

While on the subject of bird monsters, we might have a look at the origins of that giant among fabulous birds, the roc. The roc is best known to us from the tales of the voyages of Es-Sindibad, or Sindbad the Sailor. Sindbad's adventures were related in *A Thousand and One Nights*, a collection of ancient tales from the Middle East.

The size of the roc is expressed in nothing but superlatives. When Sindbad first saw the roc's egg he thought it was the dome of a great building. Then the sky darkened and Sindbad saw "a bird of enormous size, bulky body, and wide wings, flying in the air; and this it was that concealed the body of the sun, and veiled it from view." The roc, says the story, fed elephants to its young. When Sindbad angered a roc, the giant bird took its revenge by dropping stones on his ships and sinking one.

If ever there was a purely imaginary monster, the roc sounds like it. Yet there are hints that the roc was more than a legend. Marco Polo mentions the roc, and says that the Great Khan of Cathay asked for evidence of the creature. An envoy brought back to the khan a gigantic feather from the island that was supposed to be the roc's home. The khan was impressed.

Marco indicates that the island home of the roc was Madagascar, and 15 Madagascar was the home of a really gigantic bird. The bird is called *Aepyornis maximus*, or the elephant bird. It looked like a big ostrich and may have been the largest bird that ever lived. But more impressive than the size of the bird itself was the size of its eggs. They had the capacity of six ostrich eggs or 148 chicken eggs.

While *Aepyornis maximus* is definitely no longer with us, the time of its extinction is not known with any certainty. The elephant bird may very well have survived into the sixteenth century, and its extinction was probably brought about by hunters who preyed both on the huge birds and on their eggs. The trip from Madagascar to Baghdad, the city of *A Thousand and One Nights*, is a long one, but medieval Arabs were great sailors and traders. They conducted a thriving trade along the east coast of Africa, before the trade was disrupted by the Portuguese in the fifteenth and sixteenth centuries. Arab traders undoubtedly visited Madagascar, and they might have seen living specimens of *Aepyornis maximus*. Large numbers of broken eggshells of the giant bird have been found along the coast, and this has given rise to the theory that the Arab sailors themselves helped kill off the birds by stealing eggs for food and for use as convenient cups for holding liquid. Such monstrous eggshells would also have been valuable trade items and curious souvenirs to bring back to show the family and friends.

These same Arab merchants traveled as far as China and carried the tale of the roc with them to the court of the Great Khan. The "feather" shown at the khan's court could have been the frond of *sagus ruffia*, a palm tree that grows on Madagascar. This particular palm has enormous fronds. The general similarity of shape of the palm frond and a feather would not have escaped the notice of canny merchants anxious to impress the rich khan with the wonders of the Africa trade.

But the roc cannot be explained so simply, for our roc is really the *rukh*, a huge bird that figured prominently in ancient Indian mythology. Perhaps it would be more accurate to say that *A Thousand and One Nights* is really based on traditional tales of the Middle East and India, some of which date back to the third or fourth millennium BC. Therefore the legend of the roc was around a long time before anyone in the Middle East could have gotten to Madagascar to catch sight of *Aepyornis maximus*. And there are other problems with this identification. The roc is definitely a flying bird, yet *Aepyornis maximus*, like the ostrich, was flightless. Its size might well have inspired legends of giants, but not flying giants.

For the origins of the roc-rukh legends we must again turn to the eagle or other large birds of prey. These creatures seem to have played an extremely important part in the mythology of the Middle East from earliest times. Eagle-like figures pop up in the art of the Sumerians, the earliest-known civilization. After centuries of retelling, one branch of the legendary cycle that surrounded the eagle must have grown into the legends of the huge rukh. When Arab traders returned from Madagascar with tales of enormous eggs, or with the eggshells themselves, this doubtless strengthened the legend of the rukh. People could no longer doubt its existence simply because they had never seen it. With their own eyes they beheld the shells of eggs that could not have been laid by any ordinary bird. Naturally the eggs were nowhere near the size of the one described in the Sindbad tales, but those stories were avowedly fiction, and the storyteller's exaggeration was taken for granted.

Few had seen the roc alive because these monstrous birds lived in a distant island that was very hard to get to. No doubt more than one latter-day Sindbad spiced up his reminiscences of past voyages with descriptions of the roc that he was supposed to have seen. Who could dispute such a story? All of these—traditions, misinterpretations, misleading evidence, and deliberate falsehoods—converged to make the tale of the monster bird, the roc.

I suspect that most monster legends grew in a manner similar to those of the griffin and the roc. They started with observations of a real creature. These observations then became exaggerated and twisted through constant retelling, until the animal with which they had originally been associated was forgotten completely. The next step was to place this legendary animal in some distant or otherwise hard-to-reach place to explain why it was not seen more frequently. Bits of evidence like the griffin's claws or the roc's eggs were brought back to support the legend, and so it continued to flourish. Travelers' tales added an additional flavor of authenticity to the story.

Understanding the Text

1. After a discussion of centaurs, Cohen states, "It is comforting to begin a search for the origins of ancient monster legends with this story of the centaur. If only one could speak with such easy assurance about the origins of the other monsters" (par. 5). What does he mean by this statement? What other monsters does he discuss whose origins are not so easy to find?

2. Why does Cohen think that the heraldic explanation — that the griffin was created as a combination of symbols on coats of arms — is not convincing?

3. What other hybrid monsters does Cohen examine from around the world? What, if any, qualities do they have in common?

4. Cohen ends this selection with a discussion of a roc. What is a roc, and how is it different from the other monsters he examines?

Reflection and Response

5. What is it about the griffin (part-lion, part-eagle) that seems to make it a particularly powerful symbol? Are the human values attached to the griffin an accurate reflection of how we see each part (lion and eagle), or is it more than the sum of its parts? Take note of the various regions of the world where the griffin is alleged to have lived. How might the belief that the griffin originated in far distant lands affect the attitudes people have toward the griffin?

6. Cohen is best known for his children's books. Is there a connection between children's books and mythological creatures? If so, what is it? Cite examples in your answer.

7. The roc is the only monster in this selection that is not a hybrid; it is simply a vastly oversize bird. Do you think the roc qualifies as a monster? Explain your reasoning.

Making Connections

8. How do the stories about the Aztecs' and Incas' first encounters with humans on horseback relate to the experiences of Alexander the Great in India, as described in Stephen T. Asma's "Alexander Fights Monsters in India" (p. 156)?

9. Cohen lists four specific mammal-birds: the *senmurv* or *sinamru* of Persia, the *garuda* of India, the *tengu* of Japan, and the *T'ien Kou* of China. Research more about these monsters. What aspects of these mammal-bird combinations led people to regard them with terror and fear or in a more positive light?

An Ancient Crypto-Bestiary

David D. Gilmore

The world of the ancients was populated by monsters of incredible variety, especially those with combinations of human and animal features. David D. Gilmore explores the monsters of the ancient Greeks and Romans, whose mythology included not only the well-known centaurs and satyrs but also the Hydra, basilisk, and manticore. Many ancient monsters possessed human female features, such as the Harpies, the Furies, and Medusa. The classical Greeks and Romans saw their monsters as human predecessors as well. Gilmore is a professor of anthropology at Stony Brook University. He is the author of *Misogyny: The Male Malady* (2001) and *Monsters: Evil Beings, Mythical Beasts, and All Manner of Imaginary Terrors* (2003), from which this excerpt comes.

Ubiquitous° in the early civilizations, monsters reach an apogee° in classical antiquity, especially among the Greeks. Indeed the pictorial and literary representation of monsters was to reach its apex in the classical age, in the Aegean world influenced by Greece and to a slightly lesser extent in the Roman possessions, after thousands of years, during which time the Hittite, Phoenician, Syrian, Cretan, and Mycenaean civilizations all kept monster mythology alive. So common were representations of monsters in the ancient world, both in visual art and in literature, poetry, and song, that many ancients made fun of their countrymen's obsessions with them. For example, Lucian in his *True History* and Horace in his *Ars Poetica* both derided the contemporary taste for monsters, as did the art critic Vitruvius in various writings (see Mode 1973: 10–11).

In the classical Mediterranean world, monsters first appear in literary form in the Homeric legends, by 700 BC (possibly earlier), perhaps derived from Semitic prototypes, and they immediately proliferate into the richest reparatory of perhaps any ancient civilization. One of the first pictorial representations we have from Greece is a vase painting dating from around 550 BC, depicting Heracles battling against the so-called "Monster of Troy," from whose fearsome jaws the hero rescues the maiden Hesione (Mayor 2000: 157). Already venerable by the eighth century, the Monster of Troy legend repeats the threefold narrative discussed earlier concerning the manner of the monster's interaction with humanity.

---

ubiquitous: constantly around, widespread.
apogee: the highest point.

In this case, the fearsome giant suddenly appears off the coast of Troy after a flood, preying upon farmers, whom it catches and devours, in the neighborhood of the port of Sigeum. In a typical twist, often repeated in monster lore, Hesione, the king's daughter, is offered by way of propitia-tion,° but instead the hero Heracles arrives in time to kill it and set the princess free. The monster shows the usual characteristics: immense in size, hideous in appearance, destructive, and innately malevolent.

The Greek vase painting depicts Heracles and Hesione in confronta-tion with the monster depicted anatomically in skeletal form, she throw-ing stones, he shooting arrows. As the painting clearly shows, two of her projectiles have hit home, one just under the eye and another lodged in the creature's dreadful, snapping jaw; one of the hero's arrows projects from the jaw as well. The whole montage has a nightmare quality, due to the sketchily ambiguous, specter-like representation of the beast. The Mon-ster of Troy is the first in a long line of Greek fantasy monsters.

Although probably deriving such fantasy figures from the horrific 5 Middle Eastern prototypes . . . , it was the Attic Greeks who gave the most lasting visual forms to people's innate fascination with evil and who ex-pressed in most striking pictorial forms the horrors of man's nightmares. The myriad Greek monsters that follow are often the offspring of humans with animals or the product of human wickedness. Carrying such sins upon them, they represented the dark side of the classical pagan imagina-tion, the thanatotic (death-drawn), as against the erotic fantasies in the age before Christianity. For the Greeks, monsters were made by the gods to horrify, persecute, and bedevil humans, and most of all to represent the ineluctable evils of human existence. Monster and man were eternal neighbors, metaphorically intertwined in ambiguous ways.

A Greek Crypto-Bestiary

The inventory of Greek monsters is indeed a virtually endless category. The most familiar are known to every schoolchild who has studied clas-sical mythology. The briefest list would include the following. There were the Tritons, half-human sea beasts; the satyrs and silenoi, lustful goat-men who waylaid innocent maidens; the centaurs, frisky half-horse, half-man hybrids, depicted as oversexed if not necessarily evil; serpents; and of course the terrible Minotaur of Crete, a cursed creature with a bull's head and horns, the hideous fruit of miscegenation of woman and god, who demanded sacrificial maidens to slake his lust. But there were thousands

---

propitiation: a sacrifice meant to gain or regain favor or goodwill.

more, of every shape, size, and sex. Here we name just a few figuring prominently in classical mythology in alphabetical order.

The basilisk is depicted as a malignant serpent with gnashing teeth who killed people with a glance. Its eyes shot out death-dealing rays. Pliny describes the basilisk in his *Natural History*, written in Rome in AD 77, as follows:

It routs all snakes with its hiss, and does not move its body forward in manifold coils like the other snakes but advancing with its middle raised high. It kills bushes not only by its touch but also by its breath, scorches up grass and bursts rocks. Its effect on other animals is disastrous: it is believed that once one was killed with a spear by a man on horseback and the infection rising through the spear killing not only the rider but also the horse. Yet to a creature so marvelous as this—indeed kings have often wished to see a specimen when safely dead— the venom of weasels is fatal: so fixed is the decree of nature that nothing shall be without its match. (1971, 8. xxxiii)

Just as terrible was the Chimera, a title that has come down to us in English to mean a nonexistent thing, a mirage. The Chimera was a composite beast with eagle's wings, green eyes, and a dragon's tail described by Bulfinch as "a fearful monster, breathing fire" (1970: 124). Then there was the Geryon, a monster-giant eventually killed by Heracles in Tartessus near present-day Cadiz in Spain. Next was the exotic griffon [griffin], or gryphon, a powerful hybrid beast with a vulture's beak, white wings, red paws, and a blue neck. Its claws were said to be so large that people made them into drinking cups. The Greeks believed the gryphon to dwell in the east, mainly India, and to guard gold treasure. Then there were the Gorgons, a race of homicidal giants, one of whom, a female, was Medusa the snake-haired. The Greeks also feared the Hecatoncheires, or "hundred handed." These were gigantic ogres with fifty heads and one hundred arms, each of great strength. Equally bizarre was the Hydra, a reptile with nine heads, each with a razor-toothed mouth, also killed by Heracles. The Hydra's monstrosity consisted not only in its multi-cephalic° nature but also in its promiscuous mingling of realms sea and earth, and, in Homer, its ability to grow back its nine heads when lopped off by humans, and therefore to escape death.

As classicist Adrienne Mayor points out in her study of ancient cryptomorphology (2000: 196–97), many giant monsters were supposed to be multi-headed and many-mouthed like the Hydra and the Hecatoncheires,

multi-cephalic: having more than one head.

conforming to a widespread contemporary belief in a motif of anatomi-
cal superfluity° denoting superhuman powers. In addition, most of these
cryptomorphs embody the motif of mixed animal and human features
or of blended animal traits, also indicating the composite nature of monsters in general in ancient cosmology. The emphasis on the monster's
mouth is a common motif and which requires its own formal analysis.

Another composite in Greek mythology was the manticore. It had the   10
body of a red lion, a human face, three rows of teeth in each jaw, a fatal
sting like a scorpion's in the end of the tail, and poisoned spines along
the tail that could be shot, like arrows, in any direction. Some classical
monsters were fierce giants rather than composites, for example, the
great python Aksar, which was said to be sixty cubits long, and the monstrous weasel Pastinaca, which killed trees by its powerful smell (Cawson
1995: 6).

Some Greek monsters were entirely airborne or part avian. The Stym-
phalian birds were giant, death-dealing creatures. Their huge beaks and
claws were made of hardest brass, and they could shoot their feathers as
if they were arrows. In some accounts, these misshapen birds are described as vicious man-eaters, vampire-like. It was one of Heracles's twelve
labors to rid the lake Stymphalus of these monstrous birds. Another multi-
cephalic ogre was Typhoeus, a fire breathing dragon with a hundred heads
that never rested. And, lest we forget, the first werewolf was an ancient
Greek, an accursed soul named Lycaon, who tears up the scenery in the
fable by Ovid and from whom we get the term *lycanthropy*, or werewolfery
(J. Cohen 1996: 12–13).

Still other Greek monsters were amphibious or water-dwellers. In ancient times, the lakes, ponds, and rivers as well as the deep seas were full of
demonic creatures. Among the many water monsters was the dragon of
Chios, a huge sea beast that terrorized the island of that name, eating
people and cattle. Another marine terror was the so-called sea monster of
Ethiopia, killed by the hero Perseus in the rescue of the princess Andromeda and subject of a famous Renaissance painting by Piero di Cosimo.

Not all Greek monsters were represented as male. In fact a large proportion of the theriomorphic° creatures were specifically depicted as female. For example the snake-haired Medusa turned men to stone with a
look. Just one of many, the Medusa was joined by various kinds of lamias, sharp-clawed sphinx-like creatures with a woman's upper body who
attacked men and boys and sucked their blood. The lamias were said to

---

superfluity: excess, oversupply; something unnecessary.
theriomorphic: having an animal form.

inhabit all the deep forests and woods of the ancient world. But perhaps the most fearsome female monsters of all were the sea-dwelling Scylla and Charybdis. Living under the waves in the Strait of Messina, off the coast of Sicily, these two female scourges dragged down sailors making the crossing. Charybdis was represented as a man-eating, gigantic virago° who pulled down whole ships in her maw. Her cohort, Scylla, blasted ships and sailors with her six dog's heads, nine rows of sharp devouring teeth and twelve muscular legs.

To further bedevil mankind, there were the Harpies and Furies, also presented as distinctly and disturbingly female. In Greek lore, the Harpies were foul-smelling half-human, half-bird women who attacked travelers, stole their food, and befouled everything they touched. In the Aeneid, Virgil's hero describes the Harpies as the worst of the Stygian monsters:

No monster is more terrible than the Harpies, no plague, no wrath of the gods more dire, surging upwards from the Stygian waters. They are birds with the faces of young girls. Disgusting filth comes from their stomachs; their hands have claws and they are always pale from hunger. . . . Suddenly, with a fearful swoop from the mountains, they are upon us, and with a loud clang they flap their wings, plunder the feast, making every dish filthy with their dirty hands; with the foul stench comes a hideous scream. (cited in Rowland 1987: 156)

There were still other female monsters. Similar in appearance and foulness to the Harpies were the Furies, also called erinyes (meaning the "angry ones"). These were three hag-like creatures who have the head of a dog, snakes for hair and bat wings; they persecuted and pursued all those poor souls whom the gods wished to torment. Like the sphinxes, Medusa, and the Sirens, who also had birdlike qualities mixed with female traits, the Harpies and Furies rained death and destruction everywhere. They were psychopomps° who carried off the soul to the underworld, the personification of human guilt and fear.

Completing the picture of a dangerous world were specifically male figures, often with a bestial, satyr-like sexuality. These animalistic, hypermasculine spirits cavorted in woods and attacked passersby, raping females and killing men. Then there were the cyclops, a race of giant one-eyed cannibals living on remote islands in the Aegean. The most famous of these was Polyphemus, who was blinded by Odysseus in the Homeric tale after eating a number of Odysseus's men. Satyrs, centaurs, and various

virago: a loud, overbearing woman.
psychopomps: people who conduct spirits or souls to the afterworld.

other zoomorphic combinations populated Greek myths and folklore. These could be of either sex, but were usually presented as male and as both malicious and egregiously lustful.

A World Full of Monsters

Greek travelers to foreign lands often came back with reports of dragons and other fantastic monsters that they had personally witnessed, especially in modern-day Turkey and India, adding to illusions and fears held by Hellenes of foreign lands. One of these travelers was Apollonius of Tyana, an explorer and naturalist, who traveled from Asia Minor to the southern foothills of the Himalayas in the first century AD. According to Philostratus, who compiled a bibliography of Apollonius based on the sage's lost letters and manuscripts, on his return to Greece he reported that the Asian countryside was full of dragons and that "no mountain ridge was without one" (cited in Mayor 2000: 130).

Trophies of these and other dragon quests were displayed for all to see in an unidentified city the Greeks called Paraka (possibly present-day Peshawar in Pakistan): "In the center of that city are enshrined a great many skulls of dragons," Apollonius assures us, according to Mayor (2000: 131). Rather than being purely imaginary, these dragon remains were probably the bones of extinct megafauna such as the large giraffe Giraffokeryx and the colossal Siratherium, a moose-like quadruped as big as an elephant and carrying massive antlers.

Instead of dismissing these beings as silly fables, many Greek authors wrote copiously about them, taking them quite seriously. Most authorities corroborated their existence with whatever evidence they could muster. Apparently, there was a need to believe in them even among the otherwise skeptical. For example, an early philosopher, Empedocles of Acragas (Sicily), who died in 432 BC, wrote at length deploring the literal belief in monster myths and folktales in general among his countrymen. Yet, despite his doubtfulness in other matters of myth, in one passage in his surviving works, Empedocles discusses the existence of such creatures as described above, and decides that they are, or were, quite real.

Empedocles writes that in the infancy of humanity nature brought 20 forth all manner of such weird hybrids, "endowed with all sorts of shapes, wondrous to behold . . . such as human-headed oxen and ox-headed humans" (cited in Mayor 2000: 215–16). Like most Greeks and Romans, this scholar apparently accepted all the monster stories as real, yet at the same time he disputed the Olympian myths about gods and derring-do. "It is hard to escape the conclusion that Empedocles was here seeking to provide a scientific explanation of composite creatures like minotaurs, centaurs, and so on, which featured so heavily in mythology," writes Susan Blundell, a historian of ancient philosophy at University College, London (1986: 41). Another classical scholar, W. K. C. Guthrie, concurs with this assessment: the Greek philosopher "was always glad to show that his . . . system accounted for phenomena known or believed in by his countrymen" (1965: 205).

The Romans and their subject peoples were equally enthralled by weird beings. As an example of the appeal of monster myths, Empedocles's work was taken up later by the first-century BC Roman naturalist Lucretius, who was an otherwise rational and scientific observer. Seriously considering the issue of monsters, Lucretius resuscitated and refined Empedocles's theory of extinct monsters in his own work, *On the Nature of Things*. In this massive tome, he repeats his predecessors' belief that nature has indeed produced "many monsters of manifold forms" (cited in Mayor 2000: 216).

So full of monsters was classical culture, and so pervasive the belief among otherwise skeptical philosophers in the Mediterranean world, that classicist Adrienne Mayor decided there must be some rational basis for the obsession. She spent some time researching the matter and found some justification for this idea in classical archaeology. Her book *The First Fossil Hunters* (2000) shows conclusively that the Greeks and later the Romans based many of their visual images on the megafaunal fossils they observed around the shores of the Mediterranean Sea. Because of local geological conditions in the Mediterranean basin, many huge bones of dinosaurs and of extinct mega-mammals like elephants and giant bears were visible to the naked eye, literally sticking out of promontories and quarries. Since these morphologically anomalous remains could not be identified with any living animals, the Greeks took them as evidence of the extinct monsters they so fervidly believed in.

The example Mayor uses as the starting point in her study is the Monster of Troy depicted on the vase discussed above. The picture resembles nothing so much as a fossil skull of a giant Miocene giraffe that flourished in the Mediterranean area, the Samotherium. Indeed, it is in the vase painting as a large animal skull eroding out of a rocky outcrop, probably reproducing its natural provenience as seen by the naked eye (Mayor 2000: 158–60). She also writes persuasively that belief in the cyclops may have been buttressed by observation of skulls of Pleistocene dwarf elephants. These were common in the Mediterranean basin and had a large nasal cavity in the middle of the skull, which could very well have been mistaken for a single eye socket: "The great piles of bones on the cave floors might be the remains of ship-wrecked sailors—the savage Cyclopses were probably cannibals!" (35–36).

So perhaps more than some other ancient peoples, the Greeks had visual clues at hand to assist them in the task of imagining monsters. This indeed may explain the richness and diversity of their fabulous bestiaries and myths. However, as historian Rudolf Wittkower pointed out long ago (1942: 197), the Greeks simply gave new and anatomically artful forms to legends and myths shared by all the ancient peoples, from the Egyptians onward, inventing new symbols to express universal fantasies.

The Greeks tended to depict their monsters in patterned ways, adher- 25 ing to aesthetic and behavioral standards that remained steadfast up to the Christian era. Their monsters were usually immense in size, with the usual hybrid shapes predominating, and superhuman in physical power. Such beings also usually combined human and animal traits in shocking or terrifying ways. The most common fantasy was to imbue animal-like monsters, or half-animal beings, with human malice and destructiveness. Another common feature was, as we have seen, the imputation of man-eating, or, more accurately, cannibalism, as in the case of the part-human monsters like the cyclops.

Later the Romans took over most of the Greek prototypes and elaborated on them without much change or invention, continuing also the theme of heroic rescue. Indeed, according to some historians, the Romans surpassed even the Greeks in their morbid preoccupation with monsters and prodigies. Classicist Carlin Barton, in her book *The Sorrows of the Ancient Romans: The Gladiator and the Monster* (1992), writes that, more than all other people, the Romans of the late Republic and early Empire were entranced by the horrific, the miraculous, and the untoward to the point of "embracing the monster" as a central statement of their culture. Aside from their beloved gladiatorial games, a favorite Roman pastime was collection of monster artifacts, often as commercial hoaxes. For example, there was the Monster of Joppa, supposedly the remains of the monster killed by the Greek Perseus in his valiant rescue of the maiden Andromeda at Joppa (present-day Jaffa).

What happened was that, in AD 58, Marcus Aemilius Scaurus obtained skeletal remains he claimed were those of the Joppa monster and had them hauled to Rome, where they were presented with much fanfare as the centerpiece of the "marvels of Judea." Pliny tells us that the backbone was 40 feet (12 meters) long and 1.5 feet thick, with ribs taller than an Indian elephant. Mayor identifies these remains as probably those of a beached whale (2000: 138). She notes that such hoaxes were commonplace and attested to the continuing fascination with monsters, oddities, megamorphs, and all manner of inexplicable phenomena.

To summarize, the Greeks and Romans continued inherited traditions dating back to Egypt and Mesopotamia. One continuing thread from the

Pharaohs to the Caesars, aside from the usual hybrid nature and malevolence of monsters, is the sense of their antiquity. In ancient days, monsters shared the feature of being genetically ancestral to humans: they were father and mother, or in some cases both, and unimaginably old.

> "Owing to their implacable hatred toward their human offspring, the monsters provoke the first generational conflicts on record."

The monsters of the archaic civilizations are both the predecessors and the progenitors of modern humans and thus closely related. Owing to their implacable hatred toward their human offspring, the monsters provoke the first generational conflicts on record.

Later in classical antiquity, this genetic theme is repeated, but there is a slightly changed emphasis. As among their Middle Eastern predecessors, the Greeks and Romans also maintain a belief in ancient monsters ancestral to men, as in the case of the Giants and Gorgons, who must also be defeated by their heroic children. But in classical thought, the legions of everyday monsters, like the Minotaur, are often the product of miscegenation of humans and beasts or of humans and gods, or are begat by gods and are often the brothers of heroes. So the curious and fluid organic familiarity linking men and monsters continues in a slightly changed form, continuing a kinship as tortuous as it is inescapable.

A view of a preexisting world-of-monsters underlies the basic cosmo- 30 logical paradigm in classical antiquity. The Greeks and Romans thought this prior epoch was populated by huge and powerful creatures, dwarfing their present descendants. In those heroic times of yore, everything was larger, more powerful, and more impressive than today. Such a phylogenetic° paradigm of temporal "shrinkage," as Mayor calls it (2000: 201), may be regarded as a kind of a metaphor for the parent-child relation in which, ontologically,° extinct monsters symbolize the giant inhabitants of childhood: fantasized images of none other than one's own parents.

Like imaginary monsters, one's own parents are of course temporally prior and epigenetic,° occupying a mysterious prelapsarian° world of which we know little. They are also (as perceived by small children) immense in bulk, looming majestically above, all-powerful and dominating, and therefore unintentionally threatening. As Mayor points out, this element of gigantism combined with a sense of mystery and power

---

phylogenetic: based on natural evolutionary relationships.
ontologically: relating to or based on being or existence.
epigenetic: relating to the genetic precursor that forms the later animal.
prelapsarian: characteristic of the time before the Judeo-Christian Fall in the Garden of Eden.

was for the Greeks a defining feature of all monsters. In all the early religions, gigantism is identified as being both godlike, on the one hand, symbolizing the immensity of the divine, and on the other hand embodying hubris, monstrous pride.

And here once again we come to a major conundrum of monster lore, because the moral duality and the ambiguous nature of the monster signal a dualistic and troubled relationship to mankind. If the image of God incarnates the idealized father (and mother), then the monster, which parodies god, may be said to embody the demonized father (and equally demonic mother). And so we see an unsettling paradoxical unity of men and monsters, a strange but unbreakable genetic relationship.

Works Cited

Barton, Carlin A. *The Sorrows of the Ancient Romans: The Gladiator and the Monster.* Princeton: Princeton UP, 1992. Print.

Blundell, Susan. *The Origins of Civilization in Greek and Roman Thought.* London: Croom Helm, 1986. Print.

Bulfinch, Thomas. *Bulfinch's Mythology.* 1855. New York: Thomas Y. Crowell, 1970. Print.

Cawson, Frank. *The Monsters in the Mind: The Face of Evil in Myth, Literature and Contemporary Life.* Sussex: Book Guild, 1995. Print.

Cohen, Jeffrey J. "Monster Culture (Seven Theses)." *Monster Theory: Reading Culture.* Ed. Jeffrey J. Cohen. Minneapolis: U of Minnesota P, 1996. 3–25. Print.

Guthrie, W. K. C. *A History of Greek Philosophy.* Vol. 2. *The Presocratic Tradition from Parmenides to Democritus.* Cambridge: Cambridge UP, 1965. Print.

Mayor, Adrienne. *The First Fossil Hunters: Paleontology in Greek and Roman Times.* Princeton: Princeton UP, 2000. Print.

Mode, Heinz. *Fabulous Beasts and Demons.* New York: Phaidon, 1973. Print.

Pliny the Elder. *Natural History.* Trans. H. Rackham. Cambridge: Harvard UP, 1971. Print.

Rowland, Beryl. "Harpies." *Mythical and Fabulous Creatures: A Source Book and Research Guide.* Ed. Malcolm Smith. New York: Greenwood Press, 1987. 155–61. Print.

Wittkower, Rudolf. "Marvels of the East: A Study in the History of Monsters." *Journal of the Warburg and Courtauld Institutes* 5 (1942): 159–97. Print.

Understanding the Text

1. Which monsters did Heracles have to destroy in his labors? What made those monsters particularly difficult?

2. What qualities are typically connected to monsters that have female characteristics? What qualities are typically connected to monsters that have male characteristics?

3. What is Gilmore's point about the large size of monsters? How does he connect that to the parent-child relationship?

Reflection and Response

4. How does Gilmore organize his categories of monsters? Why did he use this organizational strategy?

5. What are the differences in the behaviors and threats between monsters that are just animal combinations and those that are animal-human combinations?

6. Why are all the monsters described by Gilmore evil, and why do they hold particular malice toward humans? Use multiple examples to support your position.

Making Connections

7. Gilmore notes that Greek writers and authority figures went to great lengths to legitimize belief in mythological beings, even providing evidence where they could: "Apparently, there was a need to believe in them even among the otherwise skeptical" (par. 19). Can you think of other instances in history or in your own experience in which rational, well-educated people believed something that now seems irrational?

8. Gilmore states that the earliest monsters in the Greek and Roman imagination "continued inherited traditions dating back to Egypt and Mesopotamia" (par. 28). Research the monsters of Egypt and Mesopotamia and analyze how they are connected to Greek and Roman monsters.

9. Gilmore connects monsters to the psychology of childhood, in which parents are "immense in bulk, looming majestically above, all-powerful and dominating, and therefore unintentionally threatening" (par. 31). Research what psychology says about the parent-child relationship and argue whether gigantic monsters serve as symbols for parents or not.

From Beowulf

Anonymous

The epic poem *Beowulf* is one of the few surviving texts originally written in Old English. The characters in the poem, however, are not English. Rather, they are from Germanic tribes that inhabited areas in what are now Denmark, Sweden, and other surrounding countries. This selection from the poem records the initial assault on Heorot, a mead hall that is more than just a place to eat and drink: the hall is an attempt to bring civilization to a wild, unknown world. Angered by hearing sounds of feasting and songs of praise to God, the monster Grendel invades the hall at night, slaughtering the men inside. He does so night after night, with no man able to kill him and avenge the deaths. The original text is from about 1000 CE, but the story may have originated as much as four hundred years earlier. This translation is by Seamus Heaney, a poet, playwright, and translator who won the 1995 Nobel Prize in Literature. [Editor's note: line numbers follow the Heaney translation.]

The fortunes of war favored Hrothgar.
Friends and kinsmen flocked to his ranks,   65
young followers, a force that grew
to be a mighty army. So his mind turned
to hall-building: he handed down orders
for men to work on a great mead-hall
meant to be a wonder of the world forever;   70
it would be his throne-room and there he would dispense
his God-given goods to young and old—
but not the common land or people's lives.
Far and wide through the world, I have heard,
orders for work to adorn that wall stead   75
were sent to many peoples. And soon it stood there,
finished and ready, in full view,
the hall of halls. Heorot was the name
he had settled on it, whose utterance was law.
Nor did he renege, but doled out rings   80
and torques at the table. The hall towered,
its gables wide and high and awaiting
a barbarous burning. That doom abided,
but in time it would come: the killer instinct
unleashed among in-laws, the blood-lust rampant.   85

Then a powerful demon, a prowler through the dark,
nursed a hard grievance. It harrowed him

to hear the din of the loud banquet
every day in the hall, the harp being struck
and the clear song of a skilled poet
telling with mastery of man's beginnings,   90
how the Almighty had made the earth
a gleaming plain girdled with waters;
in His splendor He set the sun and moon
to be earth's lamplight, lanterns for men,   95
and filled the broad lap of the world
with branches and leaves; and quickened life
in every other thing that moved.

So times were pleasant for the people there
until finally one, a fiend out of Hell,   100
began to work his evil in the world.
Grendel was the name of this grim demon
haunting the marches, marauding round the heath
and the desolate fens;° he had dwelt for a time
in misery among the banished monsters,   105
Cain's clan, whom the creator had outlawed
and condemned as outcasts. For the killing of Abel
the Eternal Lord had exacted a price:
Cain got no good from committing that murder
because the Almighty made him anathema°   110
and out of the curse of his exile there sprang
ogres and elves and evil phantoms
and the giants too who strove with God
time and again until He gave them their final reward.

So, after nightfall, Grendel set out   115
for the lofty house, to see how the Ring-Danes
were settling into it after their drink,
and there he came upon them, a company of the best
asleep from their feasting, insensible to pain
and human sorrow. Suddenly then   120
the God-cursed brute was creating havoc:
greedy and grim, he grabbed thirty men
from their resting places and rushed to his lair,

---

fens: lowlands covered wholly or partially by water.
anathema: one that is cursed or loathed.

flushed up and inflamed from the raid,
blundering back with the butchered corpses. 125

Then as dawn brightened and the day broke
Grendel's powers of destruction were plain:
their wassail° was over, they wept to heaven
and mourned under morning. Their mighty prince,
the storied leader, sat stricken and helpless, 130
humiliated by the loss of his guard,
bewildered and stunned, staring aghast
at the demon's trail, in deep distress.
He was numb with grief, but got no respite
for one night later the merciless Grendel 135
struck again with more gruesome murders.
Malignant by nature, he never showed remorse.
It was easy then to meet with a man
shifting himself to a safer distance
to bed in the bothies,° for who could be blind 140
to the evidence of his eyes, the obviousness
of that hall-watcher's hate? Whoever escaped
kept a weather-eye open and moved away.

So Grendel ruled in defiance of right,
one against all, until the greatest house 145
in the world stood empty, a deserted wall stead.
For twelve winters, seasons of woe,
the lord of the Shieldings° suffered under
his load of sorrow; and so, before long,
the news was known over the whole world. 150
Sad lays° were sung about the beset king,
the vicious raids of Grendel,
his long and unrelenting feud,
nothing but war; how he would never
parley or make peace with any Dane 155
nor stop his death-dealing nor pay the death-price.
No counselor could ever expect
fair reparation from those rabid hands.

wassail: a toast to someone's health.
bothies: huts.
Shieldings: or Scyldings, another name for Hrothgar's warriors.
lays: ballads or songs.

All were endangered; young and old
were hunted down by that dark death-shadow   160
who lurked and swooped in the long nights
on the misty moors; nobody knows
where these reavers° from Hell roam on their errands.

"So Grendel ruled in
defiance of right,
One against all, until the
greatest house
In the world stood empty."

So Grendel waged his lonely war,
inflicting constant cruelties on the
people,   165
atrocious hurt. He took over Heorot,
haunted the glittering hall after dark,
but the throne itself, the treasure-seat,
he was kept from approaching; he was
the Lord's outcast.

These were hard times, heart-breaking   170
for the prince of the Shieldings; powerful counselors,
the highest in the land, would lend advice,
plotting how best the bold defenders
might resist and beat off sudden attacks.
Sometimes at pagan shrines they vowed   175
offerings to idols, swore oaths
that the killer of souls might come to their aid
and save the people. That was their way,
their heathenish hope; deep in their hearts
they remembered Hell. The Almighty Judge   180
of good deeds and bad, the Lord God,
head of the Heavens and High King of the World,
was unknown to them. Oh, cursed is he
who in time of trouble had to thrust his soul
in the fire's embrace, forfeiting help;   185
he has nowhere to turn. But blessed is he
who after death can approach the Lord
and find friendship in the Father's embrace.

reavers: local officers or agents of a king.

Understanding the Text

1. Why is Grendel upset by songs of praise to God? Consider his lineage, as a descendant of Cain. How is it fitting that Grendel is part of that lineage?

2. How long does Grendel rule over the hall? At what time of day does he rule? Why is he not able to approach the throne?

3. Since the characters in the story are not Christianized, the poet says, "The Lord God, / Head of the Heavens and the High King of the World, / Was unknown to them" (ll. 181–83). What does the poet say is the result of their not knowing God?

Reflection and Response

4. In your opinion, why does Grendel attack only the mead hall and not the surrounding huts and other lodgings? Why does he attack only at night? Consider what this means about the purpose of his attacks.

5. A key feature of the Germanic tribal culture of *Beowulf* is the concept of *wergild*, in which one must seek revenge for the killing of a fellow member of the tribe. The revenge can be either another killing or receipt of a monetary payment — "the death-price" (l. 156). Since the Danes are unable to kill the monster Grendel or induce him to pay for the deaths, how does he represent a threat not only to their lives but also to their cultural values?

6. Analyze the tension that exists between the Christian poet and the pagan characters of the poem. Examine particularly the criticism the poet launches against the characters who pray at pagan shrines for relief from Grendel. How might the poet use the monster to tell a moral tale?

Making Connections

7. Consider the character of Grendel in light of Stephen T. Asma's "Alexander Fights Monsters in India" (p. 156). How is Grendel similar to the kind of monsters Alexander encounters? Asma specifically mentions *Beowulf* in connection to the idea that "macho monster fights" are "outmoded" today.

8. Read more of *Beowulf* (many texts are available online as well as in libraries) to see how the hero Beowulf ultimately defeats Grendel. Then argue whether or not the modern world still sees the need for heroes who conquer monsters.

9. The popularity of *The Hobbit* and *The Lord of the Rings*, written by J. R. R. Tolkien, has led to the creation of an entire genre of its own: an early-medieval fantasy world populated by knights, dragons, and numerous strange creatures, in which good fights against evil. Not surprisingly, Tolkien himself was a scholar of Old English who knew the story of *Beowulf* well. Consider which kinds of actions are praised and admired, and which are condemned, in *Beowulf* and in this new genre. How are the social values and actions of characters in *Beowulf* present, in one form or another, in one of Tolkien's stories or in another story in the same genre (e.g., the HBO series *Game of Thrones*)?

Alexander Fights Monsters in India

Stephen T. Asma

Imagine being in a strange land, surrounded on all sides by enemies wishing to do you harm. Add to the scene a menagerie of powerful and deadly animals that you have never encountered before — dragons, oversize crabs, and three-horned beasts — that are attempting to kill you. This is the scene encountered by Alexander the Great as he marched his Macedonian army into India. In this selection, Stephen T. Asma examines Alexander's experience with these strange creatures and his army's interpretation (or misinterpretation) of the new world around them. Asma is a professor of philosophy and Distinguished Scholar at Columbia College Chicago. He is the author of seven books, including the best-selling *Buddha for Beginners* (1996). This excerpt is taken from his book *On Monsters: An Unnatural History of Our Worst Fears* (2009).

After defeating King Porus in the Punjab region, Alexander the Great chased the tyrant farther into India. "However," Alexander reported, "it commonly happens that when a man achieves some success, this is pretty soon followed by adversity." Lost in the deserts of the Indus Valley, Alexander and his army found themselves dehydrated and demoralized by a fierce and hostile environment. Alexander relates the frightening events of that campaign in a letter to his old teacher, Aristotle. Marching through the desert, Alexander's forces were so thirsty that some of the soldiers began to lick iron, drink oil, and even drink their own urine. A devoted soldier named Zefirus found a tiny puddle of water in the hollow of a rock, poured it into his helmet, and brought it to Alexander to drink. Alexander was moved by the soldier's generosity, but he poured the water out on the ground in front of the whole army to demonstrate that he, as their leader, would suffer with them. This show of strength and solidarity gave inspiration to the troops and they marched on until they finally reached a river. But frustration rose further when they discovered that the river was poisonous and undrinkable.

In the middle of this large river sat a strange island castle. Alexander tried to communicate with the naked Indians therein, asking them where he might find good water, but they were unresponsive and took to hiding. Two hundred lightly armed soldiers were sent wading through the water to try to pressure the castle's inhabitants for help. When the soldiers were a quarter of the way through the river, a terrible turbulence began to churn and the men began screaming and disappearing underwater. "We saw emerging from the deep," Alexander explains, "a number of hippopotamuses, bigger than elephants. We could only watch and wail as they devoured the Macedonians whom we had sent to swim the river." Alexander was so enraged by this calamity that he gathered together the guides, local men who had betrayed them by leading them into this hostile land, and marched them into the deadly water. "Then the hippopotamuses began to swarm like ants and devoured them all."

After another day of marching, the exhausted and dehydrated soldiers finally came to a "lake of sweet water" and a surrounding thick forest. All the men drank their fill and regained some of their strength. They pitched camp there at the sweet water lake, cutting down huge swaths of forest to build fifteen hundred fires. They organized their legions into defense formations in case something should attack in the night, and settled down to rest. "When the moon began to rise," Alexander reports, "scorpions suddenly arrived to drink at the lake; then there came huge beasts and serpents, of various colors, some red, some black or white, some gold; the whole earth echoed with their hissing and filled us with considerable fear."

It's not hard to imagine the terror. Soldiers don't lack fear, after all; they just override it with stoic° resolve. Anyone who has ever been in a strange forest after dark knows the pulse-quickening fears that can take hold. If you've ever tent-camped in grizzly country you'll have an inkling of the dread that must have filled these soldiers. The fears of the Macedonians, however, were not just imagined but actually realized over the course of that long night.

After killing some of the serpents the soldiers were relieved to see the   5
creatures retreat. But their hopes of finally getting some sleep were dashed when dragons began to slither out of the woods toward them. They were larger than the serpents, thicker than columns, with a crest on their head, breasts upright, and mouths wide open to spew poisonous breath. "They came down from the nearby mountains and likewise made for the water." After an hour of fighting, the monsters had killed thirty servants and twenty soldiers. Alexander could see that his men were overwhelmed by the strangeness and resilience of the dragons, so he leaped into the fray and told them to follow his monster-slaying technique. Covering himself with his shield, he used nets to tangle the enemy and then struck at them viciously with his sword. Seeing his success, the soldiers rallied and finally drove back the dragons. But then came the giant crabs and crocodiles. Spears and swords were ineffective against the impenetrable shells of these

---

stoic: being free from pleasure or pain; not being moved or governed by emotion.

Alexander and his army fight a parade of monsters in India. Scene from the *Romance of Alexander*, France (Rouen), circa 1445.

enormous crabs, so the soldiers used fire to kill many of them and drive the rest back to the forest. Alexander lists the subsequent parade of foes:

It was now the fifth watch of the night and we wanted to rest; but now white lions arrived, bigger than bulls; they shook their heads and roared loudly, and charged at us; but we met them with the points of our hunting spears and killed them. There was great consternation in the camp at all these alarms. The next creatures to arrive were enormous pigs of various colors; we fought with them too in the same way. Then came bats as big as doves with teeth like those of men; they flew right in our face and some of the soldiers were wounded.

As if this onslaught were not enough, the men were astonished next to see an enormous beast, larger than an elephant, emerge from the forest. The behemoth, first appearing in the distance, headed for the lake to drink but then saw Alexander's encampment. It turned quickly, revealing three ominous horns on its forehead, and began charging toward the men. Alexander ordered a squadron of soldiers to meet the earth-shaking juggernaut head-on, but they were overrun. After engaging the monster in difficult battle for some time, the soldiers managed finally to kill it, but only after the creature had taken seventy-six Macedonian warriors to a bloody end.

Still shocked and shaken, the tattered army watched with horror as oversized shrews skulked out of the darkness and fed upon the dead bodies strewn around the beach. Dawn mercifully broke and vultures began to line the bank of the lake. The ordeal was over.

"Then I was angry," Alexander says, "at the guides who had brought us to this dreadful place. I had their legs broken and left them to be eaten alive by serpents. I also had their hands cut off, so that their punishment was proportionate to their crime."

Embellishing

Alexander's letter is almost certainly apocryphal,° but it has formed an important part of the legend and mythology of Alexander. Most of the letter's descriptions of frightening creatures come from a book about India written by Ctesias in the fifth century BCE, so, although the events of the letter are fabulous, the monsters were a commonplace in the ancient belief system. An ancient Greek or Roman citizen would have had no trouble believing this story of Alexander's difficulties in exotic India. In fact, the Roman natural philosopher Pliny the Elder (23–79 CE) reinforces the point a few centuries later, when he writes, "India and regions of Ethiopia are especially full of wonders. . . . There are men with their feet reversed and with eight toes on each foot. On many mountains there are men with dog's heads who are covered with wild beasts' skins; they bark instead of speaking and live by hunting and fowling, for which they use their nails."

The story of Alexander's monster battle at the sweet water lake may be   10 wholly invented by ancient writers, or it may be partially true with significant embellishments. Psychologists have identified a common human tendency to unconsciously exaggerate perceptions. These misperceptions are heavily influenced by our subjective emotional and cognitive states. People who are startled to discover a burglar in their home, for example, usually report the size of the intruder as much larger than he actually is. The cognitive scientist Dennis R. Proffitt has amassed significant empirical data that demonstrate the tendency of those afraid of heights to actually see a greater distance between themselves and the ground. We don't need science to deliver up commonly understood truths, but scientific validation is helpful. Proffitt speculates that perceptual exaggeration of

apocryphal: of doubtful authority; unlikely to be true or authentic.

spatial distances probably evolved as a safeguard to promote caution and prevent recklessness when our ancestors engaged in climbing activities. "With respect to fear of falling," he explains, ". . . the perceptual exaggeration of steep hills and high places increases their apparent threat, and thereby promotes caution and its adaptive advantage." Applying this Darwinian notion to our perception of monsters, it seems useful for humans to see a creature as more dangerous than it truly is.

> "Wherever we find monsters, there, too, we also find heroes."

The creatures described in Alexander's letter may have been real exotic animals, such as cobras and rhinoceroses, which were then multiplied and enlarged by fear-filled misperceptions. Add to this misperception the embellishments of self-report (e.g., the fisherman's syndrome of magnifying the dimensions of the one that got away) and you have a recipe for a fantastic monster story.

Regardless of the veracity of Alexander's description, the symbolic nature of the story is provocative. Among other things, the narrative is a testament to masculine stereotypes of courage and resilience. Wherever we find monsters, there, too, we also find heroes. The Macedonians were intensely afraid to be in such uncharted territory, then wave after relentless wave of dangerous attack came at them from out of the jungle. Yet though they took losses and even occasionally waned in commitment, they ultimately stood their ground against inhuman enemies. It's a manly story of virile strength and valor. When dawn finally broke at the sweet water lake, Alexander reminded his worn-out soldiers "to be brave and not to give up in adversity like women."

The travelers' stories of encounters with exotica are certainly filled with wonder, but they are equal parts fight stories, demonstrations and justifications of martial masculinity. According to this view, the exotic world is not benign, and we must make our way defensively and aggressively. Monsters live with the barbarians, and indeed are the most extreme form of barbarian. One cannot meet them with rational persuasion because they lack the proper faculties, nor can the arts of diplomacy pave a road to compromise.

Manliness

There is a lesson in such monster stories as Alexander's victory at the sweet water lake. Each of us will eventually encounter some awful obstacles in life, obstacles that will make us want to lie down, give up, or go away. The lesson is: don't.

As we [can] see in . . . *Beowulf* . . . , in our more liberal intellectual culture macho monster fights have become a quaint genre of outmoded heroics. After all, why must *men*, who cause these aggression problems in the first place, go around slaying dragons? The monster-killing man has become a bit of a joke, trivialized by the ivory tower° as too obvious. Hollywood, however, continues to understand this feature of the monster story very well. In 2007 Will Smith starred in a film version of Richard Matheson's 1954 sci-fi classic *I Am Legend*, playing the vampire-slaying last man in New York City. In 2005 Steven Spielberg's remake of H. G. Wells's *War of the Worlds* pitched Tom Cruise against the bloodsucking aliens from a distant planet. Or consider M. Night Shyamalan's 2002 blockbuster *Signs*, with Mel Gibson and Joaquin Phoenix fighting off the invading aliens. All these films portrayed the monster killers as fathers, family men forced to extremes to protect their children. As Robert Neville (Will Smith) in *I Am Legend* tells his daughter, "Don't worry, Daddy's going to take away the monsters." This may seem trivial, obvious, and even naïve to the cynical cognoscenti,° but what father hasn't felt this same impulse deep in his bones?

Contrary to the narrative of early twentieth-century anthropology, early humans were probably not bold, assertive predators, marching confidently through the savanna to spear their threatening competitors. Male aggression, we were told, was put to good use in the realm of the hunt and of course in primitive warfare. This kind of domination and mastery of the field was helped along by some burgeoning brain power, but such domination of the other animals led to much further cognitive and cultural progress. Barbara Ehrenreich, in her book *Blood Rites*, surveys more recent anthropology and corrects the old story. We should not think about "man the hunter" in Paleolithic times, she writes, but "man the hunted." She reminds us that humans are fragile creatures: "Our biology is alone enough to suggest an alarming level of vulnerability to the exceptionally hungry or casual prowler." If we are to infer some aspects of human psychology from the evolutionary environment in which they developed, then we had better get an accurate picture of that environment and our status in it. Early humans were not uber predators but scavengers, waiting in the bushes to sneak in and pilfer morsels. It doesn't occur to us anymore to factor in the huge role that big cats, for example, must have played in the cognitive, emotional, and imaginative lives of our progenitors,° but we

ivory tower: a place isolated from day-to-day realities; often referring to the academic world of colleges and universities, which value ideas more than practical matters.
cognoscenti: people who are knowledgeable about a subject.
progenitors: forefathers or ancestors.

were constantly harassed and victimized by them. Moreover, even in recent history, when the numbers of such predators are way down, a staggering number of deaths from lions, tigers, crocodiles, and wolves have been chronicled. "The British," Ehrenreich reports, "started recording the numbers of humans lost to tigers [on the Indian subcontinent] in 1800, and found that by the end of the century, approximately three hundred thousand people had been killed, along with 6 to 10 million farm animals." Though it may seem a remote possibility to us now, during the formation of the human brain the fear of being grabbed by sharp claws, dragged into a dark hole, and eaten alive was not an abstraction.

Men tend to respond to fear and vulnerability with aggression. The philosopher Harvey Mansfield writes, "Men have aggression to spare; they keep it in stock so as to have it ready when it is needed and even, or especially, when it is unneeded and unwanted." Before men ever fought for honor or economic gain or even turf they must have fought for their own children and mates. Monsters, both real and imagined, are bound up with our feelings of insecurity and our responses to those anxieties. Masculine audacity and bravado is the reflex response to vulnerability.

This universal paternal impulse to protect and use whatever aggression is necessary is rehearsed again in Cormac McCarthy's Pulitzer Prize–winning 2006 novel *The Road*. McCarthy gives us a powerful story about a father trying to protect his son in a postapocalyptic world of roaming cannibals. The father must safeguard his son, lest he become a captive catamite° slave whose limbs are harvested by cannibal monsters. Among other things, it is an allegorical story about the need to shelter the good, which is fragile, from the monstrous world.

To a young boy, monsters are exciting and alluring. They are invoked daily as the imaginary foes of the playground. Anyone, I think, who has raised a boy gets this point. When that boy becomes a man, however, he feels keenly, rightly or wrongly, that monsters have become his responsibility, part of his job.

catamite: a boy kept by an older man for a sexual relationship.

Understanding the Text

1. What characterizes the animals that Alexander and his men encounter at the "lake of sweet water" (pars. 3–8)? That is, what in particular makes them monstrous?

2. What explanations does Asma offer for Alexander's reports of the monsters that attacked his army? Which one or ones seem the most plausible? How does the example of the burglar relate to the reports of the beasts involved in the waves of attacks?

3. Asma argues that "in our more liberal intellectual culture macho monster fights have become a quaint genre of outmoded heroics" (par. 15). What does he mean by this? According to Asma, why does Hollywood continue to embrace this story line?

Reflection and Response

4. Asma lists several Hollywood blockbusters, as well as Cormac McCarthy's novel *The Road* (2006), all of which feature fathers as heroes combating monsters. In your opinion, what is the advantage of portraying the monster slayer in this light? What might this reflect about our times and our contemporary vision of the role of fathers?

5. Asma argues that early humans were more likely scavengers, vulnerable to the physical superiority of other creatures. Even as recently as the nineteenth century, large numbers of people were killed by such creatures. If what Asma says is true, how does this reflect our concept of monsters and our reactions to them?

6. What does Alexander's experience say about how we understand, and misunderstand, the world around us, especially creatures we may be encountering for the first time? What experiences have you had or witnessed in which a misconception on a first encounter affected a worldview?

Making Connections

7. Compare Asma's work with "Monstrous Beginnings" by W. Scott Poole (p. 176). What similarities do you see in their discussions of how people create monsters out of animals they have never seen before? What differences in perceptions are apparent in Alexander's tales about India and those of European settlers in the New World? What does this lead you to conclude about the two times and cultures?

8. Research the psychology of human perception and how accurate and inaccurate our memories can be, especially when encountering traumatic situations. How might this affect other accounts of monster sightings? Consider, for example, reports of the chupacabra in Mike Davis's "Monsters and Messiahs" (p. 46) or descriptions of mermaids in Skye Alexander's "Mermaids' Attributes, Behavior, and Environs" (p. 232). If necessary, research other examples of alleged sightings of creatures such as Sasquatch or the Loch Ness monster and examine how error in human perception may account for the details of the tales.

Cursed by a Bite

Matt Kaplan

Investigating the origins of vampires and zombies, Matt Kaplan uses history and biochemistry to decipher how the myths about these creatures could have evolved from actual events. Vampires may be the logical repository for fears about death and disease — fears that could have been exacerbated by the appearance that a human corpse has when exhumed. Zombies may have been the creation of plantation owners looking to enslave workers by poisoning them with a dangerous cocktail of anesthetics, muscle relaxants, and hallucinogens. Kaplan is a science journalist who regularly contributes to publications such as *National Geographic*, *Nature*, *New Scientist*, and the *Economist*. This excerpt comes from his book *Medusa's Gaze and Vampire's Bite: The Science of Monsters* (2012).

Slinking through the shadows of night, they come to feed on the innocent. Seemingly human in appearance, the threat that they pose becomes apparent only as needle-sharp fangs pierce the throat of their intended victim and blood is sucked away. When every last drop of this precious life essence is consumed, prey becomes predator, seeking out blood to fuel its own newly acquired supernatural hunger. Vampires are among the world's most celebrated and popular monsters, and they have an extremely complex history and biology surrounding them, supported by a long line of books and movies featuring them as both villains and heroes. Yet working out exactly which fears drove the rise of vampires is a tricky question to answer because they are such multifaceted monsters with no clear point of origin.

On the face of it, they are predators like lions and play upon the terror of being killed by a nocturnal hunter. With such a basic fear, one would expect vampires to be present during ancient times when fears of beasts lurking in the night were at their height, yet vampires as we know them today arrived on the scene only in the eighteenth century. Even so, earlier reports of creatures resembling these monsters do exist.

In the *Odyssey*, Odysseus is forced to travel to the land of the dead and confront the ghosts of people he once knew in order to gain information to aid him on his quest. The witch Circe advises that he must allow the ghosts to feed on blood freshly spilled from the body of an animal to gain their trust and knowledge. At first he is highly protective of the pool of blood that he spills on the ground, allowing only the ghost of the wise man, Teiresias, to feed and answer his questions. But then the ghost of Odysseus's mother appears and fails to recognize him as her own son.

Odysseus turns to Teiresias for answers: "Tell me and tell me true, I see my poor mother's ghost close by us; she is sitting by the blood without saying a word, and though I am her own son she does not remember me and speak to me; tell me, Sir, how I can make her know me." Teiresias replies, "Any ghost that you let taste of the blood will talk with you like a reasonable being, but if you do not let them have any blood they will go away again." Odysseus then allows the ghost of his mother to feed on the blood, and her memories of him come flooding back.

For Homer, blood is clearly a link between the dead and the living, even if it has to be spilled from an animal's body onto the ground to have this effect. However, while the spirits in the *Odyssey* are a tantalizing ancestor to the modern vampire, they are still very different, and it is not until nearly two thousand years after Homer, during the late 1100s, that creatures more like the vampires of modern fiction appear in Europe. The person who documents these monsters is William of Newburgh, an English historian who is widely thought to have had a network of trustworthy informants who helped him report on historic events that took place between the days of William the Conqueror in 1066 and those of Richard the Lionheart in 1198.

· · ·

William of Newburgh told many . . . stories of the dead rising from the 5
grave, and he had much company. In 1591, in the town of Breslau (now the Polish city of Wrocław), a shoemaker who killed himself by putting a knife through his neck, came back to haunt those around him by pressing against their necks in the night. He was ultimately found in his grave with the wound in his neck just as fresh and red as it had been when he died. In 1746, the French abbot Augustin Calmet reported, "A new scene is offered to

> "Terrified by these sights, people chopped off heads, drove stakes through hearts, and jammed bricks into decaying mouths to keep the monsters from biting anything more."

our eyes. People who have been dead for several years, or at least several months, have been seen to return, to talk, to walk, to infest the villages, to maltreat people and animals, to suck the blood of their close ones, making them become ill and eventually die."

The solution to the undead threat that locals turned to was exactly what William of Newburgh described. They dug up the graves of the offending monsters to destroy them and found that recently buried corpses often had blood on their lips, bloated stomachs that looked as if they had just fed, blood still flowing inside their bodies, fresh-looking organs, clawlike fingernails, and elongated canine teeth. Terrified by these sights, people chopped off heads, drove stakes through hearts, and jammed bricks into decaying mouths to keep the monsters from biting anything more. It must have been dreadful business, but there are no reports of the monsters ever fighting back. They are always just corpses in graves taking a beating.

Finally, after hundreds of years of terrorizing Europe, all these walking corpses and ghosts earn the name "vampire" in the second edition of the *Oxford English Dictionary* in 1745. It was described as "a preternatural being of a malignant nature (in the original and usual form of the belief, a reanimated corpse), supposed to seek nourishment, or do harm, by sucking the blood of sleeping persons." People must have been scared out of their socks.

Mortifying Misunderstanding

With so many traits and behaviors being associated with these early vampires, it is likely there were several fears merging together to form these monsters. As such, it seems best to start with the most concrete details being described: Vampires had bloody mouths, bloated stomachs, fresh blood in their bodies, and, sometimes, claws and fangs.

The Europeans who were initially digging up corpses were probably not exaggerating. After people die, bacteria living within the body often continue to be productive and generate gases that collect inside. The gas production leads to an effect that morticians refer to as "postmortem bloat," and while it has nothing to do with diet or recent feeding, it can make the belly look swollen and lead people to conclude that the corpse has recently eaten.

In addition, gas buildup inside the body can cause blood to get pushed 10 up from the lungs, passed through the trachea, and out of the mouth so that it stains the teeth and lips. This likely created the illusion that the bloated stomach was not simply full, but full of blood that the corpse had recently consumed, logically leading to the idea that the monster fed on blood.

Furthering the idea of the animated corpse, under certain circumstances bacteria-created gases can move past the vocal cords and create sound. This often occurs when bodies are handled or meddled with after death, causing corpses to make noises as if they are groaning or, in rare cases, speaking.

As for elongated canines and clawlike fingernails, there is a medical explanation for this too. After death, tissues die and waste away; the skin begins to shrink, and this leads it to be pulled back along both the nail beds and the gum line. As a result, the nails and teeth become more prominently exposed than they were at the time of burial. Of course, this is an illusion, but to early vampire hunters who had worked themselves into a lather over the perceived plague of the undead, these were fangs and claws indicative of a vampiric transformation.

All of these natural processes can explain the descriptions of early vampires and can even account for why Homer, way back in ancient Greece, suggested that the dead liked to feed on blood. But one thing that is not immediately clear is why the belief of the dead leaving their graves to attack the living gained such popularity during the 1100s when William of Newburgh was writing but not during the days of Homer. One possibility worth considering is that people being buried during William's time were not actually dead.

Today there are a lot of tools available, like blood pressure cuffs, stethoscopes, and heart monitors, that help doctors determine whether someone is alive or dead. Yet even with these devices, patients with very weak or infrequent heartbeats can easily be declared dead by mistake. As an example, in Jan Bondeson's book *Buried Alive*, which goes into great detail on how accidental burials happened (and still do), the tale is told of a Frenchman named Angelo Hays who suffered a brutal motorcycle accident in 1937. At the hospital he was not breathing, had no detectable pulse, and had a serious head injury. The doctor, using a stethoscope, could not hear anything, and Hays was sent to the morgue. Three days later, as he was buried, an insurance company realized Hays had been covered by a policy for up to 200,000 francs and sent an inspector out to investigate the accident before paying up. The inspector ordered the body exhumed to look at the injuries and to confirm the cause of death. Remarkably, the doctor in charge found the corpse to still be warm. Hays returned to the land of the living and is thought to have survived his near-death ordeal by being buried in loose soil that allowed some flow of oxygen to the coffin and by needing very little oxygen in the first place as the result of his head injury reducing all metabolic activities in the body. Bondeson relates a few more similar stories and argues that if we see such cases now, they probably were taking place somewhat more often in the past when vital sign monitoring tools were not available. Could such events of still-living but "geologically challenged" patients have been feeding into undead mythology?

Rising from the Grave

In 1938, the author, folklorist, and anthropologist Zora Neale Hurston, then a student of the noted anthropologist Franz Boas at Columbia University, proposed there might be some material basis for the stories 15 told in Haiti of individuals being raised from their graves by voodoo masters. These raised people, or zombies, legends said, were robbed of their identities, enslaved, and forced to work indefinitely on plantations. Hurston was not believed. For decades, the wider research community ignored her suggestions and in some cases actively ridiculed her, but this attitude eventually changed.

In May 1962, a man spitting up blood and sick with fever and body aches sought help at the Albert Schweitzer Hospital, a facility operated in Haiti by an American charity. Two doctors, one of whom was an American, did their best to save him, but to no avail. The man's condition deteriorated and he was declared dead shortly after his arrival. At the time of his death, he was diagnosed as suffering from critically low blood pressure, hypothermia, respiratory failure, and numerous digestive problems. What exactly caused such systemwide problems remained a mystery. The man's sister was called in to identify his body and stamped her thumbprint to the death certificate to confirm he was her brother and that he was, indeed, dead. Eight hours later he was buried in a small cemetery near his village, and ten days later a large stone memorial slab was laid over his grave.

In 1981, the sister was approached by a man at her village market who introduced himself to her using the boyhood name of the dead brother. It was a name that only she and a handful of other family members knew, so he seemed real enough. The man explained that he had been made into a zombie and forced to work on a sugar plantation with many other zombies until their master died and the zombies were freed. The media went crazy with the story, particularly in Haiti, and Lamarck Douyon, the director of the Psychiatric Institute in Port-au-Prince, made up his mind to test whether this zombie tale could possibly be true.

Douyon knew that digging up the grave would prove nothing; if the man and his zombie story were fraudulent, it would have been easy for the deceivers to remove remains from a rural village cemetery. Instead, Douyon collaborated with the family to construct the ultimate identity test. He would ask the man a series of questions that only the brother would know all the answers to. The man passed the test, and later, when the sister's thumbprint and the thumbprint on the death certificate were confirmed by Scotland Yard to be identical, Douyon concluded the man's story was likely true. There had to be something real about the zombie mythology of the island.

All of the evidence pointed to the idea that some sort of a poison had been used to make the man appear dead after making him quite ill. Then, after he was buried, he had been exhumed by his poisoner so he could be enslaved. Realizing that this was a matter for a biochemist rather than a psychologist, Douyon and other doctors in Haiti asked the Harvard ethno-biologist Edmund Wade Davis to get involved.

Davis conducted several expeditions to Haiti and collected five zom- 20
bie poison recipes from four different locations. All the poisons varied in the number of tarantulas, lizards, millipedes, and nonvenomous snakes added to the brew, but there were a handful of similarities that caught Davis's attention. All recipes contained a species of ocean-dwelling worm (*Hermodice carunculata*), a specific tree frog (*Osteopilus dominicensis*), a certain toad (*Bufo marinus*), and one of several puffer fish (also known as blowfish in some regions).

Since these organisms appeared in all the different zombie poisons, Davis focused his attention on them. He found that the worm had bristles on its body that could paralyze people, and the tree frog was closely related to a frog species that released toxins on its body that could cause blindness in those who touched it. Furthermore, the toad, he learned, was a chemical nightmare. Some of the compounds in its body functioned as anesthetics, some as muscle relaxants, and some as hallucinogens. He noted that earlier studies conducted with the toad compounds had discovered they induced a rage similar to the berserker rages found in Norse legends, and these studies suggested that compounds of closely related toads had once been consumed by ancient barbarians as they charged with reckless courage into battle and shrugged off all but the most lethal attacks. But by far the most interesting ingredients in the zombie poisons were the puffer fish.

Puffer fish, which are well known for their deadly nerve toxins, are said to be tasty. Eating them comes with the serious risk of being poisoned, but this doesn't put off the Japanese. Called fugu in Japan, puffer fish is something of a dining adventure that popularly leaves consumers with feelings of body warmth, euphoria, and mild numbness around the mouth. Of course, if the chef gets fugu preparation wrong, diners end up in the hospital. Because the fish is so popular, hospitalization occurs with relative frequency and, as a result, there is a lot of medical literature on what fugu poisoning looks like.

Common symptoms include malaise, dizziness, nausea, vomiting, very low blood pressure, headache, and initial numbness around the lips and mouth that spreads to the rest of the body and often becomes severe. Eyes become glassy, and patients who survive the experience say it felt as if their bodies were floating while they could not move. They remained fully aware of their surroundings and alert during the poisoning experience. In one dramatic account, a fourteen-year-old boy in Australia, who accidentally ate puffer fish while on a camping trip with his family, recalled his family talking in the car as he was taken to the hospital, the nurses wishing him good morning and good night, and the doctors speaking their medical mumblings all while entirely paralyzed and feeling "light."

Davis found this intriguing because when he interviewed the man who claimed to have been made a zombie, he learned that he had remained conscious the entire time, heard his sister weeping when she was told that he had died, and had the sensation of floating above the grave. These descriptions, in combination with the medical reports filed when the man had been in the hospital on the night of his "death," suggested that puffer fish poison had been at work.

Upon further investigation, Davis learned that zombie makers created 25 their poisons and exposed victims to these toxins by releasing them in the air near where the person lived or by putting them in places where the person was likely to make contact, such as on door handles or window latches. Lacing food with the poison was never done, because zombie makers believed it would kill the victim too completely.

After burial, zombie makers had their assistants pull victims out of their graves and then beat them fiercely to drive their old spirit away. This was followed by binding the exhumed person to a cross, baptizing them with a new zombie name, and force-feeding them with a paste made from sweet potato, cane syrup, and *Datura stramonium*, one of the most hallucinogenic plants known.

Davis suggested in the *Journal of Ethnopharmacology* in 1983 that these ghastly experiences, combined with the potent initial poisoning, created a state of psychosis that literally transformed people into zombies who would do anything they were told by their masters. This, he argued, explained why voodoo magic was widely perceived as raising the dead and why Hurston was right. People literally were being buried alive and then dragged back to the living world as zombies.

Undead Plague

But what of vampires? The early stories about these monsters do not support the "buried alive" theory very strongly, and there are no indications of poisons or zombie makers being involved with vampire creation. The vampire historian Paul Barber points out in his book *Vampires, Burial, and Death* that none of the early vampiric accounts actually describe vampires digging themselves out of graves, a fact that William of Newburgh's stories support. The protovampires just tend to emerge from the grave. This hints that early proponents of the vampire myth might have been making up this element of vampire behavior to explain something they were seeing in the world around them.

Today, if a person in a family falls ill with a contagious and potentially lethal disease, doctors usually have the knowledge to identify it, prescribe treatment, and suggest quarantine measures if they are needed. In the days before modern medicine, when understanding of infectious disease transmission was rudimentary, people exposed to lethally contagious individuals had a good chance of following their friends to the grave. But they would not have done so immediately. Viruses and bacteria take time to spread through the body before having noticeable negative effects. This delay, which is known in the medical community as the incubation period, varies with the disease and can range from hours for some gut and respiratory infections to years for viruses like HIV. In most cases, though, incubation for diseases is a matter of days.

Imagine what people in those days saw after a loved one died from a 30 highly lethal and contagious disease, like tuberculosis or a nasty strain of influenza. First, those who had lived with the diseased individual would fall ill upon the completion of the incubation period and run a high risk of dying. Then, those who had tended to these diseased individuals would also fall ill and transmit the disease before dying. One death would follow another in a dominolike progression. In a morbid sense, these patients were literally killing their friends and relatives, but from their deathbeds rather than from the hereafter. However, because of the incubation period, it wasn't clear to anyone how the disease was being passed along.

Driven into a panic by plagues of contagious diseases, people desperately sought an explanation. This search for answers even appears in William of Newburgh's story: The monster "filled every house with disease and death by its pestiferous breath." People were already somewhat aware of what was going on, but rather than pointing the finger at microscopic pathogens (which would have been impossible since microscopes were not even in use until the mid-1600s), they came up with the idea of the dead returning to kill off their friends and family. This led someone at some point to open up a grave and have a look. Shocked by the discovery of a bloody-mouthed corpse with a bloated belly, claws, and fangs, a connection was likely made between this horrific sight and the plague of death spreading throughout the community.

This seems logical, but it raises a question about timing. Why does the fear of vampires begin during the 1100s, when William of Newburgh was writing? Highly lethal and contagious diseases were hardly new things. In fact, Ian Barnes at Royal Holloway, University of London, published a study in the journal *Evolution* in 2011 revealing that infectious disease has played a key role in human evolution for centuries. Remarkably, this study found that humans who have been dwelling in places where population densities have been high for a long time carry genes that are particularly good at granting resistance to certain contagious diseases. This makes sense since places with higher population densities would have more humans available (and living in closer proximity) for diseases to infect and thus tend to be reservoirs where the infections could linger for long periods. People who carried genes that coded for immune systems strong enough for them to survive this pathogenic onslaught proliferated while those who did not, died out. The study specifically notes that people from Anatolia in Turkey, where dense settlements have been around for nearly eight thousand years, carry a gene granting an innate resistance to tuberculosis, a disease that wreaked havoc in ancient cities. In contrast, people with almost no history of dense urban living, like the Saami from northern Scandinavia and the Malawians in Africa, do not show similar genetic resistance.

So it seems unreasonable to argue that people started digging up graves and inventing vampires as monsters only to explain the spread of contagious disease. If this were the whole story, vampires would be expected to have emerged as monsters much earlier. There had to have been other factors associated with the rise of the modern vampire, and clues to what these might have been can be found in one of the stranger vampire traits.

The Sweet Smell of Garlic

According to some folktales, vampires are repelled by garlic, and for the most part this idea has remained tethered to the monsters for centuries. While modern enthusiasts of Gothic horror accept this trait as simply part of what vampires are, if you stop to think about it, being repelled by garlic is a rather bizarre quality to associate with a monster. The threat of sunlight makes the most sense. Evil things tend to be active in the dark and thus sunlight should naturally harm them. However, early vampire lore does not present sunlight as a threat. It is garlic that gets mentioned.

Garlic has a history of being used to protect the innocent from the 35 forces of evil. The Egyptians believed that it could repel ghosts, and in Asia, garlic has long been smeared on the bodies of people to prevent them from being targeted by the spells of witches and wizards. Is there logic to this?

Some studies have shown that garlic fights infection, reduces blood pressure, and lowers cholesterol. For this reason, you could argue that any monster conjured up to explain inexplicable diseases, including vampires, came to be viewed as "fended off" by garlic because it was helping to boost immune system function. However, there is a problem. The scientific community is nowhere near any sort of consensus on the powers of garlic because its effects are, at best, weak. So one has to wonder: If modern researchers testing garlic's potential in controlled laboratory settings are having trouble determining if it really grants substantial benefits, were ancient people able to detect benefits at all? Or was there something else going on?

Foul odors created by corpses were often covered up by powerful smells like that produced by garlic, and there is some literature suggesting that, along with strong-smelling flowers, garlic was used at funerals where the corpse was getting a bit stinky. This may have been how it came to be connected with protecting people from the evil and the walking dead. Yet a most intriguing explanation for garlic being associated with vampires stems from the field of neurology.

During the 1600s, many Romanians believed that rubbing garlic around the outside of the house could keep the undead away, that holy water would burn them like boiling oil, and that throwing a vampire's sock into a river would cause the menace to enter the water searching for the sock and be destroyed. Intriguingly, Juan Gómez-Alonso, a neurologist at the Hospital Xeral in Vigo, Spain, points out that these three things all have a connection to rabies.

In a report published in the journal *Neurology* in 1998, Gómez-Alonso explains that while the rabies virus can cause animals to become increasingly paralyzed as it spreads, in afflicted humans it can have a frightening effect on the mind leading to a condition known among medical practitioners as furious rabies. As the virus attacks their nervous system, patients become restless; some leave their beds and wander the surrounding area. They have trouble swallowing, frequently drool bloody saliva, become fiercely dehydrated and very thirsty. Worse, they often suffer from persistent feelings of terror and have a tendency to become angry and aggressive. Most important, furious rabies frequently attacks the section of the brain controlling how the body manages emergency respiratory activities like coughing and gasping.

Nerve cells in the lining of the nose, throat, larynx, and windpipe 40 become extremely sensitive to noxious fumes and liquids. For this reason, patients with furious rabies suffer from spasms and extreme fear when they are forced to endure exposure to pungent odors (like that of garlic) or are presented with water (remember, they are desperately thirsty but cannot swallow). What do these spasms look like? When confronted, rabies patients tend to make hoarse gasping noises, clench their teeth, and retract their lips like animals.

Rabies has another connection to vampires based upon the way it is transmitted. Unlike, for example, influenza and tuberculosis, which are spread invisibly by particles in the air, rabies is primarily transmitted through bites. Most infections in people occur when a rabid animal breaks human flesh with its teeth and contaminates the wound with the infected saliva. The animals that most commonly spread rabies to humans in this way are dogs, wolves, and bats, all of which have a history in legends of being associated with vampires (bats are more recent than dogs and wolves, but all have been connected to the monsters for a while). Human-to-human transmission of rabies is all but unheard of today; however, historical accounts of people being bitten by rabid individuals do exist, and it seems likely that incidents of authorities or doctors being bitten while trying to subdue or capture rabid patients have taken place. In this case, the bite wound would heal as the rabies virus incubated inside the newly infected person's body. The individual who made the bite would die, but in time a new monster would be born.

Rabies is spread not only through bites. It can also be spread through sexual activity. Furious rabies can cause hypersexuality and leave people with powerful feelings of sexual excitement. Men with the condition can develop erections that last for several days, and one individual is documented as having had sexual intercourse thirty times in a twenty-four-hour period before the disease claimed him. With such powerful sexual stimulation at work and with patients so severely mentally compromised, it is hardly surprising the rabies literature reports violent rape attempts being common.

However, as tempting as it might seem to make a direct connection between rabies and vampires, rabies is very much a disease of the living and does not suggest that anything is returning from the grave. This does not disqualify rabies from being involved with the evolution of vampires. The virus probably did inspire the concept of vampirism spreading via bite and then merged with the perception that vampires were bloodsuckers. It is the undead element of vampires that rabies does not resolve, but, as mentioned earlier, there are many contagious diseases, like tuberculosis and influenza, that could explain how people came to believe that the dead were returning from the grave to claim their loved ones.

In the end, the fears that ultimately led to the rise of vampires as they are known today may have come from people trying to make sense of two disease epidemics that took place roughly simultaneously. Tuberculosis was at epidemic levels in Europe throughout much of the 1700s just as a major rabies epidemic struck the wild dogs and wolves of the region. In one case, in 1739, a rabid wolf in France bit seventy people, and in another case, in 1764, forty people were bitten. To what extent these bites led to cases of rabid people biting one another is unknown, but if such a situation did develop at the same time as a town was suffering a tuberculosis epidemic, fears from each medical condition could have become intertwined. Even so, the idea of a curse turning man into a monster appeared long before vampires.

Understanding the Text

1. What similarities are there between the story told by the likes of William of Newburgh and modern vampire myths? What is the naturalistic explanation for the physical features of the exhumed monsters?
2. According to some accounts, how were zombies made in Haiti? List the important ingredients.
3. What is different about today's understanding of disease transmission from the way diseases were understood in the time of William of Newburgh and even for centuries thereafter? How does that past understanding connect to the powers of monsters?
4. How is rabies connected to belief in vampires?

Reflection and Response

5. Argue whether Kaplan's historical and biological explanations for the origins of the myths about either vampires or zombies are convincing or not. Does he explain all aspects of these myths, or are there elements he doesn't cover?
6. What connection does Kaplan make between the growth of population density and the rise of certain monster myths, such as those about vampires? Is his argument convincing? In what other ways has population growth caused cultural beliefs to shift?
7. What is the importance of blood in the origin myths of vampires? Examine its role as both a giver of life and a symptom of death.

Making Connections

8. Research the practice of voodoo in Haiti. Explore further its connection to zombies. You might also research the socioeconomic conditions of Haiti and how they could lead to belief in the supernatural more easily than conditions in more developed nations.
9. How are the monsters in this selection connected to their times? What about our present time has led to changes in the portrayals of these monsters, such as in the Twilight or Harry Potter series?
10. Kaplan offers biological, scientific, and historical evidence for the belief in vampires and zombies. Is this approach compatible with more philosophical and psychological arguments for the existence of these creatures? In answering the question, consider arguments presented elsewhere in *Monsters*, such as in Guillermo del Toro and Chuck Hogan's "Why Vampires Never Die" (p. 36) or Chuck Klosterman's "My Zombie, Myself: Why Modern Life Feels Rather Undead" (p. 40).

Monstrous Beginnings

W. Scott Poole

W. Scott Poole, an associate professor of history at the College of Charleston, is the author of seven books, including *Vampira: Dark Goddess of Horror* (2014), *Satan in America: The Devil We Know* (2009), and *Never Surrender: Confederate Memory and Conservatism in the South Carolina Upcountry* (2004). In this excerpt from *Monsters in America: Our Historical Obsession with the Hideous and the Haunting* (2011), Poole examines the attitudes of European settlers and explorers since Christopher Columbus toward the New World and its inhabitants. While some saw these native inhabitants as savages in need of salvation, others saw them as monsters in league with Satan, unable to be redeemed. Poole narrows his focus to the experiences of the Puritans, English Dissenters who came to America in the early seventeenth century to escape persecution in England. The Puritans perceived Native Americans as violent, hypersexual monsters who needed to be removed. Once they had taken measures to do so, they found monsters among themselves, leading to the famous Salem witch trials.

Christopher Columbus came to the "New World" seeking gold, slaves, and monsters. Columbus reported both in his personal diary and correspondence that the native peoples he encountered in the Caribbean in 1492 and 1493 told him of "one-eyed men and other men with dog heads who decapitated their victims and drank their blood." Michael Palencia-Roth notes that the Genoese explorer's private diary of the first voyage shows that finding the monsters of the New World "became an obsession for Columbus."

A long tradition of legend and theological speculation about monstrous creatures informed Columbus' beliefs about what he might find in the new world. Medieval mental maps of a world inhabited by monstrous races prepared Spanish and Portuguese explorers to encounter giants, dog-men, ape-men, and various creatures out of the medieval bestiary. Christian theological speculation about the work of the devil, combined with the ongoing geopolitical conflict with the Islamic powers of the Mediterranean world, encouraged European explorers to see these monstrous races as allied with the evil one, the enemies of God and of the church.

Some scholars argue that the first European conquerors in the New World did not think of the native people themselves as monsters. Contemporary historian Peter Burke, for example, contends that Europeans always saw the native peoples of Africa and the Americas as part of the human family, even as they categorized them as an uncivilized or even degraded branch of that family. Burke notes that, throughout the era of European expansion, a debate took place among churchly scholars over the ethnic origins of "the savages of America." The very fact that such a debate was held meant that Europeans assumed the humanity, if not the equality, of the native peoples. A monster has no ethnic origin. If Burke is correct, European explorers saw the people of the New World as vastly inferior cousins but not as monsters.

Contrary evidence, however, suggests that such an ambivalent view of the natives had very little traction among most early modern Europeans. The conquerors of the New World saw, not simply a savage version of humanity, but the monstrous races of their mythology. Even significant Enlightenment thinkers such as the French naturalist Buffon in his *Natural History* connected the creation of monstrosities with the etiology° of the "darker races." Monsters represented the progeny of these supposedly savage peoples, a concept that reappeared again and again throughout American history, with a lineage that stretches from Puritan minister Cotton Mather to the twentieth-century horror maestro H. P. Lovecraft.

New kinds of technology in the period of exploration contributed to 5 European monster mania. The print revolution of the fifteenth century, though normally seen as an important moment in the expansion of modernity, provided a way to spread the concept of the monster, locating it in the enemy other. Numerous Reformation tracts portrayed either Martin Luther or the Pope as monstrous beings empowered by the devil. In 1727 a popular Portuguese tract, *Emblema Vivente*, described a Turkish monster "fifteen palms high" with an eerie light emanating from its chest every time it breathed. Historians of early modern Europe Laura Lunger Knoppers and Joan B. Landes argue that this tract "blurs the boundaries of science and religion," in its description of the monster both as an oddity of nature and malformed beast. The monster incarnated fears of the religious other whose land it inhabited, the Ottoman Turk.

Emblema Vivente's blurring of conceptual boundaries is representative of the emerging Enlightenment view of the monster. While many eighteenth-century thinkers dismissed theological explanations for the birth of monsters, they did not reject the reality of monsters themselves. The natural scientist Buffon suggested a number of purely natural explanations for the monstrous peoples and creatures that walked the earth. In 1796 the Enlightenment Encylopedist Diderot speculated about the possible

---

etiology: all of the causes of a disease or abnormal condition.

natural origins of monsters. The New World, with its strange creatures and peoples, offered new opportunities for sightings of such creatures.

Europeans found the monsters they searched for. Not only did explorers and settlers readily believe wonder tales, they tended to ascribe morally monstrous qualities to the peoples they encountered. This process began with the early explorations of Africa and provided some of the earliest materials for the racist imagination of the modern West. Early European accounts of orangutans imagined a similarity between them and the native peoples of West Africa, the region that soon became the primary target for slave traders. Fabulous accounts written by European travelers dwelt on the monstrous appearance of the ape and on the monster's sexual proclivities. According to one account, the apes of India were "so venerous° that they will ravish their women," while an African baboon brought before a French monarch allegedly had a sexual organ "greater than might match the quantity of his other parts." These ideas had a calamitous effect on how the white mind encountered native African peoples.

Such imaginings became a familiar part of the racist folklore of the United States concerning African American men. An English naturalist, Edward Topsell, would write in 1607 of African men with "low and flat nostrils" who are "as libidinous as apes that attempt women and having thicke lips the upper hanging over the neather, they are deemed fools." Winthrop Jordan notes that these associations also drew on European folklore about the connection between apes and the devil. Contemporary demonological texts often made this connection explicit, seeing apes as incarnations of Satan or as the familiars of witches. Europeans encountering Africans in the context of the slave trade held in their minds these bizarre associations between monstrous apes, Satan, libidinous sexuality, and enormous sexual organs. They readily applied these folkloric images to the human beings they stuffed into the holds of their ships for a life of enslavement. Such poisonous associations would be reborn again and again in twentieth-century popular culture, most notably in *The Birth of a Nation* (1915) and *King Kong* (1933). They even played a role in the folklore that supported lynching, some of the most pathological violence ever to take place on American soil.

Europeans found monsters in the Americas as quickly as in Africa. Some of the earliest Spanish explorers of what would become the southeastern coast of the United States readily accepted Native American tales of monstrous peoples and saw the natives themselves as embodiments of

---

venerous: seeking gratification of sexual desires.

the marvelously monstrous. In the 1520s Spanish explorer Lucas Allyón hungrily devoured the stories of a local Native American Chicora° who spoke of all the lands north of Florida as being populated by "a race of men with tails for which they dug holes in the ground when they sat down." Chicora regaled Allyón, and later the Spanish court, with other stories of Native American tribes that stretched their children so that they became enormous giants.

Belief in the monsters of the New World influenced discussions about the moral justification for the enslavement and oppression of native peoples. These debates, with very few exceptions, assumed theological and cultural justifications for the economic exploitation of the New World. European explorers who willingly granted that the natives came from human stock often believed them to be a type of monstrous human, depraved beings whose moral leprosy had its source in the world of the demonic. Even the sixteenth-century friar Bartolomé de Las Casas, a strong proponent of the rights of Native Americans under Spanish law, saw the New World as firmly under Satan's domain. Friar Bartolomé saw the very air of the New World teeming with evil spirits who tempted and destroyed the unbaptized.

Such conceptions of the diabolism of native peoples led some Europeans to imagine the New World as a landscape of horror. Charges of perverse sexuality and inhuman appetites represent some of the most common descriptions of native peoples. Friar Tomas Ortiz described the natives of Terra Firme, colonial Panama, as flesh-eating monsters who had "no sense of love or shame. . . . [T]hey are bestial and they pride themselves in having abominable vices." Viewing them as "steeped in vices and bestialities," Friar Ortiz saw no reason their personal autonomy should be recognized. Monsters could be enslaved.

The New World itself often seemed a kind of monster to the early modern European imagination. One of the earliest allegorizations of America is Philippe Galle's 1580 *America*, in which we see a giantess with spear and bow that has cannibalized a man and triumphantly carries his severed head. Galle's own description of the image refers to America as an "ogress who devours men, who is rich in gold and who is skilled in the use of the spear and the bow." In 1595 Paolo Farinati painted an allegorical representation of the New World as a monstrous cannibal to decorate a villa in Verona, Italy. In Farinati's *America*, the artist imagines the New World as a

Francisco de Chicora: a Native American who was kidnapped by Spanish explorers in 1521, was baptized and renamed as a Catholic, and accompanied the explorer Lucas Vásquez de Ayllón to Spain, where he gave accounts of his homeland. In 1526 he returned to North America with another expedition and escaped.

giant roasting a human arm. A crucifix is shown on his right, illustrating the hope that conversion to Christianity could tame the beast.

A sixteenth-century Dutch engraving in Hans Staden's *True History* best illustrates this very common representation of the Americas. Staden's work, a captivity narrative that allegedly describes his time among the natives of Brazil, tells a tale of cannibalism that rivals anything a modern master of horror could conjure. One of the more infamous images from that work shows a gory cannibal feast that zombie auteur George Romero might have filmed. A gaggle of cannibals roast human body parts over a fire. A dwarf gnaws on a human hand. Women, sketched according to the traditional European iconography of the witch, chomp on legs, arms, and unidentified bits of human detritus.

Images of a New World filled with monstrous races and the tendency to imagine the New World itself as a kind of cannibalistic beast grew out of the deep roots of European culture. Europeans who settled in the New World brought with them a head full of monsters and a well-practiced tendency to define the cultural and religious other in terms of monstrosity. A long history of military conflict with the Islamic world converged with early modern religious tensions and age-old legends of the world beyond the borders of Europe to convince most European explorers that they would encounter new lands crawling with monsters.

Numerous scholars have examined the European tendency to construct the native peoples of North America as monstrous cannibals and demonic servants. Less attention has been paid to how supernatural beings and occurrences provided a way for white Americans in later historical periods to negotiate the meaning of the colonial period. Simplistic interpretations of folk belief in monsters have seen them as shorthand for death, sexuality, and metaphysical uncertainty. But the monster has, just as frequently, offered a way to ignore historical trauma and historical guilt, to remake the facts into a set of pleasing legends. The grotesquerie of the monster has offered relief from the gruesome facts of history. 15

• • •

Sex with the Devil

The Puritan settlements of New England have become representative symbols of early American settlement. Although not the first successful settlements in English North America (Jamestown dates to 1607), they occupy an integral place in the memory of the early American experience. There are many explanations for this importance, ranging from the dominance of New England historians and educational institutions in the writing of early American history, to the way the Puritans' own self-conceptions comport with Americans' tendency to view themselves as bearers of a special destiny.

The special place the Puritans have occupied in American memory made them multivalent° signifiers for national identity, appearing as everything from dour-faced party poopers to, ironically, the embodiment of the alleged American appreciation for the search for religious liberty. Their sermons and devotional tracts have provided the grammar of American understanding of sin, redemption, and national destiny, shaping both religious and political consciousness.

No aspect of Puritan experience lives more strongly in American memory than their fear of monsters, specifically their fear of witches that led to the trials of about 344 settlers during the course of the seventeenth century. The Salem witch trials, an outbreak of Puritan witch-hunting that ended in the executions of twenty people in 1692–1693, has become central to most Americans' perception of their early history. Salem historians Owen Davies and Jonathan Barry have noted the central role the event came to play in the teaching standards and curriculum of public schools, making knowledge of it integral to understanding the colonial era.

> "No aspect of Puritan experience lives more strongly in American memory than their fear of monsters."

For many contemporary people, Salem is read as a brief flirtation with an irrational past. At least some of the interest it garners comes from its portrayal as an anomaly, a strange bypath on the way to an unyielding national commitment to freedom and democracy. On the contrary, Salem was far from the first witch hunt in early New England. Nor did the American fascination with the witch disappear after 1693.

Puritans hunted monsters in the generation before Salem. In 1648 20 Margaret Jones of Charlestown, Massachusetts, became the first English settler accused of witchcraft, and later executed, in New England. The Massachusetts Bay Colony's first governor, John Winthrop, called Jones "a cunning woman," someone with the ability to make use of herbs and spells. Jones was further alleged to have had a "malignant touch" that caused her erstwhile patients to vomit and go deaf. Winthrop, after a bodily search of Jones by the women of Charlestown, claimed that she

---

multivalent: having many values or meanings.

exhibited "witches teats in her secret parts," which was, by long established superstition, the sign of a witch. The Puritan judiciary executed
Jones in the summer of 1648. More trials and more executions followed.

The witch embodied all the assorted anxieties that early New England
settlers felt about their new environment, their personal religious tur-
moil, and their fear of the creatures that lurked in the "howling wilderness." The Puritan movement in England grew out of the fear that the
English Church retained too many elements of the "satanic" Roman Catholic Church. The Puritan conception of the spiritual life, embodied in
John Bunyan's *The Pilgrim's Progress*, imagined the Christian experience as
a war with monstrous beings inspired by the devil. This understanding of
Christian experience as a struggle with the forces of darkness made its way
to the New World. Not surprisingly, this new world became a geography of
monsters in the minds of many of the Puritans.

Puritan clergyman Cotton Mather helped to construct a New World
mythology that not only included the bones of antediluvian° giants but
also the claim that native peoples in North America had a special relationship to Satan. In Mather's New World demonology, the Native Americans had been seduced by Satan to come to America as his special servants. This made them, in some literal sense, the "children of the Devil."
Other Puritan leaders reinforced this view, seeing the Native Americans
as a special trial designed for them by the devil. Frequently, Puritan leaders turned to Old Testament imagery of the Israelites destroying the
people of Canaan for descriptions of their relationship with the New England tribes. The Puritans believed you could not live with or even con-
vert monsters. You must destroy them.

The Puritans embodied the American desire to destroy monsters. At the
same time, the Puritan tendency toward witch-hunting reveals the American tendency to desire the monster, indeed to be titillated by it. Contemporary literary scholar Edward Ingebretsen convincingly argues that the
search for witches in the towns of New England should be read as popular
entertainment as well as evidence of religious conflict and persecution.
Ingebretsen shows that Mather makes use of the term "entertain" frequently when explaining his own efforts to create a narrative of the witch
hunts. He uses the same term to describe the effect of the testimony of
suspected witches on the Puritan courtrooms that heard them. Mather
described the dark wonders that make up much of his writings as "the
chiefe entertainments which my readers do expect and shall receive."

---

antediluvian: from the time before the biblical Flood.

Mather obviously does not use the word "entertain" in the contemporary sense. And yet his conception of "entertainment" bears some relationship to the more modern usage of the term. Mather believed that his dark entertainments warned and admonished, but a delicious thrill accompanied them as well. Mather himself sounds like a carnival barker when he promises frightening spectacles that his readers "do expect and shall receive." Historian of Salem Marion Starkey, in *The Devil in Massachusetts*, notes that for all of Mather's righteous chest-thumping over the danger the New England colonies faced from the assaults of Satan, it is hard not to see him "unconsciously submerged in the thrill of being present as a spectator." He provided his readers the same thrill.

This thrill had clear erotic undertones, underscoring the close connec- 25 tion between horror and sexuality that became a persistent thread in American cultural history. The genealogy of the witch in western Europe already included many of the ideas that aroused, in every sense, the Puritan settlements. Folklore taught that any gathering of witches, known as the "witches sabbat," included orgiastic sex, even sex with Satan and his demons. European demonologists frequently connected the tendency to witchcraft with a propensity toward uncontrolled sexual desire.

Such ideas appeared again and again in the New England witch hunts. The trial of indentured servant Mary Johnson not only included accusations that she had used her relationship with Satan to get out of work for her master, but also the assertion that she had flirted, literally, with the devil. Cotton Mather wrote that she had "practiced uncleanness with men and devils." One of the first women accused of witchcraft in Salem village had a reputation for sexual promiscuity, while male testimony against women accused of witchcraft often included descriptions of them as succubi,° appearing at night dressed in flaming red bodices. The witch was not only one of the first monsters of English-speaking America. The witch also became America's first sexy monster and one who would be punished for her proclivities.

The end of the witch trials in 1693 came with numerous criticisms of how the cases had been handled. Petitions on behalf of the accused began to appear in the fall of 1692. In October of that year, Boston merchant Thomas Brattle, a well-traveled member of the scientific Royal Society with an interest in mathematics and astronomy, published an open letter criticizing the courts. He especially critiqued the Puritan judiciary for allowing "spectral evidence," evidence based on visions, revelations, and alleged apparitions. Significantly, Brattle did not challenge the idea that supernatural agency had been involved in the trials, only that it had

---

succubi: demons that assume female form to have sex with men in their sleep.

worked by different methods than the Puritan judiciary had supposed. Brattle wrote that the evidence of witches sabbats and apparitions put forward by those who accused (and by those who confessed) represented "the effect of their fancy, deluded and depraved by the Devil." In Brattle's mind, to accept such evidence would be tantamount to accepting the testimony of Satan himself. Like many skeptics during this period, Brattle challenged the courts on how they had used the belief in monsters, without questioning the reality of the existence of monsters.

Salem did not mark the end of the witch trials in America. Fear of that old black magic remained a crucial part of early American life. Marginalized women and enslaved Africans remained the most common target of the witch hunt. In 1705–1706, a Virginia couple, Luke and Elizabeth Hill, accused Grace Sherwood of witchcraft. Although the Virginia courts at first found little evidence for the charge, the time-honored search for the witch's teat soon revealed "two things like titts with Severall other Spotts." Sherwood next underwent the infamous "water test" in which the suspected witch was thrown into water to see if she floated or sank. Sherwood floated and faced reexamination by some "anciente women" who, this time, discovered clearly diabolical "titts on her private parts." She was subjected to another trial, although the record breaks off at this point, making her fate unclear.

Enslaved Africans faced accusations of a special kind of witchcraft known as "conjuration" or, more simply, "sorcery." The use of black magic against the white master class became a common charge against the instigators of slave rebellions. In 1779 a trial of slave rebels in the territory that would later become the state of Illinois ended with the execution of several slaves for the crimes of "conjure" and "necromancy."

The Puritans clearly had no monopoly on the belief in witchcraft. 30 Even in parts of colonial America without a strong tradition of witch trials, beliefs that supported such trials remained strong. An Anglican missionary in colonial Carolina, Francis Le Jau, complained in a 1707 journal entry that the colonial court had not severely punished "a notorious malefactor, evidently guilty of witchcraft." While the Puritans pursued their obsession with the most vehemence, the belief in dark powers inhabiting the American landscape remained common throughout the eighteenth century.

Puritans found more monsters in their new world than the witch. Although we tend to picture the dour Puritans in their equally dour meetinghouses, taking in Calvinist theology and morality in great drafts, the actual Puritans lived out at least part of their experience in what David D. Hall has termed "worlds of wonder." The work of Hall, and of colonial historian Richard Godbeer, has uncovered a variety of magical traditions, astrological beliefs, and conceptions of monstrosity among the Puritans that kept alive older European wonder-lore. Puritan conceptions of original sin, for example, contributed to their interest in abnormal births, often termed as "monstrous births," that functioned as signs and omens. Spectral, shapeshifting dogs haunted the edges of the Puritan settlements, as did demonic, giant black bears.

Predictably, much of the Puritan ministry saw any portents in nature as signs of the New Englanders' divine mission. The same clergymen, just as predictably, ascribed a diabolical character to any marvel or wonders that did not fit into their theological paradigm. For Puritan clergy, it came as no surprise to find the forests of New England populated with marvelous creatures. Their new world was surrounded by evil spirits of all kinds, as numerous as "the frogs of Egypt" according to Cotton Mather.

Reaction to an alleged sighting of a sea serpent early in the Puritan experiment showcases this attitude. Puritan observers claimed to have encountered sea serpents long before the nineteenth-century sightings in Gloucester harbor. They also more quickly ascribed dark religious meanings to the appearance of the creature off their shores. In 1638 New England settler John Josselyn reported that recent arrivals to the colonies had seen "a sea serpent or a snake." Nahant native Obadiah Turner described the same creature and worried that "the monster come out of the sea" might be "the old serpent spoken of in holy scripture . . . whose poison hath run down even unto us, so greatly to our discomfort and ruin." The monster could be a portent of divine providence or judgment. The only other possible explanation was that it was a creature of Satan.

Puritans were not alone in finding monsters on the American frontier. Sea serpents swam in many American waters, and strange beasts populated the wilderness that surrounded most new American settlements. But the American response to the monsters they met was not uniform and did not always share the Puritan desire to destroy the monster and cleanse the American landscape. Some even saw the monster as a strange partner in mastering the unruly frontier.

Understanding the Text

1. Why did past experiences make it so easy for early European settlers to believe in the existence of monsters in the New World?
2. According to the New World settlers and explorers, how were the native peoples they encountered connected to monsters — and thus to Satan?
3. During the Salem witch trials, what were the signs that a woman was a witch? What was the significance of Thomas Brattle's argument against the trials?

Reflection and Response

4. What is your reaction to Poole's descriptions of the interactions between European settlers and native peoples and to the perceptions and treatment of the native peoples by the settlers?

5. Examine how the sexuality of native peoples became a weapon for European settlers to use against them. What role does sex play in justifying the perception that Native Americans were monsters? What were some of the consequences for the native peoples of the Europeans' perceptions about their sexuality?

Making Connections

6. Poole writes, "Europeans found the monsters they searched for. Not only did explorers and settlers readily believe wonder tales, they tended to ascribe morally monstrous qualities to the peoples they encountered" (par. 7). Research the social practices of Native Americans, including those regarding issues such as marriage and the family, sexual relations, warfare, and trade. Compare their practices with those of the Europeans of the time. Then argue whether the European perspective represents a misunderstanding of native cultures or not.

7. Conduct more research on the Salem witch trials. Investigate how and why accusations of sorcery were made, how they were supported during the trials, what was done to those who were convicted, and what brought the trials to an end. How did the Puritan preoccupation with evil, monsters, and Satan lubricate the process? What other "witch hunts" have caused such a frenzy or made such a mark on a culture or historical era?

4

What Is the Attraction of Monsters?

A monster is inherently dangerous, and thus off-limits—the ultimate bad boy with an attraction all its own. We are drawn to the forbidden — the desire for something outside the boundary set by society between what is acceptable and what is not. But the monster as Other isn't just dangerous; it's also exciting. After all, who wants to be normal — that is to say, boring? There is always an excitement on the edge of acceptability: never to venture past the edge is to cheapen life experience, while venturing too far could mean getting lost beyond all hope of return.

Part of what we envy in monsters is their ability to do what we cannot. Jeffrey Jerome Cohen analyzes why we are attracted to creatures that break the rules and represent an escape from our ordinary lives, which are bound by convention. In a passage from Bram Stoker's novel *Dracula*, written in the nineteenth century near the end of the Victorian era, Jonathan Harker, a young man engaged to be married, is sexually stimulated by three young female vampires who dance around him. He is excited by their presence, ignoring his sense of danger. J. Gordon Melton looks at the attraction of the vampire, from Stoker's Dracula through several movie versions of the famous Count and other vampires. The groundwork for changing the emphasis from the danger of vampires to their attraction was clearly being laid even before Stephenie Meyer penned her Twilight series, a phenomenon examined by Karen Backstein. Analyzing the new generation of vampires that Twilight's Edward Cullen and his family represent, as well as why Bella Swan is attracted to him and to life as a vampire, Backstein argues that Cullen is an update of the romantic hero. Further exploring the sexuality of the female monster, Declan McGrath interviews director Neil Jordan about his film *Byzantium* and its female vampires. One vampire turns the killing of her victims into an erotic experience for herself; her daughter, also a vampire, rejects such licentiousness, killing reluctantly, and then only those who are already old and dying. Skye Alexander explores the watery world of mermaids and mermen, discussing the allure of these creatures and the symbolism connected to them. In the epic poem *The Odyssey*, the Greek poet Homer recounts the tale of the hero Odysseus's journey home. In one of the oldest written depictions of female monsters, Odysseus, strapped to the mast of his ship, hears the song of the Sirens, who entice him to their island with their knowledge of all things. These irresistible creatures embody the double characteristics of attraction and danger. Finally, in an analysis of two representations of the same female monster, Karen Hollinger asserts that males — both human and monster — attempt to control female sexuality. Female monsters — in this case, a woman who turns into a panther — represent a threat to male dominance and control. As such, they must be tamed and the threat of their sexuality removed.

Sex has a long history of being dangerous. Libraries are filled with stories of men and women brought down by the desire for someone — or something — that is forbidden. Monsters can embody that desire, but they can also represent other attractive qualities, such as immortality or omniscience. The human desire to go beyond the limits and expectations of society can find its expression in monsters, whose presence can both attract and repel.

Fear of the Monster Is Really a Kind of Desire

Jeffrey Jerome Cohen

How can something as horrible and terrifying as a monster be considered the object of desire? In this selection, Jeffrey Jerome Cohen, as part of his larger work "Monster Culture (Seven Theses)," examines the issue of desire. He considers the various ways in which we desire to be with the monster and — better yet — to be the monster ourselves. The Other that the monster represents is not bound by the same rules and conventions that ordinary people are, and thus the monster promises a freedom from convention that we can only imagine. Cohen is an English professor and director of medieval and early modern studies at George Washington University. His books include *Monster Theory: Reading Culture* (1996), *Of Giants: Sex, Monsters, and the Middle Ages* (1999), and *Hybridity, Identity and Monstrosity in Medieval Britain: On Difficult Middles* (2006).

The monster is continually linked to forbidden practices, in order to normalize and to enforce. The monster also attracts. The same creatures who terrify and interdict can evoke potent escapist fantasies; the linking of monstrosity with the forbidden makes the monster all the more appealing as a temporary egress° from constraint. This simultaneous repulsion and attraction at the core of the monster's composition accounts greatly for its continued cultural popularity, for the fact that the monster seldom can be contained in a simple, binary dialectic° (thesis, antithesis . . . no synthesis). We distrust and loathe the monster at the same time we envy its freedom, and perhaps its sublime despair.

Through the body of the monster fantasies of aggression, domination, and inversion are allowed safe expression in a clearly delimited and permanently liminal space. Escapist delight gives way to horror only when the monster threatens to overstep these boundaries, to destroy or deconstruct the thin walls of category and culture. When contained by geographic, generic, or epistemic° marginalization, the monster can function as an alter ego, as an alluring projection of (an Other) self. The monster awakens one to the pleasures of the body, to the simple and fleeting joys of being frightened, or frightening—to the experience of mortality and corporality. We watch the monstrous spectacle of the horror film be-

egress: an exit; an act of going out.
dialectic: the juxtaposition of conflicting opposites; logical argumentation.
epistemic: relating to knowing; cognitive.

cause we know that the cinema is a temporary place, that the jolting sensuousness of the celluloid images will be followed by reentry into the world of comfort and light. Like-
wise, the story on the page before us may horrify (whether it appears in the *New York Times* news section or Stephen King's latest novel matters little), so long as we are safe in the knowledge of its nearing end (the number of pages in our right hand is dwindling) and our liberation from it. Aurally received narratives work no

> "The monster awakens one to the pleasures of the body, to the simple and fleeting joys of being frightened, or frightening — to the experience of mortality and corporality."

differently; no matter how unsettling the description of the giant, no matter how many unbaptized children and hapless knights he devours, King Arthur will ultimately destroy him. The audience knows how the genre works.

Times of carnival temporally marginalize the monstrous, but at the same time allow it a safe realm of expression and play: on Halloween everyone is a demon for a night. The same impulse to ataractic° fantasy is behind much lavishly bizarre manuscript marginalia, from abstract scribblings at the edges of an ordered page to preposterous animals and vaguely humanoid creatures of strange anatomy that crowd a biblical text. Gargoyles and ornately sculpted grotesques, lurking at the cross-beams or upon the roof of the cathedral, likewise record the liberating fantasies of a bored or repressed hand suddenly freed to populate the margins. Maps and travel accounts inherited from antiquity invented whole geographies of the mind and peopled them with exotic and fantastic creatures; Ultima Thule, Ethiopia, and the Antipodes were the medieval equivalents of outer space and virtual reality, imaginary (wholly verbal) geographies accessible from anywhere, never meant to be discovered but always waiting to be explored. Jacques Le Goff has written that the Indian Ocean (a "mental horizon" imagined, in the Middle Ages, to be completely enclosed by land) was a cultural space

where taboos were eliminated or exchanged for others. The weirdness of this world produced an impression of liberation and freedom. The strict morality imposed by the Church was contrasted with the discomfiting attractiveness of a world of bizarre tastes, which practiced coprophagy° and cannibalism; of bodily

---

ataractic: tending to tranquilize.
coprophagy: feeding on dung; the use of feces for sexual excitement.

innocence, where man, freed of the modesty of clothing, rediscovered nudism and sexual freedom; and where, once rid of restrictive monogamy and family barriers, he could give himself over to polygamy, incest, and eroticism.

The habitations of the monsters (Africa, Scandinavia, America, Venus, the Delta Quadrant—whatever land is sufficiently distant to be exoticized) are more than dark regions of uncertain danger: they are also realms of happy fantasy, horizons of liberation. Their monsters serve as secondary bodies through which the possibilities of other genders, other sexual practices, and other social customs can be explored. Hermaphrodites, Amazons, and lascivious cannibals beckon from the edges of the world, the most distant planets of the galaxy.

The co-optation of the monster into a symbol of the desirable is often accomplished through the neutralization of potentially threatening aspects with a liberal dose of comedy: the thundering giant becomes the bumbling giant.[1] Monsters may still function, however, as the vehicles of causative fantasies even without their valences° reversed. What Bakhtin calls "official culture" can transfer all that is viewed as undesirable in itself into the body of the monster, performing a wish-fulfillment drama of its own; the scapegoated monster is perhaps ritually destroyed in the course of some official narrative, purging the community by eliminating its sins. The monster's eradication functions as an exorcism and, when retold and promulgated, as a catechism.° The monastically manufactured *Queste del Saint Graal°* serves as an ecclesiastically sanctioned antidote to the looser morality of the secular romances; when Sir Bors comes across a castle where "ladies of high descent and rank" tempt him to sexual indulgence, these ladies are, of course, demons in lascivious disguise. When Bors refuses to sleep with one of these transcorporal devils (described as "so lovely and so fair that it seemed all earthly beauty was

5

---

valences: the degrees of attractiveness an individual, activity, or object possesses.
catechism: a form of religious doctrine often put in the form of questions and answers.
Queste del Saint Graal: *The Quest for the Holy Grail.*

---

[1] For Mikhail Bakhtin, famously, this is the transformative power of laughter: "Laughter liberates not only from external censorship but first of all from the great internal censor; it liberates from the fear that developed in man during thousands of years: fear of the sacred, fear of the prohibitions, of the past, of power." *Rabelais and His World*, trans. Hélène Iswolsky (Indianapolis: Indiana University Press, 1984), 94. Bakhtin traces the moment of escape to the point at which laughter became a part of the "higher levels of literature," when Rabelais wrote *Gargantua et Pantagruel*.

embodied in her"), his steadfast assertion of control banishes them all shrieking back to hell. The episode valorizes the celibacy so central to the authors' belief system (and so difficult to enforce) while inculcating a lesson in morality for the work's intended secular audience, the knights and courtly women fond of romances.

Seldom, however, are monsters as uncomplicated in their use and manufacture as the demons that haunt Sir Bors. Allegory may flatten a monster rather thin, as when the vivacious demon of the Anglo-Saxon hagiographic° poem *Juliana* becomes the one-sided complainer of Cynewulf's *Elene*. More often, however, the monster retains a haunting complexity. The dense symbolism that makes a thick description of the monsters in Spenser, Milton, and even *Beowulf* so challenging reminds us how permeable the monstrous body can be, how difficult to dissect.

This corporal fluidity, this simultaneity of anxiety and desire, ensures that the monster will always dangerously entice. A certain intrigue is allowed even Vincent of Beauvais's well-endowed cynocephalus,° for he occupies a textual space of allure before his necessary dismissal, during which he is granted an undeniable charm. The monstrous lurks somewhere in that ambiguous, primal space between fear and attraction, close to the heart of what Kristeva calls "abjection":

There looms, within abjection, one of those violent, dark revolts of being, directed against a threat that seems to emanate from an exorbitant outside or inside, ejected beyond the scope of the possible, the tolerable, the thinkable. It lies there, quite close, but it cannot be assimilated. It beseeches, worries, fascinates desire, which, nonetheless, does not let itself be seduced. Apprehensive, desire turns aside; sickened, it rejects. . . . But simultaneously, just the same, that impetus, that spasm, that leap is drawn toward an elsewhere as tempting as it is condemned. Unflaggingly, like an inescapable boomerang, a vortex of summons and repulsion places the one haunted by it literally beside himself.

And the self that one stands so suddenly and so nervously beside is the monster.

The monster is the abjected fragment that enables the formation of all kinds of identities—personal, national, cultural, economic, sexual, psychological, universal, particular (even if that "particular" identity is an embrace of the power/status/knowledge of abjection itself); as such it

---

hagiographic: relating to the lives of saints or other highly esteemed persons.
cynocephalus: a dog-headed being.

reveals their partiality, their contiguity. A product of a multitude of mor-phogeneses° (ranging from somatic° to ethnic) that align themselves to imbue meaning to the Us and Them behind every cultural mode of see-ing, the monster of abjection resides in that marginal geography of the Exterior, beyond the limits of the Thinkable, a place that is doubly dan-gerous: simultaneously "exorbitant" and "quite close." Judith Butler calls this conceptual locus "a domain of unlivability and unintelligibility that bounds the domain of intelligible effects," but points out that even when discursively closed off, it offers a base for critique, a margin from which to reread dominant paradigms. Like Grendel thundering from the mere° or Dracula creeping from the grave, like Kristeva's "boomerang, a vortex of summons" or the uncanny Freudian-Lacanian° return of the repressed, the monster is always coming back, always at the verge of irruption.°

Perhaps it is time to ask the question that always arises when the mon- 10 ster is discussed seriously (the inevitability of the question a symptom of the deep anxiety about what is and what should be thinkable, an anxiety that the process of monster theory is destined to raise): Do monsters re-ally exist?

Surely they must, for if they did not, how could we?

References

Judith Butler, *Bodies That Matter: On the Discursive Limits of "Sex"* (New York: Rout-ledge, 1993), 22.

Julia Kristeva, *The Powers of Honor: An Essay on Abjection*, trans. Leon S. Roudiez (New York: Columbia University Press, 1982), 1.

Jacques Le Goff, "The Medieval West and the Indian Ocean," in *Time, Work and Culture in the Middle Ages*, trans. Arthur Goldhammer (Chicago: University of Chicago Press, 1980), 197.

The Quest for the Holy Grail, trans. Pauline Matarasso (London: Penguin Books, 1969), 194.

morphogeneses: formations and differentiations of tissues and organs.
somatic: relating to the body.
mere: an expanse of standing water.
Freudian-Lacanian: based on the writings of Sigmund Freud (1856–1939) and Jacques Lacan (1901–1981). Freud posited that the human mind repressed unacceptable wishes that were fulfilled symbolically in dreams; Lacan argued that the human sciences were inherently unstable because of humans' own complexity and limitations.
irruption: a rushing in, forcibly or violently.

Understanding the Text

1. According to Cohen, why is it important that our exposure to monsters, whether in books or movies or on television, be temporary?

2. How do monsters represent the "margins" (par. 3)? Explain at least one of the specific examples Cohen uses in his essay.

3. What does Cohen mean by the phrase "beyond the limits of the Thinkable" (par. 9)?

Reflection and Response

4. After running through a description of a typical horror narrative, Cohen states, "The audience knows how the genre works" (par. 2). How much does genre affect the expectations of the audience? In particular regarding monsters, what are those expectations? To what extent does genre limit monsters, and why might this be a good thing?

5. According to Cohen, the monster in some ways represents the expression of the repressed. In other words, it does what we cannot. In your opinion, to what extent do monsters incorporate the forbidden? Cite specific examples.

6. Cohen says that the "simultaneity of anxiety and desire . . . ensures that the monster will always dangerously entice" (par. 7). To what extent are desire and anxiety intertwined in monsters? Aside from monsters, are there other beings or phenomena that make people both desirous and fearful?

Making Connections

7. Cohen states, "The co-optation of the monster into a symbol of the desirable is often accomplished through the neutralization of potentially threatening aspects with a liberal dose of comedy" (par. 5). How do movies in popular culture reflect this tendency? Think, for example, of the Shrek movies (2001, 2004, 2007, 2010), the Teen Wolf movies (1985, 1987), and Young Frankenstein (1974), among others, that use humor to deflect the power of the monster.

8. Cohen cites an example from Queste del Saint Graal (The Quest for the Holy Grail), in which Sir Bors resists sexual temptation by "demons in lascivious disguise" (par. 5). To what extent is sexual desire a part of the allure of monsters? Refer to other monster stories either in this book or from outside research to include specific details in your answer.

From Dracula

Bram Stoker

Bram Stoker was educated at Trinity College in Dublin, where he earned a degree in mathematics in 1870. His work as a theater manager at the Lyceum Theatre in the West End of London, however, initiated a second career in writing, and in 1897 Stoker published *Dracula*. Since then, Count Dracula has been the subject of innumerable film, stage, and literary renditions. In this excerpt, young Jonathan Harker is in Transylvania on legal matters. Against the advice of the count, of whom he is already suspicious, Harker wanders the castle and falls asleep in a room that is not his bedroom. He awakens to find himself the interest of three young ladies, and their attention is simultaneously sexually stimulating and horrifying.

15 May.—Once more have I seen the Count go out in his lizard fashion. He moved downwards in a sidelong way, some hundred feet down, and a good deal to the left. He vanished into some hole or window. When his head had disappeared, I leaned out to try and see more, but without avail—the distance was too great to allow a proper angle of sight. I knew he had left the castle now, and thought to use the opportunity to explore more than I had dared to do as yet. I went back to the room, and taking a lamp, tried all the doors. They were all locked, as I had expected, and the locks were comparatively new; but I went down the stone stairs to the hall where I had entered originally. I found I could pull back the bolts easily enough and unhook the great chains; but the door was locked, and the key was gone! That key must be in the Count's room; I must watch should his door be unlocked, so that I may get it and escape. I went on to make a thorough examination of the various stairs and passages, and to try the doors that opened from them. One or two small rooms near the hall were open, but there was nothing to see in them except old furniture, dusty with age and moth-eaten. At last, however, I found one door at the top of the stairway which, though it seemed to be locked, gave a little under pressure. I tried it harder, and found that it was not really locked, but that the resistance came from the fact that the hinges had fallen somewhat, and the heavy door rested on the floor. Here was an opportunity which I might not have again, so I exerted myself, and with many efforts forced it back so that I could enter. I was now in a wing of the castle further to the right than the rooms I knew and a story lower down. From the windows I could see that the suite of rooms lay along to the south of the castle, the windows of the end room looking out both west and south. On the latter side, as well as to the former, there was a great precipice. The castle was built on the corner of a great rock, so that on three sides it was quite impregnable,° and great windows were placed here where sling, or bow, or culverin° could not reach, and consequently light and comfort, impossible to a position which had to be guarded, were secured. To the west was a great valley, and then, rising far away, great jagged mountain fastnesses, rising peak on peak, the sheer rock studded with mountain ash and thorn, whose roots clung in cracks and crevices and crannies of the stone. This was evidently the portion of the castle occupied by the ladies in bygone days, for the furniture had more air of comfort than any I had seen. The windows were curtainless, and the yellow moonlight, flooding in through the diamond panes, enabled one to see even colors, whilst it softened the wealth of dust which lay over all and disguised in some measure the ravages of time and the moth. My lamp seemed to be of little effect in the brilliant moonlight, but I was glad to have it with me, for there was a dread loneliness in the place which chilled my heart and made my nerves tremble. Still, it was better than living alone in the rooms which I had come to hate from the presence of the Count, and after trying a little to school my nerves, I found a soft quietude come over me. Here I am, sitting at a little oak table where in old times possibly some fair lady sat to pen, with much thought and many blushes, her ill-spelled love-letter, and writing in my diary in shorthand all that has happened since I closed it last. It is nineteenth century up-to-date with a vengeance. And yet, unless my senses deceive me, the old centuries had, and have, powers of their own which mere "modernity" cannot kill.

· · ·

Later: the Morning of 16 May.—God preserve my sanity, or to this I am reduced. Safety and the assurance of safety are things of the past. Whilst I live on here there is but one thing to hope for, that I may not go mad, if, indeed, I be not mad already. If I be sane, then surely it is maddening to think that of all the foul things that lurk in this hateful place the Count is the least dreadful to me; that to him alone I can look for safety, even though this be only whilst I can serve his purpose. Great God! merciful God! Let me be calm, for out of that way lies madness indeed. I

---

impregnable: very strong; not likely to be captured by attack.
culverin: a rude musket or long cannon.

begin to get new lights on certain things which have puzzled me. Up to now I never quite knew what Shakespeare meant when he made Hamlet say:—

> "My tablets! quick, my tablets!
> 'Tis meet that I put it down," etc.,

for now, feeling as though my own brain were unhinged or as if the shock had come which must end in its undoing, I turn to my diary for repose. The habit of entering accurately must help to soothe me.

The Count's mysterious warning frightened me at the time; it frightens me more now when I think of it, for in future he has a fearful hold upon me. I shall fear to doubt what he may say!

When I had written in my diary and had fortunately replaced the book and pen in my pocket I felt sleepy. The Count's warning came into my mind, but I took a pleasure in disobeying it. The sense of sleep was upon me, and with it the obstinacy which sleep brings as outrider.° The soft moonlight soothed, and the wide expanse without gave a sense of freedom which refreshed me. I determined not to return tonight to the gloom-haunted rooms, but to sleep here, where, of old, ladies had sat and sung and lived sweet lives whilst their gentle breasts were sad for their menfolk away in the midst of remorseless wars. I drew a great couch out of its place near the corner, so that as I lay, I could look at the lovely view to east and south, and unthinking of and uncaring for the dust, composed myself for sleep. I suppose I must have fallen asleep; I hope so, but I fear, for all that followed was startlingly real—so real that now sitting here in the broad, full sunlight of the morning, I cannot in the least believe that it was all sleep.

I was not alone. The room was the same, unchanged in any way since 5 I came into it; I could see along the floor, in the brilliant moonlight, my own footsteps marked where I had disturbed the long accumulation of dust. In the moonlight opposite me were three young women, ladies by their dress and manner. I thought at the time that I must be dreaming when I saw them, for, though the moonlight was behind them, they threw no shadow on the floor. They came close to me, and looked at me for some time, and then whispered together. Two were dark, and had high aquiline° noses, like the Count, and great dark, piercing eyes that seemed to be almost red when contrasted with the pale yellow moon.

---

outrider: one who clears the way for another; a forerunner.
aquiline: curving like an eagle's beak.

The other was fair, as fair as can be, with great wavy masses of golden hair and eyes like pale sapphires. I seemed somehow to know her face, and to know it in connection with some dreamy fear, but I could not recollect at the moment how or where. All three had brilliant white teeth that shone like pearls against the ruby of their voluptuous lips. There was something about them that made me uneasy, some longing and at the same time some deadly fear. I felt in my heart a wicked, burning desire that they would kiss me with those red lips. It is not good to note this down, lest some day it should meet Mina's° eyes and cause her pain; but it is the truth. They whispered together, and then they all three laughed—such a silvery, musical laugh, but as hard as though the sound never could have come through the softness of human lips. It was like the intolerable, tingling sweetness of water-glasses when played on by a cunning hand. The fair girl shook her head coquettishly, and the other two urged her on. One said:—

> "I felt in my heart a wicked, burning desire that they would kiss me with those red lips."

"Go on! You are first, and we shall follow; yours is the right to begin." The other added:—

"He is young and strong; there are kisses for us all." I lay quiet, looking out under my eyelashes in an agony of delightful anticipation. The fair girl advanced and bent over me till I could feel the movement of her breath upon me. Sweet it was in one sense, honey-sweet, and sent the same tingling through the nerves as her voice, but with a bitter underlying the sweet, a bitter offensiveness, as one smells in blood.

I was afraid to raise my eyelids, but looked out and saw perfectly under the lashes. The girl went on her knees, and bent over me, simply gloating. There was a deliberate voluptuousness which was both thrilling and repulsive, and as she arched her neck she actually licked her lips like an animal, till I could see in the moonlight the moisture shining on the scarlet lips and on the red tongue as it lapped the white sharp teeth. Lower and lower went her head as the lips went below the range of my mouth and chin and seemed about to fasten on my throat. Then she paused, and I could hear the churning sound of her tongue as it licked her teeth and lips, and could feel the hot breath on my neck. Then the skin of my throat began to tingle as one's flesh does when the hand that is to tickle it approaches nearer—nearer. I could feel the soft, shivering touch of the lips on the super-sensitive skin of my throat, and the hard

Mina: Jonathan Harker's fiancée.

dents of two sharp teeth, just touching and pausing there. I closed my eyes in a languorous° ecstasy and waited—waited with beating heart.

But at that instant, another sensation swept through me as quick as lightning. I was conscious of the presence of the Count, and of his being as if lapped in a storm of fury. As my eyes opened involuntarily I saw his strong hand grasp the slender neck of the fair woman and with giant's power draw it back, the blue eyes transformed with fury, the white teeth champing with rage, and the fair cheeks blazing red with passion. But the Count! Never did I imagine such wrath and fury, even to the demons of the pit. His eyes were positively blazing. The red light in them was lurid, as if the flames of hell-fire blazed behind them. His face was deathly pale, and the lines of it were hard like drawn wires; the thick eyebrows that met over the nose now seemed like a heaving bar of white-hot metal. With a fierce sweep of his arm, he hurled the woman from him, and then motioned to the others, as though he were beating them back; it was the same imperious gesture that I had seen used to the wolves. In a voice which, though low and almost in a whisper seemed to cut through the air and then ring round the room he said:—

"How dare you touch him, any of you? How dare you cast eyes on him 10 when I had forbidden it? Back, I tell you all! This man belongs to me! Beware how you meddle with him, or you'll have to deal with me." The fair girl, with a laugh of ribald coquetry,° turned to answer him:—

"You yourself never loved; you never love!" On this the other women joined, and such a mirthless, hard, soulless laughter rang through the room that it almost made me faint to hear; it seemed like the pleasure of fiends. Then the Count turned, after looking at my face attentively, and said in a soft whisper:—

"Yes, I too can love; you yourselves can tell it from the past. Is it not so? Well, now I promise you that when I am done with him you shall kiss him at your will. Now go! go! I must awaken him, for there is work to be done."

"Are we to have nothing tonight?" said one of them, with a low laugh, as she pointed to the bag which he had thrown upon the floor, and which moved as though there were some living thing within it. For answer he nodded his head. One of the women jumped forward and opened it. If my ears did not deceive me there was a gasp and a low wail, as of a half-smothered child. The women closed round, whilst I was aghast with horror; but as I looked they disappeared, and with them the dreadful

---

languorous: with weakness or weariness.
coquetry: a flirtatious act or attitude.

bag. There was no door near them, and they could not have passed me without my noticing. They simply seemed to fade into the rays of the moonlight and pass out through the window, for I could see outside the dim, shadowy forms for a moment before they entirely faded away.

Then the horror overcame me, and I sank down unconscious. 15

Understanding the Text

1. What observation does Harker make as he passes through the rooms in Count Dracula's castle? What does this say about his character?

2. On the morning of May 16, Harker observes in his diary, "Whilst I live on here there is but one thing to hope for, that I may not go mad, if, indeed, I be not mad already" (par. 2). Why is Harker afraid that he is going insane?

3. Count Dracula, in pushing away the three sisters, says, "This man belongs to me!" (par. 10). In response, they say that he never loved. What do they mean by this?

Reflection and Response

4. Why does Jonathan Harker make so many comments about possible past inhabitants of Count Dracula's castle? How does alluding to the past instead of finding comfort in "modernity" (par. 1) provide him with a sense of normalcy in a place that seems anything but normal?

5. Harker comments that writing in his diary "must help to soothe me" (par. 2). How can the act of writing be therapeutic, especially given the horrific events he encounters?

6. When Harker becomes aware of the sisters, his feelings are conflicted. At one point, he comments, "There was something about them that made me uneasy, some longing and at the same time some deadly fear" (par. 5). How are sexual desire and danger intermingled in this passage? What is the basis of his contradictory feelings?

Making Connections

7. How does this selection compare with movie or television versions of *Dracula* you have seen? Be specific in your answer.

8. Read John Polidori's *Vampyre* (free reproductions are available online). How is Polidori's version of the vampire different from Stoker's, and what do these differences reveal?

9. Compare Stoker's female vampires with the female vampires in Neil Jordan's movie *Byzantium*, as described in Declan McGrath's "Life among the Undead: An Interview with Neil Jordan" (p. 221). How do their differences reflect changes in attitudes toward the role of women in society from the nineteenth century to today?

Sexuality and the Vampire

J. Gordon Melton

J. Gordon Melton is a religious studies specialist at the University of California, Santa Barbara. He has published more than thirty-five books and numerous articles and also coedited the second edition of *Religions of the World: A Comprehensive Encyclopedia of Belief and Practice* (2010). In this excerpt from *The Vampire Book: The Encyclopedia of the Undead* (originally published in 1998), Melton investigates how vampires have appeared as sexual creatures since Bram Stoker's *Dracula* was published in 1897. He covers not only literary but also movie and stage versions of vampires. In particular, he focuses on the evolution of vampires as sexual beings, detailing their progression from monsters to romantic heroes.

Essential to understanding the appeal of the vampire is its sexual nature. While it frequently has been pointed out that traditional vampires cannot engage in "normal" sexual activity, the vampire is not necessarily asexual. As twentieth-century scholars turned their attention to the vampire, both in folklore and literature, underlying sexual themes quickly became evident. The sexual nature of vampirism formed an underlying theme in *Dracula*, but it was disguised in such a way that it was hidden from the literary censors of the day, the consciousness of the public, and probably from the awareness (as many critics argued) of author Bram Stoker himself. Carol Fry, for example, suggested that vampirism was in fact a form of "surrogate sexual intercourse."

Sexuality in *Dracula*

The sexual nature of vampirism manifested initially in *Dracula* during Jonathan Harker's encounter with the three vampire brides residing in Castle Dracula. Harker confronted them as extremely appealing sex objects but who embody an element of danger. Harker noted, "I felt in my heart a wicked, burning desire that they would kiss me with their red lips" (chapter 3). Stoker went on to describe the three as sensual predators and their vampire's bite as a kiss. One of the women anticipated the object of their desire. "He is young and strong; there are kisses for us all." And as they approached, Harker waited in delightful anticipation.

Attention in the novel then switched to the two "good" women, Lucy Westenra and Mina Murray. Lucy, as the subject of the attention of three men, reveled in their obvious desire of her before she chose Arthur

Holmwood, the future Lord Godalming, as her betrothed. Mina, to the contrary, was in love with Jonathan and pined in loneliness while he was lost in the wilds of Transylvania. While preparing for her wedding, however, Lucy was distracted by the presence of Dracula. While on a seaside vacation in Whitby, Lucy began sleepwalking. One evening, Lucy was discovered by Mina in her nightclothes across the river. As Mina approached, she could see a figure bending over Lucy. Dracula left as Mina approached, but she found Lucy with her lips parted and breathing heavily. Thus began Lucy's slow transformation from the virtuous and proper, if somewhat frivolous, young lady, into what Judith Weissman termed a "sexual monster." By day she was faint and listless, but by night she took on a most unladylike voluptuousness. Shortly before her death, she asked Arthur to kiss her, and when he leaned toward her, she attempted to bite him.

Stoker's understanding, however unconscious, of the sexual nature of the vampiric attack became most clear in the blood transfusions that were given to Lucy in the attempt to save her life. Arthur, who never was able to consummate his love for Lucy, suggested that in the sharing of blood he had, in the eyes of God, married her. The older and wiser Abraham Van Helsing rejected the idea, given the sexual connotation for himself and the others who also gave her blood. But by this time, the sexual interest of Dracula in women was firmly established and led directly to the most sexual scene in the book.

Having given Lucy her peace (and, by implication, returned her virtue) in the act of staking and decapitating her, the men called together by Van Helsing to rid the world of Dracula, were slow to awaken to his real target—Mina. When they finally became aware of this, they rushed to Mina's bedroom. There, they found Dracula sitting on her bed forcing her to drink from a cut on his chest. Dracula turned angrily to those who had interrupted him. "His eyes flamed red with devilish passion. . . ." Once Dracula was driven away and Mina came to her senses, she realized that she had been violated. She declared herself unclean and vowed that she would "kiss" her husband no more. 5

The Sexual Vampire of Folklore

While there is little evidence that Stoker was intimately aware of eastern European vampire lore, he could have found considerable evidence of the vampire's sexual nature—particularly in the folklore of the Gypsies and their neighbors, the southern Slavs. For example, corpses dug up as suspected vampires occasionally were reported to have an erection. Gypsies thought of the vampire as a sexual entity. The male vampire was believed to have such an intense sexual drive that his sexual need alone was sufficient to bring him back from the grave. His first act usually was a return to his widow, whom he engaged in sexual intercourse. Nightly visits could ensue and continue over a period of time, with the wife becoming exhausted and emaciated. In more than a few cases, the widow was known to become pregnant and bear a child by her vampire husband. The resulting child, called a *dhampir*, was a highly valued personage deemed to have unusual powers to diagnose vampirism and to destroy vampires attacking the community.

> "The male vampire was believed to have such an intense sexual drive that his sexual need alone was sufficient to bring him back from the grave."

In some cases the vampire would return to a woman with whom he had been in love, but with whom he had never consummated that love. The woman would then be invited to return with him to the grave where they could share their love through eternity. The idea of the dead returning to claim a living lover was a popular topic in European folklore. By far the most famous literary piece illustrating the theme was Gottfried August Bürger's ballad "Lenore," known in English by Sir Walter Scott's translation.

The folklore of Russia also described the vampire as a sexual being. Among the ways in which it made itself known was to appear in a village as a handsome young stranger. Circulating among the young people in the evening, the vampire lured unsuspecting women to their doom. Russian admonitions for young people to listen to their elders and stay close to home are reminiscent of the ancient Greek story of Apollonius, who saved one of his students from the allure of the *lamiai*, whom he was about to marry.

The *langsuyar* of Malaysia was also a sexual being. A female vampire, she was often pictured as a desirable young woman who could marry and bear children. *Langsuyars* were believed to be able to live somewhat normally in a village for many years, revealed only by their inadvertent involvement in an activity that disclosed their identity.

The Modern Literary Vampire

While overt sexual activity was not present in *Dracula*, sexual themes were manifest in the vampire literature of the previous century. The original vampire poem written by Goethe, "The Bride of Corinth," drew upon the story from ancient Greece concerning a young woman who had died a virgin. She returned from the dead to her parents' home to have sexual experiences with a young man staying temporarily in the guest room. The strong sexual relationship at the heart of Samuel Taylor Coleridge's "Christabel" was expanded in "Carmilla," the popular vampire story by Sheridan Le Fanu.

In the story, Carmilla Karnstein moved into the castle home of Laura, her proposed victim. She did not immediately attack Laura, but proceeded to build a relationship more befitting a lover. Laura experienced the same positive and negative feelings that Harker had felt toward the three women in Castle Dracula. As she put it:

Now the truth is, I felt unaccountably toward the beautiful stranger. I did feel, as she said, "drawn towards her," but there was also something of repulsion. In this ambiguous feeling, however, the sense of attraction immensely prevailed. She interested and won me; she was so beautiful and so indescribably engaging.

Carmilla went about her assault upon Laura while seducing her cooperation. She would draw Laura to her with pretty words and embraces and gently press her lips to Laura's cheek. She would take Laura's hand while at the same time locking her gaze on her eyes and breathing with such passion that it embarrassed the naive Laura. So attracted was Laura to Carmilla, that only slowly did she come to the realization that her lovely friend was a vampire.

The Sensuous Vampire on Stage and Screen

Carol Fry, author of the article "Fictional Conventions and Sexuality in *Dracula*," has properly pointed out that Dracula was in part a stereotypical character of popular nineteenth-century literature, the rake.° The rake appeared in stories to torment and distress the pure women of proper society. The rake was to some extent the male counterpart of the vamp;° however, the consequences of falling victim to a seductive male were far more serious for a woman than they were for a man victimized by a seductive woman. The man who loved and left was thought to have left behind a tainted woman. Just as a state of "moral depravity" contaminated the fallen woman, so vampirism infected the one bitten. The vampire's victim became like him and preyed on others. The fallen

---

rake: a dissolute person; a libertine; a person of low moral standards.
vamp: a woman who uses her charm or wiles to seduce and exploit men.

Christopher Lee's Count Dracula represented a stronger sexual appeal in *Taste the Blood of Dracula* (1970).
© Photos 12/Alamy

woman might become a vamp, professional or not, who in turn led men to engage in her immoral ways.

Once brought to the stage, Dracula's rakish nature was heightened. No longer hovering in the background as in the novel, he was invited into the living rooms of his intended victims. In this seemingly safe setting, he went about his nefarious business, though what he actually did had to be construed from the dialogue of those who would kill him. Only after the play was brought to the screen, and the public reacted to Bela Lugosi, did some understanding of the romantic appeal of this supposed monster become evident to a widespread audience. However, not until the 1950s would the vampire, in the person of Christopher Lee's Dracula, be given a set of fangs and allowed to bite his victims on screen.

Interestingly, the obvious sexuality of the vampire was first portrayed   15 on screen by a female vampire. In retrospect, the scene in *Dracula's Daughter* (1936) in which the female vampire seduced the young model was far more charged with sexuality than any played by Lugosi. A quarter of a century later, Roger Vadim brought an overtly sensual vampire to the screen in his version of "Carmilla," *Blood and Roses* (1960). In 1967 French director Jean Rollin produced the first of a series of semi-pornographic features, *Le Viol du Vampire* (released in English as *The Vampire's Rape*). The story centered around two women who believed that they were cursed by a vampire to follow his bloodsucking life. The sexuality of "Carmilla" was even more graphically pictured in *The Vampire Lovers*, Hammer Films' 1970 production, in which the unclad Carmilla and Laura romped freely around their bedroom.

From these and similar early soft-core productions, two quite different sets of vampire films developed. On the one hand were pornographic vampire films that featured nudity and sex. Among the earliest was *Dracula (The Dirty Old Man)* (1969), in which Count Alucard kidnapped naked virgins to fulfill his sexual and vampiric needs. Spanish director Jesus Franco produced *La Countess aux Seins Nus* (1973) (released in video in the United States as *Erotikill*), in which Countess Irena Karnstein (a character derived from Carmilla) killed her victims in an act of fellatio. (These scenes were cut from the American version.) The trend toward pornographic vampire movies culminated in 1979 with *Dracula Sucks* (also released as *Lust at First Bite*), a remake of *Dracula*, that closely followed the 1931 movie. It starred Jamie Gillis as Dracula. More recent sexually explicit vampire movies include *Dracula Exotica* (1981), also starring Gillis; *Gayracula* (1983), a homosexual film; *Sexandroide* (1987); *Out for Blood* (1990); *Princess of the Night* (1990); and *Wanda Does Transylvania* (1990). Most of these were shot in both hard-core and soft-core versions.

The Vampire in Love

The pornographic vampire movies were relatively few in number and poorly distributed. Of far more importance in redefining the contemporary vampire were the novels and films that transformed the evil monster of previous generations into a romantic lover. The new vampire hero owed much to Chelsea Quinn Yarbro's St. Germain. In a series of novels beginning with *Hotel Transylvania* (1978), St. Germain emerged not as a monster, but as a man of moral worth, extraordinary intellect, and captivating sensuality. He even occasionally fell in love. He was unable to have ordinary sexual relations because he could not have an erection. However, his bite conveyed an intense experience of sexual bliss that women found to be a more than adequate alternative.

At the time Yarbro was finishing *Hotel Transylvania*, a new stage production of *Dracula, The Vampire Play in Three Acts* had become a hit on

Broadway. The play was the first dramatic production of *Dracula* to rein-troduce the scene in which Dracula forced Mina to drink from his blood. The scene, a rapelike experience in the novel, had been transformed into one of seduction. In 1979 the larger populace was introduced to this more sensual Dracula when Frank Langella re-created his stage role for the motion picture screen. He presented Dracula as not only a suave for-eign nobleman, but as a debonair, attractive male who drew his victims to him by the sheer power of his sexual presence. The scenes in which Lucy, over the objections of her elders, rushed to Carfax to join her lover and drink his blood completed a transformation of Dracula from mere monster into a hero who lived up to the movie's billing: "Throughout history he has filled the hearts of men with *terror*, and the hearts of women with *desire*."

Langella's Dracula directly informed the more recent production of *Bram Stoker's Dracula* under the writing and direction of Francis Ford Coppola. Coppola not only brought the vampire into proper society but turned him into a handsome young man who, with his money and for-eign elegance, was able to seduce the betrothed Mina from her wimpish fiancé. He returned the final blood drinking scene to her bedroom, re-vealed Dracula at his most human, and made their lovemaking the sen-sual climax of the movie's love story subplot, which Coppola had added to explain Dracula's otherwise irrational acts against the British family he had assaulted.

The transformation of the vampire into a hero lover was a primary 20 element in the overall permeation of the vampire myth into the culture of late-twentieth-century America (which included the emergence of the vampire in humor and the vampire as moral example). As such, the con-temporary vampire has had to deal with a variety of sexual patterns. Television detective Nick Knight developed an ongoing relationship with a researcher who was trying to cure him. Mara McCuniff, the centuries-old vampire of Traci Briery's *The Vampire Memoirs*, was overtaken by her sexual urges for three days each month at the time of the full moon. In *Domination*, Michael Cecilone placed his vampires in the world of sado-masochism. Lori Herter's romance novels elevated the vampire as the object of female fantasies.

The response to the conscious development of the vampire as a sexual being has almost guaranteed future exploration in fictional works. *Prisoners of the Night*, a periodical of vampire fiction that appears annu-ally, has focused on sexuality in several issues. Editor Mary Ann B. McKinnon has added an impetus to exploring the theme in her fanzine, *Good Guys Wear Fangs*, which covers good-guy vampires, most of them romantic heroes. Such sexualizing of the vampire, while departing from the common image of the vampire as mere monster, has not been foreign to the creature itself. From the beginning, a seductive sexuality has existed as an element of the literary vampire, comingling with that of the monstrous, and goes far to explain the vampire's appeal relative to its monstrous cousins.

Sources

Fry, Carol L. "Fictional Conventions and Sexuality in *Dracula.*" *The Victorian Newsletter* 42 (1972): 20–22.

Weissman, Judith. *Half Savage and Hardy and Free: Women and Rural Radicalism in the Nineteenth-Century Novel.* Middletown, CT: Wesleyan University Press, 1987. 342 pp.

Understanding the Text

1. What are the different attitudes projected by Lucy Westenra and Mina Murray, as Melton describes them? How do those attitudes prefigure the women's ultimate fates?

2. Melton cites Judith Weissman as calling Lucy a "sexual monster" (par. 3). What does Weissman mean by this?

3. How does Melton establish the premise that the vampire is a sexual creature? What examples, apart from Bram Stoker's *Dracula*, does he present?

Reflection and Response

4. Why did the vampire monster legend provide a useful framework for talking about homosexual experiences, such as in "Carmilla" by Sheridan Le Fanu? Why does vampirism lend itself to the exploration of sexuality?

5. How are blood, love, and sex connected in the vampire myth? Cite specific examples.

Making Connections

6. Melton's book appeared before Stephenie Meyer's Twilight series was published. How does Melton's argument reveal that the groundwork for Meyer's Edward Cullen, the romantic hero/vampire, was laid by other authors and filmmakers?

7. Melton states that many early vampires were female. Indeed, Bram Stoker's *Dracula* features three female vampires who are subordinate to Count Dracula. The selection presents other examples of female vampires as well, such as Carmilla, who undertakes a slow seduction of Laura. Research the female vampire—in the far past, the near past, and the present—and argue why the male vampire has largely usurped the female vampire in literature and film.

8. Melton states, "From the beginning, a seductive sexuality has existed as an element of the literary vampire, comingling with that of the monstrous, and goes far to explain the vampire's appeal relative to its monstrous cousins" (par. 21). Investigate what other monsters have sexual appeal. What is the basis of their appeal, and how does that appeal differ from that of the vampire?

(Un)safe Sex: Romancing the Vampire

Karen Backstein

With a Ph.D. in cinematic studies from New York University, Karen Backstein has written on film and dance in both academic journals and popular magazines. Her book credits include several children's books, including *The Blind Men and the Elephant* (1992) and *Little Chick's Easter Surprise*

(1993). This article initially appeared in *Cineaste*, a magazine that covers the art and politics of the cinema. Backstein argues that newer vampire stories, such as the Twilight series and *True Blood*, have altered the traditional sexual dynamic of the vampire narrative. In the past, the vampire combined sexual allure and evil, emphasizing that the woman who is the target of the vampire's desires needs to remain chaste. Now the vampire is a romantic hero who protects the female protagonist from evil humans as well as other vampires, and sexual energy between vampire and human abounds. The woman is no longer the passive, chaste object of desire, but an active, sexually aware force of her own.

In the horror universe, the popularity of vampires never seems to die. This makes sense: forever young and beautiful, they are, as *Twilight*'s Edward Cullen points out to his inamorata,° Bella, specifically designed to be irresistible to humans. But if the greatest (and most filmed) of literary bloodsuckers, Count Dracula, served as a warning about what would happen to the pure Victorian woman who succumbed to the lure of the mercurial° and seductive man, the contemporary vampire often is a very different figure altogether. Just as the eternally living creature within the narrative must adapt to the passing centuries in dress and manner, the fictional construction of the protagonist has had to shift in order to survive as a meaningful symbol for audiences with modern sensibilities.

Across every medium, from books to films to television, today's vampire—at least, that particular type of vampire who serves as the narrative's male lead and the heroine's love interest—has transformed into an alluring combination of danger and sensitivity, a handsome romantic hero haunted by his lust for blood and his guilt for the humans he killed in the past. No bats, no capes, and perhaps just a touch of white pallor to provide a whiff of the grave (the black vampire remains a rarity in mainstream texts)—and so much the better if he shimmers in the manner of

---

inamorata: a woman whom one loves.
mercurial: being eloquent or ingenious.

Twilight's Edward and resembles an Armani model. He's often courtly, too, in the fashion of another age—the age, in fact, when he was born and lived as a human before "being made." At the same time, the vampire's power can never be underestimated: the very notion of "devouring" and "eating" someone is redolent° of sex (and, in some cases, rape), and he could have what he wants for the taking. "When we taste human blood," Edward hesitatingly says, "a sort of frenzy begins."

But he has now become too evolved and moral to engage in that frenzy: "I don't want to be a monster." In part, the modern vampire story is one about self-control, about man struggling to master his worst impulses—perhaps even his essential nature—through whatever means necessary, be it with synthetic substances (*True Blood*) or by finding other sources of food (*Twilight*). In an almost Victorian ethos, this "civilizing impulse" is strengthened by the arrival of the heroine, who cements the vampire's determination not to succumb to his bloodthirst. To further stress the point, a "bad vampire" usually throws the hero's chivalrousness into relief: *Twilight's* vicious and murderous tracker James contrasts with Edward, while *True Blood* juxtaposes the gentlemanly Bill Compton with the imperious and manipulative (but equally sexy) Eric Northman, *The Vampire Diaries* has two divergent brothers, and Buffy had Angel and Spike.

But the complex qualities of the hero—his mix of sex and sensibility—is not the only reason women seem to have such an insatiable appetite for vampires today; another attraction may be the point of view these texts adopt. They are female-centered narratives that strive for audience identification with the heroine—with her strength, her extraordinary capabilities, her status as an object of desire, or a combination of all these traits. She is the focus of the story, whether she's narrating it (*Twilight*) or the active visual center of the screen image (*Buffy the Vampire Slayer, True Blood*).

Apart from the pioneering works of Anne Rice (who a while ago set 5 aside Lestat and company in favor of Jesus, anyway), many of these modern vampire narratives have been directed primarily to teen females and spotlight young heroines—perhaps all the better to stand out against their centuries-old paramours. *Twilight, True Blood*, and *The Vampire Diaries*, to name but a few, all have their origins in young adult novels aimed specifically at girls. They then crossed over to capture a huge audience of older women, who lapped up their Gothic atmosphere, dreamy heroes, and romantic focus. *True Blood*, in particular, is pure Southern

---

redolent: suggestive.

Gothic that moved into adult mode in its TV incarnation, with its graphic sex scenes and its use of the vampire to signify "the Other." Imagining a world where an artificial blood allows vampires to live among us without feeding, the series plays with the idea of "interspecies mixing" as miscegenation—a metaphor that encompasses sexual fear and potency, as well as a social critique. Vampire Bill Compton is literally a refugee from the Civil War, when he was brought over, and the credits feature assorted images from the Old South, including a Klansman.

Despite their dissimilarities, and varied approaches to the construction of vampire life and rules, all these supernatural stories are driven largely by female desire and the female voice. The virginal Victorian ladies of *Dracula* may have needed Jonathan Harker to tell their tale; no longer. Ever since *Buffy the Vampire Slayer* came on the scene, the ladies have spoken for themselves. This is not to say that vampire narratives are necessarily feminist. Their degree of girl power varies, with Buffy perhaps the strongest, rarely in need of rescue and able to slay multiple neck biters with a single kick and knife thrust—and master them romantically, too. (A point wittily made in a fan-created viral video that juxtaposed shots of Buffy at her fiercest with images of a dreamy, clearly smitten, and physically passive Edward from *Twilight*. Rolling her eyes at his persistent advances, the Buffster resisted his charms and killed.) Like Buffy, singled out among all girls as the one in her generation to be the Slayer, Sookie in *True Blood* is not quite human; possessing extra-normal skills (including the ability to read minds and a strange kind of electrical energy that sometimes flows from her hands), she sidesteps the many lures that drag down her fellow townsfolk, family, and friends.

But no heroine, and no relationship, seems to have enthralled female readers and spectators like that of Bella and Edward in the *Twilight* saga. Unlike much in the horror genre, *Twilight*—both the book and the film—is the product of women: novelist Stephenie Meyer, screenwriter Melissa Rosenberg, and director Catherine Hardwicke. (Hardwicke was replaced by Chris Weitz for the sequel, *New Moon*, a more male-focused and presumably more action-centered narrative in which Bella cedes some of the spotlight to the Native American character Jacob, a werewolf. The removal of Hardwicke is particularly fascinating for Hollywood watchers given the box-office success of *Twilight*—over $70 million the first weekend—as compared to the critical and financial disaster that was Weitz's *Golden Compass*.) It would be impossible to overestimate the popularity of the novels. At a time when the publishing industry is collapsing, sales of Meyer's books played a huge role in ensuring the financial health of Little, Brown, *Twilight*'s publishing house. As was the

In *Twilight* (2008), Bella Swan (Kristen Stewart) falls for fellow student Edward Cullen (Robert Pattinson), who, since he's a vampire, is truly a boyfriend to die for.
© AF archive/Alamy

case when the final *Harry Potter* tome came out, bookstores stayed open at midnight on its release day, hosting parties to draw in readers eager to get their hands on the next installment as soon as possible. When casting for the movie adaptation was announced, its unknown leads became instant celebrities, and the film not unexpectedly was a blockbuster, too. Despite the fact that *Twilight* is remarkably poorly written and astonishingly repetitive, clearly Meyer has her finger on the pulse of young female America.

Twilight tells the story of Bella Swan, a teenager who reluctantly leaves her home in sunny Phoenix to come to the gray and rainy climes of Forks, Washington, where her father is sheriff. The move is nothing less than a sacrifice, prompted by her mother's remarriage; Bella generously gives her mom the space, time, and freedom to travel with her new husband as he pursues his career. Almost immediately upon her arrival, however, Bella, formerly an outsider, finds herself the center of attention at school, with a group of friends and plenty of male interest. But her eye is drawn irresistibly to Edward Cullen and his four sisters and brothers, all startlingly beautiful and supremely standoffish. Bella is shocked when

BACKSTEIN (Un)safe Sex: Romancing the Vampire **215**

Edward initially reacts to her presence with pure, overt hostility. The truth will out, however, when she discovers that his coldness was just a ploy: he is so deeply drawn to her, and so scared he might harm her in the throes of passion, that he tried to resist his feelings. For Edward and his entire family are vampires—albeit vampires who wish to live peacefully with humans—and this love appears to be star-crossed. Bella and Edward's relationship grows ever more passionate, but always with Edward attempting to make Bella feel a healthy sense of fear at what he is. The true danger, however, comes in the form of a different group of neck biters, including a "tracker" who hunts down humans forever until he catches the prey he wants. And he wants Bella.

Why have female audiences of all ages so embraced the series, both on the page and on screen? Why, like the character of Edward Cullen himself, has it proven so irresistible? And how do both hero and heroine differ from their vampire/human counterparts—and what do those differences mean? First, although vampire stories generally fall within horror—and *Twilight* has its share of blood and violence—in many ways it has just as much in common with the romance novel, except with a paranormal twist. Other than his fondness for the taste of blood, Edward is the perfect dark, brooding, romantic hero; tormented by his past and so protective of the woman he loves that he willingly pushes her away for her own good. Only, he happens to have extra vampire powers to help him safeguard the woman better—and to make him even more compelling to viewers.

As with any romantic hero, Edward's worth has to be established within the narrative, which measures him against both vampire and man (and eventually werewolf) in order to validate him as a singular figure and force in any world. On the human side are Bella's male schoolmates, almost all with a crush on her, and all boyish and immature in contrast to Edward (who of course is many years older than them). Sweet and welcoming, into sports and the prom, they represent a normalcy Edward can never have; they also are roundly rejected as boyfriend material by Bella, who gently guides them instead to more appropriate girls.

Also human are the men who try to rape Bella one evening in town; in the book, which is actually scarier than the film's depiction of it, they slyly "herd" a lost Bella to an abandoned cul-de-sac where she has no hope of escape. In the movie, Bella first glimpses two young men at the end of an alleyway after she emerges from a bookstore at night; apprehensively, she heads in the opposite direction, but the pair chase her to a clearing. There, they and a group of drunken friends surround and menace her; as the camera turns slowly around the leering circle of men, a series of nervous jump cuts follows the tormentors' movements as they close in on Bella. Just as she finally tries to defend herself, Edward zooms up in his car, wheels squealing, to act as her savior. The implication is clear: not all dangers come from the paranormal. That the scene is lit to have the same gray-green mistiness as ones featuring several vampire-caused murders further links the human and the undead.

Additionally, this almost-rape by flesh-and-blood males acts [as] a mirror image to James's even more sadistic abduction of Bella, both in its elaborate entrapment and Edward's rescue operation. Both these sequences stand out in this otherwise romantic movie for their terror, explicit threat to Bella's body, and dependence on male physical violence. After luring Bella in, James presses up against her stroking her hair, adding a sexual element to the kidnapping. Unlike the earlier sequence, a long time elapses before Edward arrives and the brutalization is visualized. When Bella tries to escape, James flies to intercept her, using techniques familiar to fans of martial arts films. The surface grace of his airborne trajectory contrasts with Bella's body, which goes into flight in a different way: by being thrown. The crack of her "fragile little human" bones is audible. And James films it all to torment Edward, in what is one of *Twilight*'s several interesting and negative references to still and movie cameras in relation to women.

> "While the vampire, in almost every artistic incarnation, symbolizes impossible desire and transgressed boundaries—the romantic idea that sex = death—. . . *Twilight*'s operative equation is love = death."

While the vampire, in almost every artistic incarnation, symbolizes impossible desire and transgressed boundaries—the romantic idea that sex = death—*Twilight* shifts the paradigm in interesting ways. *Twilight*'s operative equation is love = death, which Bella reaffirms in a voice-over at the start, a ghostly reference to a later point in the story when she expects to die. The gentlemanly Edward not only refuses sex because of the danger to Bella, he also swoops in to pluck her out of sexually threatening situations. In fact, as we've seen, whenever someone in *Twilight* does want sex, or cannot control his desires, he is evil. *Twilight* makes an argument for abstemious love, no surprise given that the story sprung from the pen of a Mormon writer. In a day when the romance novel is packed with explicit semipornographic depictions of bedroom activities far beyond the old-fashioned bodice ripper, *Twilight* harks back to a time when sexual attraction was implied, not acted upon. In this regard, Bella stands apart from such heroines as Buffy and Sookie who consummate both human and vampire relationships. There is perhaps a touch of Heath-cliff and Catherine° in Edward and Bella, an affirmation of a powerful love that transcends the limits of human life. For young readers especially, there may be a kind of safety in a story that steers clear of perilous sexual territory and that suggests gazing into one another's eyes and holding hands are the most sublime joys.

At the same time, however, the narrative is packed with sexual substitutes, so the vampire retains his potency even if he pulls back. It is always clear that when the time comes (and it does, in later novels) that sex is permissible, he will be the perfect lover. Perhaps the book, a little more than the film, overtly emphasizes the power of Edward's vampiric touch and kiss, which induces an almost orgasmic reaction in Bella (who faints). Nonetheless, the film finds its stand-in for Meyer's intricately physical descriptions in a soaringly romantic cinematic style. Manipulation of motion becomes one of the movie's hallmarks, a slowing down or hastening of time, most notably to capture Edward's vampire superspeed, but also to indicate perceptual awareness, self-consciousness, and even grace. In lengthy wordless and lushly scored sequences, cameras circle the Pacific Northwest landscape from up high, flying with Bella and Edward as he carries her up trees and cliffs, or looking down upon them lying in the grass. His near-magical powers, and his speed, his ability to bring her into a different world, imply sexuality, skill, and thrill, enhanced by the vertiginous° patterns traced by the cinematography. And a large percentage of the audience comes armed with a knowledge of the written text, which will influence their reading of the cinematic images.

Twilight the novel is told almost exclusively from Bella's perspective, which the film to some extent replicates, through her voice-overs placed throughout, as well as through the use of point of view. It is Bella who first sees the Cullens, through the slats of the school windows, moving in graceful slow motion, outdoor light falling on them. "Who is that?" she asks. Edward's glance only later meets her originating gaze; with him, she is rarely the "looked at," but the one doing the looking or an equal in an exchange of glances—except at night, when Edward sneaks in simply to watch her sleep. (But we only see that when she wakes suddenly and catches him, so we never share his point of view of her vulnerable body.) And not only does the camerawork emphasize Edward as visual object through lingering shots, but actor Robert Pattinson, a former model, assumes the photographic poses and runway walks of a

15

Heathcliff and Catherine: the tormented lovers in Emily Brontë's *Wuthering Heights* (1847).
vertiginous: causing or likely to cause a feeling of dizziness.

self-aware performer. Even when we know he is looking at her because of an eyeline match, he stays the visual object for the audience. The usual paradigm of female viewed/male viewer has shifted thoroughly, especially as Bella makes clear how much she despises being the center of attention when under the curious stares of her fellow students.

In one of the most telling scenes, students mill about in front of the school and Angela, a photographer and Bella's friend, aims her camera at something we cannot see; "Oh my God," she exclaims, lowering it, and we cut to a classy sports car from which Bella and Edward emerge. Pattinson plays it with the enigmatic smile of a model or movie star on the red carpet who knows all eyes are on him. "Well, everyone's staring," [actress Kristen] Stewart's unsmiling Bella points out, and we cut to her point of view. As the camera moves forward into the crowd, the scene alternates between normal and slow motion as if emphasizing the sense of unreality Bella feels.

In fact, Bella is defined through scent more than look, a more difficult quality to convey visually, hence the constant verbal allusions to her smell. But when she walks into her science classroom—where she will be seated next to Edward—she steps in front of a fan, again as slowly as the Cullens strode into the lunchroom where Bella first glimpsed them. The wind ruffles her hair, and the film cuts to Edward as the paper on the desk in front of him sharply blows as her *bella aroma* reaches his nose. His body quivers and his hand reaches up to cover his nose and face. When the scene cuts back to Bella, still standing in front of the room, her smile fades. This scene repeats, to more ominous effect, when the wind blows through her hair when James and his more vicious vampires meet Bella; hiding among Edward's family, the breeze alerts him to a human presence.

The vampire's effect on his victim has always been one of transformation, but a negative one: the draining of blood, the draining of energy, the draining of life. *Twilight*, unlike its predecessors, tells a story of transformation in a more positive sense. While it has elements of horror, particularly near the end with James's attack, it more closely resembles a fairy tale—Bella and the Beast, if you will, with elements of Cinderella. At the start of the story, Bella comes to the town of Forks without ever having had a boyfriend, and indeed having had few friends at all. But in this new territory, she turns into the central object of desire for every man, and finds her "beast" who is really a prince in disguise. Like a fairy-tale heroine, her qualities are innate, not just the beauty that's de rigueur,° but even her smell, which shocks Edward into submission and draws the

---

de rigueur: required by fashion, etiquette, or custom; proper.

deadly attention of James. And, as in a fairy tale, all females are secondary to her: helpmates whose own interior lives remain obscure.

Given this generic shift, it is logical that the vampire hero is moved out of the night and into the light, not just able to see the sun but also to sparkle brilliantly in it. *Twilight*, as a film, rejects Expressionist or neo-*noir* style: it is not a film of jagged angles or darkness, but of fog and the mossy, hazy green of the Northwestern forest. Water, mountains, and majestic trees form the backdrop for Bella and Edward's intimate talks, substituting for the moors that Heathcliff and Cathy wandered. The vampires have homes, not coffins, and because they are not limited to sundown, the night is no more threatening than the day. Bella, though a figure who can articulate her desire, becomes an object in need of protection, this time by the vampire rather than from him. Edward rescues his princess from careening cars, a roving band of human rapists, and a vampire who hunts his prey without cease. Ultimately, what Edward would most like to save her from is himself, the one task where he cannot succeed.

Understanding the Text

1. How does the character of Edward Cullen from the Twilight series differ from more traditional portrayals of vampires, particularly Count Dracula?

2. Backstein argues that the new vampire stories are "driven largely by female desire and female voice." What evidence does she give to support this statement?

3. In discussing *Twilight*, Backstein focuses on Bella's scent. How does scent work in terms of making Bella an object of desire for Edward, as well as the prey hunted by James?

Reflection and Response

4. Backstein makes much of the physical attractiveness of Robert Pattinson, the actor who plays Edward Cullen in the Twilight movies. How does this support her argument that the new vampire stories have more in common with romance novels than with horror stories?

5. Backstein argues that the vampire story has always been a story of "transformation" (par. 18). How and why has the transformation changed from the days of Bram Stoker and older movie versions of *Dracula* to contemporary images of vampires as presented in *Twilight*, *Buffy the Vampire Slayer*, *True Blood*, and other stories?

6. In analyzing the scene where Edward saves Bella from the gang of potential rapists, Backstein writes, "The implication is clear: not all dangers come from the paranormal" (par. 11). What do you make of this statement? What does this scene say about humanity?

Making Connections

7. Compare the Twilight movies with *Interview with the Vampire*, a movie based on the books by Anne Rice. The movie features Brad Pitt, Tom Cruise, and Antonio Banderas at the peak of their physical attractiveness. How do their good looks function to create horror in the film? Contrast that with Pattinson's portrayal of Edward Cullen. How does his role function in relation to Backstein's argument that in the old-fashioned vampire story "sex = death," but in *Twilight* the equation is "love = death" (par. 13)?

8. In Bram Stoker's *Dracula* (p. 196), the male hero, Jonathan Harker, is surrounded one evening by three female vampires who inspire in him "some longing and at the same time some deadly fear." How has Stephenie Meyer kept the longing and lost the fear in her Twilight series?

9. In the nineteenth century, when Bram Stoker was writing *Dracula*, repression of sexuality was the norm. How are modern changes in morality and sexual expression in other aspects of life—including the entertainment world—reflected in the newer portrayals of "bad boys" and vampires, as seen in *Twilight*, *Buffy the Vampire Slayer*, *True Blood*, *The Vampire Diaries*, and other stories?

Life among the Undead: An Interview with Neil Jordan

Declan McGrath

Mother-daughter relationships can be difficult. In the movie *Byzantium* (2012), Eleanor appears to be a lonely, outcast teenager whose mother, Clara, works as the madam at a brothel. But what could be a teenage melodrama has an important twist: both mother and daughter have been vampires for more than two hundred years. Clara is full of joy and kills with a pleasure that is virtually sexual. Eleanor disapproves of her mother; she kills only people who are already very old and wish to die. Their conflict is set in two time frames—the present and the early 1800s. In this interview, director Neil Jordan discusses the convention of having female leads who are not victims of monsters, but rather the monsters themselves. Jordan is also the director of *The Crying Game* (1992), *Interview with the Vampire* (1994), and *The End of the Affair* (2002), among many other movies. He most recently created, wrote, and frequently directed the television show *The Borgias* (2011–2013). Declan McGrath is a frequent contributor to *Cineaste*, a magazine that covers the art and politics of the cinema, from which this selection is taken.

Neil Jordan's *Byzantium* is so full of preoccupations that feature regularly throughout his thirty-year career as a prose writer and film director that it is surprising to discover that he did not write the screenplay. Indeed, directing other people's scripts is unusual for Jordan. Before becoming a director, he made his name as a writer in 1976 with the publication of his short-story collection *Night in Tunisia* and has since published five works of fiction. The latest is the contemporary Gothic thriller *Mistaken* (2011). Of his sixteen features before *Byzantium*, there are only two on which he does not have a screenwriting credit. One was *We're No Angels* (1989), scripted by David Mamet and which Jordan has subsequently described as "a director for hire job," the experience of which led him to focus on smaller films where he would be in control of realizing his own screenplays. The other was *Interview with the Vampire: The Vampire Chronicles* (1994), adapted by Anne Rice from her best-selling novel, a film for which, although Jordan is not credited as cowriter, he did contribute extensively to the screenplay.

Byzantium was written by Moira Buffini, screenwriter of *Jane Eyre* (2011) and *Tamara Drewe* (2008), as an adaptation of her 2008 play, *A Vampire Story*. Her screenplay has allowed Jordan to not only rework recurring themes but also to flex his skill as a filmmaker. Depicting mythical subject matter seems to allow him an even greater than usual freedom to reimagine our world unfettered by realism. The result is stylish and poetic and, in its confident command of the craft of cinema, is perhaps Jordan's most self-assured feature since *The Butcher Boy* (1997).

Whereas *Interview with the Vampire* and Jordan's take on the werewolf myth, *The Company of Wolves* (1984), are mostly situated in an imaginary and costumed past, *Byzantium*'s central storyline is set in a contemporary and somewhat rundown England. With this film, he and Buffini have taken the opportunity to reinvent the vampire myth. *Byzantium*'s mythological creatures refer to themselves as revenants° and soucriants° rather than vampires. Though blessed (or burdened) by immortality, they are also very human, and struggle to survive without superpowers on the margins of society. Furthermore, Jordan and Buffini have contributed their own creation myth that mixes an ancient pagan Irish mythology of undead sorcerers (*neam-hmairbh*) with Christian notions of a watery rebirth offering eternal life to "only those prepared to die."

The story centers on Clara (Gemma Arterton) and her daughter Eleanor (Saoirse Ronan), both vampires who have lived for over two hundred years. Clara, brassy and sexually provocative, works in the sex trade and kills men as if sexually ravishing them. Eleanor is a melancholy teenage loner who disapproves of her mother's behavior and kills only elderly victims who are ready and willing to die. This contemporary story is intercut with events from their lives two hundred years ago that gradually explain the present. It is Eleanor's writing about this past and the reading of her writings by others that intermittently brings us back to their history, along with her daydreams and nightmares of the period (stories within stories and dreams are, of course, familiar territories for Jordan). As the narrative becomes clearer, Jordan (again typically) challenges our initial judgment of the characters' behavior. Clara, the ruthless killer and brothel madam, proves to have a captivating joie de vivre° and is admirably protective of her daughter, her toughness partly explained by a history of exploitation and abuse by a deeply sexist society. Conversely, the somewhat prim Eleanor is at times unable to control her basic emotional desires, no matter how much she tries.

Jordan has created distinct visual and aural moods for each of the two timelines, past and present, and the different worlds within them. Clara's realm of the nightclub, brothel, and fairground is seedy yet vibrant, pre-   5

revenants: ones who return after death or a long absence.
soucriants: also spelled "soucouyants"; bloodsucking Caribbean folklore characters who take the form of an old hag by day.
joie de vivre: a feeling of happiness or excitement about life.

sented through dynamic camera movement and a color design of vivid blues and (sometimes literally) blood reds. With the passive, melancholy Eleanor, the camera is more subdued; she is filmed in icy blues and grays, often by the shore and accompanied by the lonely sound of the sea. Contrasting with this modern world is the more mannered and Gothic-costumed melodrama of the historical story, within which is found the mythical and surreal heart of the film, the origin of the vampires. A story within stories, this is portrayed by spectacular images of blood-red waterfalls, swirling birds, living-dead doppelgängers,° and soaring cliffs.

Aesthetic pleasures aside, some viewers have found these shifting timelines and disparate styles convoluted and unsettling. It is seventy minutes before the fragments make sense as a whole and Jordan's detached style will not succumb to sentiment in order to pull us in. The film is grounded by the subtle performance of Saoirse Ronan as Eleanor and her communication of adolescent ennui and loneliness. While Jordan may create dreamscapes and present a refracted version of reality, he does so to explore the psychologically authentic. So, at its core, *Byzantium* is a poignant coming-of-age story. It features not only the obligatory first romance but also the lesser explored dynamic of the passionate mixture of love and hate that can afflict a daughter and mother relationship. To bring out these themes, Ronan's performance is supplemented by that of the more physical Gemma Arterton as Eleanor's instinctive mother and that of a fragile Caleb Landry Jones as Frank, a fellow outsider and Eleanor's potential soulmate.

Cineaste spoke with Jordan in June at his home in Dalkey, Co. Dublin, in Ireland, at which time he was still recovering from a knee injury, with his leg in a brace, and walking with a cane. His temporary disability wasn't preventing him from continuing to write, however, or agreeing to meet with us to discuss his new film.—Declan McGrath

CINEASTE: *It is unusual for you to direct from someone else's script. How did that come about?*

NEIL JORDAN: Stephen Woolley, a producer with whom I have worked many times, had liked a play he had seen called *A Vampire Story*. He got the play's writer, Moira Buffini, to write a script, which he then sent to me, I suppose, because we had made *Interview with the Vampire* and *The Company of Wolves* together. There was a strange interface with a lot of films I had done:

---

doppelgängers: ghostly counterparts of living persons; doubles.

a young girl was trying to tell her story and that story was viewed through successive people as it went along; it went between present and past; it was about a mother and daughter; it was set in an out-of-season holiday resort. It was like a gift, really. The only thing that worried me was that it was another movie about vampires.

CINEASTE: *Was the fact that you had made* Interview with the   10
Vampire *a negative when you were asked to make*
Byzantium?

JORDAN: I was mainly worried whether people wanted to see another vampire movie after the Twilight series. In a way, *Byzantium* was a female companion piece to *Interview with the Vampire*, with Eleanor and Clara as a female version of Lestat and Louis. One is a reluctant person who has received this gift, the other is an exultant person who has received it.

CINEASTE: *A lot of the best vampire movies have realistic themes as subtext. Did such themes attract you to* Byzantium?

JORDAN: That was the main thing that attracted me. *Byzantium* could almost survive as a story if there weren't vampires. I believe that in the play, which I never saw, the entire story could have been a deranged girl's imagination. Actually, the first draft of the script I was sent was quite unsatisfactory. You weren't sure whether the characters following the two women were vampires or not. They were disguised as psychiatrists or social workers. I told Moira, "Don't be afraid of it being a vampire film. Don't be afraid of things that speak genre like blood and horror."

CINEASTE: *You say that the cutting between past and present attracted you, but did you also worry that it might confuse the audience?*

JORDAN: It's a little bit worrisome but it made it really interest-   15
ing to me. That is the center of the script, really. The point is that Eleanor is telling a story. As different people read the story, it is revealed to us. That is what I did in *Company of Wolves*. It's what I did in a movie called *The Miracle*. It's what I did in *The End of the Affair* to a certain extent. I am attracted by the idea of examining fictional realities.

CINEASTE: *While moving between the different timelines in Byzantium, the performances ground the viewer. Was casting important?*

JORDAN: Oh, yeah. There were only two rules I made in this movie because I know the way they try to squeeze you on independent movies nowadays. I said, "If I can't cast it right, I am not going to do it, and if I can't find the right location to shoot in, I am not going to do it." We were lucky. Both Saoirse and Gemma were perfect. Both wanted to do it and, when I began to rehearse with the two of them, they rapidly complemented each other in emotional intensity. They have two totally different and contrasting energies.

CINEASTE: *They work very well together. The other main character is Eleanor's love interest, portrayed by Caleb Landry Jones.*

JORDAN: Caleb was great but English people don't like it when you cast Americans in English roles. But I thought, let's not force him into an English accent; let us imagine his father is American and he is transplanted in England. There is, however, a slight awkwardness in the script. It has a kind of "non-*Twilight*" originality but, in the middle of it, there is a teenage love story between these two characters, which was the essence of *Twilight*. So amid this original series of takes on the whole idea of vampirism, there is something quite conventional in the center. That is a bit of a weakness, I think, in the screenplay.

CINEASTE: *But only because the Twilight films exist?*

JORDAN: I suppose that is the case. I thought the way Moira had written those scenes was quite moving, simple, and quite innocent. It depicts an adolescent love affair where they hate each other and then love each other. That is the way kids relate.

CINEASTE: *Are you concerned with reviews?*

JORDAN: I read some of them. Why?

CINEASTE: *Some of the film's critics would have preferred that you stayed in one timeline. Interestingly, there is no consistency, since some of them prefer the modern story, while others prefer the nineteenth-century story.*

20

JORDAN: The problem with this script was the question of which story are you actually telling? Is the nineteenth-century story there to reinforce the contemporary story or the reverse? Normally, when I work with a script written by other writers, I do a draft myself. I deliberately didn't do so on *Byzantium* because Moira's voice was very distinctive and she was insistent that she had gone back to the earliest nineteenth-century versions of vampire legends in English literature, a scrap by Lord Byron and a scrap by Polidori. The characters in the Polidori story were called Ruthven and Darvell [*the names of characters played by Jonny Lee Miller and Sam Riley in* Byzantium]. Because she had imagined these characters so clearly, I didn't want to interfere and I decided that, if I wanted someone to rewrite the script, I would ask her to do it herself. I am aware there are some clunky expositional statements, particularly in the dialogue in the eighteenth-century sequences. But I thought it had its charm as well.

25

> "The fact that the vampires in this story are women who are not victims but protagonists with the power of life and death was interesting to me."

CINEASTE: *She has written quite a feminist take on the vampire myth. Did that appeal to you?*

JORDAN: The fact that the vampires in this story are women who are not victims but protagonists with the power of life and death was interesting to me. A feminist or female writer of the seventies would never have presented a character like Clara, with her rather shocking ability to use her sexuality and to treat killing as a kind of an orgasm. They would never have had a character exulting in their sexuality. I think it could only be written in the present day because the masculine-feminine dialogue has changed. And it's something I could never have written.

CINEASTE: *You have said you did not like the early Hammer vampire movies.*

JORDAN: It's not that I did not like them. It is just when I was making *Interview with the Vampire*, the studio kept saying to me, "Make it really scary." And I was saying, vampire movies are creepy, unsettling, and make you feel uneasy, but they are rarely "jump out of your seat" scary the way *The Exorcist, Paranormal Activity*, or *Saw* is scary. You would be unsettled by vampire movies but not scared.

CINEASTE: *But did you not say you found the Hammer films too* 30
camp?

JORDAN: Some of them are great, of course, but let's face it, Christopher Lee is not the best actor in the world, although he is interesting. Today people seem to love them for their relative cheesiness. The vampire movies that I like include Murnau's *Nosferatu*, Carl Dreyer's *Vampyr*, Werner Herzog's version of *Nosferatu*, Kathryn Bigelow's *Near Dark, Let the Right One In*, and the first Bela Lugosi ones. Francis Coppola's *Bram Stoker's Dracula* was great because he introduced grandeur and spectacle to the vampire myth. The *Buffy the Vampire Slayer* TV series was incredibly smart and well written, especially the knowingness of the whole thing, situating it in a high school. The point is that if there is an interesting way to interpret the metaphor, you can make an interesting movie. And people always will. The camp enjoyment is not that interesting, really.

CINEASTE: Byzantium *may not be camp enjoyment but you do have some fun with Clara's character.*

JORDAN: I just enjoyed her jumping on men, the game she played with them, and the way she killed them. I thought parts *of Byzantium* were very funny, particularly the idea that Eleanor is going nuts begging for a normal life while her mother says she has to work as a prostitute to put some food on the table.

CINEASTE: Byzantium *has received good reviews in specialized magazines such as* Diabolique *and* Fangoria. *These are the cognoscenti of the genre. Does that please you?*

JORDAN: Absolutely. I do love the genre. I do love horror. It is 35
what I do best in a way.

CINEASTE: *Were you aware of the vampire myth from early on?*

JORDAN: I grew up in Dollymount in Dublin and, in order to go to the cinema, I had to pass Bram Stoker's house. If it was too late to get the bus home, I had to walk past it, which was creepy. I used to confuse Bram Stoker with Dracula and so I imagined I was going past Dracula's house. So I was aware of Dracula from a young age. I saw my first vampire movie when I was about eight. It was Bela Lugosi and it really terrified the life out of me.

CINEASTE: *Did you read* Dracula *when you were a kid?*

JORDAN: I did. It is one of the great Gothic books. It influenced the film in a sense. Moira had written an origin myth of these vampires based on the Byronic stories where you got turned into a vampire by finding an ancient graveyard in Asia Minor. We couldn't afford to go there, and it also didn't fit the story because it was unbelievable that the characters would travel that distance. Since Bram Stoker was Irish and he got the character of Dracula through the stories told by his Catholic nanny, I said, "Let's look into *droch fhola* [*the Irish for bad blood*], the origin of Dracula, and Irish legends about the undead." Moira read about these things and she got very excited. So we came up with an island based on the Skelligs [*a monastic island off the coast of southwest Ireland*] with a Christian monastic hut that sat on a more pagan residue of belief. I love the Christian and pagan interface of the early Celtic sites.

CINEASTE: *That island is visually stunning, particularly its water-* 40 *falls of blood. You said there were effects you could not achieve in* Company of Wolves *because the technology at the time did not allow you to do so. Are you now appreciating what you can do with computer-generated imagery (CGI)?*

JORDAN: I was referring to the transformations in *Company of Wolves* that used the animatronic technology of the time. When it came out on DVD a few years ago, some of those transformations seemed unbelievably clunky to me. But there is almost no CGI in *Byzantium*. We couldn't afford it. To turn that waterfall red, we put dye in the lake above the water and then color correcting it in postproduction. The only CGI in the movie is the birds.

CINEASTE: *It is your first digitally shot movie. Was that to achieve a different feel?*

JORDAN: It is my first digital movie but, for the first season of *The Borgias*, we used an early version of the Sony digital camera and it was not thrilling. We would have been better off using film but, as it was television, we couldn't afford to. For the second season, we tested the new Arri Alexa camera. It has extraordinary tolerance. You can expose for both the darkness and the brightness in any frame. I love film but I thought this is a different form of photography, which I would like to explore, and so I asked the cinematographer Sean Bobbitt to look at the camera. Originally, we were going to shoot the eighteenth-century sequences on film and the contemporary sequences on digital, which of course makes no sense because there was no film in the eighteenth century. The idea was that one format is older and the other is new. We did a series of tests and shot the same scenes on film and then on the Arri Alexa and we honestly couldn't tell the difference. So we decided to shoot it all digitally.

CINEASTE: *The result is visually stunning and evidences a real mastery of all the elements of your craft, not only the photography but also the editing, the production design, and the music. Is that the result of experience?*

JORDAN: No, that is just what I like to do. I like to create imaginative spaces. I like to create images that you don't normally see in real life. That's the reason I make movies. It gives you the opportunity to do that. Making movies allows you to close your eyes and see things and say, "Let's do this." This script gave me the opportunity to do that more than anything I have had for a long, long time.

CINEASTE: *Are you tempted to use 3-D to create your imagined spaces?*

JORDAN: I don't like 3-D. Because it really is 3-bloody-D! It seems to me to be a terrible reduction of the photographic image. There is a plane in the background that is like a theatrical flat, there is stuff in the middle distance that pokes at your eyes, and then there is stuff in the foreground that jumps right out at you. I have never seen a 3-D movie that has been multidimensional except for James Cameron's *Avatar*.

45

I couldn't finish Martin Scorsese's 3-D movie. Any sense of spatial reality was totally destroyed. I am not a fan.

CINEASTE: *You have said you find reality "boring." Why?*

JORDAN: The Irish imagination has always seemed to me to take flight in some kind of escape from reality, rather than in descriptions of reality. Or maybe the kinds of works that I like: Oscar Wilde, W. B. Yeats, Flann O'Brien, most of the poetry of the Gaelic tradition, and all of the Gothic fictions of the Anglo-Irish tradition. They all create alternatives to a social and historical reality that was harsh, poor, wet, riven with division, and governed by the logic and the language of an empire next door that obeyed its own, very rational rules. So I kind of see the creation of fantasies as a response to a certain powerlessness, an inability to control one's own reality and destiny. And this is quite apart from the tradition of oral folklore, which creates ghost stories out of every available field and whitethorn tree.

I always choose a story where the world as it is presented to you is not as it seems. In *Mona Lisa*, for example, Bob Hoskins thinks he is helping this young girl portrayed by Cathy Tyson by rescuing her from a life of child prostitution and perdition and discovers that he is finding her a lover. In *The Crying Game*, Stephen Rea falls in love with a woman who turns out to be a man. In *The End of the Affair*, Ralph Fiennes imagines that Julianne Moore has a lover with whom she is betraying him only to discover that she has promised herself to God. I like these kinds of stories and that is the reason that I was attracted to a werewolf story in *Company of Wolves*, to vampires in *Interview with the Vampire*, and to these souciants in *Byzantium*.

Understanding the Text

1. Director Neil Jordan and scriptwriter Moira Buffini wanted to create vampires that were different from the traditional depictions (such as in Jordan's own *Interview with the Vampire*). Thus, Eleanor and Clara in *Byzantium* call themselves "revenants and soucriants" (par. 3) rather than vampires. How are they different from traditional depictions of vampires? What different cultural history and background went into the creation of their characters?

2. What part of *Byzantium* bothered Jordan as being too close to the Twilight movies?

3. According to Jordan, why are vampire movies "creepy" and "unsettling" but not "scary" (par. 29)? Why is this distinction important?

Reflection and Response

4. In *Byzantium*, the traditional vampire movie's dynamic of sexual attraction is turned on its head, with Clara being the seductive killer and men her victims. Jordan states that in the 1970s, doing a movie with this dynamic would not have pleased feminists. Could Clara be described as a feminist? Why or why not?

5. Is Eleanor, as a reluctant killer and perpetual teenager, truly a monster? Why or why not?

Making Connections

6. Consider the character of Clara in light of the theories about male attempts to dominate female sexuality and power presented by Karen Hollinger in "The Monster as Woman: Two Generations of Cat People" (p. 243). In what ways is Clara like Irena in the two movie versions of *Cat People*? Compared with the social attitudes that Hollinger sees as restricting both portrayals of Irena, how is Clara's embrace of her own sexuality, and her own vampirism, reflective of a new attitude toward the male-female dynamic today?

7. McGrath observes that "a lot of the best vampire movies have realistic themes as subtext" (par. 12). Do you agree? Does this statement extend beyond vampire movies to other monster movies? Use specific examples to support your answer.

8. Jordan says that people love the older movie versions of the vampire story "for their relative cheesiness" (par. 31). Watch an older vampire film starring either Christopher Lee or Bela Lugosi and argue whether Jordan's comments are valid or not. Are the older films less frightening because of their restraint, or do they require the viewer's imagination to supply what could not be shown on the screen at the time? What role do the expectations of today's filmgoers contribute to the manner in which monstrous characters and acts of violence are portrayed?

Mermaids' Attributes, Behavior, and Environs

Skye Alexander

Mermaids are some of the oldest and most enduring creatures in mythology. A union of human and fish, the mermaid (or merman) is simultaneously known and unknown. The mermaid is considered particularly alluring—and dangerous—because her singing can lead sailors to their doom. Sometimes, however, the mermaid can aid sailors. Depictions of mermaids are rife with symbolism, whether of good or evil, fortune or misfortune. Skye Alexander has written more than two dozen books of fiction and nonfiction, including *Wine, Women, and the Many Passions of Max McCoy* (2013) and *Mermaids: The Myths, Legends, & Lore* (2012), from which this selection is taken.

In addition to their fishy tails and human torsos, the traits and behaviors of mermaids are similar in the various mythologies of the world. These attributes became more homogenized° during the middle of the second millennium CE, as trade routes expanded and seamen journeyed far and wide, sharing their "fish stories" with peoples of various lands. Later, immigrants and slaves brought their mermaid legends with them when they relocated, and those tales merged with the folklore that already existed in their new homes.

However, certain common mermaid characteristics figured prominently in the mythology of diverse cultures, long before the periods of travel and exploration in the late Middle Ages and the Renaissance. Chief among these are mermaids' enchanting voices, their sensuality, and their destructive potential—all of which lie at the core of the mermaid mystique.

The Mermaid's Song

According to nearly all legends and stories, a mermaid's voice isn't merely melodious enough to rival the greatest of operatic divas. It's so mesmerizing that men who hear it go wild with delight and jump from their boats or rush into the sea—and subsequently drown. Some sailors, captivated and disoriented by the mermaid's hauntingly beautiful singing,

---

homogenized: made uniform or similar.

run their ships aground on rocky shores and, in a state of delicious delirium, they go to their watery graves. . . .

Literary Accounts of Mermaids' Songs

The ancient *One Thousand and One Nights* says that mermaids' songs rendered sailors helpless and lured them to their doom. The infamous Sirens of ancient Greek myth are presented as melodious but malevolent temptresses—no man could resist their tantalizing singing. In the 3,000-year-old *Odyssey*, Odysseus (or Ulysses in Latin) is warned about the Sirens' powers; he therefore ties himself to his ship's mast and his sailors put wax in their ears so they won't be driven mad by the enchantresses' songs. Our modern-day word "siren," rooted in the Greek myths of the Sirens of old, has the connotation of a seductive and potentially dangerous human femme fatale.

Folklore remains pretty quiet on the subject of mermen's singing ability. Some sources report the males as having "silvery" or "fluted" voices, though nothing as exquisite as those of the females. One Cornish legend tells of a handsome young man from the town of Zennor who goes to live with the mermaids—yet people in the town still say they hear his beautiful tenor voice wafting on the waves. But just because mermen don't possess the bewitchingly beautiful voices of the females of the species doesn't mean that they lack musical talent. The Scandinavian Havman is said to be an accomplished violinist who enchants women with his skillful playing, and the Greek Triton blew a conch shell like a trumpet.

> "Mermaids, it seems, are as changeable as the sea—serene one moment and tumultuous the next."

Deadly Beauties

Do mermaids intend to sing mariners into "the big sleep"? Or do their victims simply overreact when they hear the otherworldly beauty of the music? It's a subject for debate. It's been speculated that sailors, upon observing mermaids floating in the waves, think they see drowning women and jump overboard to rescue them—but in the process the well-meaning seamen drown instead.

Some stories say that mermaids drag men they fancy down into the depths and accidentally drown them, not realizing that humans can't breathe underwater. Other tales say humans who've been drawn into the mermaids' underwater realms remain there, transformed into merfolk themselves.

Hans Christian Andersen's popular fairy tale "The Little Mermaid" offers yet another perspective. In it the author explains that the mermaid's song is a compassionate attempt to calm the fears of sailors who are about to drown in a storm at sea. "They had more beautiful voices than any human being could have; and before the approach of a storm, and when they expected a ship would be lost, they swam before the vessel, and sang sweetly of the delights to be found in the depths of the sea, and begging the sailors not to fear if they sank to the bottom."

The Tempest

Many legends link mermaids with storms and even blame them for whipping up tempests at sea in order to sink ships. Some old English stories portrayed mermaids as evil omens and portents of bad luck. It's said that if a sailor spotted a mermaid, it meant bad weather was coming and he'd never return home again.

Another belief, explained in the twelfth-century text known as the *Speculum Regale* or *The King's Mirror*, states that when seafarers saw a mermaid at the onset of a storm, she served as an oracle and her actions let them know if they'd survive or perish. According to this theory, the mermaid dives underwater and brings up a fish. If she plays with the fish or throws it at the boat, death is imminent. If she eats the fish or tosses it back into the water, away from the ship, the sailors will make it through the tempest alive.

Ominous depictions of mermaids were encouraged by the Catholic Church during the Middle Ages. Medieval church fathers linked mermaids with the deadly sins of vanity and lust, as well as the alluring powers of women in general. Some churches displayed images of mermaids swimming with fish or starfish (which symbolized Christians) as warnings against sexual temptations. If a mermaid held a fish in her hands, it signified that a Christian had succumbed to the sin of lust.

Bearers of Good Fortune

Not all legends portray mermaids as dangerous. The African water deities known as Mami Wata, who often appear as mermaids, are said to heal the sick and bring good fortune. In Caribbean tradition, the water spirit/mermaid Lasirèn guides people (usually women) underwater where she confers special powers on them. Some European folklore acknowledges their potential dangers, but reminds us that mermaids, like the sea itself, can bring good things to humanity as well as bad.

Mermaids, it seems, are as changeable as the sea—serene one moment and tumultuous the next. The *Physiologus* or Bestiary (originally written in Greek, probably in the third or fourth century CE) was one of the most popular books during the Middle Ages. It characterized a mermaid as "a beast of the sea wonderfully shapen as a maid from the navel upward and a fish from the navel downward, and this beast is glad and merry in tempest, and sad and heavy in fair weather."

Psychologically, mermaids have been said to represent the complexity of women's emotions, ranging from playful to stormy, as well as the light and dark sides of the human psyche. Like the fairy, whom movies and children's stories have also trivialized, mermaids can be both alluring and dangerous. . . .

Luxurious Locks

You'll never see a picture of a mermaid with a pixie or brush cut. One of 15 her defining attributes is her long, flowing hair. Seafarers often report seeing a mermaid's sinuous tresses floating on the waves or twining around her body like seaweed. In some cases, artists (such as those who "cleaned up" the Starbucks logo) depict her modestly covering her breasts with her luxurious locks—something unabashed mermaids wouldn't even think of doing.

As far as the color of merfolk hair is concerned, green seems to be popular. The ancient Greek Tritons supposedly sported green hair, and legends of merfolk from Ireland and the British Isles also mention their green hair. And tales from Down Under say that the local water spirits known as yawkyawks have long hair that looks like seaweed or green algae.

In Scandinavia, however, where human blondes predominate, so do stories of golden-haired mermaids. Other folktales and sightings report that mermaids' hair can vary from palest blonde to black—and everything in between, especially the colors that remind us of the sea: green, blue, turquoise, purple, white, and silver.

Combs and Mirrors

If you believe what you read in mermaid myths, these lovely ladies devote a lot of time to personal grooming—specifically, combing their hair. Although they may appear devoid of other possessions—even clothing—mermaids throughout the world carry their combs and mirrors with them when they set out to entice human seafarers into their watery worlds. Countless stories speak of mermaids sitting on rocks near the ocean with their glistening tails curled about them, while they comb their long, flowing tresses and examine themselves in hand-held mirrors.

Mythology and art present numerous links between mermaids and 20 Venus/Aphrodite, the Roman/Greek (respectively) goddess of love and beauty. Botticelli's famous painting *The Birth of Venus* depicts the goddess with abundant auburn hair, long enough to discreetly conceal her "lady parts." So perhaps it's no surprise that we see mermaids gazing into their mirrors and combing their lustrous, flowing locks—just as human women are known to do.

If you're familiar with astrology or astronomy you may notice the similarity between the mermaid's hand-held mirror and the glyph° for the planet Venus (named for the Roman goddess). It's probably no accident. Take a look at that symbol—it's a circle above a plus sign—which suggests that mermaids descended from this ancient goddess of beauty and love.

Seductive Attributes

A woman's hair has long been counted among her most seductive attributes. Her hair was considered so enticing, in fact, that until the latter part of the twentieth century Catholic women covered their hair when they attended Mass, lest they distract men with their feminine charms. Until recently, Catholic nuns shaved their hair and veiled their heads. Buddhist nuns, too, shave their heads. Traditionally, Orthodox Jewish women wore wigs or otherwise concealed their natural hair in public. In Islamic culture today, women shroud their heads to signify modesty. So do women in Amish, Mennonite, and other conservative communities.

Obviously, there's more to a mermaid's hair than meets the eye. Barbara Walker, author of *The Woman's Dictionary of Symbols and Sacred Objects*, proposes that when a mermaid combs her hair she's performing a type of magic. Because hair traditionally represents strength, the mermaid's act of attending to her long, lustrous hair signifies her efforts to nurture and enhance her personal power.

The image of the mermaid combing her hair can also be linked to a purification ritual practiced in the Irish church, explains Patricia Radford

---

glyph: a sculptured figure or relief carving; a hieroglyph or pictograph.

in "Lusty Ladies: Mermaids in the Medieval Irish Church." Priests groomed their own hair with special liturgical combs in a rite intended to cleanse both body and soul. Thus, the mermaid's behavior could symbolize not only physical indulgence but transcendence as well.

A Mermaid's Abode?

According to the accounts of sailors and people who live by the sea, mermaids frolic on the waves far out in the ocean, but also come close to shore where they sit on rocks and preen themselves. Celtic legends say they can also be found in marshes and fens, and European tales claim merfolk reside in rivers, lakes, and waterfalls. Like their water-spirit predecessors, mermaids seem at home in freshwater as well as the salty seas.

In his 3,000-year-old epic *Theogony*, the poet Hesiod wrote that the   25
Greek merman Triton and his parents, Poseidon and Amphitrite, lived in a golden palace at the bottom of the sea. Some legends say mermaids make their homes in coral caves in the ocean's depths. Other tales suggest that mermaids inhabit the long-lost continents of Atlantis and Lemuria, which supposedly sank to the ocean floors eons ago.

Published in 1891, *The Folk-Lore of the Isle of Man*, by A. W. Moore, stated that the people of the Isle of Man believed "a splendid city, with many towers and gilded minarets, once stood near Langness, on a spot now covered by the sea." Here, merfolk dwelt, surrounded by treasure they'd accumulated from the ships they'd caused to sink.

Considering that people all over the world have reported seeing mermaids in all sorts of environments and locations, we can assume these mysterious and versatile creatures are capable of living almost anywhere—even on land, at least for a while. Ultimately, though, they reject the land-based lives they've embarked on and return to their true home: the sea.

Understanding the Text

1. What are the common features of mermaid stories as told in late medieval and early Renaissance times?
2. Explain the symbolism of the mermaid's mirror and comb.
3. What is important about the changes that Hans Christian Andersen made to the mermaid myth?

Reflection and Response

4. Why did the medieval church feel compelled to embrace the existence of mermaids as a means of teaching about the sins of lust and vanity? How does the fact that the mermaid is unable to fully consummate a relationship with a man — by virtue of being half-fish — complicate that portrayal?

5. What makes the mermaid a monster? Is it her half-human, half-fish form? Is it the allure of her beauty and singing, which can lead men to their deaths? Or is it that she is a representative of an entirely different world, largely unknown to humans? What does this say about how a monster is defined?

Making Connections

6. What are some contemporary portrayals of mermaids in popular culture, such as in film, television, or books? How do these portrayals either reinforce or contradict the more traditional portrayals of mermaids that Alexander describes?

7. Read the excerpt from Homer's *Odyssey* (p. 239), in which Odysseus fills his men's ears with wax and then has them tie him to the ship's mast so that only he can hear the song of the Sirens but cannot respond to their call. How can the danger the Sirens represent be compatible with their symbolic connections to creativity and fertility? Do the Sirens, being female, represent a threat to male power represented by Odysseus? Consider Alexander's assertions about mermaids and what they represent, keeping in mind that their history predates Homer.

8. Alexander refers to portrayals of mermaids and mermen in non-European cultures, including the Mami Wata in Africa and the water spirit Lasirèn in the Caribbean. Investigate myths and stories connected to merfolk around the world. What elements do these stories have in common, and how are they different? What may be the significance of the similarities and differences? What overall picture can you draw of the relationship between humans and merfolk?

From The Odyssey

Homer

After the ten-year war in Troy, described in Homer's *Iliad*, Odysseus, the king of Ithaca, is thwarted in his attempt to sail home by the god Poseidon. This journey, which takes an additional ten years, is the subject of Homer's epic poem *The Odyssey*. The following passage is from Book 12, in which Odysseus resumes his journey after spending a year as the witch Circe's lover. Circe warns him about the Sirens — half-woman, half-bird creatures whose singing lures sailors to their deaths — and tells him that only he must hear their song. There is much uncertainty about the dates of Homer's life, and consequently the dates of *The Iliad* and *The Odyssey*, but he is generally thought to have lived in the eighth or ninth century BCE. [Editor's note: line numbers follow the Fagles translation.]

At those words Dawn rose on her golden throne
and lustrous Circe made her way back up the island.   155
I went straight to my ship, commanding all hands
to take to the decks and cast off cables quickly.
They swung aboard at once, they sat to the oars in ranks
and in rhythm churned the water white with stroke on stroke.
And Circe the nymph with glossy braids, the awesome one   160
who speaks with human voice, sent us a hardy shipmate,
yes, a fresh following wind ruffling up in our wake,
bellying out our sail to drive our blue prow on as we,
securing the running gear from stem to stern, sat back
while the wind and helmsman kept
          her true on course.
At last, and sore at heart, I told my
          shipmates,
"Friends . . . it's wrong for only one
          or two
to know the revelations that lovely
          Circe
made to me alone. I'll tell you all,
so we can die with our eyes wide open now   170
or escape our fate and certain death together.
First, she warns, we must steer clear of the Sirens,
their enchanting song, their meadow starred with flowers.
I alone was to hear their voices, so she said,
but you must bind me with tight chafing ropes   175
so I cannot move a muscle, bound to the spot,

> *"*We must steer clear of the Sirens, their enchanting song, their meadow starred with flowers.*"*

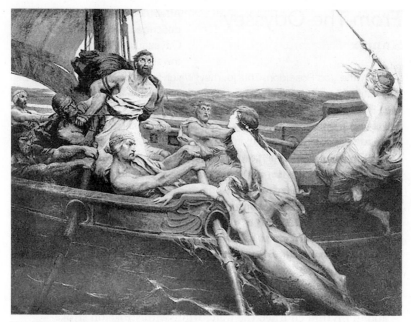

The Sirens attempt to lure a bound Odysseus to their island.
© Ivy Close Images/Alamy

erect at the mast-block, lashed by ropes to the mast.
And if I plead, commanding you to set me free,
then lash me faster,° rope on pressing rope."

So I informed my shipmates point by point,   180
all the while our trim ship was speeding toward
the Sirens' island, driven on by the brisk wind.
But then—the wind fell in an instant,
all glazed to a dead calm . . .
a mysterious power hushed the heaving swells.   185
The oarsmen leapt to their feet, struck the sail,
stowed it deep in the hold and sat to the oarlocks,
thrashing with polished oars, frothing the water white.
Now with a sharp sword I sliced an ample wheel of beeswax

faster: stronger, tighter.

down into pieces, kneaded them in my two strong hands   190
and the wax soon grew soft, worked by my strength
and Helios'° burning rays, the sun at high noon,
and I stopped the ears of my comrades one by one.
They bound me hand and foot in the tight ship—
erect at the mast-block, lashed by ropes to the mast—   195
and rowed and churned the whitecaps stroke on stroke.
We were just offshore as far as a man's shout can carry,
scudding° close, when the Sirens sensed at once a ship
was racing past and burst into their high, thrilling song:
"Come closer, famous Odysseus—Achaea's° pride and glory—   200
moor your ship on our coast so you can hear our song!
Never has any sailor passed our shores in his black craft
until he has heard the honeyed voices pouring from our lips,
and once he hears to his heart's content sails on, a wiser man.
We know all the pains that the Greeks and Trojans once endured   205
on the spreading plain of Troy when the gods willed it so—
all that comes to pass on the fertile earth, we know it all!"

   So they sent their ravishing voices out across the air
and the heart inside me throbbed to listen longer.
I signaled the crew with frowns to set me free—   210
they flung themselves at the oars and rowed on harder,
Perimedes and Eurylochus springing up at once
to bind me faster with rope on chafing rope.
But once we'd left the Sirens fading in our wake,
once we could hear their song no more, their urgent call—   215
my steadfast crew was quick to remove the wax I'd used
to seal their ears and loosed the bonds that lashed me.

Helios: Greek god of the sun, father of Circe.
scudding: moving rapidly.
Achaea: a region in southern Greece.

Understanding the Text

1. Homer's poem says that Circe sent a gift, "a fresh following wind ruffling up in our wake" (l. 162). Why, then, are the men later paddling with their oars?

2. What do the Sirens say they know and will reveal to Odysseus in their song? What do they say happens to those who hear their voices?

3. How does Odysseus respond to hearing the Sirens' song?

Reflection and Response

4. Homer does not spend any time on descriptions of the Sirens, so presumably he expected that his audience would already know that they were half-woman, half-bird creatures. What about the woman-bird combination seems particularly suited to the type of danger they represent?

5. The Sirens sing, "All that comes to pass on the fertile earth, we know it all!" (l. 207). Note that Odysseus, listening to them, wishes to be freed of his bonds and sail to them. Why is the temptation of knowledge so alluring? Can you think of other similar examples of people being tempted by knowledge? What does this say about the human condition?

Making Connections

6. How are the Sirens similar to other composite monsters, such as those described in Chapter 2, especially woman-animal combinations? Do further research on the Sirens, mermaids, or some other monster (like those in Chapter 2) that combines women's features with those of another creature. What role does the composite woman-animal monster play in relation to Karen Hollinger's argument about the need for men to control the power of female sexuality ("The Monster as Woman: Two Generations of Cat People," p. 243)? In answering the question, consider the point Skye Alexander makes that the Christian church used the mermaid as a symbol of lust and vanity—powerful urges the church felt needed to be controlled ("Mermaids' Attributes, Behavior, and Environs," p. 232).

7. Investigate other monsters that Odysseus came across during his ten-year journey home. Learn about the origins and dangers of the monsters. What might these monsters have represented culturally to the ancient Greeks, and why might they appear in Homer's poem?

The Monster as Woman: Two Generations of Cat People

Karen Hollinger

Most monsters are male, or at least seem to represent a male incarnation. Frequently, the monster's victim — or at least the attempted victim — is female. Thus, when the monster is female, there is an opportunity to explore the social messages behind the female monster.

Karen Hollinger examines two versions of the movie *Cat People*, the first made in 1942, the second in 1982. Hollinger is a professor of English at Armstrong State University who focuses on film studies and gender studies. She is the author of numerous books, including *The Actress: Hollywood Acting and the Female Star* (2006) and *Feminist Film Studies* (2010). This article originally appeared in the scholarly journal *Film Criticism* in 1989.

> . . . [I]t could well be maintained that it is women's sexuality, that which renders them desirable—but also threatening—to men, which constitutes the real problem that the horror cinema exists to explore, and which constitutes also and ultimately that which is really monstrous.
>
> —STEPHEN NEALE, *GENRE*

As Stephen Neale suggests, an intimate relationship seems to exist among the filmic presentation of the horror monster, the castration anxiety it evokes, and the cinematic representation of the female form. The complexity of this relationship has been suggested by several critics, but its theoretical articulation, how it works in specific horror films, and the social and historical implications it has for the positioning of women in patriarchal society still remain to be more fully examined. A possible step in this direction involves an inquiry into the filmic presentation of the monster as woman.

Critics have been slow to investigate the connection between the representation of the horror monster and that of the female image because the horror monster traditionally has been presented as male. From classic monster films like *The Cabinet of Dr. Calgari* through *Nosferatu, Frankenstein, Dracula, The Wolf Man, King Kong*, and *The Mummy* to the contemporary psychopath-as-monster films like *Texas Chainsaw Massacre* and *Halloween* or the monstrous creature-as-phallic-symbol films like *Jaws* the monster is overtly, even excessively, masculine. A closer look at theoretical approaches to the iconography of the horror monster and that of the female cinematic form, however, reveals striking similarities. The traditional maleness of the horror monster can be explained in Freudian terms as an expression of the connection between the image of the monster and the filmic representation of castration anxieties. It has been proposed that the essential nature of narrative is Oedipal,° that it involves the reactivation and eventual management of the castration anxieties for the male subject. If so, the monster film can be said to combine in the figure of its monster the fascination, fear, and anxiety that this reenactment of the Oedipal trauma evokes. Stephen Neale, for instance, argues that the traditional male horror monster mobilizes castration anxieties by his portrayal of the lack that represents castration to the male subject (*Genre* 43–44). It is this reenactment of the male Oedipal trauma in the figure of the horror monster that accounts for the male spectator's simultaneous attraction to and repulsion from the monster film and its monstrous central character.

Thus, the monster film is centrally concerned with problems of sexual difference. This concern, according to Neale, acts not to undermine the male spectator's filmic pleasure by using the monster merely to expose the lack upon which castration anxieties are founded, but rather to entertain the spectator by filling this lack (*Genre* 43–44). The monster not only represents castration, but also disavows it and provides filmic pleasure for the male viewer by soothing castration fears. The avenues of this disavowal fall into two categories: fetishistic scopophilia° and sadistic-investigative voyeurism. The horror monster by his very presence and by the spectacular nature of this presence serves fetishistically to reassure the spectator by masking the castration fear that is the real concern of the film. As Neale suggests, the positioning of the monster as a fetishistic figure of disavowal explains both why so much is made of the details of the monster's construction and why so many of the resources of costume and make-up are expended to make his appearance both spectacular and believable (*Genre* 45). He must not only frighten but also convince the spectator of the credibility of his existence and appearance if he is to disavow castration as well as symbolize it.

The rhythm of presence and absence that the horror film sets up in regard to the monster's appearance also represents an aspect of this fe-

---

Oedipal: relating to Sigmund Freud's Oedipus complex and castration anxiety, in which the young boy fears that his father may castrate him as punishment for his attraction to his mother.
fetishistic scopophilia: the displacement of erotic interest and satisfaction to the act of looking, such as at naked bodies or pornography.

tishistic avenue of disavowal. The random appearances of the monster throughout the horror film work, as Neale points out, to create a reassuring rhythm of presence and lack that serves to regulate and contain the irrevocable lack, castration (*Genre* 44). Thus, for the monster to ward off castration anxiety effectively, he must be shown, and if possible even unmasked, in the course of his filmic appearances so that he can visually enact his fetishistic role.

The monster's evocation of castration anxieties can be controlled not only visually by his fetishization, as Neale suggests, but also narratively by plots that involve fetishistic and sadistic-investigative aspects. In fact, the overreacher and discovery plots, two classic forms of monster film narrative, parallel these twin forms of disavowal. The overreacher plot enacts narratively the monster's positioning as a fetishistic figure by setting him up as the embodiment of his creator's lofty and unattainable dreams of reaching a god-like relationship to nature and of creating a perfect human being. Thus, we see inscribed even in the narratives of these monster films disavowal, overvaluation, and fetishistic substitution. An exemplary text in this regard is James Whale's *Frankenstein* (1931), in which Henry Frankenstein's creation of a violent and destructive monster is explained as the result of his desire to assemble a magnificent creature with a superior human brain.

The discovery plot, on the other hand, works to manage the monster and the castration anxieties that he evokes in a slightly different way. Rather than completely disavowing castration through fetishistic substitution and overvaluation, the discovery plot seeks to control the monster by a process of demystification. This narrative movement culminates in the devaluation and/or punishment of the monster or at least in the acquisition of sufficient knowledge of his mysterious behavior to find a way to deal with his threatening presence.

A comparison of this Freudian description of the filmic presentation of the horror monster and Laura Mulvey's analysis of the iconography of the female form in narrative cinema shows them to be quite similar. According to Mulvey, the figure of the woman, like that of the monster, also mobilizes castration fears in the male subject. She is "the bearer of the bleeding wound," the signifier of the male Other, and the symbol of the castration threat by her real absence of a penis (7). For Mulvey, the project of narrative cinema as a whole is both to represent this lack and to disavow it in its presentation of the female form, just as the monster film works both to represent and to disavow the threat of the castrated and castrating monster. The two avenues of disavowal for the threat of castration embodied in the filmic image of woman are also sadistic-investigative voyeurism (the investigation of the woman's mystery) and fetishistic scopophilia (the substitution of the fetish object or the turning of the represented figure itself into a fetish through overvaluation).

While a relationship thus seems to exist between the image of woman in cinema and that of the monster in the horror film, the nature of this relationship is obscured by classic monster films, which position women as victims of the monster's aggression. Just as the classic horror monster is commonly defined as male, so the primary object of his desire is almost exclusively female. As Neale points out, patriarchy positions women as subject to men and to their power, and the horror film simply "rehearses and restates this ideology" ("*Halloween*" 28), but, as Linda Williams suggests, beneath this assertion of male power that positions women only as victims there lies a sympathetic affinity and identification between woman and monster. Williams argues that the look of the female victim at the monster in the horror film reveals not only an acknowledgment of her punishment for usurping the male power of the look but also a recognition of her similar status to the monster "in patriarchal structures of seeing" (85).

The positioning of woman as victim in the classic monster film, therefore, functions as a method of masking what is really presented as monstrous and threatening in these works. The fear that lurks behind castration anxieties and the fetishized horror monster can be seen as a fear not of the lack represented by the horror monster but of the potency of female sexuality and the power of woman's sexual difference. Both Neale and Mulvey perceive the threat of the horror monster and of female sexuality to the male in terms of its evocation of a weak, castrated female form. For them, the image of the woman and of the monster recalls for the male spectator his childhood Oedipal trauma during which he came to regard his mother as rendered weak and helpless by castration. It also reactivates the Oedipal fear that he too could be reduced through castration to her situation of powerless deformity and mutilation.

This conception of female sexuality as threatening to the male in terms of its representation of the castrated female's weak and helpless state is called into question by the affinity between woman and monster. If the woman is related to the monster in that they both are seen by patriarchy as representing sexual difference and castration fears, then she is allied not to a representation of weakness but to one of power in sexual difference. For the classic male horror monster, as symbol of the male Other, is not only a castrated victim of male society, but also a powerful, potentially castrating nemesis to the male hero, and he gets his power from the very fact of his dangerous difference from the normal male, from his positioning as "a biological freak with the impossible and threatening appetites that suggest a frightening potency precisely where the normal male would perceive a lack" (Williams 87).

The inadequacy of the Freudian rendering of woman as a symbol only of the lack that is castration and nothing more has led revisionist psychoanalytic theorists like Susan Lurie to challenge traditional Freudian notions of the nature of the male Oedipal experience. According to Lurie, the male child's trauma involves not his fear of being castrated and thus reduced to his mother's state of helpless mutilation, but rather a recognition that his mother, although she lacks a penis, is not, in fact, powerless or helpless. The whole notion then of woman as representing castration can be read, according to Lurie, as really a disavowal of this unsettling discovery, as a lie that covers up the male child's recognition of his mother's power in difference. Applying this theory to the monster film suggests that an interpretation with greater explanatory power than those of Neale and Mulvey in assessing the socio-historical implications of the monster as woman in patriarchal society involves a recognition that the underlying fear that informs these texts and that lies behind the fear of castration is the threat of the potency of non-phallic sexuality. As Williams, building on Lurie's theories, suggests, it is not a recognition of the weakness but of the power in difference that woman, as sexual Other and as a potentially castrating force to the male, represents (89–90).

This fear of female sexuality is carefully masked, disavowed, and displaced in the classic monster film with its male monster, fetishistic and investigative plots, and positioning of woman as victims. With the introduction of the female monster, however, this careful cover-up is destroyed because the twin avenues of disavowal no longer disavow. Castration anxieties, the underlying threat of non-phallic female sexuality, and the power in sexual difference explode from the text. Extraordinary means, therefore, must be taken to control and diminish the resulting effects on the traumatized male spectator.

A consideration of the filmic presentation of the female monster demonstrates that her existence threatens to destroy the tight control that the classic monster film imposes on the evocation of castration fears and on the portrayal of the female sexual threat that lies behind castration. From the very beginning of her cinematic career, the female monster's threatening nature was evoked only to be forcefully suppressed. James Whale's *Bride of Frankenstein* (1935) provides an early example of this suppression. The major portion of the film is devoted to a sympathetic rendering of the male Frankenstein monster. He is shown to be a pitiful creature in search of friendship and kindness who kills only when attacked and endures brutally cruel treatment, even visual crucifixion, by his captors. Much is also made in the film of the creation of the female monster, but when she does finally appear, it is only to be quickly disposed of. Despite her wild hairdo and the hissing sound she makes when approached, she is, in fact, not at all a very threatening creature: she clings submissively to Henry Frankenstein, is terrified of the male monster, and is incapable even of protesting when her rejected would-be mate sets out to destroy them both. She seems created only to act as the ultimate victim for the male monster's final demonstration of power. Clearly, however, the female sexual threat in this film, symbolized in the female monster's capacity to reject her mate, is perceived as too dangerous to allow her more than a few moments of screen time.[1]

If the female threat is forcefully controlled in *Bride of Frankenstein* by quick and total destruction, it is allowed to demonstrate its overwhelming power in Jacques Tourneur's *Cat People* (1942). Tourneur, a director noted for his subtle visual suggestion of horror, allows his female monster to triumph over all male efforts to control her. Attempts are made to utilize the traditional monster film's methods of disavowing the female sexual threat, but they are exposed here as pitifully inadequate to control the horror of the female monster. Irena (Simone Simon), the cat woman, is pursued by two men, each of whom represents one avenue of disavowal. Oliver Reed (Kent Smith) is a non-threatening male presence who tries to control Irena's sexual threat by converting her into a fetishistic figure, placing her in the cult of the beautiful and sexually provocative, but unknowable and untouchable woman. Oliver describes their relationship as involving his being drawn to Irena by the force of her sexual attraction, which holds him against his will. He confesses:

I'm drawn to her. There's a warmth from her that pulls at me. I have to watch her when she's in the room. I have to touch her when she's near, but I don't really know her. In many ways we're strangers.

In direct contrast to Oliver's passive fetishism and embodying the sadistic-investigative avenue of disavowal is the aggressive sexual threat represented by the psychiatrist Dr. Judd (Tom Conway). He sets out actively to counter Irena's dangerous sexuality with the force of his phallic

15

---

[1]Elsa Lancaster plays two roles in the film: as Mary Shelley in the prologue and later as the female monster. Shelley is presented in the prologue as an angelic Victorian woman who has demonstrated her suppressed wickedness by writing a naughty book. This positioning of the woman anticipates Tourneur's *Cat People*, in which it is suggested that the female monster is finally controlled by her own internalization of patriarchal standards.

Irena Reed (Simone Simon) in *Cat People* (1942), a horror film about a race of women who transform into panthers when sexually aroused.
Hulton Archive/Getty Images

presence. His aggressive sexuality is symbolized in his walking-stick, which contains within it a hidden sword. The sword connects him visually to another phallic power in the film, King John of Serbia, whose statue Irena keeps in her apartment. As she tells Oliver, the legendary King John rescued her village by driving out evil invaders who had led the villagers to witchcraft and devil worship. Since Irena's statue portrays King John with a panther impaled on his sword, a connection is made between the devil worshipers, whom Irena describes as having escaped King John's invasion by fleeing to the mountains, and the cat women, whom she later mentions to Dr. Judd under hypnosis. The image of a primitive, evil matriarchy threatening to male power is thus suggested. As Dr. Judd relates Irena's description of the cat women, they are:

women who in jealousy or passion or out of their own corrupt passions can turn into great cat-like panthers. And if one of these women were to fall in love and if her lover were to kiss her, take her into his embrace, she would be driven by her own evil to kill.

Irena believes herself related to these evil creatures, and Dr. Judd sets out to disprove this belief. The conflict between Irena's determination to cling to her conviction that she is, in fact, a cat woman and Dr. Judd's attempts to "cure" her becomes a struggle for power and domination. Judd initially attempts to gain control over Irena by mastering her secrets, investigating her while she is under hypnosis. After their first session together, he taps his little black notebook and tells her that although she remembers nothing of what she has revealed to him, he has it all at his command. Later, when they meet again at the zoo, she asks how he knew where to find her, and he answers with a look of mastery that makes her visibly uncomfortable, "You told me many things." Judd's attempts to control Irena do not stop with his investigation of her psyche. They culminate in his sexual advances, their kiss, and her transformation into a panther. In the resulting battle, the shadowy forms of the panther and the phallic walking-stick/sword are seen in violent conflict. The panther, although wounded, is still victorious: Judd is killed, and the walking-stick/sword is later discovered to have been broken in the battle, half of it left embedded in Irena's body.

If Judd's active attempts to exert male control result only in his death, Oliver's passive reaction to Irena's sexual threat leads him to a different fate. He turns to a seemingly asexual union with his female friend and co-worker, Alice (Jane Randolph), who describes their relationship in this way:

I know what love is. It's understanding. It's you and me and let the rest of the world go by. It's just the two of us living our lives together happily and proudly, no self-torture and no doubt. It's enduring and it's everlasting. Nothing can change it. Nothing can change us, Ollie. That's what I think love is.

There is no sexuality here. Alice offers Oliver a safe, secure, and non-threatening affection, but it is also presented as an asexual one. As they stand over Irena's dead body in the film's concluding scene, Oliver comments to Alice, "She never lied to us," reconfirming the horrible reality of Irena's sexual threat. It is a real threat to Oliver, and one that must never touch his ideal relationship with Alice, a relationship that is safe in its asexuality.

Although Irena's threatening sexuality is managed at the film's conclusion through her violent destruction, it is never brought under the sway of male dominance. Both Oliver and Dr. Judd fail to control her, and she is left to destroy herself by deliberately opening the gate to the panther's cage in the zoo and exposing herself to its attack. Acting in accord with the patriarchal standards that she has internalized, Irena punishes herself for a sexual nature that she has come to see as evil. This self-induced punishment, however, does not diminish the power of her sexual difference, and Tourneur's film remains a strong statement of female power in difference, which is controlled only by the woman's internalization of patriarchal standards.

Tourneur's version of *Cat People* thus illustrates the forceful expression 20 of the female threat to the male in the character of a female monster. A consideration of this film makes it tempting to see the female monster as defying the usual filmic avenues of disavowal and expressing a threat beyond narrative control. A comparison of Tourneur's film with Paul Schrader's 1982 remake, however, demonstrates clearly that the female monster, in fact, can be controlled by a strong, even brutal evocation of phallic power. Schrader's film, in its crudely explicit narrative presentation of horror, acts as a reassertion of the phallic control that Tourneur's subtle, visually and thematically suggestive style intentionally eschews.

The project of Schrader's *Cat People* is much like that of the male child who finally has come to see his mother's non-phallic power and wants desperately to disavow it. Schrader's film works to represent the female as a weak, castrated figure and to reaffirm her submission to the phallic dominance of the male. This reaffirmation involves the transformation of the original film's representative of failed phallic power, Dr. Judd, into a much more threatening male monster who can assert the force of the male sexual threat even in death. This figure is Irena's brother Paul (Malcolm McDowell), another cat person who in his panther form is responsible for many brutal murders. He brings Irena (Natasia Kinski) to live with him, hoping that an incestuous relationship with her, another cat person, will prevent his transformation into a panther.

Thus, Irena is introduced in this film not as a powerful sexual threat, but as a potential victim to Paul's threatening sexuality. This portrayal is immediately established in the film's opening scenes depicting primitive tribal ceremonies in which young women are offered as sexual partners to male panthers. A comparison of this representation of the origin of the cat people legend to that presented in the Tourneur version is informative. Whereas in the original, the cat women are seen as powerful witches and devil worshipers who escape King John's male domination by fleeing to the mountains, in Schrader's version, they become ritual sacrifices to the lust of male panthers. Irena's connection to these primitive female victims is made visually by the transition from these opening scenes to her arrival in New Orleans to meet Paul. A dissolve superimposes a close-up of Irena's face as she searches through the airport for her brother over the face of one of these female sacrificial victims.

Throughout the film, in scenes depicting his post-coital attacks on his sexual partners, Paul's strength is contrasted to Irena's weakness. Even in death, Paul maintains significant power. He is killed while in his panther form not by Irena or Oliver (John Heard), her zookeeper lover, but by Alice (Annette O'Toole), Oliver's female co-worker, who represents the asexual non-threatening femininity characteristic of her counterpart in the original version. Male power in Schrader's as in Tourneur's film thus is at least partially subdued by a voluntary female renunciation of sexuality, but Paul is not really completely subdued. After his death, his corpse in its panther form is subjected to an autopsy by Oliver. When the carcass is opened up, a noxious gas is released that affects Oliver so strongly that he is sent to a hospital to recover, and the panther's body disintegrates, leaving behind only a green slime associated earlier in the film with Paul's transformations from one physical form into another. The suggestion is made that even after his death Paul remains a threatening creature capable of inflicting bodily harm on others and of escaping any attempts to understand and thus to control him. Irena, on the other hand, does not demonstrate a very powerful or threatening nature. She is shown only once with blood on her mouth after an apparent attack on a rabbit. While the phallicly potent Paul rips off a zookeeper's arm and devours unsuspecting female sexual partners, Irena can only stalk rabbits. A castrated cat, she is reduced to small acts of viciousness.

"The presence of the female monster brings to the surface . . . the underlying threat of female sexuality and of the power of sexual difference that shapes it."

When she does finally accept her sexual power and have sex with Oliver, she takes on her panther form but then refuses to attack him; instead, she goes off into the night to find another victim. Even though Irena is shown in her panther state, the details of her animal brutality are not presented. She does kill in order to return to her human form, but she murders the custodian of Oliver's cabin; he is, significantly, an old man well past the age of sexual potency. Thus, the force of her threat to the sexually active male is reduced. The actual attack itself is not shown. In contrast to the graphic portrayals of Paul's victims' mutilations, Irena's victim is simply shown in what appears to be a non-mutilated state. He could as easily have died from fear as from Irena's attack. Irena is not seen again until she has returned to her human form and awaits Oliver in his cabin. The visual presentation of this scene is significant. The shadows from the cabin window screens cast a cage-like pattern on Irena. She seems to have willingly sought out her own imprisonment. Her lover has sought her out as well, and she begs him to kill her. When he refuses, she asks that he use his phallic power to return her to her animal state so that she can be freed from the torment of her sexual potency. He agrees, ties her to the bed in his cabin, and performs his rites of transformation.

Extraordinary means are here taken to reaffirm the power of male 25 sexuality and to minimize the female sexual threat. In order to accomplish this reaffirmation, the non-threatening male in the film is converted into a benevolent sexual despot. He provides for the weak female a way out of the horror of her sexual potency; she can find salvation if she submits to his mastery. The final scene in the film recapitulates this theme as Oliver stands outside a panther's cage and allows the cat (by implication, Irena in her animal form) to eat from his hands through the bars. The zookeeper shows kindness and concern but remains completely in control. The panther growls but finally can only submit to his dominance. It is a scene that shows the threat of female power effectively subdued and the final triumph of the male complete.

A comparison of Tourneur's film to Schrader's indicates that the filmic evocation of the female sexual threat through the figure of the female horror monster involves a complex formulation related not only to the psychic needs of its male spectators and to the internal requirements of the textual systems of the films themselves, but also to the social conditions under which the films were made. Tourneur's 1942 film speaks to a patriarchy secure in its control of female power yet on the brink of the wartime initiation of women's challenges to that control. It, therefore, rehearses and restates in symbolic form a reassuring confidence in women's internalization of patriarchal standards and of images of female power as evil. This symbolic restatement of the patriarchically correct positioning of women in 1942 also involves a strong expression of women's potential power in difference and the threat it poses to a male-defined hegemony.° This expression could be tolerated by a society that still felt sure of male social dominance.

By 1982, however, when Schrader became attracted to the notion of redoing *Cat People*, women had made so many threatening advances against male power that the patriarchal assumption of women's internalization of its cultural standards and codes no longer could be confidently entertained. It became necessary to reassert male dominance in the only other way possible, through the use of force. Thus, in a period of growing

hegemony: domination; the exercise of control and influence over others.

assertion of female power against patriarchal hegemony, Schrader's film acts as a historically conditioned response to Tourneur's version. It attempts to master through generic variation the evocation of the female sexual threat in the original film and to reassert crudely, but effectively, the phallic control that is only subtly suggested in Tourneur's work. In both films, however, the presence of the female monster brings to the surface of the text the underlying threat of female sexuality and of the power of sexual difference that shapes it.

Works Cited

Lurie, Susan. "Pornography and the Dread of Women." *Take Back the Night.* Ed. Laura Lederer. New York: Morrow, 1980. 159–73.

Mulvey, Laura. "Visual Pleasure and Narrative Cinema." *Screen* 16 (Autumn 1975): 6–18.

Neale, Stephen. *Genre.* London: British Film Institute, 1980.

———. "*Halloween*: Suspense, Aggression, and the Look." *Framework* 14 (Spring 1981): 25–29.

Williams, Linda. "When the Woman Looks." *Revision: Essays in Feminist Criticism.* Ed.-Edited by Mary Ann Doane, Patricia Mellancamp, and Linda Williams. Frederick, MD: U Pub. of America and American Film Institute, 1984. 83–99.

Understanding the Text

1. What does Hollinger mean when she says that the horror monster evokes "castration anxiety" (par. 1)? How does the female monster evoke this anxiety differently than the male monster?

2. Explain what Susan Lurie means when she challenges the traditional Freudian interpretation of the male Oedipal experience. What is the "lie" she refers to (par. 11)?

3. What are "two classic forms of monster film narrative," and how do they parallel the "twin forms of disavowal" (par. 5)?

4. How are the two main male characters in the 1982 version of *Cat People* different from those in the 1942 version? According to Hollinger, what is the significance of those differences, given the forty years that separate the two films?

Reflection and Response

5. Do you find male or female monsters more frightening? More sexual? How might your gender affect your answer?

6. Hollinger states, "It is this reenactment of the male Oedipal trauma in the figure of the horror monster that accounts for the male spectator's simultaneous attraction to and repulsion from the monster film and its monstrous central character" (par. 2). How do male monsters embody this attraction/

repulsion for a male spectator? Do female monsters change how the attraction/repulsion works? If so, how?

7. In addition to the *Cat People* movies, Hollinger also examines *The Bride of Frankenstein* (1935), in which the female monster, or the Bride, is almost immediately killed by the male monster when she rejects his advances. Hollinger argues that the female monster represents the power of female sexuality (even the power to reject) that must be brought under male control, reflecting society's larger demand that female sexuality be kept within acceptable confines. Do you agree with her argument? Cite representations of monsters and other characters in specific films to support your answer.

Making Connections

8. Do representations of other female monsters, particularly those in movies, confirm Hollinger's central thesis about the desire to control female sexuality? Cite specific examples to support your answer.

9. Investigate the theories of Sigmund Freud, particularly those related to the Oedipus complex and castration anxiety, and the threat posed by female sexuality. Also investigate critics of Freud, particularly feminist critics, regarding these issues. Is the use of these theories in the interpretation of film fair and appropriate? Why or why not?

5

Is the Monster within Us?

There is a certain comfort in the concept of the Other: that indescribable thing that commits such horrible atrocities and is so very different from us. But nowhere in literature are there vampires, werewolves, aliens, or other monsters that can destroy and kill with the ferocity — and senselessness — of real-life humans. Indeed, at times we are the monsters. How can we account for the actions of human monsters such as serial killers, cannibals, murderous autocrats, and others who do things that go far beyond the realm of what is typically termed "human"? The psychology of a serial killer, the rationalizations of a cannibal, the bloodlust of a tyrant — these are characteristics of monsters that might make even Count Dracula return to his coffin in revulsion.

Within the memory of many people still living today was one of the most horrific examples of the savage human monster. Adolf Hitler, writing in jail after a failed attempt to overthrow the German government in 1925, outlined his belief in racial superiority in his book *Mein Kampf* ("my struggle"). In the selection included in this chapter, he explains how the race he deemed superior must not only reject association with lower races but should eliminate them as well. His ravings were ignored by many at the time, but he would eventually put his words into action during the Holocaust leading up to and lasting throughout World War II. Turning to the monsters of today, the Christian ethicist Patrick McCormick bemoans the tendency to create nonhuman monsters — aliens, dragons, and beasts — that people revel in killing. As he points out, on some level we identify and sympathize with monsters possessing human qualities, such as Frankenstein's creature, werewolves, and vampires, but we don't think twice about blasting aliens and other nonhuman monsters to smithereens. These attitudes can carry over into real life, as people become less tolerant and accepting of marginalized people and their struggles. Jason Huddleston undertakes a Freudian analysis of John Carpenter's film *Halloween*, a seminal movie in the horror genre. The main character, Michael Myers, acts out his confusion and sexual frustration by murdering the women who stimulate him — or the men who stand in his way. Michael hides behind a mask that hides all human emotion, making him a killing machine. Crime reporter Anne E. Schwartz looks at a killer wearing a different sort of mask: the mask of normalcy. Living in Middle America, Jeffrey Dahmer did not look the part of a serial killer and cannibal, but that's exactly what he was. Schwartz gives an exciting, detailed account of Dahmer's arrest, as well as a look into the mind of this most unusual monster. Richard Tithecott continues the theme of Dahmer being an "Average Joe" on the surface and explores how masks — such as the blank white mask of Michael Myers, the hockey mask of Jason in *Friday the 13th*, and the placid face of Dahmer — hide the truth. Dahmer was as much a zombie as a serial killer, going through the same mechanical motions with the bodies of all his victims. Finally, philosophy professor William Andrew Myers examines the challenge presented by what he calls "extreme perpetrators" — people whose actions are beyond the pale of normal bad behavior. Looking at the murderous dictator, serial killer, and ideological killer, Myers analyzes how they represent a moral challenge for us. He argues that we do a disservice to ourselves if we see them as the Other, pushing them aside as being barely human. When we dismiss such people, we fail to see the origins of evil in the world.

Human monsters are the greatest monsters of them all, for they are real and therefore the most dangerous. We can attribute evil qualities to a Medusa or Minotaur, wonder at mermaids and sphinxes, fear Dr. Frankenstein's creature or a werewolf in the woods, be attracted to or repelled by vampires or Sirens, but in the end, the greatest challenge is to confront the human monster, to explore what it means to be human in all its various forms.

Nation and Race

Adolf Hitler

Few human beings have ever had as immense an impact on the human race as Adolf Hitler. After Germany's humiliating defeat in World War I and the passage of the economically ruinous Treaty of Versailles, Hitler was able to take advantage of national resentment to come to power, rebuild the German war machine, and launch a new war largely targeted at those he considered weaker than his own race. By the end of the war, nearly fifty million people had died in the European theater. Among the casualties were nine million people who had died in concentration camps, including six million Jews and three million Communists, Gypsies, homosexuals, disabled persons, and others. What sort of monster would do these things? In this excerpt from Hitler's book *Mein Kampf* (1925), which he began writing in jail after a failed coup attempt against the German government, he explains his brutal philosophy by which the strong must by necessity conquer the weak.

There are some truths which are so obvious that for this very reason they are not seen or at least not recognized by ordinary people. They sometimes pass by such truisms as though blind and are most astonished when someone suddenly discovers what everyone really ought to know. Columbus's eggs° lie around by the hundreds of thousands, but Columbuses are met with less frequently.

Thus men without exception wander about in the garden of Nature; they imagine that they know practically everything and yet with few exceptions pass blindly by one of the most patent principles of Nature's rule: the inner segregation of the species of all living beings on this earth.

Even the most superficial observation shows that Nature's restricted form of propagation and increase is an almost rigid basic law of all the innumerable forms of expression of her vital urge. Every animal mates only with a member of the same species. The titmouse seeks the titmouse, the finch the finch, the stork the stork, the field mouse the field mouse, the dormouse the dormouse, the wolf the she-wolf, etc.

Only unusual circumstances can change this, primarily the compulsion of captivity or any other cause that makes it impossible to mate within the same species. But then Nature begins to resist this with all possible means, and her most visible protest consists either in refusing

---

Columbus's eggs: brilliant ideas or discoveries that seem obvious afterward.

further capacity for propagation to bastards or in limiting the fertility of later offspring; in most cases, however, she takes away the power of resistance to disease or hostile attacks.

This is only too natural.

5

Any crossing of two beings not at exactly the same level produces a medium between the level of the two parents. This means: the offspring will probably stand higher than the racially lower parent, but not as high as the higher one. Consequently, it will later succumb° in the struggle against the higher level. Such mating is contrary to the will of Nature for a higher breeding of all life. The precondition for this does not lie in associating superior and inferior, but in the total victory of the former. The stronger must dominate and not blend with the weaker, thus sacrificing his own greatness. Only the born weakling can view this as cruel, but he after all is only a weak and limited man; for if this law did not prevail, any conceivable higher development of organic living beings would be unthinkable.

> "The stronger must dominate and not blend with the weaker, thus sacrificing his own greatness."

The consequence of this racial purity, universally valid in Nature, is not only the sharp outward delimitation of the various races, but their uniform character in themselves. The fox is always a fox, the goose a goose, the tiger a tiger, etc., and the difference can lie at most in the varying measure of force, strength, intelligence, dexterity, endurance, etc., of the individual specimens. But you will never find a fox who in his inner attitude might, for example, show humanitarian tendencies toward geese, as similarly there is no cat with a friendly inclination toward mice.

Therefore, here, too, the struggle among themselves arises less from inner aversion than from hunger and love. In both cases, Nature looks on calmly, with satisfaction, in fact. In the struggle for daily bread all those who are weak and sickly or less determined succumb, while the struggle of the males for the female grants the right or opportunity to propagate only to the healthiest. And struggle is always a means for improving a species' health and power of resistance and, therefore, a cause of its higher development.

If the process were different, all further and higher development would cease and the opposite would occur. For, since the inferior always predominates numerically over the best, if both had the same possibility of preserving life and propagating, the inferior would multiply so much

---

succumb: to yield to a superior power; to die as a result of destructive forces.

more rapidly that in the end the best would inevitably be driven into the background, unless a correction of this state of affairs were undertaken. Nature does just this by subjecting the weaker part of such severe living conditions that by them alone the number is limited, and by not permitting the remainder to increase promiscuously,° but making a new and ruthless choice according to strength and health.

No more than Nature desires the mating of weaker with stronger indi- 10 viduals, even less does she desire the blending of a higher with a lower race, since, if she did, her whole work of higher breeding, over perhaps hundreds of thousands of years, might be ruined with one blow.

Historical experience offers countless proofs of this. It shows with terrifying clarity that in every mingling of Aryan° blood with that of lower peoples the result was the end of the cultured people. North America, whose population consists in by far the largest part of Germanic elements who mixed but little with the lower colored peoples, shows a different humanity and culture from Central and South America, where the predominantly Latin immigrants often mixed with the aborigines on a large scale. By this one example, we can clearly and distinctly recognize the effect of racial mixture. The Germanic inhabitant of the American continent, who has remained racially pure and unmixed, rose to be master of the continent; he will remain the master as long as he does not fall a victim to defilement of the blood.

The result of all racial crossing is therefore in brief always the following:

(a) Lowering of the level of the higher race;

(b) Physical and intellectual regression and hence the beginning of a slowly but surely progressing sickness.

To bring about such a development is, then, nothing else but to sin against the will of the eternal creator.

And as a sin this act is rewarded.

When man attempts to rebel against the iron logic of Nature, he comes 15 into struggle with the principles to which he himself owes his existence as a man. And this attack must lead to his own doom.

Here, of course, we encounter the objection of the modern pacifist, as truly Jewish in its effrontery as it is stupid! "Man's rôle is to overcome Nature!"

Millions thoughtlessly parrot this Jewish nonsense and end up by really imagining that they themselves represent a kind of conqueror of

promiscuously: indiscriminately; not restricted to one class or sort of person.
Aryan: a word used by the Nazis to indicate non-Jewish Caucasians, especially those having Nordic features.

Nature; though in this they dispose of no other weapon than an idea, and at that such a miserable one, that if it were true no world at all would be conceivable.

But quite aside from the fact that man has never yet conquered Nature in anything, but at most has caught hold of and tried to lift one or another corner of her immense gigantic veil of eternal riddles and secrets, that in reality he invents nothing but only discovers everything, that he does not dominate Nature, but has only risen on the basis of his knowledge of various laws and secrets of Nature to be lord over those other living creatures who lack this knowledge—quite aside from all this, an idea cannot overcome the preconditions for the development and being of humanity, since the idea itself depends only on man. Without human beings there is no human idea in this world, therefore, the idea as such is always conditioned by the presence of human beings and hence of all the laws which created the precondition for their existence.

And not only that! Certain ideas are even tied up with certain men. This applies most of all to those ideas whose content originates, not in an exact scientific truth, but in the world of emotion, or, as it is so beautifully and clearly expressed today, reflects an "inner experience." All these ideas, which have nothing to do with cold logic as such, but represent only pure expressions of feeling, ethical conceptions, etc., are chained to the existence of men, to whose intellectual imagination and creative power they owe their existence. Precisely in this case the preservation of these definite races and men is the precondition for the existence of these ideas. Anyone, for example, who really desired the victory of the pacifistic idea in this world with all his heart would have to fight with all the means at his disposal for the conquest of the world by the Germans; for, if the opposite should occur, the last pacifist would die out with the last German, since the rest of the world has never fallen so deeply as our own people, unfortunately, has for this nonsense so contrary to Nature and reason. Then, if we were serious, whether we liked it or not, we would have to wage wars in order to arrive at pacifism. This and nothing else was what Wilson, the American world savior, intended, or so at least our German visionaries believed—and thereby his purpose was fulfilled.

In actual fact the pacifistic-humane idea is perfectly all right perhaps 20 when the highest type of man has previously conquered and subjected the world to an extent that makes him the sole ruler of this earth. Then this idea lacks the power of producing evil effects in exact proportion as its practical application becomes rare and finally impossible. Therefore, first struggle and then we shall see what can be done. Otherwise mankind has passed the high point of its development and the end is not the domination of any ethical idea but barbarism and consequently chaos. At this point someone or other may laugh, but this planet once moved through the ether for millions of years without human beings and it can do so again some day if men forget that they owe their higher existence, not to the ideas of a few crazy ideologists, but to the knowledge and ruthless application of Nature's stern and rigid laws.

Everything we admire on this earth today—science and art, technology and inventions—is only the creative product of a few peoples and originally perhaps of *one* race. On them depends the existence of this whole culture. If they perish, the beauty of this earth will sink into the grave with them.

However much the soil, for example, can influence men, the result of the influence will always be different depending on the races in question. The low fertility of a living space may spur the one race to the highest achievements; in others it will only be the cause of bitterest poverty and final undernourishment with all its consequences. The inner nature of peoples is always determining for the manner in which outward influences will be effective. What leads the one to starvation trains the other to hard work.

All great cultures of the past perished only because the originally creative race died out from blood poisoning.

The ultimate cause of such a decline was their forgetting that all culture depends on men and not conversely; hence that to preserve a certain culture the man who creates it must be preserved. This preservation is bound up with the rigid law of necessity and the right to victory of the best and stronger in this world.

Those who want to live, let them fight, and those who do not want to 25 fight in this world of eternal struggle do not deserve to live.

Even if this were hard—that is how it is! Assuredly, however, by far the harder fate is that which strikes the man who thinks he can overcome Nature, but in the last analysis only mocks her. Distress, misfortune, and diseases are her answer.

The man who misjudges and disregards the racial laws actually forfeits the happiness that seems destined to be his. He thwarts the triumphal march of the best race and hence also the precondition for all human progress, and remains, in consequence, burdened with all the sensibility of man, in the animal realm of helpless misery.

Understanding the Text

1. What does Hitler mean by giving the analogy that animals mate only with animals of their own species? How does he jump from species to race?

2. What does Hitler say happens when a higher-level race mates with a lower-level race? Why, in his view, is this bad for the higher race?

3. What does Hitler mean when he argues that man has not conquered nature?

Reflection and Response

4. What is the logical fallacy that occurs when Hitler compares the segregation of animals by species and the segregation of humans by ethnicity? How does that affect the rest of his argument? To what extent does the idea that different races of humans represent different species underlie his entire philosophy?

5. A key part of Hitler's argument rests on observations of nature. In fact, he argues that humans are subject to nature and cannot escape it. Yet much of the Judeo-Christian tradition calls on humans to rise above their animalistic tendencies. How does Hitler's philosophy serve as a justification for his later, monstrous actions, such as the Holocaust?

6. Many of the readings in this book broadly define a monster as something "unnatural" or "different," yet Hitler's entire argument is based on his view of nature and sameness. What do you make of this contradiction?

Making Connections

7. Research the Holocaust, which involved the systematic execution of nine million people, including six million Jews. How did the philosophy described in this passage justify the extermination of so many? What is the difference between the destruction wrought by Hitler and that caused by many of the monsters described in previous chapters of this book?

8. Hitler states, "All great cultures of the past perished only because the originally creative race died out from blood poisoning" (par. 23). Research some of the great civilizations of the past and argue whether this statement is true or not.

Why Modern Monsters Have Become Alien to Us

Patrick McCormick

A professor of Christian ethics at Gonzaga University, Patrick McCormick teaches and speaks regularly on issues of social justice. Since 1994, he has written a regular column on Christianity and character for *U.S. Catholic*, the magazine in which this selection originally appeared. His other publications include *Sin as Addiction* (1989) and *A Banqueter's Guide to the All-Night Soup Kitchen of the Kingdom of God* (2004). In this article, McCormick argues that, traditionally, monsters have been warped manifestations of ourselves. Creatures such as Count Dracula, Frankenstein's monster, and the Hunchback of Notre Dame have an element of humanity with which we identify. We can, in fact, even find ourselves sympathizing with them. McCormick points out that today's monsters — often aliens — have no trace of humanity, which allows us to cheer unabashedly as they are destroyed. The effect of this disconnection may be to lessen our own sensitivity to people in the real world who are in need of comfort and understanding.

Late autumn has arrived and with it comes the dark magic of Halloween—and, of course, the murky thrill of monsters. Yet our appetite for a good monster knows no season. Ever since ancient times we have been fascinated with all sorts of tales about monsters and intrigued by myths and legends about those wild half-human beasts who haunt the edges of our forests and lurk in the recesses of our oceans. The sphinxes, Minotaurs, and Sirens of early mythology gave way to Beowulf's Grendel and Saint George's dragon, then to the mermaids, trolls, and one-eyed giants of our fairy and folk tales, and finally to those 19th-century Gothic classics. Nor are these stories on the wane, for the monster tales that made Lon Chaney, Boris Karloff, and Bela Lugosi stars of the silver screen continue to draw megacrowds six and seven decades later.

In 1994 Kenneth Branagh and Robert De Niro brought us [a] reincarnation of Shelley's story of Frankenstein's tortured creature, and Tom Cruise and Brad Pitt starred in *Interview with the Vampire*, the first installment of Anne Rice's homage to Stoker's *Dracula*. Meanwhile, Andrew Lloyd Webber's musical production of Gaston Leroux's *Phantom of the Opera* continues to pack in audiences from London to L.A.

Much of the initial appeal of monster stories comes from the fact that they, like their twisted siblings, "creature features" and "slashers," both terrify and fascinate us with their ghoulish brand of horror. It's the rattling-the-tiger's-cage kind of thrill that Scout and Jem Finch got from sneaking onto Boo Radley's° porch under a pale moon. Reading or watching great monster stories, we get to accompany the frightened heroes or heroines as they descend into the dragon's lair; crane our necks over the tops of books or movie seats and peek into the dank recesses of the giant cyclops' cave; stretch out our trembling hands and actually touch the monster's reptilian scales, hairy paws, or cloven hoofs; and then run screaming like a banshee the instant it wakes from its slumber. What a rush!

> "[In] classic monster stories we are also haunted by an underlying sense of sympathy — and, yes, responsibility — for these misshapen men."

As frightening as these creatures are, in monster stories it is always the beast that ends up taking the fall, which means that this is a place where we not only get to tangle with evil's most daunting and dangerous minions but to vanquish them with regularity. Pretty heady stuff. No wonder we never seem to tire of these tales.

And yet the truth is that the best of these stories are much more than simple-minded creature features. In the original versions of *Frankenstein, The Hunchback of Notre Dame, Phantom of the Opera, Jekyll & Hyde,* and   5 even *Dracula* we aren't simply terrified and enraged by these ghouls trolling about in our dungeons, sewers, or bell towers. Instead, in such classic monster stories we are also haunted by an underlying sense of sympathy—and, yes, responsibility—for these misshapen men. In their deaths and destruction we experience some pathos, some tragedy, perhaps even some shred of regret for the ways they have been abused, goaded, and abandoned.

Nowhere is this so clear as in *Frankenstein.* When, at the end of Shelley's novel, her narrator, Walton, finally sets eyes on Victor Frankenstein's dreaded creature, he describes him as having "a form I cannot find words to describe; gigantic in stature, yet uncouth and distorted in its proportions. . . . Never did I behold a vision so horrible as his face, of such loathsome yet appalling hideousness. . . . I dared not again raise my eyes to his face, there was something so scaring and unearthly in his ugliness."

Still, Walton, like the reader, feels "a mixture of curiosity and compassion" toward this disfigured beast. The very monster who has murdered

---

Scout, Jem Finch, and Boo Radley: characters in Harper Lee's novel *To Kill a Mockingbird* (1960).

all of Frankenstein's loved ones is himself a tortured soul, and the strange, misshapen creature—who has studied Plutarch and read Milton—cries out to his human maker in such eloquent anguish that we cannot help being moved.

Then, must I be hated, who am miserable beyond all living things. . . . Oh Frankenstein, be not equitable to every other, and trample upon me alone, to whom thy justice, and even thy clemency and affection, is most due. . . . Accursed creator! Why did you form a monster so hideous that even you turned from me in disgust? God, in pity, made man beautiful and alluring, after his own image; but my form is a filthy type of yours, more horrid even from the very resemblance.

   At first glance, Stevenson's story of *Dr. Jekyll & Mr. Hyde* doesn't seem to invite much pity for the villain Edward Hyde, the murderous dwarf whom the character Dr. Lanyon describes as "something seizing, surprising and revolting" and who, according to Henry Jekyll, "alone in the ranks of mankind, was pure evil." Still, when Jekyll's manservant Poole hears the poor creature "weeping like a woman or a lost soul," he admits to having come "away with that upon my heart" and comments "that I could have wept too." The truth is that for all his physical and moral deformities, Hyde, too, is but "a filthy type" of his maker, a doppelgänger of Henry Jekyll, "knit to him closer than a wife, closer than an eye," and the physical manifestation of all his vile and unruly passion. And though he is not as eloquent as Frankenstein's beast, Hyde could well have quoted Milton's *Paradise Lost* to his all-too-human creator.
   "Did I request thee, Maker, from my clay to mold me man? Did I solicit thee from darkness to promote me?"
   And even in *Dracula* there is a trace of compassion for the monstrous Prince of the Undead, the viper who takes a dozen repulsive forms. In Stoker's original narrative the vampire hunter Van Helsing, unlike so many modern action heroes, is not out simply to avenge himself against Dracula and his minions; he actually wants to redeem their lost and tortured souls. Even in visages that do not show up in mirrors, Van Helsing is capable of recognizing a shared humanity and, indeed, of feeling some pity for their frightful plight. And at the end of Stoker's novel, Mina Harker, who has more than enough reason to despise this foul creature of the underworld and to savor his destruction, describes Dracula's death with a note of unrestrained sympathy. "I shall be glad as long as I live that even in that moment of final dissolution, there was in the face a look of peace, such as I never could have imagined rested there." Stoker's vampire is not so much murdered as forgiven.

10

These stories, again and again, remind us that in biology and myth monsters are disfigured versions of ourselves, fun-house mirrors of our own frail and sometimes monstrous humanity. Monster stories, then, by confronting us with these disfigured embodiments of ourselves, invite us to reflect on our own humanity, and, indeed, our inhumanity. In a way that is not so very different from Luke's parable of the Good Samaritan, these Gothic tales challenge us to recognize the humanity of the beast and to acknowledge the beastliness of our own inhumanity. Indeed, the best of them are reminders and warnings about the ways in which we make and become such beasts.

Victor Hugo's 1831 classic *The Hunchback of Notre Dame* (so pathetically sanitized in Disney's [1996] animated version) may be one of the best modern monster stories we have. Even the name of the misshapen bell ringer, Quasimodo, tells us that this brutish creature is but "half-formed," and, like Frankenstein's beast, Hugo's disfigured monster seems cruelly fashioned of mismatched parts, his body a tortured terrain, his face a terrifying visage. As one critic writes:

Nowhere on earth was there a more grotesque creature. One of his eyes was buried under an enormous cyst. His teeth hung over his protruding lower lips like tusks. His eyebrows were red bristles, and his gigantic nose curved over his upper lip like a snout. His long arms protruded from his shoulders, dangling like an ape's.

Further, not unlike Stevenson's brutal Hyde, Quasimodo is a henchman of the night, a stalker of darkened alleys, and a hunter of women, finding cover by day deep within the bowels of Notre Dame. Here, it seems, is a fiend to haunt the nightmares of children and whip mobs into a fury.

Still, as Hugo's narrative unfolds, it is not Quasimodo but the cathedral's archdeacon, Claude Frollo, who is revealed as the novel's real monster. Like Frankenstein and Jekyll, the ascetic scholar and priest Frollo is a man who cannot abide the limits of his own mortality or acknowledge the all-too-human passions that burn within him. But Frollo's attempts to fly above this mortal flesh, or to bury it within the cathedral's shadowy vaults and Gothic spires, are all in vain. And in the end, it is he who dispatches Quasimodo—his own Mr. Hyde—to stalk and kidnap the Gypsy Esmeralda; it is he who will destroy her; and it is he who—like the thoughtless Victor Frankenstein—cruelly abandons the tortured beast he was sworn to protect.

The real fiends, then, in so many classic monster stories, are the Frankensteins, Jekylls, and Frollos who cannot abide their own humanity and   15 cannot or will not show any compassion for those whose disfigured humanity has made them outcasts. It is the men who cannot recognize their own deformities writ large on the faces of these brutes—who feel no mercy, no responsibility, no pity—who are the true monsters, and indeed, the creators of monsters.

Even in *Richard III*, Shakespeare's tale of the sociopathic "Hunchback of York," there is some reminder that monsters are fashioned not of some brutish ugliness but of our own failure to acknowledge the humanity of the stranger. In Richard of Gloucester Shakespeare has created a twisted fiend of unparalleled malice, a misshapen stump of a man who neither evidences nor invites pity. Here is a Shakespearean villain without a shred of conscience, a Renaissance Ted Bundy, Gary Gilmore, or, as Ian McKellen suggests in his [1989] production, Adolf Hitler. But this disfigured regent believes that he has the same complaint against the world, the same cause for rancor,° as Frankenstein's creature—which is that he is not, and indeed cannot be, loved.

I, that am rudely stamped, and want love's majesty . . . that am curtailed of this fair proportion, cheated of feature by dissembling nature, deformed, unfinished, and sent before my time into this breathing world . . . have no delight to pass away the time . . . and therefore, since I cannot prove a lover . . . am determined to prove a villain." (act I, scene i)

Indeed, Ken Magid and Carole McKelvey argue in *High Risk: Children without a Conscience* (M & M Publishers, 1987), sociopaths are all too often the products of emotional abandonment, children who have never been able to form an attachment or bond with a loved one.

Such insights are, of course, not really so different from the central argument of monster stories like *Frankenstein*. As the creature says to his maker/parent:

I am thy creature, and I will be even mild and docile to my natural lord and king, if thou wilt also perform thy part, that which thou owest me. . . . I ought to be thy Adam, but I am rather the fallen angel, whom thou drivest from joy for no misdeed. . . . I was benevolent and good, misery made me a fiend. Make me happy, and I shall again be virtuous.

The underlying message of these stories is that monsters are made, not born, and that they are fashioned out of our inability to accept our own limits and care for others. We don't make monsters by playing God or

rancor: deep-seated ill will.

fooling with Mother Nature. We make monsters by failing to be human and recognize and respect the humanity of others.

Maybe that's why it bothers me that monster stories seem to be being   20
replaced by a kind of tale that has no sense of our own responsibility for evil and no compassion for the disfigured creatures who serve as the stories' foils or foes. In the '50s and '60s the monsters in most creature features were often the result of some nuclear explosion or radiation experiment gone awry and so reflected some consciousness of our guilt or anxiety about the cold war and arms race. Today, however, we seem to be facing a new breed of monstrous creatures, for whom we are invited to feel neither responsibility nor sympathy. Instead, we're just to blast those little suckers out of the sky.

In a number of films the monster in question has been a beast from outer space, an alien creature to whom we are not related and who we can hunt and destroy with all the heat-seeking missiles and nuclear arsenals at our command. Meanwhile, in Michael Crichton's *Jurassic Park* (1993) we're confronted with a brood of dinosaurs from 65 million years in the past and given permission to blast and fry these reptilian sociopaths with nothing short of glee.

Nowhere, however, is this trend so evident as in [1996's] biggest blockbuster *Independence Day*—one of Bob Dole's° recommended family films and a feel-good movie that lets us blow the living daylights out of the meanest pack of really illegal aliens that ever came to town. What a thrill to be able to mount a nuclear Armageddon without the slightest concern about political or radioactive fallout of any sort, to finally find an enemy who it's not politically incorrect to hate, and to live in a world of such stark moral clarity and simplicity, where good and evil are so sharply polarized and where we are the absolutely innocent good guys. (Watching the movie, I thought I was at a Pat Buchanan rally.)

I confess to liking action films. Still, I am concerned about the presence of what seem to me to be some very dangerous trends leading to the production of more and more movies where evil is being projected onto an enemy so foreign and alien that it can be destroyed without any trace of regret. My concern is not just that such stories keep us unconscious of our own responsibility for evil and that movies like *Independence Day* help us forget that "the problem, dear Brutus, lies not in the stars, but in ourselves,"° but that they may well be tapping into some very unhealthy rage and bias in our culture.

Bob Dole, Pat Buchanan: candidates for the 1996 Republican nomination for president. **The problem, dear Brutus, lies not in the stars, but in ourselves:** a misquote of William Shakespeare's *Julius Caesar*, Act I, Scene II, lines 140–41: "The fault, dear Brutus, lies not in our stars, but in ourselves. . . ."

When you start designing movies to be theme park rides and video games, they stop being stories. It's not that stories don't or shouldn't entertain, and it's not that stories can't have thrills and chills. But real stories, at least good stories, have depth and character and plot. They wrestle with ambiguity, conflict, even paradox; pose questions—often very unsettling ones; and are open to interpretation on various levels.

Stories inspire, upset, disturb, and haunt us. They engage, not replace, 25 our imagination, challenge our moral sensitivities, and invite us to wrestle with the mystery of being human. They're about suffering, guilt, remorse, passion, anguish, even redemption.

Video games and theme parks, on the other hand, are about adrenaline. They are engineered to stimulate the fight or flight response, and, as a rule, they're geared for 12- to 14-year-olds. Like pornography, they have the thinnest of plot lines—hunt down and kill or flee from danger—and their "characters" are strictly cartoon stuff. In the midst of an adrenaline rush you don't have the time or inclination to wonder about the moral ambiguity of this situation, or the humanity of the foe. You just duck and shoot.

A second problem with these features is that their monsters turn out to be not so foreign after all, but rather poorly disguised surrogates of our rage against women and immigrants. You'd think [conservative radio host] Rush Limbaugh had written the scripts. In the Alien trilogy° Sigourney Weaver finds herself battling against a matriarchal colony of insect-like beasts, whose eggs she is always destroying. Indeed, in the second film *Aliens*, Weaver's major confrontation is with the queen bee of this monstrous breed, while the advertisements for *Alien 3* excitedly proclaim that "The Bitch is Back!"

Likewise, [British novelist] Marina Warner points out that the dinosaurs in *Jurassic Park* are dangerous females who outflank their keepers by figuring out how to propagate without males. In *Species* the alien is a Jackie the Ripper from outer space, a praying mantis who is looking for a good mate. The most dangerous monster in the universe, according to these films, is a woman having a child without permission. It's hard to miss the underlying rage against welfare moms and pregnant teens in these movies.

Meanwhile, in *Predator*, Arnold Schwarzenegger faces off against a murderous extraterrestrial who inhabits the jungles of Central America, and when Danny Glover confronts the alien's replacement in *Predator 2*,

---

Alien trilogy: the movies *Alien* (1979), *Aliens* (1986), and *Aliens 3* (1992), starring Sigourney Weaver as Warrant Officer Ellen Ripley.

the monster has decided to visit Los Angeles, of all places. One wonders just which aliens these movies are talking about. In a time when so much political rage is directed at illegal aliens, it can't be all that surprising that films like *Independence Day* would be such a hit.

Finally, there is the little matter of the bomb, or bombs. Explosives 30 are, by far and away, the most popular special effect in these video-arcade movies. It would be impossible to imagine a contemporary action film or creature feature that isn't littered with the detritus of demolitions, preferably nuclear. Not only do these toys give us the biggest bang for the buck, they are also the perfect tool for obliterating an enemy for whom we feel nothing but rage. Bombs are macho and impersonal, how perfect.

Until, of course, they start going off in the World Trade Center, in front of a government building in Oklahoma, aboard a TWA flight out of New York, or at a disco outside the Olympic Village. Then bombs are murderous, insane, cowardly, craven, and—yes—monstrous.

We need to pay attention to the kinds of monster stories we tell. They could come back to haunt us.

Understanding the Text

1. What reason(s) does McCormick give for the enduring popularity of monster stories?

2. McCormick argues that in the best monster tales, we are "haunted by an underlying sense of sympathy — and, yes, responsibility — for these misshapen men" (par. 5). What specific examples of this does he provide, and how are we responsible for them?

3. Who does McCormick believe are the real villains in *Doctor Jekyll and Mr. Hyde*, *Frankenstein*, and *The Hunchback of Notre Dame*? Why?

4. McCormick says that contemporary monster movies lack a story. What does he mean? What does he think is necessary in order to have a story?

Reflection and Response

5. McCormick states, "The underlying message of these [monster] stories is that monsters are made, not born, and that they are fashioned out of our inability to accept our own limits and care for others" (par. 18). Do you agree or disagree? Support your answer with specific examples.

6. McCormick cites aliens and dinosaurs as examples of contemporary monsters that lack humanity. Do you agree with his statement that such monsters are "rather poorly disguised surrogates of our rage against women and immigrants" (par. 27)? Include specific examples in your response.

Making Connections

7. In discussing Shakespeare's characterization of Richard III, McCormick makes a connection to real-life people he sees as monstrous: Ted Bundy, Gary Gilmore, and Adolf Hitler. What is it about these people — or others like them — that connects them to monsters? Explain your answer.

8. Update McCormick's 1996 argument about nonhuman monsters using some of today's creatures. What political messages are being sent by current representations of nonhuman monsters such as zombies, aliens, dinosaurs, dragons, and the like?

Unmasking the Monster: Hiding and Revealing Male Sexuality in John Carpenter's Halloween

Jason Huddleston

Halloween (1978) is one of the most popular and influential films of the horror genre. Its main character, Michael Myers, is a prototype of the indestructible psychotic killer. A key aspect of Michael is the mask he wears. Jason Huddleston analyzes the role of the mask in the film, arguing that it not only hides the killer's identity but actually remakes it. In struggling with sexual insecurity, Michael derives power from the mask. He needs it to slay the women who sexually excite him and the men who protect them. This article was originally published in 2005 in the *Journal of Visual Literacy*. Huddleston is an associate professor of English and literature and chair of the Department of Communications at Tennessee Temple University.

The masked killer of the slasher film usually has something to hide. Whether he is disfigured, insecure, discreet, or simply psychologically disturbed, he is almost always "distinctly male," as Carol Clover (1992) notes, and is "unmistakably sexual in both roots and expression [. . .]" (p. 42). In fact, sex and the slasher film are rarely mutually exclusive. From Hitchcock's *Psycho* to Harron's *American Psycho*, the perpetrator is typically a man fixated on destroying those demonstrating irresponsible or wanton sexual behavior, primarily women. Yet, what has become another trademark of these slasher films is the concealed identity of the killer via an often-common yet uniquely horrifying mask.

The critical question, then, becomes psychoanalytic in nature: Why does the killer need a mask? It is, of course, important to note that the mask itself within these films has taken many forms, from transvestitism (as in *Psycho* and *Dressed to Kill*) to sculptured latex or plastic (as in the Halloween and Friday the 13th series). However, it is the man beneath this cosmetic covering that we, the audience, want revealed—both physically and psychologically. Surely, we protest, the slasher has a reason for donning a disguise—some trauma from childhood or adolescence that can explain his motives and behavior to us. Indeed, many films within the horror genre are predictable and formulaic in regard to the killer's psychosexual profile, reducing him to a sexually impotent male who uses violence/murder to "rape" (a form of vicarious sex) his female victims. Yet, other, more "classic" horror films—those whose stories are often embedded with intelligent symbols and images of socio-political and/or in-depth psychological meanings—have either set the precedent for (on which the alloyed imitators have been based) or redefined the psychogenic° nature of the slasher film "monster." One of the more prevalent (and often complicated) explanations is Freud's Oedipus complex,° which traces the root of the killer's neurosis to his relationship with his mother. Other theories, such as those posited by Vera Dika (1987) in her essay "The Stalker Film, 1978–81," explore the elements of perception and the audience's identification with the killer, as well as the subsequent objectification of the story's victimized women. Still others, like Carol Clover (1992), use Freudian models to emphasize the gender identity of both the stalker and the remaining female "victim," whom Clover names "The Final Girl" in her essay "Her Body, Himself."

> "The audience, when gazing upon the often-emotionless features of the mask, is given a glimpse into the disturbed psychosexual world of the man it is meant to conceal."

Yet, among these theories, the issue of the mask remains largely unaccounted for. Many of these films that utilize this rather ordinary prop have at least implicitly suggested the significance of its function within the story and have often used the mask itself to capitalize on their slasher-hero's commercial popularity. What seems most important, however, is that the mask somehow mirrors its wearer; that the audience, when gazing upon the often-emotionless features of the mask, is given a glimpse into the disturbed psychosexual world of the man it is meant to conceal. Thus, throughout these films, the mask seems to allow the slasher to hide who he is, compensate for who he is not, and enable him to release the anxiety created by his own sexual repression.

The first of the Halloween series seems to best demonstrate this idea of hiding and revealing male sexuality. The story opens on Halloween night, 1963. Using the camera as the primary vantage point of Michael Myers, Carpenter allows his audience to see through the killer's eyes. At the beginning of the film, Michael is six years old (a crucial age in Freudian psychoanalysis, as will be discussed later). What he witnesses will not only impair his psychosexual development but will become the

---

psychogenic: originating in the mind or in mental or emotional conflict.
Oedipus complex: a psychological condition that develops from the sexual desire a boy feels toward his mother and the jealousy he feels toward his father.

primary source of psychoanalysis for most of the remaining films in the series. Michael's gaze is directed toward an open, but slightly veiled living room window. He watches as his older, teenaged sister, Judith, makes out with her boyfriend on the family couch. There are two crucial aspects to this scene: that Judith's boyfriend's sexual foreplay is both encouraged and reciprocated by Judith, and that Judith's boyfriend takes Michael's Halloween mask and holds it to his face during this foreplay.

The significance of the first aspect is that Michael seems to be vicari- 5 ously introduced to male sexuality via Judith's boyfriend. In the few seconds that the couple is on the couch, both are exchanging words and actions that are clearly suggestive of something Michael may (as a six-year-old boy) construe as illicit: adult sex. From the moment the audience becomes aware that they are viewing this scene (through the window) through the eyes of a six-year-old, the implication is that he (Michael), by intentionally partaking in an act of voyeurism, is either simply curious or already psychologically disturbed.

Nonetheless, Michael viewing the scene between his sister and her boyfriend seems to have a direct (and perhaps new) effect on him. He is sexually aroused; yet, as a boy, he is unable to both comprehend and responsibly control or respond to this sensation. As J. P. Telotte (1987) contends, the six-year-old Michael "can hardly be expected to understand the complexities of adult sexuality. [. . .] Hence, whatever he does see must remain something of a harsh mystery to him, one in which one person [the boyfriend] pleasurably assaults an apparently willing victim [Judith]" (p. 117). This is not to say that Michael, before this scene, had never encountered a sexual image or scenario. It is, however (for the viewing audience, at least, who knows nothing more of Michael's childhood than this scene), the first time he chooses to murder in response to sexual titillation.

After their interlude on the couch, the boyfriend enthusiastically suggests that he and Judith go upstairs, to which Judith enthusiastically assents. What is interesting to note here is that Michael does not immediately follow and kill them both. In fact, it appears as though he waits until the boyfriend leaves the house before entering the house himself, picking up the mask, and stabbing Judith to death as she sits (naked) before her vanity mirror. This moment in the film (though one of only a few) contradicts Carol Clover's (1992) argument that, in the slasher film, "[n]o male character of any stature lives to tell the tale" (p. 296). Why, then, is Judith's boyfriend allowed to survive? Certainly it is not because of the physical disparities between the boyfriend and Michael, for Michael's ability to mercilessly stab his adult sister (hence, any unarmed adult) implies his strong (if not remarkable) physical stamina—even if enhanced by a sharp butcher knife. Perhaps, then, the boyfriend is allowed to live because, at least at this initial stage in Michael's sexual development, he represents the virile man—that which Michael simultaneously aspires to be and knows he is not. Again, it is the boyfriend—who dons the mask in mockery of his own (as well as Michael's) childishness—who represents the virile man, the one whom his sister desires. There is a perverse reverence, then, given to the boyfriend here. Yet, Michael must also now find an outlet for his sexual arousal, which he finds in the woman who sexually rejects him by rejecting the mask that represents him.

The second aspect is equally significant, for Michael watches the boyfriend as he hovers over Judith, taunting her with and pretending to kiss her through the mask. This leads Judith to say, "Take off that thing!" Although (at least to Carpenter's audience) Judith is not seriously offended by her boyfriend wearing the mask (evidenced by her laughter and mutually playful gestures), her remark may be interpreted literally as one of disgust by the young, sexually naive Michael, who may then identify the mask as something that sexually capable men (like Judith's boyfriend) do not need in order to receive sexual gratification from women; this identification with the mask as an object of sexual immaturity—that is, an object worn only by young boys (or puerile° men)—distances Michael the child (and, ultimately, Michael the adult) from the sexually virile man (embodied in Judith's boyfriend), as well as from the sexualized woman. Telotte (1987) notes something similar to this, suggesting that the mask "functions not only to cloak his human features, but also to effectively divorce him from the world of the living, his victims" (p. 119). What becomes relevant, though, is that Michael's sexual puerility is defined by the mask. Michael may then be seen as using this mask to hide the fact that he is unable to live up to the standard of male sexuality as determined by the boyfriend and reinforced by his sister.

The violence against Judith may at least be explained in Freudian terms. For Michael, Judith represents the woman (and all women Michael will thereafter encounter and destroy) who rejects him solely on the grounds of his not being the virile man (like her boyfriend). The seemingly incestuous interpretation of this scene, where Michael "rapes" Judith with the "phallic knife" (Telotte, 1987, p. 117), is perhaps only one interpretation; that is, Michael does not necessarily kill/rape Judith because she is his sister who refuses to have sex with him. Michael is at the fringe of Freud's phallic stage in adolescent development, which includes

puerile: silly or childish.

boys between three and six years of age. At this stage, boys become aware of their sexual uniqueness, that which distinguishes them from girls (Boeree, 1997). This does not, of course, make them more prone to kill the opposite sex. However, Michael's "rape" of Judith may be seen as a sort of unresolved Oedipus complex with his mother. Although we only see Michael's mother once in the film—in a silent scene of discovery after Michael has killed Judith and walked outside the house—one might argue that, somewhere during this phallic phase, Michael's sexual desire for his mother was rejected by her. If so, then Judith logically serves as a surrogate for this desire; he transfers this desire onto Judith, which explains his need to kill her after she has sex with the boyfriend. In this context, the mask allows Michael to compensate for his own sexual puerility. Rejected by his mother, he pursues the older (implicitly mothering) sister. For whatever reasons his Oedipal desire remained unresolved with Mrs. Myers, Michael makes up for it by pursuing, and ultimately killing, Judith, covering his face (and his insecurities) with the clown mask. What is important to remember, though, is that Michael (at six) is in the last year of this phallic stage. If his Oedipal desire remains unresolved—as it was with his mother and now seems to be with Judith (through her sexual relationship with the boyfriend and, more importantly, her rejection of Michael's mask)—then he will be "afraid or incapable of close love" (Stevenson, 1966). In fact, unresolved Oedipal desire may lead to neurotic tendencies. In Michael's case, the failure to resolve leads to violence, to murder. For Michael, the mask enables him to express (though certainly not anonymously, since his sister dies while calling out his name) his unresolved desire for her. . . .

The primary focus of *Halloween* is Michael's obsession with Laurie 10 Strode, who, as revealed in *Halloween II*, is Michael's second sister, the one born to the Myerses after Judith's death and Michael's institutionalization. In the sequel, it is revealed that, although Michael was never meant to know about Laurie, he learns of his relationship to her from files at the state hospital. Knowing of another sister—another Oedipal surrogate—warrants the escape from the hospital but also prompts Michael to don a new mask.

The mask, which would immortalize Michael as "The Shape," is appropriately expressionless and, as Loomis implies, ironically similar to Michael's true facial features: "blank, pale, [and] emotionless [. . .]" with "the darkest eyes, the devil's eyes." In fact, Loomis says that he later realized that "what was living behind [those] eyes was purely and simply evil." The mask—a sculptured latex mask—has two holes for the eyes. This may be a crucial feature of the mask, for it suggests that the eyes are the only part of the man revealed; if these eyes are indeed "purely and simply evil," then the mask becomes an extension of the evil that it attempts to conceal. For Michael, the selection of the mask is perhaps arbitrary, limited to what was available at the time he stole it from the hardware store. Yet, the mask's languid features only reflect the personality, the evilness, of its wearer. Although the identity of the robber is never disclosed, Michael is the one who apparently steals the mask—along with some rope and knives, according to the local sheriff—from a hardware store (a significant symbol of masculinity in this context) in Haddonfield, Michael's (and Laurie's) hometown. Yet, prior to this, we first see Michael (shadowed, unmasked, and only from behind) in Haddonfield standing behind (or masked by) the darkened front screen door of his old, abandoned home. He is watching Laurie walk up to the door to leave a spare key for her father, a local real estate agent trying to sell the Myers house. The audience then watches her as she walks away from the house and down the sidewalk (away from the camera), over the partially visible left shoulder of Michael. Laurie is heard singing "I wish I had you all alone / just the two of us" within Michael's earshot. Although Laurie is unaware of Michael's presence, the lyric itself seems to be a sexual tease; for this is all Michael is allowed to hear—suggesting that his first encounter with Laurie is related to her (albeit vicarious) expression of sexual feelings for a man through the lyrics of a song—and it is this scene where Michael begins his more deliberate pursuit of Laurie. It is only as Laurie moves further away from Michael and the song becomes less audible (by the second line) that we are able to hear Michael breathing heavily. This is significant due to the fact that he has yet to wear the mask; thus, his heavy breathing is a result of his sexual arousal from the lyrical tease. This may indeed suggest his motive for later stealing the mask from the hardware store, for he is unable to maturely or responsibly control his desire and must therefore conceal his feelings of inadequacy with the mask.

The mask is at last revealed in a sequence of brief scenes, where Laurie questions whether or not she really sees this elusive figure. Laurie (the audience) first sees him masked while he is standing directly across the street from Laurie's classroom. He later appears to Laurie again among the hanging laundry outside her house. Yet, the most significant occurs when Laurie, Annie, and Lynda walk down the sidewalk together (toward the camera), discussing their plans for that night (Halloween). Annie teases Lynda, who says that she has to find a way to get out of taking her brother trick or treating, by suggesting that Lynda has treats waiting for Bob, Lynda's boyfriend. At this point, Michael is standing at the end of the adjoining lot, but is only seen by Laurie (Lynda having already entered her house, Annie digging through her purse). Laurie stops and tells

Annie to look "behind the bush"—a strong feminine metaphor for Michael's Oedipal repression—behind which Michael has now disappeared. Annie pursues, finds no trace of him, and says, "Poor Laurie scared another one away." The suggestion here is that Laurie's more "masculine" qualities (her bookishness, her plain appearance, her sense of responsibility) have intimidated yet another potential suitor. Indeed, he is intimidated, but perhaps more by the fact that two women are approaching him (rather than simply a "masculine" one). The mask certainly conceals his identity, but it has yet to serve to compensate for what he is not, a sexually confident man. He must instead retreat "behind the bush."

As night (a mask itself) sets in, Michael seems to slowly gain confidence, bolstered by the prospects of nightfall: a darkness that may further conceal his identity. And while Laurie seems to be his primary target, Michael realizes that he must first eliminate her friends, Annie and Lynda, who sexually tease him. They are not necessarily obstacles he must overcome to reach Laurie, although there is some logic to this methodology (i.e., eliminate all others until only the primary target remains). Instead, they, too, represent sexual surrogates. Their earlier talk of sex could have certainly aroused and provoked him to seek further arousal (via watching them through windows or, as will be discussed later, through a bedroom sheet). Yet, they, too, will deny him, further frustrating his Oedipal desires.

In (now characteristic) voyeuristic fashion, Michael stands outside the house (once more amid the bushes) where Annie is babysitting. He overhears her speaking to Laurie about Ben Tramer—a guy Annie has set up as Laurie's date for the homecoming dance. Annie tells Laurie how attracted Ben is to her and how excited he became by the idea of taking Laurie out. At this point, we hear the heavy breathing of the now masked Michael as he moves closer to the nearest window. After Annie spills popcorn oil on herself, she begins to remove her shirt (to reveal that she is braless) and then her pants, remaining only in her panties and knee-high socks until she is able to find a long, white shirt to cover her near naked body. Michael's breathing through the mask becomes more intense. Obviously aroused but unable to release the tension sexually, he pulls down a ceramic flowerpot suspended between himself and the window. Annie hears the pot break but dismisses it.

To vent his sexual frustration, Michael chokes the family (male) dog, 15
Lester, which has been barking at him since his arrival at the window and has now been allowed outside. Although it does not presume to directly associate Michael with bestiality, this particular scene with Lester is nonetheless symbolic. The audience watches as Annie finishes the popcorn, frustrated by Lester's incessant barking (the former is still at the

In John Carpenter's *Halloween* (1978), Michael Myers (Tony Moran) watches as
Annie (Nancy Kyes) undresses and then talks to her boyfriend on the phone.
© Compass International Pictures/Photofest

window while the latter is briefly shown standing directly in front of
Michael). Suddenly, the dog's loud bark becomes a whimper, followed by
silence. Annie interprets the silence as Lester finding "a hot date." The
implication in her tone is that she, too, would like to be with a guy right
now, rather than babysitting; that she, too, wants sex. But Lester's silence
is due to being strangled by Michael. What the audience sees of this may
be interpreted as symbolic, for the camera is directed at Michael's waist
and the lower half of Lester's dying body. At first, the dog's legs and tail
are curled up, tensed; then, as Michael's breathing through the mask becomes harder, and as the dog slips into death, the legs and tail relax and
uncurl down the length of Michael's own legs. Lester's body could be
symbolic of Michael's penis, which, made erect by watching Annie, is
now limp after releasing the tension through violence on the dog.
However, this has only allowed him to partially express his sexual anxiety. He watches as Annie takes her stained clothes to the laundry and,
later, while she talks with her boyfriend Paul, where she accuses him of
always thinking about sex and even suggests that he come over so that

they can "get down to doing" the (sexual) things that she's been thinking about. Aroused further by her own sexual arousal with Paul, Michael waits patiently to kill her from the backseat of the family's car, which Annie must use to pick up Paul in order to engage in sex. In a scene similar to the one where Laurie sings while walking down the sidewalk, Annie—emotionally elated by the idea of being with Paul—sings, "My, Paul! I give you all!" while en route to the parked car. Michael most likely hears these words from the backseat and is, perhaps, both aroused and enraged by them, for Paul, and not he, is the object of her desire, the one who will receive "all" of her sexual attention. It is important to note that, during the car scene, Annie is only killed immediately after becoming aware of Michael's presence (after noticing that the windshield has been fogged by his breathing). Her death may indeed be inevitable, but Michael's timing seems calculated; for Michael kills her because she threatens to discover his identity, to reveal the sexual insecurity that he wishes to conceal. And, like the dog, Annie is strangled to death, though she is never able to see the lifeless face of the man who (sexually) attacks and destroys her. Now, at least in terms of Annie, Michael is able to vent his frustration. Yet, he remains unsatisfied.

Lynda, the more blatant, sexually wanton female character of the film, is first seen that night with Bob as they pull up to the now empty house (where Annie had been sitting) where they have arranged to have sex. Both are laughing, drinking beer, and sexually excited. After they enter the house, discover Annie is absent, and begin to make out on the nearest couch, Michael is shown standing in the shadows, watching them from across the room. Bob and Lynda retreat upstairs to the master bedroom for sex, where Michael, whose shadow is seen on the wall to the right of the bed, again watches them. After a quick orgasm, Bob descends to the first floor to get Lynda a beer. It is during this scene—while Bob and Michael are in the kitchen—that Michael seems to abandon his childhood reverence for the virile man. Instead, he is enraged by and perhaps even jealous of him. In this scene, Bob now represents both a virile man (who needs only glasses to see but no other facial covering to be sexually acceptable for Lynda) and the one who serves as an obstacle for Michael, who is sexually aroused by watching Lynda have sex with Bob. Bob's death is almost immediate: a knife through the stomach that pins his body against the door. His death, though quick, is not insignificant; for Michael, who stands back from the body, watches it carefully, as if admiring it. At the same time, one may also see this disturbing postmortem inspection as time Michael uses to devise a scheme to bring himself closer to Lynda.

As Lynda files her fingernails in bed, waiting for Bob to return, the door slowly opens to reveal Michael (whom Lynda mistakes for Bob) standing in the doorway, wearing a white bed sheet (with two eyeholes torn through) and Bob's glasses. Lynda, excited by his return, sits up and lowers the sheet that covers her to reveal her breasts. "See anything you like?" she asks. Upon receiving no response (Michael stands motionless at the door), she asks, "What's the matter? Can't I get your ghost, Bob?" For Michael, this is significant: he has deceived Lynda into believing that he is her boyfriend. He can now vicariously have sex with her. His sexual insecurity is certainly demonstrated by his need to wear a second mask before a sexually powerful woman (Lynda).

Yet, this double masking also allows Michael the potential to release his repressed sexual anxiety (created by watching Lynda and Bob). As Bob, he can become (at least through Lynda's eyes) the virile man. It seems evident that Michael is aroused yet again, this time by Lynda's mistaken sexual advances; for he remains at the door, motionless, and more willing to be enticed by her than to immediately kill her. Irritated by "Bob's" silence, his lack of responses to her blatant advances, Lynda gets out of bed to call Laurie. It is only here, at the point where Michael feels his security threatened, that he chooses to kill Lynda. The implication here is that, had Lynda remained in bed and persisted in her advances, Michael would have been allowed to have sex with her while double masked; in fact, such sex may even have been deemed kinky by the licentious Lynda (a literal sex between the sheets).

David Hogan (1997), in his book *Dark Romance: Sexuality in the Horror Film*, attempts to argue that the deaths of Bob and Lynda during these scenes are in fact "not a result of their sexual habits, but of an unreasoning force that kills men and women with equal vigor [. . .]" (p. 252). In part, this is true; but while Michael may kill both men and women in this film, the ultimate objects of his wrath are the women, and only because they sexually arouse and, finally, reject him. Thus, since Lynda rejects him—even as Bob—he must destroy her, for she has (like all women thus far) left him sexually unfulfilled. She is another Judith and Annie. While strangling Lynda with the phone cord, Michael's secondary mask (the sheet) is slowly removed as Lynda's body sinks to the floor, revealing Michael's primary mask. Throughout the strangulation, Michael's belabored breathing is heard through the mask. In an almost symbolic gesture, he takes the phone and places it to the mask's ear, as if to hear Laurie on the other end. This simple action is significantly deceptive: the audience now sees Michael's mask as his real face; thus, the phone is raised not to the mask (through which he would be unlikely to hear clearly) but to his own ear. Michael too is deceived in this way, believing that the mask is indeed his own face, denoting the sense of confidence that the mask seems to give him. Yet again, although he is able to release the anxiety, his Oedipal urge remains unresolved.

As if by Michael's design, only Laurie remains. Unlike his encounters 20 with Annie and Lynda, Michael does not seem to be sexually stimulated by Laurie. Yet, the audience is given unmistakable signs as to his state of sexual repression. Laurie, as the primary target of his rampage against Haddonfield, is the remaining Oedipal surrogate (following Mrs. Myers and Judith). And while Annie and Lynda have served more as temporary surrogates, Michael's only hope of resolving his now fifteen-year obsession is to destroy the last woman in his bloodline.

Clover (1992) describes her as "The Final Girl." She alone remains not only to flee from the stalker but to turn on and ultimately destroy him:

She is introduced at the beginning and is the only character to be developed in any psychological detail. We understand immediately from the attention paid it that hers is the main story line. She is intelligent, watchful, levelheaded; the first character to sense something amiss and the only one to deduce from the accumulating evidence the pattern and extent of the threat; the only one, in other words, whose perspective approaches our own privileged understanding of the situation. (p. 44)

In *Halloween*, Laurie meets this criterion from the very beginning of the film. Not only does she demonstrate the characteristics of Clover's Final Girl, but she also has very maternal instincts that make her an ideal target for Michael to resolve his unresolved Oedipal issues. Among her friends (namely, Annie and Lynda), she proves to be the most responsible. On Halloween night, while Annie works strategically to get together with Paul, and while Lynda takes Bob to the upstairs bedroom of the house where Annie (hired to watch the house and keep the family's daughter) has arranged for them to have sex, Laurie not only keeps Tommy but Lindsey, as well—the latter being left with Laurie by Annie, who leaves so that she can spend some time with Paul. Laurie also plays the role of a maternal comforter to Tommy, whose fear of "the bogeyman" becomes more intense as stories he has been told are compounded by actual sightings of "The Shape" across the street.

After discovering the corpses of her friends (now strategically placed in the home where Annie was babysitting), Laurie finally encounters Michael as he (rather, the mask, since the darkness of the house cloaks the rest of his body) appears from behind. He is able to stab at her left arm, but she falls over the banister before he can kill her. The following scene, where Michael proceeds to descend the staircase in pursuit, best demonstrates what many psychoanalytic critics have interpreted as Michael's phallic use of the knife to penetrate his female victims. In fact, the knife may even be a signifier of his own level of sexual arousal; for, as he descends the staircase, Michael holds the knife in a horizontal position close to his right hip; due to the enveloping darkness, the knife could be construed as an extension of his penis. As the chase intensifies, the knife is turned upward to an almost complete vertical position, suggestive of Michael's erection. Thus, Carpenter himself may have been fully aware of the obvious phallic significance of Michael's knife. But it is the mask that is given the most direct attention toward the end of the film.

The final chase scene seems to be reaching its climax; Carpenter's piano music is becoming more intense while Laurie is forced into the only remaining space available to hide: the upstairs bedroom closet. As Michael breaks through the closet, Laurie fashions a makeshift knife from a dangling wire coat hanger, which she uses to stab Michael in the eye. Here, Michael himself has been "raped" by Laurie's own "penis," somewhat demonstrating Clover's (1992) idea of the Final Girl's symbolic castration of the male killer (p. 49); however, what is more important here is that Michael's mask has been penetrated. If the eyehole is the only place on the mask that directly reveals the man underneath, then Michael's sense of security—provided by the mask—has been violated by the source of his Oedipal frustration.

After Laurie relaxes against the doorframe, believing Michael to be dead, she is attacked once more from behind. This time, however, Michael is without a knife; hence, he has no desire to "rape" her, only to destroy her as he did Judith fifteen years ago. In her struggle to free herself from his grasp, Laurie attempts to remove Michael's mask, lifting it over his face. He quickly releases her and pulls away. Here, he has been exposed, returned to the stage of insecurity that he felt as a child while looking at Judith and her boyfriend through the living room window.

If the mask has both compensated for what he is not and enabled him to release this tension, then being unmasked by Laurie (i.e., Judith and his mother) is the ultimate form of self-awareness. He does not seem to interpret this as a message from Laurie that he is too virile to hide behind a mask (as Judith conveyed to her boyfriend); on the contrary, he steps back to quickly pull the mask over his face again. Instead, he may interpret this as Laurie's rejection of him entirely.

As the mask is restored—hence, as Michael attempts to regain his sense of male sexuality—Dr. Loomis arrives and shoots him. In fact,

Loomis waits until the mask has covered Michael's face before shooting him. As Michael retreats to the next room, Loomis follows him, only to see Michael's silhouette standing before him, breathing even harder than before. This hard breathing may certainly be due to being shot by Loomis (although he has been injured quite severely prior to this without such a display of exertion), but it may also suggest that Michael is responding to being rejected by Laurie. Michael is then shot five more times before falling (seemingly to his death) from the outside balcony to the ground below. By the end of this film, then, his Oedipal urge remains as yet unresolved, and the audience must await the sequel and anticipate yet another deliberate pursuit to destroy Laurie (along with numbers of other victims along the way).

Although the mask of Michael Myers continues to serve a function in the subsequent films of the series—even *Halloween III*, whose story line has nothing to do with Michael or any of his victims—its role in the first film has the most direct associations with Michael's sexual frustrations. Carpenter's ability to allow his audience to see what Michael sees enables us to not only become first-hand witnesses of his slayings but to put on the mask itself and, at times, to become the killer. Yet, despite how close we may come, the mask always belongs to Michael, whose childhood Oedipal frustrations are never truly resolved.

References

Boeree, C. George. (1997). *Personality Theories: Sigmund Freud*. Retrieved 13 April 2003, from Shippensburg University, Dr. C. George Boeree's Homepage: http://www.ship.edu/~cgboeree/freud.html.

Carpenter, J. (Director). (1978). *Halloween* [Motion picture]. United States: Compass International Pictures.

Clover, Carol. (1992). *Men, Women, and Chainsaws: Gender in the Modern Horror Film*. New Jersey: Princeton U.

Dika, Vera. (1987). "The Stalker Film, 1978–81." In Gregory A. Waller (Ed.), *American Horrors: Essays on the Modern American Horror Film* (pp. 86–101). Chicago: U of Illinois P.

Hogan, David J. (1997). *Dark Romance: Sexuality in the Horror Film*. NC: McFarland.

Stevenson, David B. (1966). *Freud's Psychosexual Stages of Development*. Retrieved 1 May 2003, from http://65.107.211.206/science/freud/Psychosexual Development.html.

Telotte, J. P. (1987). "Through a Pumpkin's Eye: The Reflexive Nature of Horror." In Gregory A. Waller (Ed.), *American Horrors: Essays on the Modern American Horror Film* (pp. 114–128). Chicago: U of Illinois P.

Understanding the Text

1. According to Huddleston, what is the importance of the mask in the horror genre, including in films such as *Psycho* and *American Psycho*?

2. What is the importance of the male character Michael Myers does not kill, Judith's boyfriend? How does Huddleston interpret his relationship to Michael?

3. How does Laurie turn the tables on Michael as he attempts to kill her?

Reflection and Response

4. Argue how male sexual power and virility — or sexual insecurity — is important in analyzing Michael's character and actions.

5. Huddleston states, "The mask [is] something that sexually capable men (like Judith's boyfriend) do not need in order to receive sexual gratification from women" (par. 8). Why does Michael need his mask? Consider the origin of the mask, what Michael does with and without it, and his use of the double mask when he kills Lynda.

6. Michael's mask is notable for its lack of detail: it is a blank white covering with eyeholes. Why is this image potentially more frightening than a mask with more distinctive characteristics?

Making Connections

7. Huddleston writes, "One of the more prevalent (and often complicated) explanations [of why the killer needs the mask] is Freud's Oedipus complex, which traces the root of the killer's neurosis to his relationship with his mother" (par. 2). Research the Oedipus complex. Then examine the lives of real-life killers such as John Wayne Gacy, Ted Bundy, and Jeffrey Dahmer and argue whether Freud's theory explains such killers or not.

8. In Karen Hollinger's article "The Monster as Woman: Two Generations of Cat People" (p. 243), she argues that the horror monster evokes "castration anxiety" and the horror film is often about "the potency of female sexuality and the power of woman's sexual difference." Read Hollinger's article and analyze the character of Michael in view of her ideas.

9. How does the role of the mask in *Halloween* compare with that of masks in other slasher movies?

Inside a Murdering Mind

Anne E. Schwartz

Two cops were nearing the end of their beat on a blistering-hot night in Milwaukee when they encountered a short, skinny black man with a handcuff on one wrist and an incredible tale of a crazy white man. Their investigation led to the discovery of one of the most gruesome and famous human monsters of our time: Jeffrey Dahmer. Anne E. Schwartz was a reporter for the *Milwaukee Journal Sentinel* at the time. These excerpts come from her book *The Man Who Could Not Kill Enough* (1992) and details not only Dahmer's crimes and his trial but also the psychology of this unusual serial killer.

Police Officers Rolf Mueller and Robert Rauth were finishing their four p.m.–to–midnight shift in Milwaukee's Third Police District. They had been driving along the 2600 block of West Kilbourn Avenue, a grimy neighborhood on the fringes of the downtown area near Marquette University, the highest crime area in the inner city. To the north, the main thoroughfare was peppered with strip bars and small, corner grocery stores. Faded, tattered signs in the windows advertised: WE TAKE FOOD STAMPS.

The neighborhood included drug dealers, prostitutes, and the unemployed mentally ill, who collected state aid because they managed to live on their own or in one of the area's numerous halfway houses. They would carry their belongings in rusty metal grocery carts and sleep in doorways. There was evidence of the area's glory days: expansive turn-of-the-century Victorian homes, rambling apartment complexes, and stately cathedral-style dwellings. For the police, the district has the dubious distinction of being the place where more than half the city's homicides have occurred in the last five years.

That Monday, July 22, [1991,] felt oppressively hot and humid, the kind of heat that would cling to the body. For cops on the beat, the sweat would trickle down their chests and form salty pools under their steel-plated bulletproof vests. Their gun belts would hang uncomfortably from their waists, and the constant rubbing chafed their middles. The squad cars they patrolled in reeked of burning motor oil and the body odor of the last prisoner who sat in the back seat. It was on nights like this that they could not wait to go home.

Anxious to see his wife and daughter, Mueller hoped to make it to the end of the shift without stumbling into any overtime. Mueller, thirty-nine, was a ten-year veteran of the Milwaukee Police Department.

Born in Germany, he had moved to America as a youngster but he spoke a little German at home with his daughter to preserve his heritage. He sported a mass of perpetually tousled blond curls on top of his six-foot frame. Mueller enjoyed horror movies and always talked about how much he loved a good scare.

Mueller's partner, Bob Rauth, forty-one, had spent thirteen years in the department. His strawberry-blond hair had begun to thin, exposing a long scar on his forehead from a car accident that pushed his face through the windshield. His stocky build seemed more suited to a wrestler than a policeman. Like many police officers, Rauth was divorced. His fellow officers knew he consistently took as much overtime as he could get, anxious to find an assignment so he could squirrel away some extra money for a couple more hours' work, something cops call "hunting for overtime." To work with Rauth was to "work over." Other cops described Rauth as one of those guys to whom all the strange, almost unbelievable things happen on the job. Fortunately, Rauth had a self-deprecating sense of humor and would frequently keep the station in stitches about something that happened to him on an assignment or "hitch."

Sitting in their squad car waiting to take a prisoner to jail, Mueller and Rauth were approached by a short, wiry black man with a handcuff dangling from his left wrist. Another summer night that brings out the best in everybody, they thought.

"Which one of us did you escape from?" one of the officers asked through an open window in the car.

The man was thirty-two-year-old Tracy Edwards. While someone coming down the street with a handcuff dangling from his wrist would be an attention-grabber in Milwaukee's posher suburbs, on 25th and Kilbourn it's nothing out of the ordinary. Police calls in that area can range from a man with his head wrapped in aluminum foil spray-painting symbols on houses to a naked man directing traffic at a major intersection. The area is filled with "MOs," citizens brought to the Milwaukee County Mental Health Complex for "mental observation" rather than taken to jail when arrested.

Rauth and Mueller were hesitant to let Edwards go on his way in case he had escaped from another officer, so they asked whether the scuffed silver bracelets were souvenirs of a homosexual encounter. Cops practice the cover-your-ass motto with every shift they work. They don't want to stand in somebody's glass office the next day, trying to explain their way out of a situation that went bad after they left and citizens called screaming their name and badge number to the Chief.

As Edwards stood next to the squad car, he rambled on about a "weird dude" who slapped a handcuff on him during his visit to the dude's apartment. After initially rebuking Edwards, telling him to have his "friend" remove the handcuffs, the two officers eventually listened to Edwards's story. It would not have been unusual for the two men to write the incident off as a homosexual encounter gone awry, but Rauth sniffed overtime and asked Edwards to show him where all this happened. That's how close Jeffrey Dahmer came to not getting caught that day. Criminals sometimes escape arrest because they are stopped at the end of a cop's shift or because an officer, tired from working late the night before, does not want to spend the next day tied up in court and then have to report for work.

The two officers decided to go with Edwards to apartment 213 in the Oxford Apartments at 924 North 25th Street. They were not familiar with the building, a reasonably well maintained three-story brick structure. They were rarely called there because most of its occupants held jobs and lived quietly. Once inside the building, the officers were struck by the rancid odor hanging heavy in the air as they approached the apartment.

But all these places stink around here, they thought. A variety of smells greet the police when they are sent to check on the welfare of an apartment full of children who, officers discover, have been sitting alone for several days in their own feces and who have been using the bathtub and the toilet interchangeably while their mother sits at a tavern down the street. Foul smells are as much a part of the inner city as crime.

"Milwaukee police officers," Rauth shouted for all to hear as he rapped loudly with his beefy hand on the wooden door of apartment 213.

Jeffrey Dahmer, thirty-one, an attractive but scruffy, thin man with dirty blond hair and a scar over his right eye, opened the door and allowed the officers and Edwards to enter.

Inside, Mueller and Rauth talked to Dahmer about the incident with 15 Edwards and asked him for the key to the handcuffs. This way, if they got the right answers, they could "advise" the assignment, meaning they could handle the problem and leave without writing a ticket or making an arrest.

Dahmer talked to the officers in the calm voice that, we would later learn, had manipulated so many victims and officials in the past. He told them that the key was in the bedroom. But before Dahmer left the room, Edwards piped up that they would find there a knife that Dahmer had used to threaten him.

It did not appear that Mueller would get home on time, but maybe they could still "advise" the situation if they discovered no knife. Mueller told Dahmer to stay put and went into the bedroom.

Mueller peered into an open dresser drawer and saw something he still describes with difficulty: Polaroid photographs of males in various stages of dismemberment, pictures of skulls in kitchen cabinets and freezers, and a snapshot of a skeleton dangling from a shower spigot. He stopped breathing for a time as he stood frozen, staring at the gruesome Polaroids that barely seemed to depict humans.

In a tremulous voice Mueller screamed for his partner to cuff Dahmer and place him under arrest. "Bob, I don't think we can advise this any more," he shouted, with that gallows humor cops use to keep a safe distance from the stresses of their jobs.

Realizing he was bound for jail, Dahmer turned violent. He and Offi- 20 cer Rauth tumbled around the living room floor until Dahmer was safely in handcuffs. Mueller emerged from the bedroom clutching several photos in his hand.

"You're one lucky son of a bitch, buddy," Mueller told Edwards. "This could have been you," he added, his hands shaking as he waved a photo of a severed human head at Edwards.

Edwards looked wide-eyed at Mueller and told him how Dahmer "freaked" when he went toward the refrigerator to get a beer. "Maybe he's got one of those heads in there," Edwards said uncomfortably. "Yeah, right, maybe there's a head in there." Mueller laughed at Edwards's fear.

Mueller opened the refrigerator door to taunt Edwards, then let out two screams from deep in his gut that neighbors would later recall had awakened them. Mueller slammed the door shut and shouted, "Bob, there's a fucking head in the refrigerator!"

• • •

An unassuming third-shift worker at the Ambrosia Chocolate Co. in Milwaukee, Jeffrey Dahmer fancied roses, his fish tank, and his laptop computer.

Until July 23, 1991, chances were that no one knew of his very secret 25 desires.

But who would have?

Many people fit the profile of a mass murderer, according to Dr. James Alan Fox, dean of the College of Criminal Justice at Northeastern University in Boston and a nationally recognized expert on mass murder. There are thousands of angry, depressed people out there, and there is no way to tell in that haystack of humanity who is going to be a killer.

Fox, co-author, along with Northeastern University sociologist Jack Levin, of *Mass Murder: America's Growing Menace*, studied serial killers for eleven years. He has testified before Congress on the subject of crime in America. I came to know him while he was working on a new book, *Overkill*, a study of different varieties of serial murder that [would] include a chapter on Jeffrey Dahmer.

A 1992 mugshot of Jeffrey Dahmer, the Milwaukee serial killer who was sentenced to fifteen life sentences.
© Corbis

The terms *serial killing, mass murder,* and *massacre* are often used inter-changeably but in fact refer to distinguishable phenomena. According to Fox, mass murderers typically target people they know and conduct the murders simultaneously. Serial killers kill over a period of time, killing one person at a time and usually using the same method each time. Family massacres are the most common type of mass murder and gener-ally do not attract national publicity. They involve private conflicts in private places, and the victim count usually is modest compared, for ex-ample, to the large number of bystanders killed at random in a restaurant shooting.

As I delved into Dahmer's childhood, I believed I would uncover 30 something sinister that would explain how a person could come to com-mit such acts. For my own peace of mind, I just had to have an explana-tion. If I discovered that he felt neglected as early as age six, that his mother had abandoned him, and that he was fascinated with dead ani-mals, I could explain why he did it. Fox told me my effort was futile.

"There was nothing we could have done to predict this [tragedy] ahead of time, no matter how bizarre the behavior," Fox explained. "[Dahmer] had an alcohol problem in high school. So do a lot of kids, and they don't all become serial murderers. Most serial murderers do tend to have difficult childhoods, but so do lots of other people. Victims of abuse are just as likely, if not more likely, to grow up and become ruthless businessmen and victimize unsuspecting consumers for pleasure—not just for profit, but because they get pleasure out of other people's pain—as they are to grow up to become serial killers."

Fox believes that some experiences of adolescence and early adulthood are just as critical in determining the fate of someone as their youths, for example, how well he fit in in high school, whether he had lots of friends, what sort of successes he had. It was apparent that Dahmer was devastated when his mother left him and took his little brother with her. But it would take a giant leap to blame Joyce Flint Dahmer or Lionel Dahmer somehow for what happened.

"Ever since Sigmund Freud, we blame everything bad that kids do on their parents, and that's unfortunate and it doesn't make sense," Fox said. "What we do is scare lots of innocent people who are suffering in their own way for what their kids did. The culprit is Dahmer. Not his father, not his family, not the police."

> "I think he knew exactly what he was doing and how he was going to do it. There's nothing wrong with Jeffrey Dahmer."

Fox, who knew many parents of serial murderers, said they go through hell. "In a sense they've lost a child, too, but they don't get lots of sympathy from us," he said. "We should have lots of sympathy for the families of the victims but we obviously have no sympathy for the family of the killer. We think of them as a Dr. Frankenstein who created a monster. We blame them and we hound them."

Hillside Strangler Kenneth Bianchi's mother was hounded out of her Rochester, New York, home by the media, and she still lives in hiding. Yet she never committed the crime; her son did.

"You have psychiatrists who want to theorize that the reason why all these people died is because a child hated his parents and wanted to get back at them indirectly by killing these people," Fox said. "When [Florida killer] Ted Bundy was executed, there was a psychiatrist who said he hated his mother and that's why he killed all the women. We focus too much on the childhood.

"If Dahmer had grown up to become the vice president of a corporation, we would have looked at his background and said that he became a stronger individual because of it."

As I watched the Dahmer case unfold in Milwaukee, I saw our focus shift from the actual killer to a scapegoat for his deeds. As soon as people found out that cops had had contact with Dahmer and his fourteen-year-old victim, we seemed to push aside the fact that Dahmer was the one who committed the murders. Except for the days when Dahmer appeared in court, the papers and newscasts were filled with tales of police insensitivity and community outrage—but not outrage so much toward Dahmer as toward the police.

In Fox's eleven years of studying serial killers, he told me, Jeffrey Dahmer stood out. "He's different than the usual serial killer. He more fits the stereotype of someone who really is out of control and being controlled by his fantasies," Fox said. "The difference is most serial killers stop once the victim dies. Everything is leading up to that. They tie them up; they like to hear them scream and beg for their lives. It makes the killer feel great, superior, powerful, dominant. He rapes her or him while the victim is alive, and when the person is dead, they take the body somewhere and leave it where it won't be found. That's the typical pattern.

"In Dahmer's case, everything was post-mortem. In a certain way, he 40 was merciful, because he drugged his victims. They didn't have the same sort of terror and horror the victims of other serial killers have had. For Dahmer, all of his 'fun' began after the victims died."

Dahmer did not overpower his victims to get them to come to his home; they returned willingly with him to his apartment. He fed them a drugged drink and strangled them when they were unconscious. The victims probably never knew anything terrible was happening to them. Dahmer confessed that he had had sex with some of the victims before he killed them, but for the most part, his efforts were concentrated on them after they were dead. He had oral or anal sex with the corpses and took elaborate measures to pose their lifeless bodies for photographs, using the camera as a means to enhance his fantasy life. He dismembered the victims, preserved some of their body parts, and disposed of the rest.

It would have been a small comfort to share with the families that at least their loved ones did not appear to have suffered before their deaths. But the families were caught in the horror of what happened to them after they were dead.

We know that Dahmer liked to experiment on drying out animal pelts with his chemistry set as a child. Some psychiatrists believe that torturing small animals stands out as a precursor of cruelty to human beings, and that the torture of dogs and cats is more of an indicator of future violent behavior than that of flies, toads, and turtles. When Dahmer performed his experiments on the pelts of squirrels and raccoons, the majority of people I talked to in Ohio did not think he had killed the animals himself but, rather, had collected road kills.

Based on their research, Fox and Levin assembled a composite profile of a mass murderer:

He is typically a white male in his late twenties or early thirties. In the 45
case of simultaneous mass murder, he kills people he knows with a hand-
gun or rifle; in serial crimes, he murders strangers by beating or strangulation. His specific motivation depends on the circumstances leading up
to the crime, but it generally deals directly with either money, expedi-
ency, jealousy, or lust.

Rarely is the mass murderer a hardened criminal with a long criminal
record, although a spotty history of property crime is common. Mass murder often follows a spell of frustration when a particular event triggers
sudden rage; yet, in other cases, the killer is coolly pursuing some goal he
cannot otherwise attain.

Finally, though the mass killer often may appear cold and show no
remorse, even denying responsibility for his crime, serious mental illness
or psychosis is rarely present. In background, in personality, and even in
appearance, the mass murderer is "extraordinarily ordinary," Fox said.
This may be the key to his extraordinary talent for murder. "After all,
who would ever suspect him?" Fox added.

Dahmer did have something in common with other serial killers in
that he led a rich fantasy life that focused on having complete control
over people and was controlled by it.

Fox continued, "That fantasy life, mixed with hatred, perhaps hatred of
himself which is being projected into his victims. If he at all feels uncomfortable about his own sexual orientation, it is very easy to see it projected
into these victims and punishing them indirectly to punish himself."

"He hated anyone who was more gay than he. This was his method of 50
punishment. He could be attracted to these people and then feel extremely horrible about it, and he lashes out at them as opposed to himself. So it's a combination of his hatred for these victims, mixed in with
some racial hatred, combined with fantasies that do involve this idea of
cutting up people."

While most of Dahmer's victims were black—and a great deal was
made of that fact by Milwaukee's black community—it was not clear
whether he hated blacks enough to target them deliberately. Our only
indication of an animosity toward blacks was the various racial slurs that
former prisoners at the Milwaukee County House of Correction and his
Army bunk mates remember him uttering.

"Murders instigated by racial hatred are surprisingly rare in a country
that has experienced so much racial conflict and violence," Fox said.
Interestingly enough, while blacks commit half the homicides in this
country (in Milwaukee, 75 percent of the city's 1991 homicides were
committed by blacks, who are 40 percent of the population), only one in
five mass killers is black, according to Fox.

Fox characterized the serial killer as a "skillful practitioner" because he murders repeatedly without getting caught. In most cases, police do not realize that a number of homicides were the work of one person until the killer is apprehended.

In a bizarre sort of way, Jeffrey Dahmer's crimes seemed very matter-of-fact when discussed clinically with someone like James Fox. But sociology aside, there will always be those who like to bring the explanation down to basics: "He was crazy."

At the January 1992 trial, Dahmer's attorney, Gerald Boyle, used the insanity defense in an unsuccessful effort to keep Dahmer out of prison and locked away in a state mental hospital. On September 10, 1991, at his pretrial hearing, Dahmer pleaded not guilty by reason of mental disease or defect. Under Wisconsin law, a person is not responsible for criminal conduct if at the time of the offense that person was suffering from a mental disease and lacked either the capacity to distinguish right from wrong or to conform his conduct to the law. Therefore, if convicted, Dahmer would be committed to a state mental hospital for no specific term but instead would be held until a judge or jury concluded that he no longer posed a danger to the community.

Criminally insane patients cannot be committed for longer than the maximum prison terms for their crimes, in this case, life. A 1988 *Milwaukee Journal* study of criminally insane patients found that the average confinement was five years for patients committed for first-degree murder. Patients such as Dahmer, who were involved in particularly brutal or highly publicized cases, usually were confined much longer, the study showed.

Although not confined to any sort of treatment facility in the past, Jeffrey Dahmer was under the care of psychiatrists during his probation for assaulting the brother of Konerak Sinthasomphone in 1988. A psychiatric treatment professional who met Dahmer observed, "For some men their only means of expressing things is through sex. Men express their feelings very poorly, according to the common lore. The crimes may reflect anger first—sex is only the medium for that." The doctor said Dahmer disclosed nothing and was very guarded about his formative childhood years.

A psychologist who worked with inmates for the Wisconsin Department of Corrections said Dahmer had an illness that was likely transmitted through heredity, if newspaper reports of Joyce Flint Dahmer's alleged mental illness were true. The psychologist noted that Lionel Dahmer's self-described strict religious leanings could indicate rigidity about other matters, such as sexual morality, and [he] probably had great difficulty accepting his son's sexual preference. "Most parents don't

55

298 Is the Monster within Us?

handle it too well when their kids diverge from the norm," the psychologist said.

The psychologist talked about Dahmer's confessions. "There may be some psychological dynamics to his confessions. There could be some relief in being caught. Whatever pain he had is finally over. Or there could be some charge for him for all of this confessing."

He described Dahmer as a formidable liar who used untruths to blanket and protect parts of his life. "Sometimes the man has lied so often that the lie becomes the truth. He tells the lie so often, he starts to believe it himself." 60

After his conviction for sexual exploitation of a child in 1989, court-appointed psychiatrists prescribed at least two drugs for Dahmer, lorazepam, an antianxiety drug, and doxepin, an antidepresssant. He also had an old prescription for Halcion, a drug akin to Valium, which he gave to Konerak Sinthasomphone's brother in 1988. Psychiatrists often prescribe antianxiety drugs, similar to barbiturates, to treat what they regard as major mental disorders. The drugs are intended to chemically control anxiety, nervousness, tension, and sleep disorders. The antidepressants cause frequent effects like drowsiness, lethargy, and difficulty thinking. The drug Halcion has come under fire for allegedly causing aberrant behavior in some of its users.

Several psychiatrists probed Dahmer's mind after his pleas of not guilty and not guilty by reason of mental disease or defect on September 10, 1991. A two-part trial was scheduled: the first phase would determine if Dahmer had committed the killings, and the second would determine if he was insane at the time. Despite his insanity plea and what Boyle called his client's depressed condition, Boyle had already established early on that Dahmer was mentally competent to go to trial and to assist in his own defense.

A number of the families were eager to talk to me after Dahmer made his plea in court in September 1991. They felt the not guilty plea was a disgrace.

"I was mad as hell," said Carolyn Smith, Eddie Smith's sister. "The man's just got it too good. Everywhere I turn it's just like everything's catered for Dahmer, and to have him just turn my life upside down. Well, it's just not right."

Inez Thomas, mother of David Thomas, rejected the claim of insanity. 65 "I think he knew exactly what he was doing and how he was going to do it. There's nothing wrong with Jeffrey Dahmer."

Understanding the Text

1. Why were Officers Rauth and Mueller initially reluctant to let Tracy Edwards go on his way? To what extent did this play a role in the discovery of Jeffrey Dahmer?

2. What are the differences between a mass murderer and a serial killer, as defined in "Inside a Murdering Mind"?

3. What does Dr. James Alan Fox argue are the problems with blaming childhood traumas for the formation of serial killers?

Reflection and Response

4. After his victims were dead, Dahmer sometimes had sex with their bodies, cut them up, and even ate their flesh. Yet Dr. Fox says, "In a certain way, he was merciful, because he drugged his victims. They didn't have the same sort of terror and horror the victims of other serial killers have had" (par. 40). What is your reaction to these details? How do they differ from the pattern of the typical serial killer? Were Dahmer's crimes more monstrous or less monstrous than those of other serial killers?

5. Schwartz refers to the issue of Dahmer's need for control. How can the quest for control of self and others lead to monstrous behavior?

Making Connections

6. Dr. Fox states, "Ever since Sigmund Freud, we blame everything bad that kids do on their parents, and that's unfortunate and it doesn't make sense" (par. 33). Consider Dahmer's story in light of Jason Huddleston's "Unmasking the Monster: Hiding and Revealing Male Sexuality in John Carpenter's *Halloween*" (p. 275). Pay special attention to Huddleston's discussion of the Oedipus complex at work in the movie. In what ways are the fictional character Michael Myers and the real-life Dahmer alike in terms of the psychology behind their actions?

7. Research additional information about Dahmer — his crimes, his trial, and his death. In what ways can his story be called a monster story? Was there any humanity left in Dahmer in the end?

The Horror in the Mirror: Average Joe and the Mechanical Monster

Richard Tithecott

The horror of Jeffrey Dahmer was that he was so ordinary, so unremarkable, just an "Average Joe," and yet he was capable of such horrific deeds. The question then becomes how we can reconcile the idea of normalcy with the facts of killing, necrophilia (an erotic interest in corpses), dismemberment of corpses, and cannibalism. Much rests upon how we define ourselves as human and how we answer the question of what constitutes normal and natural. Richard Tithecott is the author of *Of Men and Monsters: Jeffrey Dahmer and the Construction of the Serial Killer* (1997).

To Randy Jones, one of Dahmer's neighbors, Dahmer seemed "like the average Joe" (*Newsweek*, 5 August 1991: 41). Helping us to disseminate a picture of Dahmer in court, a caption in Anne E. Schwartz's book describes Dahmer as an "average-looking man." To Tracy Edwards, whose escape from Dahmer's apartment led to Dahmer's arrest, Dahmer "seemed like a normal, everyday guy," and presumably in order to justify that characterization, Edwards agrees with Geraldo Rivera's suggestion that he and Dahmer were out to "hustle some chicks" (*Geraldo*, 12 September 1991). Dahmer "is a very gentle man" according to his attorney, and "that's what makes it so absolutely intriguing and unbelievable to see how a fellow like that you saw in court today could have done all these horrific acts" (*Larry King Live*, 17 February 1992). To make it even more intriguing, as a *Washington Post* columnist notes, Dahmer is not from one of the "nation's urban areas with more of a reputation for cold-bloodedness," but from Wisconsin, "America's heartland" (1 August 1991: C3). . . . The idea that "appearances are deceptive" is repeated in article after article: "Concealed amongst all this normality lies dormant evil." Like the surrealists, in the banal we see, and perhaps like to manufacture, something extraordinary.

Average Joe often has a story to tell about himself and his friends that calls into question his claim to his name. This celebrated embodiment of middle America is often hiding something. His normality, we say, is an illusion. But when we look at our monsters and wait for the true gargoyle within to burst through that familiar shell, sometimes we experience a more horrifying or thrilling possibility: the monster that appears actually is Average Joe; what is unspeakable turns out to be impossible to put into words not because it is so extraordinary but because it is so ordinary. Thus, we have a twist on the story behind Daniel Vigne's *The Return of Martin Guerre* or Jon Amiel's *Sommersby*: not an intruder in the guise of familiarity, but familiarity in all its glory. It is a possibility that Hannah Arendt describes in *Eichmann in Jerusalem*: "[The prosecutor] wanted to try the most abnormal monster the world had ever seen. . . . [The judges] knew, of course, that it would have been very comforting indeed to believe that Eichmann° was a monster. . . . The trouble with Eichmann was precisely that so many were like him, and that the many were neither perverted nor sadistic, that they were, and still are, terribly and terrifyingly normal" (Arendt 276). The "trouble" with Eichmann is the trouble with our serial killers, both new and old. "I shall clip the lady's ears off . . . wouldn't you?" asks Jack the Ripper in a letter to his fellow man. As Martin Tropp suggests, the writer "speaks directly to his readers, implying by his words and literacy (despite the [possibly intentional] misspellings) that he is one of them" (113) and that this is why he is so difficult to catch.

Halloween director John Carpenter, commenting on the success of *The Silence of the Lambs*, remarks, "I think we're all frightened of the unknown and also of the repressed people in our society. There's a duality that touches off sparks in all of us" (*People Weekly*, 1 April 1991: 70). Those sparks are theorized by Jonathan Dollimore thus: "Since, in cultural terms, desiring the normal is inseparable from and conditional upon not desiring the abnormal, repression remains central to identity, individual and cultural" (246). We often figure the serial killer as failing to repress the desire for the abnormal. Joan Smith, for example, figuring identity in hydraulic terms, says, "The otherwise inexplicable actions of a serial killer . . . can . . . be understood as a survival mechanism, a means of coping with intolerable stress. The fact that they commit such terrible crimes enables them to function normally in the periods between their crimes" (3). Our desire for normality, our fetishization of Average Joe, inevitably means that abnormality is constructed as something that *needs* to be repressed, something that inevitably becomes desirable, mysterious, sexy. As it comes into focus, our depiction of the serial killer as "letting off steam" is also a picture of Average Joe who has given in to his deeper desires. Our monster turns out to be not something monstrous disguised as Joe but Joe who has let it all hang out.

Attempting to satisfy our hunger for horror, we revert sometimes to what John Carpenter says indicates fifties conservatism: the cheap scare.

Eichmann: Adolf Eichmann (1906–1962), a prime Nazi architect of the Holocaust.

Our monsters, more animal than human, spring at us from behind bushes, prey on us, return to their lairs far from everyday, familiar society. At such times we might, like Dahmer's neighbor, John Bachelor, compare Dahmer to Jason in *Friday the 13th* (*Los Angeles Times*, 24 July 1991: A14)—he who, like Lecter,° we like to conceal behind a hockey-mask—or we might,

"Our monster turns out to be not something monstrous disguised as Joe but Joe who has let it all hang out."

like Robert Dvorchak and Lisa Holewa, describe Dahmer's reported "wailing" and "screeching" when he is arrested as "all those forces seething inside him erupt[ing] to life" (Dvorchak and Holewa 8). But we are generally movie-literate people, and to truly scare ourselves, we want sometimes to be a little more subtle, to show that we can write and speak a little more fully, a little more *knowingly* about those "forces." At these times, we must be able to mistake our monsters for ourselves—or ourselves for them. We must build a house of mirrors.

If we are white, scaring ourselves in this way is a little easier. Average 5 Joe is white, and so is Average Joe, the serial killer. Average Joe has power, the power of being average, of being a representative of middle America. And so does Average Joe, the serial killer. The sister of one of Dahmer's many black victims is curious about why her fellow guest on *The Maury Povich Show* should be so fascinated with Dahmer that she regularly attends his trial: "Did you want to read about the man [Joachim Dressler] that sat up there and cut up 11 people in Racine. Did you want to read about him? No, see, you don't even remember him. But he was—came from an insane place. But see, that's not big news. This white man that killed almost all minorities, he is big news" (*Maury Povich*, 4 February 1992). Not that the whiteness of a serial killer becomes an issue—but his "normality" does. We not only place the white Dahmer or the white Bundy or the white Gacy on the covers of magazines, we give them the power to look back at us. And that's a thrill.

Looking at our monsters is a good way of finding out who we think we are, or who we think we might be, or even who we want to be. They can be figures who have realized our frightening or fantastic potentials. The trick is to identify how subtle we are being. Take, for example, the representation of Dahmer as automaton. Seizing on classmates' memories of Dahmer's ritual walk to the school bus—four steps forward, two back, four forward, one back (Masters 1991, 267)—we deal with his lack

---

Lecter: Hannibal Lecter, cannibalistic serial killer, a fictional character in novels by Thomas Harris and film adaptations, such as *The Silence of the Lambs* (1991).

of feeling towards his victims by constructing an image of Dahmer as boy-machine who develops into something which, when arrested, "looked so emotionless, so harmless, as if he were a robot being led away" (Norris 1992, 41). In court his face is "passionless" (*Geraldo*, 12 September 1991), his eyes "almost vacant" (*Newsweek*, 3 February 1992: 45). For the *Washington Post*, Dahmer, "his face . . . pale and impassive," "walked with the near-drop pace of a zombie" (7 August 1991: B1). *People Weekly* magazine, countering the claims of his lawyer that he was in a "state of anguish," says, "but Jeffrey Dahmer was impassive in court as he was charged with first-degree murder" (12 August 1991: 32). While defense and state attorneys differ in their assessments of Dahmer's responsibility for his actions, their portrayal of him as unfeeling, inhuman, and machinelike are indistinguishable. Dahmer's attorney, Gerald Boyle, describes him in court as a "steamrolling killing machine," "a runaway train on a track of madness, picking up steam all the time, on and on and on," while Michael McCann for the prosecution describes Dahmer as a "cool, calculating killer who cleverly covered his tracks" (*New York Times*, 16 February 1992: 24).

Such estrangement can be of the unsubtle variety, a case of "pathologizing and thus disavowing the everyday intimacies with technology in machine culture" (Seltzer 98), but it can also indicate not so much a disavowal as an expression of anxiety on our part about modern humanity or, more specifically, modern man in "machine culture." Klaus Theweleit describes the masculine self of members of the First World War German Freikorps as "mechanized through a variety of mental and physical procedures: military drill, countenance, training, operations which Foucault° identified as techniques of the self'" (Rabinbach and Benjamin in Theweleit 1989, xvii), and Mark Fasteau, among others, describes the stereotype of the contemporary male self in similar terms, a stereotype which we are still struggling to outgrow. In *The Male Machine* Fasteau describes the ideal image to which the title refers as

functional, designed mainly for work. He is programmed to tackle jobs, override obstacles, attack problems, overcome difficulties, and always seize the offensive. . . . He has armor plating which is virtually impregnable. His circuits are never scrambled or overrun by irrelevant personal signals. He dominates and outperforms his fellows, although without excessive flashing of lights or clashing of gears. His relationship with other male machines is one of respect but not

Michel Foucault (1926–1984): French philosopher and critic known for his theories on power and knowledge.

intimacy; it is difficult for him to connect his internal circuits to those of others. In fact, his internal circuitry is something of a mystery to him. (Fasteau 1)

Fasteau's "male machine" is a frightening but familiar image. It corresponds with the way we often figure our monsters: "If there's anything monstrous about [Dahmer], it's the monstrous lack of connection to all things we think of as being human—guilt, remorse, worry, feelings that would stop him from hurting, killing, torturing" (Davis Silber, quoted in Dvorchak and Holewa 141). It corresponds with the way we represent our mostly male psychopaths who can be diagnosed as such by demonstrating, among other things, "a shallow understanding of the meaning of words, particularly emotional terms" and by not showing "the surge of anxiety that normal people exhibit" when they are about "to receive a mild electric shock" (*New York Times*, 7 July 1987: C2). And, apparently keen to confer buddy-status on as many of society's others as possible, Fasteau's male ideal also corresponds with necrophiles° and schizophrenics.° "According to Eric Fromm's findings," says Brian Masters, necrophiles "often have a pallid complexion, and they speak in a monotone. . . . They are fascinated with machinery, which is unfeeling and antihuman" (quoted in Masters 1991, 266). *In Cold Blood* examiners of Lowell Lee Andrews produce a diagnosis of "schizophrenia, simple type," and by "simple," Capote tells us, "the diagnosticians meant that Andrews suffered no delusions, no fake perceptions, no hallucinations, but the primary illness of separation of thinking and feeling" (Capote 315). How different are our killing machines from our male machines? While we are familiar with and still sometimes valorize the male machine, how sensitive are we to the idea that it is logical for such machines also to regard their others as mirror-reflections of themselves, as unfeeling, interesting only as mechanical objects? While Dahmer the schoolboy explains to a classmate his reason for cutting up the fish he catches—"I want to see what it looks like inside, I like to see how things work" (Dvorchak and Holewa 41)—the adult Dahmer confesses to the police "in the uninflected language of an affidavit" that he disassembles his human victims "to see how they work" (*Newsweek*, 5 August 1991: 40). Our construction of the serial killer resembles a figure of masculinity, or rather a reassembled figure of masculinity, who has turned on all that frustrates masculinity either within himself or without. When we repre-

necrophiles: people with an erotic interest in corpses.
schizophrenics: people with a psychotic disorder characterized by the loss of contact with the environment, a noticeable deterioration in the level of functioning in everyday life, and the disintegration of personality.

sent serial killers, necrophiles, psychopaths, schizophrenics, and a male ideal in similar ways, we sometimes refuse to identify links between them, but sometimes we allow the representations to merge, to form an almost conflated image in which the other is seen through the familiar self, the familiar self seen through the other. An uncanny effect, as Freud might say.

What Freud *does* say is that the uncanny hints at "nothing new or foreign, but something familiar and old established in the mind that has been estranged only by the process of repression" (Freud 1953, 47). In the same essay he mentions the uncanniness of mechanization: "Jentsch has taken as a very good instance [of the uncanny] 'doubts whether an apparently animate being is really alive; or conversely, whether a lifeless object might not be in fact animate'; and he refers in this connection to the impression made by wax-work figures, artificial dolls and automatons. He adds to this class the uncanny effect of epileptic seizures and the manifestations of insanity, because these excite in the spectator the feeling that automatic, mechanical processes are at work, concealed beneath the ordinary appearance of animation" (31). A *Newsweek* article on Dahmer describes serial killers as "taking their cues from some deranged script" (5 August 1991: 40) and concludes with a quotation from Park Dietz: "These people are the most controlled people you can imagine" (41). While Dahmer was found to be *in control*, not out of it, his actions perceived to be those of a man who knew what he was doing, he is also represented as someone/something being controlled. The figure of the killer as unfeeling, programmed machine—the writer of the program remaining a mystery—is one with which the Gothic and our representation of serial killers are particularly occupied. And contributing to our sense of the uncanny is the defining characteristic of the serial killer, the repetitiveness of the killing act. For Freud, "repetition-compulsion" is "based upon instinctual activity and probably inherent in the very nature of the instincts—a principle powerful enough to overrule the pleasure-principle, lending to certain aspects of the mind their daemonic character" (Freud 1953, 44). In other words, "repetition-compulsion" can signify oxymorons such as "mechanized nature" or "natural machine."

With Freud's understanding of the uncanny in mind, the mechani- 10
cally repetitive serial killer is a construction which can suggest for us the power of "natural instinct," an instinct whose naturalness we may or may not wish to question. But whether we see the power of "mechanized nature" or of a "natural machine," our particular representation of the body as machine may appear as both a powerful fantasy and a fantasy of power. Mark Seltzer, who argues that "the matter of periodizing persons, bodies, and desires is inseparable from the anxieties and *appeals* of the

body-machine complex" (my italics; Seltzer 98), refers to the type of fantasy which "projects a transcendence of the natural body and the extension of human agency through the forms of technology that supplemented it" (99). And just as dreams about technology can reflect more than just our anxieties, our construction of mechanized monsters, as I mentioned earlier, can indicate more than just our worries about humanity's "naturalness" or its future in a technological age. Gilles Deleuze says, "Types of machines are easily matched with each type of society—not that machines are determining, but because they express those social forms capable of generating and using them" (Deleuze 6). Reinventing Deleuze's comment, one might say that our constructions of automated monsters, rather than indicating what we fear machines are doing to us, indicate what kind of a culture is "capable of generating and *using them.*"

In the mythology of modern America the serial killer is a character able both to scare and thrill us in unsubtle and subtle ways. He can be monstrous, but he can also demonstrate a monstrosity which is familiar. The figure of the mechanized serial killer—the serial killer as automaton, unable to stop—offers us a version of familiar, "natural," and to some extent "appealing" behavior "that has been estranged only by the process of repression."

References

Arendt, Hannah. *Eichmann in Jerusalem.* New York: Penguin, 1963.

Capote, Truman. *In Cold Blood: A True Account of Multiple Murder and Its Consequences.* London: Hamish Hamilton, 1966.

Deleuze, Gilles. "Postscript on the Societies of Control." *October* 59 (1992): 3–7.

Dollimore, Jonathan. *Sexual Dissidence.* Oxford: Clarendon Press, 1991.

Dvorchak, Robert J., and Lisa Holewa. *Milwaukee Massacre.* New York: Dell, 1991.

Fasteau, Mark Feigen. *The Male Machine.* New York: McGraw-Hill, 1974.

Freud, Sigmund. "The Uncanny," in *Standard Edition of the Complete Psychological Works.* Trans. under the general editorship of James Strachey, in collaboration with Anna Freud, assisted by Alex Strachey and Alan Tyson. Vol. 17. London: Hogarth Press, 1953.

Gerald. Investigative News Group, Inc.

Larry King Live. Cable News Network, Inc.

Masters, Brian. "Dahmer's Inferno." *Vanity Fair* (November 1991): 183–269.

The Maury Povich Show. Paramount, Inc.

Norris, Joel. *Serial Killers: The Growing Menace.* New York: Doubleday, 1988.

Schwartz, Anne E. *The Man Who Could Not Kill Enough.* New York: Birch Lane Press, 1992.

Seltzer, Mark. "Serial Killers (1)." *Differences* 5 (Spring 1993): 92–128.

Smith, Joan. "The Fear and the Fantasy." *The Guardian* (sec. 2), 18 (June 1993): 2–3.

Theweleit, Klaus. *Male Fantasies*. Vol. 1. *Women, Floods, Bodies, History*. Foreword by Barbara Ehrenreich. Trans. Stephen Conway in collaboration with Erica Carter and Chris Turner. Minneapolis: University of Minnesota Press, 1987. Vol. 2. *Male Bodies: Psychoanalyzing the White Terror*. Foreword by Jessica Benjamin and Anson Rabinbach. Trans. Erica Carter and Chris Turner in collaboration with Stephen Conway. Minneapolis: University of Minnesota Press, 1989.

Tropp, Martin. *Images of Fear: How Horror Stories Helped Shape Modern Culture, 1818–1918*. Jefferson, N.C.: McFarland, 1990.

Understanding the Text

1. Tithecott says, "Average Joe often has a story to tell about himself and his friends that calls into question his claim to his name" (par. 2). What does he mean by this?

2. What does *Halloween* director John Carpenter mean by the "cheap scare" in regard to horror (par. 4)? Why does Jeffrey Dahmer not represent that sort of scare?

3. According to Tithecott, how is race connected to serial killers and our perceptions of them?

Reflection and Response

4. Tithecott quotes John Carpenter as saying, in reference to the movie *The Silence of the Lambs*, "I think we're all frightened of the unknown and also of the repressed people in our society. There's a duality that touches off sparks in all of us" (par. 3). Do you agree? Why or why not? Cite examples to support your argument.

5. Consider how serial killers have become celebrities: people know their names and want to learn details about their upbringing, their killings, and how they were ultimately caught. Many killers have "fans" even as they serve time in prison. There are serial killer trading cards and a serial killer trivia game. What does this suggest about our cultural values?

Making Connections

6. Tithecott cites a report from the *Washington Post* stating that Dahmer "walked with the near-drop pace of a zombie" (par. 6). How was Dahmer like a zombie? Research other texts about zombies, including Chuck Klosterman's essay "My Zombie, Myself: Why Modern Life Feels Rather Undead" (p. 40). Argue whether or not contemporary serial killers, such as Jeffrey Dahmer, are zombies.

7. Much is made of the issue of control in discussing serial killers. In fact, Tithecott states, "while Dahmer was found to be *in control*, not out of it, his actions perceived to be those of a man who knew what he was doing, he is also represented as someone/something being controlled" (par. 9). How does that observation relate to other monsters such as vampires and werewolves, or even the creation myths of creatures such as the Minotaur, and the level of control they have — or don't have — over their own actions? Use specific details to develop your answer.

Ethical Aliens: The Challenge of Extreme Perpetrators to Humanism

William Andrew Myers

There are criminals, and there are murderers, and then there are what William Andrew Myers calls "extreme perpetrators" — those whose actions are so evil, so beyond our ability to understand, that they seem like a different species: aliens. Murderous dictators, serial killers, and ideological killers qualify because their actions seem to negate their own humanity. In Aristotle's terms, they act more bestial than merely wicked. In an essay originally published in 2009, Myers examines these extreme perpetrators not to salvage them, but to save us: we must recognize the human in them in order to recognize the human in all of us. Myers is professor emeritus of philosophy at St. Catherine University.

S ocieties have many ways of marking off individuals and groups, both to establish social and political hierarchies and to create categories for exclusion from a normative mainstream. The specific functions of these markers vary with time, place, and application, but no society, it seems, can get along without them. And categories established within societies have pragmatic consequences: members of out-groups are treated differently, and the different treatment is sanctioned, itself as normative as the categories themselves. We create images of the poor, of ethnic and religious minorities, of the insane, of criminals, and we justify our different treatment of them by reference to their out-group status. Yet the categories and the treatment based on them may or may not stand up to scrutiny. The exclusionary marker I want to explore here is the category, perpetrator of extreme harm.

Part of our experience as humans includes awareness, if not direct experience, that some people are quite extraordinarily vicious. Some behavior seems to go beyond ordinary criminality, so far beyond that we struggle to comprehend it as human action. I call people who behave so badly extreme perpetrators. Their behavior leads us to grope for comprehension and to dismiss them as utterly alien. But should we regard such individuals as so distinct from the human community? And what does our attitude toward extreme perpetrators say about our understanding of what it means to be human? I will argue that uncritical acceptance of the social mechanisms that treat extreme perpetrators as absolute outsiders, barely or not even human, impermissibly limits our shared beliefs about what it means to be human—and hence our self-understanding—but also constricts our conception of the humane.

Extreme Perpetrators

In a brief passage in the *Nicomachean Ethics* Aristotle distinguishes between ordinary human wickedness and bestiality:° "Bestiality is less 'evil' than vice," he says, "though more horrible." He continues that in contrast to the wicked person, whose "highest part," that is, the intellect or reason, is corrupted, in the bestial individual it is not corrupt "but entirely lacking." Aristotle thought the wicked person could do much more harm than a bestial person, but that in terms of moral character the two are not comparable. "[I]t is like comparing an inanimate with an animate thing [*apsychon* versus *empsychon*: literally, an unsouled with an ensouled thing], and asking which is the more evil; for the badness of a thing which has no originating principle—and intelligence is such a principle—is always less capable of mischief." Thus Aristotle regards bestiality as something outside the range of our framework of ethical concepts. Extreme behaviors and the minds they evince cannot even count as vice—excess or deficiency—in our calculations of the mean that constitutes excellence or virtue. In the sentences just preceding the quoted passage he notes that the concepts of moderation and profligacy° do not pertain to lower animals because they "have neither the faculty of choice nor of calculation," and he adds, "they are like men who are insane." So we get here a comparison between lower animals, who lack *nous*, intellect—and therefore cannot make rational choices—and the bestial person, who likewise cannot make rational choices due to insanity.

> "Uncritical acceptance of the social mechanisms that treat extreme perpetrators as absolute outsiders . . . impermissibly limits our shared beliefs about what it means to be human."

Perhaps because this is merely an aside in Aristotle's discussion of vices, he gives us no examples here of bestial human behavior; in fact he seems to dismiss it as outside the topic. But his point seems to be that the actions of some persons are so far outside the range of ordinary human wickedness that we can safely ignore them in constructing a descriptive

bestiality: the manifestation of the traits or desires of a lower animal.
profligacy: excessive or immoral behavior; wastefulness.

and normative account of human ethical life. What interests me in the distinction Aristotle makes between the wicked or vicious person and the bestial is that his dismissal of the latter conforms to modern ways of regarding some perpetrators of extreme harm as inhuman, or alien. And indeed, clearly some acts do challenge our norms of behavior that is merely criminal.

Hannah Arendt speaks of the abyss between a normal society's moral   5
and legal frames of reference and the revelations of Nazi depravity at the end of WWII. "What meaning has the concept of murder when we are confronted with the mass production of corpses?" she asks. Most moral theory, not just Aristotle's and its modern descendants, addresses norms ill suited to comprehend, say, the creatively sadistic serial killer or the willing participant in mass murder. And the social determinants that lead us to dismiss the extreme perpetrator as outside the range of ethical reflection are strong. Richard Tithecott, in his analysis of the social construction of the serial killer, which focuses on Jeffrey Dahmer, comments, "With our condemnation of Dahmer as evil, we say, simply, *he happened*: there is no need to explain the crime, to speculate about context, only to deal with him, the criminal." But to show that this dismissal of the extreme perpetrator as absolutely alien has undesirable consequences, I must now be more specific about what counts as the extreme in this context.

A Description

To be more precise about who counts as an extreme perpetrator I must refer to some distinctions among theories of evil. Three emphases have emerged in the recent philosophical literature. The first looks to the actual damage a person causes, the second to motivations, intentions, or the will, and the third to the feelings a person has about the actions. As Daniel M. Haybron points out, none of these emphases is sufficient on its own to provide a "robust bad/evil distinction." But my purpose here is not to develop a theory of evil, nor to examine in any detail Haybron's attempt; I merely wish to use these emphases to ground a description of extreme perpetrators.

First, we do commonly measure harm, suffering, and injury as indicators of the extreme. In its crudest form, a harm-based view literally counts the victims. Thus a planner and implementer of mass murder (Heinrich Himmler,° say) is widely regarded as being in a different cate-

---

Heinrich Himmler (1900–1945): a Nazi leader of the infamous SS, a paramilitary organization under Adolf Hitler.

gory from that of a man who kills a store clerk during a robbery. A perverse manifestation of this kind of thinking treats serial killers as sports heroes, scoring their total victims like game statistics. (There are, I read, even serial killer trading cards.) Despite such aberrations, the scope of damage done does figure importantly in our sense of the extreme.

Another harm-based marker of the extreme is sadistic cruelty. Christopher Browning, in his study of "ordinary men" induced to commit atrocities during the Nazi mass murder program in Poland, reports that a few of the men ordered to shoot women, children, and elderly persons face to face, one by one, in Józefów, Poland, in July of 1942, were unable to comply; while these men were treated by their fellows as cowards, they suffered no serious reprisals for their unwillingness to carry out the orders. We may applaud such a small triumph of human decency in terrible circumstances, but there are plenty of other cases in the bloody twentieth century in which multiple murders were carried out with a maximum of cruelty and humiliation to the victims. At least some perpetrators take obscene pleasure in their work. [Lavrenty] Beria, Stalin's henchman who oversaw the murderous infighting in the dictator's inner circle, personally tortured arrested members of the leadership (some former friends) and their wives, raping the women before murdering them.

The wantonness of such actions, the depravity it reveals, seems to mark such perpetrators as Beria as fundamentally different from those who, we may say (without in any way discounting the suffering they cause), merely murder. Extent of harm caused and sadistic cruelty thus are important markers of an extreme perpetrator. Note that the cruelty of actions treated in a harm-based account reflects only measures of the perpetrator's actual actions: that victims were in fact tortured, for example. In the case of someone whose actions spring from a deformed character, the character of one who derives pleasure from inflicting suffering on others, motivations may well count in our assessment and subsequent judgment that the individual represents an extreme. A deranged form of pleasure-seeking might be behind the actions of someone who tortures victims before killing them. Nevertheless, it remains the actual harm done, including its manner, that predominates in our delimiting of the extreme.

Second, the inner life of the perpetrator does count in our assessment 10 of the ethics of ordinary actions, but at the extremes motives and intentions become far less weighty, for two reasons. For one thing, the scale of harm can overwhelm our willingness to dissect and analyze motives. Contemplating events such as the 1994 genocidal massacres in Rwanda, our ordinary moral sensibilities, including for example such attitudes as that children should be nurtured and the elderly cared for, are so completely violated that no account of individual motivations seems relevant to our ethical assessments. As Arendt says, the mass production of corpses makes ordinary concepts of murder meaningless. While we may indeed be curious to understand the linkages between what a person thought and what he did to bring about extraordinary harms, in extreme cases like those at various levels of the Nazi mass murder programs accounts of motives notoriously fail to align with the scale of the atrocity we seek to understand. (This is the paradox of the banal perpetrator as described by Arendt.)

Moreover, motives, though they may be constituted by extraordinary malice, cannot be a sufficient condition for identifying an extreme perpetrator. For instance, we can imagine an individual so consumed with malice against some group that almost her entire mental life is devoted to imagining horrors she wishes to visit upon members of that group, whereas in fact she never does anything about these fantasies. We would hardly be justified in calling her an extreme perpetrator, or a perpetrator at all. And if she revealed publicly her mental life to be what it is, we would probably counsel therapy, regarding her pathological ideation as unhealthy rather than criminal. She may have the necessary *mens rea,*° but lack the means and opportunity to act. It is actual perpetrators who seem to merit classification as the worst of the worst.

Similarly, affect pales in significance before the scale of some atrocities. Whereas in everyday contexts it matters to us whether someone took pleasure in doing harm or felt remorse later, for extreme perpetrators these aspects of their actions do not help us to describe the extremes of our moral universe. As Haybron notes, "We don't particularly care whether Hitler cried into his pillow every night. We care about the millions of lives he destroyed." That is, we assess the moral characters of ordinary perpetrators on the basis of their actions, their motives, and how they feel about themselves and their actions. For extreme perpetrators, it appears to be actions alone that we take as primary, though we might also at times reason from those actions to judgments of depraved character.

With this background now, we can distinguish extreme perpetrators from ordinary malefactors as *those who commit acts so heinous in extent or in cruelty that they stand outside the norms of mere criminality,* even when they commit acts that are prosecutable. This concept of the extreme perpetrator is based on an idea of degrees: there are many ways to be bad, even very bad, but some people create so much mayhem—including real

---

mens rea: Latin for "a guilty mind"; a legal term used to mean a person's knowledge or intention to commit a crime.

suffering—that their actions set them apart from ordinary malefactors. The idea of the extreme perpetrator is a harm-based concept because it is the extremes of injury and suffering to which we refer in our horror at the actions of some people. Recognizing people at this extreme of evil leads to the various distancing strategies we see.

Keeping Our Distance

Societies have various mechanisms to distance themselves from the worst of the worst. Each of the three principles of exclusion I will describe here (not by any means an exhaustive list) marks those it refers to as irretrievably Other, aliens in the fullest sense. That in each case there is a huge descriptive and analytical literature and a vast array of popular entertainments devoted to them reveals our fascination with the extremes; but these productions also *create* the alien as a category.

The Murderous Dictator

National leaders who carry out programs of genocide or other mass atrocity, 15
claiming to act on behalf of the nation, are outside our normative moral framework.

Some of the people we want to distance ourselves from include murderous dictators, like Stalin, Idi Amin, or Pol Pot. Distancing is easy in this kind of case because these figures are physically and often culturally distant to start with. Their actions seem inexplicable when we learn of them, and in many cases we do not learn of the extent of their damage until long after they have died or fled the scene. The discovery of mass graves, publications of survivor narratives, reports of truth commissions, even films such as *The Killing Fields,* may give us insight into their atrocities, but typically the perpetrators remain shadowy and their story is revealed only slowly over time as historians and biographers do their patient scholarship. In some cases, prosecutions in the International Criminal Court at The Hague will elicit testimony that reveals the nature and extent of a leader's depravity. Such knowledge can itself be an alienating factor. The mere fact that a person has had the power to act on his darkest fantasies without—for a time—reprisal separates the murderous dictator from the rest of us.

Such people need others acting with complicity, often in large numbers, to carry out their depredations, but it is the leader himself (nearly always male) who bears the full onus of the atrocities—in the public mind if not legally. For the rest of us, especially those outside the sphere of operation, the murderous dictator is an inexplicable and alien being. Distance from the worst of the worst of humanity seems built in for those of us fortunate enough to be outside the ambit° of their power to do harm.

The Serial Killer

People who commit murder repeatedly, depending on their methods and numbers of victims, are outside our normative moral framework. The enormous industry that has developed over the last twenty-five years devoted to mythologizing the serial killer in America through novels, movies, and television programs has had the effect of creating a new kind of outlaw (a somewhat perverse replacement for the defunct Western gunslinger); it has exaggerated in the popular mind both the number of such killers and the number of their victims; and it has made it harder for us to see through the various constructions to the people who actually commit multiple murders. As Philip Jenkins comments,

From being a person whose sickness derived from family or social circumstances, the serial killer of the 1980s was increasingly seen as a ruthless incomprehensible monster undeserving of sympathy and meriting only destruction. . . .

The monstrous is even more titillating when it involves forbidden practices, such as occult rituals or cannibalism. "In constructing the characteristics of dangerous outsiders, tales and legends usually focus on their supposed inversion of normal culture," Jenkins notes. Serial killers capture the public imagination for many reasons, but one of them is surely that, until apprehended, such people represent an atavistic° terror of the secret and secretive predator among us, able to strike at any time. The real and justified fear communities feel when, for example, young women or children are going missing, lends itself easily to the construction of the predatory monster, the Other in its most threatening form.

The Ideological Killer

People who commit atrocities for religious or ideological reasons are outside our   20
normative moral framework.
Finally, there are ideological killers, motivated by religious or political convictions that lead them to attack, sometimes suicidally, innocent people. We can distance ourselves from someone like Timothy McVeigh, who constructed and planted the bomb that blew up the federal building in Oklahoma City in 1995 with a loss of 168 lives, many of them chil-

---

ambit: the range or limit that is covered by something (such as a law).
atavistic: exhibiting behavior connected to a much earlier generation or time period.

dren, because we see the appalling gap between his grievance against the U.S. Government and his attack on a building full of ordinary people. Similarly, the hijackers and pilots of the airliners that crashed into the World Trade Center towers and the Pentagon [in 2001] seemed to be motivated by such aberrant beliefs we find ourselves at a loss to see ourselves in them.

This construction of the Other runs somewhat counter to my claim that the primary marker of the extreme perpetrator is the harm done rather than motivation. Here the harm done is certainly primary; but part of the alienation we experience springs from contemplation of the fanaticism of the perpetrator. "How could anyone *do* that?" we ask. But then we find that the answer to that question is as confounding as the act itself, given that most of us, though we may have passionately held beliefs, would not commit mass murder on their behalf. The very idea of the *fanatic* marks someone so labeled off from the normative mainstream.

Distancing strategies based on these principles (and others like them) portray the perpetrator as so different from us that we are empowered to regard the actual individual voyeuristically, titillated by accounts of his or her crimes (those trading cards!). And being so empowered, we are able to cancel out any sense of common humanity that might intrude on our objectification. Perhaps, I speculate, we need these distancing principles because we cannot countenance seeing ourselves in the lives and actions of extreme perpetrators. This is not a failure of empathy, but a genuine blocking of the imaginative processes by which we might see ourselves as potentially like them. Tithecott says, "How much easier it is to comprehend the serial killer as akin to a bolt of lightning than as something whose origin lies within histories we can write for ourselves." In contrast, forensic psychiatrist Dorothy Lewis comments that her attitude toward many of the severely damaged individuals on death rows all over the U.S. whom she has studied and extensively interviewed has been, "There but for the grace of God go I." I submit that hers is a highly unusual attitude (she notes that it differs even from that of her co-researcher, neurologist Jonathan Pincus). Most of us would recoil at the suggestion that we have anything important in common with sadistic serial murderers like Jeffrey Dahmer or John Wayne Gacy.

We could never ever do such things, we like to think. And for the most part, we are correct. But regarding the extreme perpetrator as being in a category utterly unlike us leads us to regard such persons as totally beyond the scope of our humane concern. I hasten to add that I am not recommending in any way that we should regard extreme perpetrators empathetically or that we should imaginatively try to see the world through their eyes. In fact that might be quite dangerous for our own psyches. I do recommend that we resist the distancing mechanisms that society imposes on us to the extent that we can recognize extreme perpetrators as individuals and as part of the human community regardless of their aberrant histories.

This point obviously runs counter to the tradition of regarding some 25 people as moral monsters, and dismissing them accordingly. But as Haybron points out, an ascription of evil character (as opposed to mere badness) carries with it considerable simplification of a person's actual biography. He says,

If I am correct about the simplifications involved in ascribing evil, then regarding individuals as evil amounts to treating them as moral write-offs, as monsters who are not fully human and certainly not fit for any kind of society.

But, one may ask, isn't such categorization exactly what such people deserve? Hasn't their evil behavior itself marked them irrevocably as beyond the pale of human society? Shouldn't the purpose of studying such monsters be the purely pragmatic one of learning how to protect ourselves from them?

The pragmatic purpose is certainly valid, and the point should be taken further: it is highly valuable for us to understand the family, social, and educational conditions in which moral monsters arise, insofar as any generalizations can be drawn about causation. But my point here is that, however we assess culpability and just deserts for extreme perpetrators, writing them off as outside the scope of moral regard damages *our* self-understanding. It is our ability to recognize our full human potential that is at stake.

The Human and the Humane

Though my topic here is not the culpability of people who commit atrocities, in the conditions of some people who do terrible things we do find factors that we should take to reduce their legal and moral responsibility for their actions. Virtually all of the large number of death row inmates, including juveniles, examined by Lewis and Pincus over twenty years were discovered to have brain damage caused by childhood abuse, injury, and accident. Commonly, the damage took the form of disconnecting the frontal lobes of the cerebral cortex, responsible for controlling or modulating impulses from the limbic system; the result of such damage is an inability to control impulses. Such damage can explain the extraordinarily rageful violence sometimes seen, such as extreme mutilation of already dead victims. These diagnostic facts about certain individuals do mark significant differences between us and them. Should this matter to us? Regardless of the organic condition of the brains of some extreme perpetrators, don't we still need to keep them incarcerated once they are caught lest they do further harm? Certainly. But part of the social dynamic of distancing described here is to keep the details out of sight; it is the harms caused by extreme perpetrators that allow us to construct them as alien. The factors that may explain their extraordinary behavior may at the same time go too far in mitigating it, and we need them to be as alien as possible to justify our treatment of them in our justice systems, particularly those we execute.

And yet, despite the vast difference between extreme perpetrators and the mainstream "us," there are common threads. People who do depraved and vicious acts, even on a large scale, remain, in some sense, part of the human family. There are basic universals that pertain to all human beings, and among these are the fact that we are born (our natality), we are dependent on others and live among others (our plurality), and we all die (our mortality). Other universals, such as embodiment, could be added to this list (derived from Hannah Arendt), but the point is that the minimum conception of humanity is that as human we are united in inescapable ways. The rhetoric that constructs the extreme perpetrator as an alien, as inhuman or bestial, contradicts that conception, with the consequence that while we may study our worst perpetrators, write books and make movies about them, regard them as objects of curiosity and even entertainment, our distancing strategies tend to narrow the scope of our understanding of what it means to be human.

And by thus constricting our self-understanding, we also cut off the 30 scope of our humanity, in the sense of the set of attitudes and beliefs which, when acted upon, constitute such traits as kindness and moral regard for others. This is a huge topic in itself; here I wish only to indicate that putting extreme perpetrators in the category of Other (particularly those in our own society and time) invites us to limit our moral regard to those we see more as peers and to respond with indifference to cruelties visited upon those outside that circle. It also blinds us to the origins of evil in our own humanity. In [Dostoyevsky's] *The Brothers Karamazov*, Ivan complains, "People speak sometimes about the 'animal' cruelty of man, but that is terribly unjust and offensive to animals, no animal could ever be so cruel as a man, so artfully, so artistically cruel." We do not have to be as cynical as Ivan to see that understanding ourselves as fully human includes paying attention to the details of the extremes, the Other in all its forms, as Us.

Bibliography

Arendt, H., *The Portable Hannah Arendt*, edited by P. Bachr. Penguin, New York, 2003.

Browning, C., *Ordinary Men: Reserve Police Battalion 101 and the Final Solution in Poland*. HarperCollins, New York, 1998.

Dostoyevsky, F., *The Brothers Karamazov*, trans. R. Pevear and L. Volokhonsky. Alfred A. Knopf, New York, 1992.

Haybron, D. M., "Moral Monsters and Saints." *The Monist* 85:2, April 2002, pp. 260–284.

Jenkins, P., *Using Murder: The Social Construction of Serial Homicide*. Aldine de Gruyter, New York, 1994.

Lewis, D. O., M.D., *Guilty by Reason of Insanity*. Ballantine, New York, 1998.

Tithecott, R., *Of Men and Monsters: Jeffrey Dahmer and the Construction of the Serial Killer*. University of Wisconsin Press, Madison, 1997.

Understanding the Text

1. What is the distinction that Aristotle makes between "ordinary human wickedness and bestiality" (par. 3)? Why is that distinction important? How does it connect to what Myers terms "extreme perpetrators"?

2. What are the three emphases in the theories of evil Myers refers to? How does he use them to describe approaches to extreme perpetrators?

3. Why does Myers want to examine only the actions of extreme perpetrators, rather than take into account their motivations or emotions?

4. According to Myers, how have serial killers in particular captured the public's attention?

Reflection and Response

5. Myers quotes Richard Tithecott as saying, "With our condemnation of Dahmer as evil, we say, simply, *he happened*: there is no need to explain the crime, to speculate about context, only to deal with him, the criminal" (par. 5). What, according to Myers, are the "undesirable consequences" that might result from this attitude? Does the public put itself more at risk by ignoring the motivations of the extreme perpetrator or not? Support your response with specific details.

6. Analyze the difference between a murderer and an extreme perpetrator, as argued in this selection. What problems for society result from this distinction, not simply in terms of protecting itself physically but also in coming to terms with extreme perpetrators?

7. Myers calls the serial killer "the Other in its most threatening form" (par. 19). Do you think this characterization is appropriate? Why or why not?

Making Connections

8. Myers alludes to a number of people from the twentieth century, including Lavrenty Beria, Pol Pot, and Heinrich Himmler, among others. Choose one of these people and research how he is an extreme perpetrator, committing crimes beyond the norm of conventional murderers.

9. Describe the ways in which our culture has created an industry devoted to "mythologizing the serial killer" (par. 19). How is this phenomenon like or unlike our treatment of celebrities? In what ways does publicity help or hurt extreme perpetrators — and us? Use research to support your response.

10. Myers quotes Ivan from *The Brothers Karamazov*: "People speak sometimes about the 'animal' cruelty of man, but that is terribly unjust and offensive to animals, no animal could ever be so cruel as a man, so artfully, so artistically cruel" (par. 31). Research how different thinkers, writers, and artists have attempted to explain the human capacity to commit evil. Which ones seem more persuasive to you? Why?

Acknowledgments (continued from page iv)

Skye Alexander. From Ch. 3, "Mermaids' Attributes, Behavior, and Environs" from *Mermaids: The Myths, Legends, & Lore* by Skye Alexander. Copyright © 2012 by F+W Media. Reprinted by permission of F+W Media, DBA Adams Media.

Stephen T. Asma. "Alexander Fights Monsters in India" (2,520 words approximately, pp. 19–25) from *On Monsters: An Unnatural History of Our Worst Fears* by Stephen T. Asma (2011). By permission of Oxford University Press.

Stephen T. Asma. "Monsters and the Moral Imagination." Copyright © by Stephen T. Asma. Reprinted by permission of the author.

Karen Backstein. "(Un)safe Sex: Romancing the Vampire" by Karen Backstein from *Cineaste*, Winter 2009, Vol. 35, Issue 1, pp. 38–41. Copyright © 2009 by Cineaste Publishers, Inc. Reprinted by permission of Cineaste.

Beowulf. From "Attack on Heorot" from *Beowulf*, translated by Seamus Heaney. Copyright © 2000 by Seamus Heaney. Used by permission of W. W. Norton & Company, Inc.

Jose Luis Borges. From "Foreword to the First Edition: *An Anthology of Fantastic Zoology*," "The Centaur," "The Minotaur," "Sirens," and "The Sphinx" from *The Book of Imaginary Beings* by Jose Luis Borges with Margarita Guerrero, translated by Andrew Hurley. Copyright © 1967 by Editorial Kier, S.A.; translation copyright © 2005 by Penguin Group (USA) Inc. Used by permission of Viking Penguin, a division of Penguin Group (USA) LLC and in Canada by permission of Penguin Canada Books, Inc.

Peter H. Brothers. "Japan's Nuclear Nightmare: How the Bomb Became a Beast Called Godzilla" by Peter H. Brothers from *Cineaste*, Summer 2011, Vol. 36, Issue 3, pp. 36–40. Copyright © 2011 by Cineaste Publishers, Inc. Reprinted by permission of Cineaste.

Daniel Cohen. From "The Birth of Monsters" from *A Modern Look at Monsters* by Daniel Cohen. Copyright © 1970, 1997 by Daniel Cohen. Used by permission of the Author and his agents, Henry Morrison, Inc.

Jeffrey Jerome Cohen. "Fear of the Monster Is Really a Kind of Desire. Monster Culture: Seven Theses" (pp. 16–20) from *Monster Theory*, edited by Jeffrey Jerome Cohen (University of Minnesota Press, 1996). Copyright © 1996 by the Regents of the University of Minnesota. Reprinted by permission of the University of Minnesota Press.

Mike Davis. "Monsters and Messiahs" from *Grand Street*, 16.1 (1997): 34. Reprinted by permission of the author.

Guillermo del Toro and Chuck Hogan. "Why Vampires Never Die" from *The New York Times*, July 31, 2009. Copyright © 2009 The New York Times. All rights reserved. Used by permission and protected by the Copyright Laws of the United States. The printing, copying, redistribution, or retransmission of this Content without express written permission is prohibited.

Ted Genoways. "Here Be Monsters" by Ted Genoways from *The Virginia Quarterly Review*, Winter 2005, Vol. 81. Copyright © 2005 by The Virginia Quarterly Review. Reprinted by permission of The Virginia Quarterly Review.

David D. Gilmore. "An Ancient Crypto-Bestiary" (pp. 37–46) from *Monsters: Evil Beings, Mythical Beasts, and All Manner of Imaginary Terrors* by David D. Gilmore. Copyright © 2003 by University of Pennsylvania Press. Reprinted with permission of the University of Pennsylvania Press.

Susan Tyler Hitchcock. "Conception" from *Frankenstein: A Cultural History* by Susan Tyler Hitchcock. Copyright © 2007 by Susan Tyler Hitchcock. Used by permission of W. W. Norton & Company, Inc.

Adolf Hitler. "Nation and Race" from *Mein Kampf* by Adolf Hitler, translated by Ralph Manheim. Copyright © 1943, renewed 1971 by Houghton Mifflin Company. Reprinted by permission of Houghton Mifflin Harcourt Publishing Company and Random House UK. All rights reserved, and in Canada by Random House Group Limited.

Karen Hollinger. "The Monster as Woman: Two Generations of Cat People" by Karen Hollinger from *Film Criticism*, Winter 1989, 13.2. Copyright 1989 by Film Criticism. Reprinted by permission.

Homer. From *The Odyssey*, "Book 12, The Cattle of the Sun," by Homer, translated by Robert Fagles. Translation copyright © 1996 by Robert Fagles. Used by permission of Viking Penguin, a division of Penguin Group (USA) LLC.

Jason Huddleston. "Unmasking the Monster: Hiding and Revealing Male Sexuality in John Carpenter's *Halloween*" by Jason Huddleston from *Journal of Visual Literacy*, Autumn 2005, 25.2. Copyright © 2005 by Journal of Visual Literacy. Reprinted by permission.

Matt Kaplan. "Cursed by a Bite" from *Medusa's Gaze and Vampire's Bite: The Science of Monsters* by Matt Kaplan. Copyright © 2012 by Matt Kaplan. Reprinted with the permission of Scribner Publishing Group, a division of Simon & Schuster, Inc. All rights reserved.

Bruce F. Kawin. "Composite Monsters: *Island of Lost Souls* and *The Fly*" from *Horror and the Horror Film* by Bruce F. Kawin. Copyright © 2012 by Bruce F. Kawin. Reprinted by permission of Anthem Press.

Stephen King. "Why We Crave Horror Movies" by Stephen King. Copyright © Stephen King. Originally appeared in *Playboy* (1982). All rights reserved. Used with permission.

Chuck Klosterman. "My Zombie, Myself: Why Modern Life Feels Rather Undead" by Chuck Klosterman from *The New York Times*, December 5, 2010. Copyright © 2010 The New York Times. All rights reserved. Used by permission and protected by the Copyright Laws of the United States. The printing, copying, redistribution, or re-transmission of this Content without express written permission is prohibited.

Konstantinos. "Birthright" from *Werewolves: The Occult Truth* by Konstantinos. Copyright © 2010 by Konstantinos. Reprinted by permission of Llewellyn Worldwide.

Elizabeth A. Lawrence. "Werewolves in Psyche and Cinema: Man-Beast Transformation and Paradox" from *Journal of American Culture*, Vol. 19 Issue 3, Fall 1996. Copyright © 2004 by John Wiley and Sons. Reprinted by permission of John Wiley and Sons via Copyright Clearance Center.

Patrick McCormick. "Why Modern Monsters Have Become Alien to Us" by Patrick McCormick from *U.S. Catholic*. Copyright © 1996 by U.S. Catholic. Reproduced by permission from the November 1996 issue of *U.S. Catholic*. Subscriptions: $29/year from 205 West Monroe, Chicago, IL 60606; call 1-800-328-6515 for subscription information or visit www.uscatholic.org/subscribe.

Declan McGrath. "Life among the Undead: An Interview with Neil Jordan" by Declan McGrath from *Cineaste*, Fall 2013, pp. 10–14. Copyright © 2013 by Cineaste Publishers, Inc. Reprinted by permission of Cineaste.

J. Gordon Melton. "Sexuality and the Vampire" from *The Vampire Book: The Encyclopedia of the Undead*, Third Edition, by J. Gordon Melton, Ph.D. Copyright © 2011 by Visible Ink Press®. Reprinted by permission of Visible Ink Press.

William Andrew Myers. "Ethical Aliens: The Challenge of Extreme Perpetrators to Humanism" by William Andrew Myers (pp. 91–101) from *Something Wicked This Way Comes: Essays on Evil and Human Wickedness*, edited by Colette Balmain and Lois Drawmer. Reproduced with permission of Rodopi in the format Educational/Instructional Program via Copyright Clearance Center.

Ovid. From "The Battle of the Lapiths and Centaurs" from *Metamorphoses* by Ovid, translated by David Raeburn (Penguin Books, 2004). Translation copyright © 2004 by David Raeburn. Reprinted by permission of Penguin Group (UK). All rights reserved.

W. Scott Poole. From "Monstrous Beginnings" from *Monsters in America: Our Historical Obsession with the Hideous and the Haunting* by W. Scott Poole. Copyright © 2011 by Baylor University Press. Reprinted by permission of Baylor University Press.

Index of Authors and Titles